EXPLORING SUBURBIA

The Suburbs in the Contemporary Australian Novel

Nathanael O'Reilly

AMHERST, NEW YORK

Copyright 2012 Nathanael O'Reilly

All rights reserved
Printed in the United States of America

No part of this publication may be reproduced, stored in or introduced into a retrieval system, or transmitted, in any form, or by any means (electronic, mechanical, photocopying, recording, or otherwise), without the prior permission of the publisher.

Requests for permission should be directed to:
webmaster@teneopress.com, or mailed to:
Teneo Press
PO Box 349
Youngstown, NY 14174

This book has been registered with the Library of Congress

ISBN 978-1-93484-494-6 (alk. paper)

Exploring Suburbia

For Tricia and Celeste

TABLE OF CONTENTS

Acknowledgments ix

Introduction xi

Chapter 1: Patrick White's *Riders in the Chariot* (1961) 1

Chapter 2: Patrick White's *The Solid Mandala* (1966) 45

Chapter 3: Establishing and Perpetuating the Anti-Suburban
          Tradition 83

Chapter 4: A New Generation Perpetuates the Anti-Suburban
          Tradition 137

Chapter 5: Creating Suburban Fantasies 191

Chapter 6: Taking Suburbia Seriously 249

Chapter 7: Celebrating Suburbia 303

Conclusion 335

Bibliography 339

Index 361

Acknowledgments

My deepest appreciation goes to Gwen Tarbox, Allen Webb, Todd Kuchta, and Nicholas Birns for their insightful and helpful commentary on earlier versions of this project. Gwen Tarbox deserves immense thanks for unparalleled advice, support and advocacy over the past decade. I'd like to thank Nicholas Birns for ten years of advice, opportunities, and friendship, and the members of the American Association of Australasian Literary Studies for their support. I am grateful to Lisa Cohen Minnick, Jill Larsen, Jon Adams, Nic Witschi, Arnie Johnston, Bethlyn Sanders, Judy Lockyer, Hui Wu and Brad Lucas for mentorship and professional assistance. I'd like to thank the students in the courses on Australian literature that I taught at Western Michigan University, Albion College, The University of Texas at Tyler and Texas Christian University; their insights and enthusiasm led me to a deeper and more nuanced understanding of the field.

I began work on this project almost ten years ago and have encountered a number of editors who argued that the topic of suburbia in Australian literature is not important, worthy of intensive study, or of interest to readers, which confirms my belief that the anti-suburban intellectual tradition remains pervasive. However, while working on this book I was fortunate to also encounter scholars and editors who encouraged and/or published my work – many thanks to John Scheckter, Carolyn Bliss, Jack Bennett, Bruce Bennett, Paul Kane, David Callahan, Peter Mathews, Mike Griffiths, Nicholas Dunlop, Lyn McCredden, David McCooey, Nicholas Jose, Frances Devlin-Glass and Paul Richardson.

My parents, Paul and Moira O'Reilly, have my deepest gratitude for instilling in me a passion for literature, supporting my academic pursuits, and sending books and articles from Australia. My best mate, Sean Scarisbrick, has provided over twenty years of friendship on three continents. My deepest thanks go to my wife, Tricia Jenkins, for thirteen wonderful years of marriage, constant support, putting up with my workaholic tendencies, setting the bar high, and believing in my abilities. Finally, I wish to thank my daughter, Celeste, for reminding me daily that there are more important things than writing literary criticism.

Introduction

Australia, Suburbia and Literature

Australia's most important national narratives, such as the stories of Ned Kelly, Burke and Wills, and Gallipoli, take place in the bush, the outback and overseas. In *National Fictions*, Graeme Turner contends that the country, usually the bush or the outback, is preferred "as the authentic location for the distinctive Australian experience" (26). However, Australia has been one of the most suburban societies on earth, rather than a predominantly rural society, since the mid-nineteenth-century, decades before the six British colonies on the Australian continent and the island of Tasmania federated to become a nation in 1901 (Davison, "Australia" 60). In Donald Horne's classic study of Australian society, *The Lucky Country*, he claims that Australia "may have been the first suburban nation" (29). Despite the fact that the vast majority of Australians live in suburbia, Australian narratives are rarely suburban (Gilbert 37; Powell 127). Turner notes that after World War Two, Australian fiction writers gradually began to address urban and suburban society (31). Nevertheless, when post-war Australian writers set their novels in suburbia, the majority depicted it negatively, "coloured by the tradition of anti-suburbanism amongst Australian intellectuals ... which sees suburbia as a cultural wasteland" (Powell 127). Robin Gerster claims that most Australians have been "disenfranchised" by "the virtual restriction" of the representation of suburbia to "satire and ridicule" (574).

Literary novels dealing with suburbia make up a small portion of Australian literature. Research conducted using the AustLit database, the most comprehensive source for bibliographic information on Australian literature, reveals that on those rare occasions when suburbia is the subject for works of Australian literature, those works take the form of poetry and short stories much more often than novels.[1] Of the "Top Forty Australian Books" selected by the Australian Society of Authors in 2003, just four of the thirty-two novels on the list are set in suburbia. While historians, sociologists, comedians, screenwriters, poets and writers of short fiction have devoted significant attention to Australian suburban life, the nation's novelists and literary critics have given suburbia scant serious attention, largely due to the dominance of the anti-suburban tradition amongst Australian novelists and critics. For most of Australian history, novelists and literary critics have deemed suburban life an unworthy subject.

SUBURBIA IN BRITISH AND AMERICAN LITERATURE

In his influential essay, "Heaven and a Hill's Hoist: Australian Critics on Suburbia," Tim Rowse notes that the term "suburbia" is "part of a wider intellectual culture common to Britain and North America. Among social critics of these countries, 'suburbia,' 'suburban' and 'suburb' have been used to describe a certain form of social life which emerged in the metropolises of Europe" (3). Rowse states that suburbs "became the typical mode of domestic living for the majority of people in ... [developed] countries" (3). Although the representation of suburbia in Australian literature has not garnered much critical debate, suburbia is the subject for considerable scholarly activity in other developed nations, especially Britain and the United States. According to the WorldCat database, between 1999 and 2012 1040 non-fiction books on suburbia were published in English

Introduction   xiii

worldwide.² Thus, while little criticism has been written on suburbia in Australian literature since the publication in 1998 of a special issue of *Australian Literary Studies* entitled *Writing the Everyday: Australian Literature and the Limits of Suburbia*, edited by Andrew McCann, the broader topic of suburbia has generated much scholarship and interest from publishers and readers worldwide. The 1040 aforementioned books include works on contemporary British and American fiction, television, film, urban planning, politics, religion, race, class, education and architecture. Even though few scholars have examined suburbia in Australian literature, the topic of suburbia is clearly important globally, within both literary studies and wider academic circles.

In Dominic Head's survey, *The Cambridge Introduction to Modern British Fiction, 1950-2000*, he acknowledges "the dramatic spread of suburbia" (209) and its influence on fiction, noting that British cultural connotations of the term are mostly negative:

> ... for many people, the adjective 'suburban' defines a state of mind characterized by narrow middle class aspirations ... Perceived as embodying a world-view, the 'suburban state of mind' can be ridiculed, consigned to the intellectual margins, just as its actual physical space notionally occupies the urban margins. In the popular imagination, then, suburbia is Middle England; it is preoccupied with shopping and cars; it breeds narrow attitudes ... and it is mystified by artistic endeavour. (213)

Head argues that British novelists "have played their part in establishing suburbia as an object of ridicule" (213). However, he concludes that negative fictional representations of suburbia signal a failure on behalf of novelists "to recognize the sociological importance of suburbia" (Head 214). Head finds the negative depiction of suburbia by British novelists problematic, since suburbia has rapidly become "a constant fact of recent human geography" and commentators tend to accord it "a central place in the explanation of twentieth-century experience" (214). Similarly, Roger Silverstone argues that suburbia is central to contemporary culture and that understanding suburbia is an integral part of the project of understanding everyday life in contemporary industrialized and industrializing societies ("Introduction" 3; "Preface" ix).

Head describes post-war British fictional engagement with suburbia as consisting of stereotypical representations of suburban life that depict it as "deadening, unimaginative, [and] representative of a low or restricted common denominator" (218). Head questions whether suburban life can really be as homogenous as British fiction has depicted it, suggesting that much diversity exists "beneath the surface uniformity" (218). Moreover, Head argues that "the centrality of suburbia hinges on the paradoxes and contradictions it generates and sustains. There are many fissures that make suburban life exemplary of contemporary experience, and make it more surprising than it appears" (218). Head's analysis of the treatment of suburbia by British authors and critics demonstrates that suburbia occupies the same space in British literature that it does in Australian literature. Moreover, Head's recognition of the rarely acknowledged importance of suburbia in contemporary British life and the rich potential it holds as a setting for fiction mirrors my argument regarding suburbia in Australian society and literature.

In Susan Brook's analysis of Hanif Kureishi's seminal novel *The Buddha of Suburbia* (1990), she notes, like Head, that the stereotype of suburbia "as homogenous and conformist is pervasive, not only in popular culture but also in contemporary literary and cultural criticism, where the suburb tends to feature negatively, if it features at all" (209). Brook notes that in both Britain and the United States, the suburb is represented as

> the (often demonized) other of city life: safe where the city is dangerous; conformist where the city is heterogeneous; monotonous and enervating where the city is diverse and stimulating; the site of heterosexual family life where the city opens up the potential for sexual experimentation and possibility. (209)

Introduction   xv

Brook argues that if critics want to understand cities they need to examine the complexity of suburban life (210). Emphasizing the often-shallow engagement with suburbia by British critics, Brook argues that critics of suburbia falsely act as if "there were no distinctions between different kinds of suburbs. The binary opposition between the city and suburbs persists because of the vagueness of the idea of 'the suburbs,' which enables it to function as the other of a range of urban experience" (212). Like Head, Brook posits that false representations of suburbia as a homogeneous zone serve to conceal difference (212). Furthermore, Brook argues that negative judgments of suburbia "are often judgements aimed at the lower middle class" and that anti-suburban criticism says little about suburban life, but reveals much about the prejudices of "those who make such judgements" (212). Moreover, Brook claims that anti-suburban criticism is the product of both class anxieties and sexism (212-13).

Negative stereotypes of suburbia are by no means confined to British and Australian culture and literature; they are also pervasive in American culture and literature. Although widespread suburbanization began later in the United States than in Britain and Australia (the American population was still predominantly urban in 1920), the movement of population from American cities and rural areas to suburbia and the subsequent growth of the suburbs was so substantial that by the 1970 census more Americans dwelt in suburbia than in cities or rural areas, and by the 1990 census the number of suburbanites was greater than the combined number of rural and city residents (Jurca 160). In response to the suburbanization of American society, scholarly work on suburbia has proliferated in the United States in fields such as geography, urban planning, architecture, sociology and history. Robert M. Fogelson, author of *Bourgeois Nightmares: Suburbia, 1870-1930*, notes that

> The literature [of the history of suburbia] is so vast that it is easy to forget that almost all of it has appeared in the past forty-five years. Indeed, it is so vast that historians have already begun writing arti-

cles about the historiography of suburbia, the history of its history. (3)

Fogelson argues that the suburbanization of America was driven largely by fear: "fears of disease, crime, immorality, poverty, immigration, and public disorder drove many Americans from the center of the city to the periphery" (4). Furthermore, the actual physical development of the suburbs and the widespread use of legislation such as restrictive covenants to exclude specific races and classes from the suburbs and prevent certain behaviors, such as hanging laundry outside to dry, were indicative of "a host of deep-seated fears that permeated much of American society in the late nineteenth and early twentieth centuries" (Fogelson 24).[3] Lynn Spigel argues that planning and building policies have constructed American suburbia as a "hostile and alienating terrain" (237).

Although developers intended the American suburbs to be sites of escape, security and exclusion, American literature dealing with suburbia criticizes it for possessing the very features that attract tens of millions of Americans to make it their home. In Edith Wharton's 1925 essay "The Great American Novel," she launches a typical anti-suburban attack, claiming that "modern America" has

> reduced relations between human beings to a dead level of vapid benevolence, and the whole of life to a small house with modern plumbing and heating, a garage, a motor, a telephone, and a lawn undivided from one's neighbor's. Great as may be the material advantages of these diffused conveniences, the safe and uniform life resulting from them offers to the artist's imagination a surface as flat and monotonous as our own prairies. (Qtd. in Jurca 3)

Despite Wharton's exhortations, numerous American writers set novels in suburbia in the decades after her essay appeared. Wharton's "failure to dislodge 'the little suburban house' from the twentieth-century American novel" is readily apparent in the works of writers such as Frederick Barthelme, James M. Cain, Richard Ford, Sinclair Lewis, John Updike, Sloan Wilson and Richard Yates (Jurca 4).

Introduction

In Catherine Jurca's study of American literary engagement with suburbia, *White Diaspora: The Suburb and the Twentieth-Century American Novel*, she argues that suburban narratives "have become a national literary specialty" (160). Jurca claims that, as in Australia and Britain, suburbanization "has been one of the most significant social and political facts of modern American life" (5). Jurca demonstrates that anti-suburban attitudes dominate American suburban novels, following much the same pattern as Australian and British suburban novels. Jurca notes that twentieth-century American novelists writing about suburbia "present their work as a critique of its culture" (6) and that the novels are marketed as anti-suburban, based "on the assumption that although millions of people choose to live there [in suburbia], it is the environment that we love to hate" (161). American suburban novels contain "ubiquitous complaints about mass production, standardization, dullness, and conformity, which novelists have developed and refined in the context of a broad-based intellectual resistance to the suburb" (Jurca 6). The anti-suburban intellectual tradition that Jurca identifies in American literature is also prevalent in British and Australian literature.

Defining the Terms "Suburbia," "Suburb" and "Suburban"

In this book I use the terms "suburbia," "suburb" and "suburban" frequently. Because the term "suburbia" often carries negative connotations, it is imperative that I explain my use of the term and related terms. The *Oxford English Dictionary* defines "suburbia" as "A quasi-proper name" for the suburbs that is frequently disparaging. I use the term "suburbia" to refer to the suburbs as a whole, and *do not* intend the word to carry a negative connotation. The *OED* defines a suburb as "The country lying immediately outside a town or city; more particularly, those residential parts belonging to a town or city that lie immediately outside and adjacent to its walls or boundaries" and as "Any of such residential parts, having a definite designation, boundary, or organization." I use the term "suburb," in the Australian context, to refer to a specific, named, defined, primarily residential area outside of the city's central business district (CBD). In cities such as Melbourne and Sydney, which have hundreds of suburbs, there is much variation from suburb to suburb with regard to factors including population, geographical size, age, distance from the CBD, population density, property size and value, and ethnic and demographic composition. Therefore, there is no such thing as a typical Australian suburb, although it is useful to employ terms such as "inner," "outer," "middle-class," "working-class," "established," "newly-developed," "exclusive," "affordable" and "expensive" to refer to individual suburbs or groups of suburbs.

The *OED* defines "suburban" as "Of or belonging to a suburb or the suburbs of a town; living, situated, operating, or carried on in the suburbs" and as "Having characteristics that are regarded as belonging especially to life in the suburbs of a city; having the inferior manners, the narrowness of view, etc., attributed to residents in suburbs." I use the term "suburban" to refer to characteristics associated with a suburb or group of suburbs, or to literature that deals with the suburbs, but I do not intend *any* negative connotation. For example, when I write that a character "resides in suburban Melbourne," I merely wish to convey that the character is a resident of a Melbourne suburb, not to imply that the character possesses any negative characteristics that may be associated with Melbourne suburbs or suburbs in general. I also use the phrase "built environment" to refer to both the city and the suburbs in order to avoid using gender-biased language, such as "man-made."

The Development of Australian Suburbia

Before discussing the anti-suburban tradition in Australian society and outlining my argument regarding suburbia in the contemporary Australian novel, it is necessary to provide a brief history of the development of Australia's suburbs. The historian Graeme Davison notes the discrepancy

Introduction   xix

between the reality and mythology of Australian society, arguing that Australia "liked to present itself to the world as a frontier society ... inhabited by a hardy breed of bushmen," even though "the frontier that most Australians were busy pioneering was not a land of sweeping plains, but a land of sprawling suburbs" ("Australia" 1). The suburbanization of Australia began almost eighty years before the six Australian colonies federated in 1901; the process was underway by the late 1820s in Sydney and by the 1850s in Melbourne, when "Australia" still consisted of six English colonies (Gilbert 33). Thus, in Sydney's case, suburbanization began about forty years after initial English settlement, and in the case of Melbourne, less than twenty years after settlement.

Davison highlights the deep connections between colonialism and suburbanization, pointing out that suburban development "was consciously promoted by the country's founders and expressed the social aspirations of immigrants drawn largely from the cities of the United Kingdom where the suburban idea had first taken root" ("Australia" 2). In another sense, the English colonies in Australia functioned as the farthest suburbs of Britain, with "the suburban imperative" in Australian society being "intimately bound up with the essentially British caste of colonial society" (Davison, "Australia" 7). As John Hartley argues, suburbia is "an imperial invention" (184). By the late 1820s, wealthy businessmen and government officials in Sydney began a movement to create English-style villa suburbs; in 1828, Governor Ralph Darling "authorized the subdivision of Woolloomooloo Hill ... overlooking the harbor about a mile east" of Sydney (Davison, "Australia" 4). In the same year, in Van Diemen's Land, Lieutenant Governor George Arthur issued regulations for suburban development in Hobart (Davison, "Australia" 6).

Within less than a decade of the first government-authorized subdivisions, Sydney's commercial elite began moving to the suburbs, where they imitated and adapted English architectural fashions (Davison, "Australia" 4; "Colonial" 7). Davison argues that the development of suburbia in Australia differed from British and American suburban development in "the swiftness with which the ideal was diffused and the low barriers that colonial society presented to its attainment" ("Australia" 5). An increase of assisted immigration in the 1830s also increased the need for suburban development (Davison, "Australia" 5). Immigrants in the nineteenth century were predominantly from England, Scotland and Ireland, where home ownership was often unattainable for the lower classes (Davison, "Colonial" 8).

Although suburban development began early in Sydney and Hobart, it was not until the 1850s that living in suburbia became an attainable reality "for the majority of Australian town dwellers"; previously, most residents of suburbia were from the upper class. However, the introduction of the horse-drawn omnibus and the development of railway networks enabled the "suburban idea [to] become a democratic reality" (Davison, "Australia" 7). The ideal of a home in the suburbs was promoted by immigration agents for over a century, "from the gold rushes of the 1850s to the Second World War and beyond" (Davison, "Australia" 8). Thus, the promise of a new life in the constantly expanding suburbs of Australia's cities was a major motivation for immigrants, who were rarely property owners in their homelands and often wrote letters to relatives and friends at home describing their dreams of acquiring a suburban home and subsequent success in doing so (Davison, "Australia" 9). The history of suburbia in Australia is an integral part of both the history of Australia's relationship with Britain and the history of immigration in Australia. Indeed, many of the novels discussed in this book address the role of immigrants in suburbia, whether they hail from Britain or other places, such as Germany, Armenia, Greece, Italy and Lebanon.

The immigrants of the 1850s influenced the physical development of the suburbs immensely, making them substantially different from "the bourgeois utopias" of London and the early villa suburbs of Sydney and Hobart (Davison, "Australia" 9). In Melbourne, the one-hundred-foot frontages created by government surveyors were "divided, subdivided, sold, and resold" into allotments with frontages as narrow as twelve-

and-a-half feet, so that instead of picturesque English-style suburbs, Melbourne's inner suburbs became "a messy jigsaw of villas, truncated terraces, cottages, corner shops, pubs, workshops, stables, and vacant lots" (Davison, "Australia" 9). Davison argues that the "free, skilled immigrants of the 1850s" modified "the once-aristocratic suburban idea," giving it a "radical democratic twist" ("Australia" 9). The names of Australian suburbs reflect the role working-class immigrants played in suburban development. Australian suburbs were often named after leafy London suburbs, such as Richmond, Paddington, Kensington and Camberwell, rather than the "densely settled neighbourhoods from which the immigrants had probably come – Stepney, Whitechapel, Clerkenwell and Bethnall Green," since the immigrants were aspiring to a better life and chose names reflecting their aspirations (Davison, "Colonial" 9).

The arrival of immigrants and their settlement in new suburbs caused Australia to possess "one of the highest proportions of city dwellers in the world" by the late nineteenth century (Horne 29); the development of suburbia continued steadily as the century progressed. Melbourne's population increased from 268,000 to 473,000 in the 1880s, with 70% of the growth occurring in the suburbs (Gilbert 33). Similarly, by 1891, Sydney had 107,652 residents in the inner city, while 275,631 resided in the suburbs (Rowse 4). Gilbert argues that "The lure of the suburbs was a persistent social force" due to the rapid expansion of transport networks after 1875 and "an abundance of suitable land" on the edge of the cities, which made the suburbs a "marvelous compromise" between the city and the bush (33, 35; Rowse 4).

In his article "The Rise of the Suburbs," published in 1891, the English journalist Sidney Low demonstrated remarkable insight, noting that "The suburban type is just as pronounced in some of our colonies [as it is in England]," arguing that instead of being a "dashing pastoralist," the average Australian "lives in his own house, provided with a verandah and a piano" and reads the newspaper as he commutes to work "by the train or tramcar" (Qtd. in Kuchta 179). By the end of the nineteenth century all of Australia's capital cities were "predominantly suburban in character," while Melbourne, with a population approximately one-eighth of London's, already covered an area twice as large as the Empire's capital (Davison, "Australia" 10). At the start of the twentieth century, "the dominance of the capital cities, combined with their marked low-density character, combined to make Australia the most suburbanized nation on earth" (Davison, "Australia" 11).

The most prevalent form of housing in Australian suburbs has always been the detached, single-family home, often located on a quarter-acre block. Sophie Watson states,

> The single detached home on the quarter-acre block is one of the most striking visual symbols of urban Australia. Roughly three-quarters of dwellings are of this kind. Flats, terraces, [and] low- and high-rise apartment blocks characteristic of European cities are relatively rare even in the more dense urban areas. In outer Brisbane and Melbourne over nine in ten households live in separate houses. (Qtd. in Kapferer 111)

Davison states that the bungalow "originated in India, but made its way to Australia during the earliest years of New South Wales where it became the prototype of the Australian house in both city and country" ("Australia" 11). Anthony D. King argues that the suburb "was instrumental in producing the architectural form of the bungalow, just as the bungalow was instrumental in producing the spatial form of the suburb" (56). The detached suburban house represents "economic and political independence," both much sought after by immigrants and native-born Australians (Davison, "Colonial" 10).

Although many families aspired to live in single-family homes, local, state and federal governments also played a significant role in making the detached single-family home the dominant mode of living in Australia through the promotion of home-ownership and the construction of public housing. State governments created housing commissions or departments to construct and administer public housing, usually in the form of

Introduction xxiii

estates comprised of detached single-family dwellings. In 1909, the Royal Commission for the Improvement of Sydney and its Suburbs concluded that "the tenement or flat system of housing [prevalent in Europe and America] would not meet the requirements of Australian workmen," and recommended "that on social and on hygienic grounds, workmen ... be encouraged to live in separate houses in the suburbs" (Qtd. in Hoskins 4). In 1912, J.R. Dacey, the Colonial Secretary for New South Wales, sought to alleviate urban congestion and promote "peace, order and good government" by drafting a proposal for the construction of a model suburb (Hoskins 6-7). In the same year, the establishment of the NSW Housing Board and "The passage of the 1912 Housing Act ... cleared the way for the erection of a government-funded model suburb," named Daceyville in honor of Dacey who died that year (Hoskins 7). However, it was not until the late 1930s that state governments began large-scale construction of public housing (Hayward, "Anything" 1). The Second World War greatly exacerbated the housing shortage in Australia and led to a post-war housing boom (Powell 47, 52; Hoskins 2); government estimates "put the housing shortfall at about 300,000 dwellings in the mid-1940s" (Badcock 257). On November 19, 1945, the State and Commonwealth governments signed an agreement under which the Commonwealth government agreed to provide low-cost loans to fund the construction of public housing (Hayward, "Introduction" 1).

Home ownership is a central facet of the Australian dream, just as it is central to the American dream. For over 150 years, Australians have sought to own their own homes, usually in suburbia. In Sydney, rates of home ownership increased from 40% in 1947 to 60% in 1954, and then to 71% in 1961 (R. White 49). A survey conducted in 1959 of British immigrants to Australia revealed that 90% of couples sought to buy a home, despite the fact that "less than one-third had been owners in their homeland" (Davison, "Colonial" 12). Gilbert notes that "there seems to be much less emphasis on the social importance of home-ownership in continental Europe than there is in Australia ... In suburban Sydney in the mid-1970s, over 80% of all private houses were owner-occupied" (36).

The 1950s, 1960s and 1970s have been described as the "Golden Age" of home ownership in Australia; during this period almost 90% of households owned a home "at some stage of their lives" and almost half of the construction in Australian cities took place (Badcock 254). Thus, the bulk of the suburbanization of Australia's cities was driven by the desire of working and middle-class Australians to own a detached single-family home.

Blair Badcock observes that the construction of "equally modest homes on similarly sized building blocks in the suburbs" led to the suburban bungalow occupying a central position in popular notions of a prosperous, egalitarian society (254). A home in the suburbs became physical evidence of both individual and community success, a symbol of an industrialized democratic nation in which individuals had the freedom and opportunity to prosper and live comfortably. Home-ownership rates approached 72% in the mid-1960s and have remained relatively static since then (Badcock 263). However, Badcock questions the ability of Australian society to continue to provide access to home-ownership to the vast majority of citizens, noting decreasing access to home-ownership in the 1990s, especially among lower-income households, citizens under thirty years of age, persons living alone, and single-parent households (260, 261, 263). Badcock concludes that "the illusion that [home-ownership] ... is accessible to all 'ordinary' Australians" is sustained by the middle-classes, who have reaped the financial benefits of home ownership (266). Australian novels set in suburbia tackle issues such as home ownership, egalitarianism, democracy, freedom, and prosperity and question the reality behind the suburban mythology.

Despite the fact that the dream of home ownership in the suburbs may be less attainable for Australians now than in past decades, due to factors such as sharply rising property values in the early years of the twenty-first century,[4] life in the suburbs is still the "preferred mode of existence for millions of ordinary Australians" (Kapferer 125). Sociologist Judith Kapferer argues that "the suburbs present a vision of a liberal democratic workers' paradise to the world outside" and that "the suburban home is still conceptualized as enshrining egalitarianism, individualism and that freedom of choice which is believed ... to lie at the very heart of a liberal capitalist democracy" (116). As Gilbert notes, "there has been surprising *continuity* since the 1850s in the attitudes, values and motives underlying suburbanization" (36, original emphasis).

The suburbs in Australia's five largest cities - Sydney, Melbourne, Brisbane, Adelaide, and Perth - have developed similarly. As Diane Powell states in *Out West: Perceptions of Sydney's Western Suburbs*,

> All Australian cities have similar cartographies: older inner areas gentrified since the 1970s; prestigious suburbs in geographically attractive locations; older, established middle-class areas; and, usually in the outer circle, the newer dormitory suburbs, the mass-planned housing estates, where services are minimal, the populations younger and more culturally diverse, the families newer and their incomes lower than those in the rest of the city. (xiv)

Like Powell, Kapferer points out that the outer suburbs are home to the marginalized and disadvantaged: "blue-collar workers are exiled to the outer suburbs as are the 'non-productive' – single-parent households, the unemployed and pensioners" (120). In Australia, property values, prestige and access to services usually decrease the further a suburb is from the CBD, which is the opposite of the typical American pattern, in which inner urban areas are usually low-income, and affluent, exclusive suburbs are often located on the outer fringe of cities.

THE ANTI-SUBURBAN TRADITION IN AUSTRALIAN CULTURE

In his introduction to the essay collection *Beasts of Suburbia*, Chris Healy notes that in Australian culture "there is a relatively long history of intellectuals and others seeking to delineate the suburb. The positions and orientations of these commentaries range from pure hatred to mad love" (xv); however, the negative commentaries far outweigh the positive.

Likewise, Andrew McCann states that a dominant anti-suburban ethos has existed within Australian intellectual life since the late nineteenth century ("Introduction" vii), while Garry Kinnane notes that anti-suburbanism "has long been a deep current in the Australian artistic and intellectual mainstream" ("Shopping" 41). In addition to influencing Australian culture as a whole, the anti-suburban intellectual tradition has heavily influenced both the literature dealing with suburbia and the criticism of that literature.

One of the earliest and most striking examples of the anti-suburban tradition is Louis Esson's essay "Our Institutions," which was published in 1912 along with his play *The Time is Not Yet Ripe*. Kinnane argues that Esson's "notorious diatribe" reflects "the sentiments of nearly every artist and poet of his era" ("Shopping" 41). Esson declares:

> The suburban home must be destroyed. It stands for all that is dull and depressing in modern life. It endeavours to eliminate the element of danger in human affairs. But without dangers there can be no joy, no ecstasy, no spiritual adventures. The suburban home is a blasphemy. It denies life. (73)

Esson goes on to claim that "it would be better to live in a slum area than in a bourgeois suburb," arguing that "slums have more character ... and more potentialities. Life is more vivid and picturesque there. People dance, and have passions, and live ... dangerously. In the suburbs all is repression, stagnation, a moral morgue" (73). Esson's equation of suburbia with domesticity, boredom, depression, conservatism, repression, safety and predictability has been echoed and repeated by numerous Australian intellectuals for a century. As Gerster notes, "Esson's wildly romantic rhetoric ... supplies a representative attitude" (567-68). Gilbert also identifies Esson's rhetoric as romantic, arguing that "Anti-suburbanism is heir to the recurrent anathema that Romanticism has pronounced for more than a quarter of a millennium against the rationalism, meliorism and materialism of the modern world. Suburbanites are criticized because they feel safe, and because their lives are comfortable" (40).

Introduction   xxvii

Rowse argues that Australian intellectuals, including Vance and Nettie Palmer, Esson, W.K. Hancock and Frederic Eggleston, "all equated 'suburbia' with a stifling materialism of outlook" and that "The generation of intellectuals who came to maturity just before, during or just after the First World War inaugurated a use of the term 'suburbia' in an overwhelmingly pejorative sense" (7). Kinnane claims that anti-suburbanism was "adopted in succession" by individual intellectuals and groups including the Heidelberg school of painters, the Lindsays, "Hugh McCrae, Kenneth Slessor, the Palmers, the Meldrumites, the Montsalvat lifestylers, the Boyds, the 'Heide' modernists ... Sidney Nolan, Russell Drysdale, George Johnston, Patrick White ... and the *Meanjin* 'school' of the 1960s" ("Shopping" 41-42).[5] Rowse identifies the anti-suburban tradition in Australian intellectual life as a conflict between "the cosmopolitan and the suburban," arguing that the conflict was "not one that existed between nations, say Britain and Australia," but one that "took place in every country. It was a contest between two attitudes to life: one whose intellectual horizons were broad ... and one that was [allegedly] narrow, self-satisfied, materialistic and parochial" (5).

Gilbert argues that when intellectuals criticize suburbia for being an environment that promotes "'mindless conformism,'" they are critiquing "values and attitudes shared *across* the entire suburban culture" (37, original emphasis). Therefore, since the vast majority of Australians live in the suburbs, the anti-suburban tradition is in effect an anti-Australian tradition, a manifestation of the cultural cringe and an expression of dissatisfaction with the nation as a whole. Since Australian intellectuals have been made to feel inferior by their former colonial masters, they resort to an attack on members of their own society whom they see as inferior, namely the lower-middle and working classes. In cases where intellectuals are themselves suburbanites, their attacks on suburbia are an expression of self-loathing. Furthermore, as Gilbert notes, "anti-suburbanism, as a specific, systematic cultural critique, may be more powerful in Australian life than elsewhere" (37). Hence, in Australia one finds the seemingly paradoxical situation of the most suburban society on earth also possessing the strongest expressions of anti-suburbanism.

Just as Rowse notes that a generation of intellectuals in the period surrounding the First World War disparaged suburbia, Robert Dixon states that in the period from "the late 1940s to the mid 1960s" another generation of intellectuals "mounted a sustained critique of suburbia," attacking "commodification, industrialisation, standardisation, secularisation, [and] the 'levelling down' effect of mass culture" ("James McAuley's" 20). Although the anti-suburban position has dominated Australian intellectuals' engagement with suburbia, Rowse argues that by the early 1950s some critics came to view suburbia "in a more positive light – as an innocent utopia" (7). Furthermore, Rowse claims that in the 1950s, suburbia

> ... was coming to be seen not so much as an aberration of the Australian spirit, but as its abiding manifestation ... as "suburbia" became accepted as an authentic image of the way ordinary Australians lived, the critical connotations of the term began to lose their force, giving way to a gentle irony and even to an aloof benediction. No-one did more to facilitate this shift than Barry Humphries. (8)

The comedian Barry Humphries' characters, especially Dame Edna Everage and Sandy Stone, are "truly 'suburban,'" according to Rowse; he argues that Everage "apes but violates the conventions of taste, status and worldliness" while "Stone's life is a pathetic shell of would-be gentility and conformity" (8). Delys Bird argues that Humphries' "attack on the assumed conservative mediocrity of suburban Australia is itself ultimately conservative" (189). Moreover, Rowse notes, as time has passed, the "authenticity and familiarity" of Everage and Stone has "come to undercut the critical edge of Humphries' satire" and "an undeniable element of sentimental patriotism in the appreciation of Humphries' work" has developed (8). Rowse's last point is even more pertinent thirty years after the publication of his article, since Dame Edna Everage is now an iconic figure in Australian culture. The historians Graeme Davison and Tony

Dingle argue that the residents of suburbia who laughed at Dame Edna's jokes in the 1950s and 1960s did so knowing that "she was not really one of them," since by the time Dame Edna became a star, "the suburbs had become far too diverse ethnically, culturally and socially to be encapsulated in a single stereotype" (4).

Hugh Stretton, author of *Ideas for Australian Cities* (1970), has been described by Kapferer as "the high priest of suburbia in Australia" (111), while Rowse claims that Stretton presented "an articulate and philosophic case" for suburban life (10-11). Likewise, Kinnane identifies Stretton as one of the first to question the anti-suburban tradition ("Shopping" 43), while Gerster describes Stretton as a champion of suburbia (573). Stretton countered some of the standard criticisms of suburbia while simultaneously emphasizing its advantages:

> You don't have to be a mindless conformist to choose suburban life. Most of the best poets and painters and inventors and protestors choose it too. It reconciles access to work and city with private, adaptable, self-expressive living space at home ... For children it really has no rivals. At home it can allow them space, freedom and community with their elders; they can still reach bush and beach in one direction and in the other, schools to educate them and cities to sophisticate them. (Qtd. in Rowse 11)

Despite Stretton's obvious championing of suburbia, the final phrase of the above passage reveals a common anti-suburban idea, namely that sophistication cannot be obtained within suburbia, that one must spend time in the city in order to attain cultural knowledge and cosmopolitan manners.

Donald Horne was another prominent Australian intellectual who bucked the anti-suburban tradition. Rowse credits Horne with rejecting "the interwar snobbery about suburbia" because "it effectively dismissed the whole nation. Instead, he defended the vitality of the Australian lifestyle" (8). In *The Lucky Country*, Horne claims that "'suburbanism' ... is likely to be the target of practically all intellectuals. And since most

Australians live in the suburbs of cities this means that intellectuals hate almost the whole community" (28). Horne notes that "recognition of the essentially suburban character of Australia has been slow, partly because old myths have remained virulent" (29). Countering ideas about suburbia espoused by intellectuals such as Esson, Horne argues,

> The profusion of life doesn't wither because people live in small brick houses with red tile roofs. It is the almost universal failure of Australian writers to realize this that causes them to either caricature Australian life, or to ignore it ...almost all Australian writers – whatever their politics – are reactionaries whose attitude to the massive diversities of suburban life is to ignore it or condemn it rather than discover what it is. (30)

Despite the strenuous defense of suburbia by Stretton and Horne, the majority of the Australian intelligentsia "hated suburbia. They despised it" (Gilbert 38). For intellectuals, the suburbs represented the "epitome of all the worse characteristics of the city – a distillation of pure mediocrity, alienation and false consciousness" (Gilbert 39). Gilbert points out that the anti-suburban tradition is essentially elitist and arrogant, since "the notion of suburban consciousness as false consciousness lies at the heart of Australian anti-suburbanism" (40). However, anti-suburbanism is not only elitist and arrogant, it is founded partly upon what Gilbert terms "ignorance or misconception" (47), since it ignores or fails to recognize the diversity, complexity and benefits of suburban life. As Rowse notes, the use of the term "suburbia" often "suggests a homogeneity in Australian society" that does not exist (4). Because critics are "preoccupied by a search for the 'average' Australian home and its life-style," they fail to see "important ethnic and class differences" (Rowse 4). Davison and Dingle argue that Australian intellectuals "easily succumbed to the belief that because the houses looked the same, the people who lived in them must also have lived, thought and voted the same" (4). The novels analyzed throughout this book clearly demonstrate that suburbia is not homogenous; in fact, suburbia contains a great deal of ethnic, class, sexual, religious and economic diversity.

Introduction   xxxi

Suburbia has long been associated with feminine domesticity, usually in a negative manner (Gilbert 35). As Silverstone puts it, "suburban culture is a gendered culture" ("Introduction" 7). The negative depiction of domesticity also usually entails a negative depiction of women, and sometimes outright misogyny. As Rowse notes,

> A rough equation that seems to be employed is: women + domesticity = spiritual starvation. (Men + wide open spaces + achievement = heroism of the Australian spirit.) The female influence in the "culture" is often taken to amount to an obsession with status and difference. (13)

As Gerster puts it, "The unspoken assumption ... is that suburbia is an essentially *female* domain. It's no place for a man" (567, original emphasis). Thus, not only is the anti-suburban tradition in Australian culture elitist and arrogant, it is often misogynistic.

In his 1966 article "Godzone 3: Myth and Reality," Allan Ashbolt attacks suburbia, highlighting the alleged domesticity, conformity, consumerism and repetitive nature of suburban life, and mocks the suburban male:

> Behold the man – the Australian man of today – on Sunday mornings in the suburbs, when the high-decibel drone of the motor-mower is calling the faithful to worship. A block of land, a brick veneer, and the motor-mower beside him in the wilderness – what more does he want to sustain him, except a Holden to polish, a beer with the boys, marital sex on Saturday nights, a few furtive adulteries, an occasional gamble on the horses or the lottery, the tribal rituals of football, the flickering shadows in the lounge-room of cops and robbers, goodies and baddies, guys and dolls? (373)

Ashbolt derides the suburban Australian male as "hardly rational or purposeful," claiming that "things merely happen to him or around him" in a world that is "mass-produced and mass-manipulated" (374). Ashbolt's caricature of the suburban male retires at age sixty-five and "imagines that he is about to begin living, not knowing that he died many years before" (374). Many of the standard criticisms that have been part of the anti-suburban tradition for almost a century appear in Ashbolt's caricature of suburbia. The poet and critic Chris Walllace-Crabbe also disparaged suburbia in the 1960s, arguing that "outer suburbia" contains a "double deprivation," since "one loses contact with the lively core of the city and the suburb offers no compensating sense of community" (168).

According to Davison and Dingle, the published social commentary of the 1950s and 1960s expressed "an immense collective sneer towards the inhabitants of the suburbs" (3). In her 1993 study, *Out West: Perceptions of Sydney's Western Suburbs*, Diane Powell reveals that the attitudes of the intelligentsia towards suburbia changed little between the 1960s and the 1990s: "today's cultural elite still tends to see suburbia as a place where nothing worthwhile ever happens and nothing worth writing about ever occurs" (127). In 1995, the Melbourne architect Epaminondas Katsilidis gave a perfect example of the attitude of the cultural elite that Powell refers to when he dismissed suburbia as "neither city nor country. It's terrible, vacuous, isolated, [with an] awful lack of information and interaction" (Qtd. in Kapferer 128).[6] In an issue of the *Griffith Review* published in 2005, Julianne Schultz notes that "suburban life has been a lightening rod for intellectual criticism in Australia for generations," noting that the stereotype of suburbia as "dull, ordinary, [and] predictable has been an article of faith, even as its accuracy diminished" (8). Interestingly, Schultz suggests that the stereotypes regarding suburbia were once accurate and perhaps are still accurate to an extent; she certainly does not declare the stereotypes false. In the same issue, Margaret Simons' essay "Ties That Bind" examines the differences between Melbourne's inner and outer suburbs and their residents. Simons states that the suburbs are viewed by intellectuals "as boring at best, vacuous, mean and racist at worst" (28). Clearly, the anti-suburban tradition is still pervasive and influential in Australian culture.

Introduction xxxiii

The Anti-Suburban Tradition in Australian Literature and Literary Criticism

Given the cultural history of Australian suburbia, one may ask how widely-held anti-suburban attitudes are manifested in Australian literature and literary criticism. Australian literature is one of the many components that make up Australian culture, and as such, it is subject to the prevailing attitudes within that culture. Anti-suburbanism has both influenced Australian literature and been perpetuated by it. Kinnane describes anti-suburbanism in Australian culture as "almost exclusively" privileging "the city and the bush as the two poles of experience that matter," arguing that the privileging of the city and the bush "is clearly reflected in our fiction writers, who from Lawson through Vance Palmer to Prichard, White, Johnston, Hal Porter, Keneally, Moorhouse, Garner [and others] … have idealised or found heroic suffering in the bush and the outback, or else have explored the fascinations of city waste" ("Shopping" 42). The single most significant effect of the anti-suburban tradition on Australian fiction is that it has led Australian writers to set the vast majority of their works *outside* suburbia, hence the small body of work that may be deemed "Australian suburban fiction."

> McCann argues that "post-war Australian writing … concerned with suburbia"
>
> reflects anxieties about the suburbs [that] are not just anxieties about the everyday experience of life in Australian cities, its social and political effects and cultural possibilities … [but] are also anxieties about the 'everyday' itself as an experiential category referring to the mundane cycle of work, consumerism and domesticity. ("Introduction" vii)

The concerns McCann identifies as present within fiction about suburbia mirror those espoused by the intellectuals who created and perpetuated the anti-suburban tradition. McCann also notes that fiction about suburbia "solicits fantasies of escape or flight" ("Introduction" viii). Indeed, the protagonist of McCann's novel *Subtopia* flees suburbia, and characters in Johnston's *My Brother Jack*, Malouf's *Johnno*, Winton's *Cloudstreet* and Lucashenko's *Steam Pigs* all flee suburbia or fantasize about doing so.

In 1990, Robin Gerster published "Gerrymander: The Place of Suburbia in Australian Fiction"; his article is the most useful of the few works of criticism on suburbia in Australian fiction. Gerster argues,

> The denigration of the suburbs by Australian writers ... is inveterate ... suburbia is not only attacked by the pedlars of the bush mythology, but it is habitually dismissed with cosmopolitan contempt by urban-oriented writers as a place fit solely for satire, if indeed it is worth writing about at all. Whereas the intellectual enclaves and working-class slums of the inner city are celebrated for their ideological attraction and aesthetic potential, for their cultural energy and diversity, for their LIFE, suburbia is used as a metonym for living death. (565-566, original emphasis)

Gerster describes the attitude of Australian novelists to suburbia as a "combination of fear and contempt," arguing that they "are unwilling to explore beyond the 'surface'" and that they "shrink from close encounters with the suburbanites, perhaps because they are afraid to see an image of themselves" (566). Gerster posits that Australian artists cultivate a "sense of difference from the mainstream culture" that "prohibits close communication" and "empathy" with suburbanites, thus "satire and blank neglect become convenient refuges" (566). Furthermore, Gerster claims that the difference between satire and "gratuitous insult" is often impossible to discern (567).

Kinnane argues that it is not the suburbs that are "refuges of conformity" as anti-suburban intellectuals have contended, but "the clichés about suburbia" themselves, which he describes as "the sanctuaries of attitudinal smugness" and "substitutes for critical thinking" ("Shopping" 54). As a result, Kinnane claims,

Introduction   xxxv

> The anti-suburban tradition in Australia has largely outlived its relevance, and writers of fiction who remain under its spell are in danger of blinding themselves to some of the more interesting, significant and dramatic material available to them ... suburbia is not a desert but a rich field of opportunities for narrative, character, drama and action. ("Shopping" 54)

Despite the decision by the majority of Australian novelists to ignore suburbia and the tendency of most writers who address suburbia to disparage it, a number of authors have taken suburbia seriously and engaged with it in a detailed, nuanced and unbiased manner. Gerster identifies Marion Halligan, Peter Goldsworthy and Gerald Murnane as members of a group of writers who treat suburbia seriously, without contempt (573); I add Peter Carey, Jonathan Bennett, Liam Davison, Neil Boyack, Christos Tsiolkas, Shaun Tan, Steven Carroll, Damian McDonald, Judy Pascoe, Lillian Ng, Amanda Lohrey, Murray Bail, Tim Winton (in his short fiction) and Patrick White to the list. About half of the works under discussion in this book were published after Gerster's article, and I suspect that if he were writing today he would include the authors I mention alongside Halligan, Goldsworthy and Murnane.

In addition to the neglect of suburbia by Australian novelists, critics have largely ignored the importance of suburbia in Australian fiction, even in works that obviously address suburbia; this critical neglect is evidenced by the dearth of criticism on the subject. As McCann noted in 1998, comparing criticism of recent fiction to that of Patrick White's works, "the persistence of an anti-suburban strain in more recent Australian fiction has attracted less criticism and comment" ("Introduction" vii). For example, a search for criticism on the subject of "suburbia" in the AustLit database returns just sixty-five results, many of which focus on poetry and plays, rather than fiction.[7] A search for criticism on the subject of "suburbs" returns one hundred and three results, while a search for criticism using the keyword "suburban" delivers just forty-eight results. Alternatively, a search for criticism on the subject of "the bush" returns 1071 results, "city" returns 335 results, and "urban" garners 591 results. The bulk of the small body of criticism that addresses Australian fiction set in the suburbs deals with White's novels *Riders in the Chariot* and *The Solid Mandala*, and George Johnston's *My Brother Jack*, although the majority of the criticism on these novels deals with issues *other* than suburbia. For example, none of the works of criticism on *Riders in the Chariot* focus on the suburban setting, nor do any of the works on *The Solid Mandala*, which is remarkable given the fact that White is often described as an anti-suburban writer. Therefore, although it is rare for critics to write about Australian fiction set in suburbia, it is *even rarer* for critics to address the manner in which authors explore suburbia.

The body of criticism on many of the writers addressed in this book is quite small. The scholarship on Gerald Murnane and the two of his novels I examine consists of two monographs and thirteen chapters and journal articles. Despite Tim Winton's tremendous popularity and numerous awards, there is only one collection of essays on his work, one monograph, and twenty-two journal articles and book chapters dealing with *Cloudstreet*, arguably Australia's most popular novel. Although Melissa Lucashenko's *Steam Pigs* was published fifteen years ago, it is the subject of just three journal articles and one book chapter. A.L. McCann's *Subtopia* (2005) is the subject of four journal articles. To date, not a single journal article or book chapter has been published regarding Steven Carroll's trilogy of suburban novels, despite the many accolades Carroll has received. The literature on David Malouf's work is extensive, including five monographs and twenty-six articles dealing in whole or in part with *Johnno*. Likewise, Peter Carey's popularity with both audiences and critics is matched by the extent of the criticism of his work, which consists of seven monographs, one essay collection, and thirty articles and chapters dealing with *Bliss* and *The Tax Inspector*. White remains the most written-about Australian author; there is more criticism regarding White's work than that of any other Australian writer.[8]

While there is a substantial amount of criticism regarding the novels by White, Malouf, Carey and Winton, the majority of the criticism focuses on aspects of the novels *other* than the suburban setting and the impact of the suburban environment on the characters. In 1998, Andrew McCann, the critic and author of the novel *Subtopia*, edited a special issue of *Australian Literary Studies* entitled *Writing the Everyday: Australian Literature and the Limits of Suburbia*, which contained an introductory essay and an essay on White by McCann, plus eight essays by other scholars on suburbia in Australian novels, poetry and non-fiction prose. Apart from three essays on White, between McCann's special issue in 1998 and Rodney Wetherell's essay on McCann's *Subtopia* in 2006, there was an eight-year critical silence on the topic of suburbia in Australian novels. Additionally, suburbia is often neglected in histories, introductions and companions to Australian literature. Although it contains 760 pages and claims to be comprehensive, *The Oxford Companion to Australian Literature* does not include a single entry on "suburbia," "suburbs," or "suburban." Likewise, *The Cambridge Companion to Australian Literature* contains references to suburbia in Australian fiction on just six of 326 pages; the references to suburbia are brief and usually made in passing. However, Nicholas Birns and Rebecca McNeer's *A Companion to Australian Literature Since 1900*, published in 2007, lists "suburbs" in the index and contains references to them on twenty-nine pages, which is a welcome departure from the past neglect of the topic in such works.

THE ARGUMENT OF EXPLORING SUBURBIA

As I have demonstrated above, the anti-suburban tradition in Australian literature stems from a Western worldview that equates suburban life with anti-intellectualism and a postcolonial obsession with national self-image. I am interested in examining the effects of the anti-suburban tradition on the contemporary Australian novel; therefore, this book focuses on novels set in Australian suburbs which were published from the 1960s (when Patrick White and George Johnston published their canonical suburban novels) to the present and explores how novelists have dealt with and moved beyond the anti-suburban tradition, using suburbia as a site in which to address many of the central social issues in Australian culture. As I seek to demonstrate a progression over almost five decades within the body of work that could be called "the Australian suburban novel," rather than focusing on just a few authors, novels or a narrow time-period, I closely examine fourteen novels published between 1961 and 2007. The novels are Patrick White's *Riders in the Chariot* and *The Solid Mandala*; George Johnston's *My Brother Jack*; David Malouf's *Johnno*; Tim Winton's *Cloudstreet*; Melissa Lucashenko's *Steam Pigs*; A.L. McCann's *Subtopia*; Gerald Murnane's *A Lifetime on Clouds* and *Landscape with Landscape*; Peter Carey's *Bliss* and *The Tax Inspector*; and Steven Carroll's *The Art of the Engine Driver*, *The Gift of Speed* and *The Time We Have Taken*.

I selected the novels for the following reasons: first, so that my project covers a time-frame of almost fifty years and reveals a progression within the suburban novel; second, to provide a mixture of canonical, little-known and recent works; third, to include works by both well-known, internationally-recognized authors and little-known, obscure, neglected or emerging writers; fourth, to include novels by writers of a variety of ages and more than one ethnic background; fifth, to include works set in suburbs around Australia; sixth, to include novels set in a variety of types of suburbs, such as inner, outer, working-class, middle-class, established and newly-developed; and seventh, to include novels that deal with a range of social issues. By examining fourteen novels, I demonstrate that the corpus of suburban novels includes some of the most widely-read and critically-acclaimed Australian novels, despite its numerically marginal place within Australian literature. Moreover, I reveal that the suburban novel encompasses a range of styles, from journalistic realism to experimental post-modernism; spans numerous locations within suburbia, including inner and outer suburbs, working class, middle class and upper class suburbs; that much suburban fiction does not fit into the anti-suburban/pro-suburban binary; and, most importantly, that utilizing the suburban setting allows novelists to engage with some of the most important issues in Australian society, such as immigration, environmental degradation, racial and class conflict, consumerism, religion and spirituality, and domestic violence. Moreover, I demonstrate that suburbia is a central concern of Australia's leading novelists.

Exploring Suburbia is the first book-length study of suburbia in Australian literature; it addresses a long-neglected and under-examined area within Australian literature and analyzes novels by some of Australia's most important writers from a new perspective, in addition to examining novels previously neglected by critics. This book provides new insights and perspectives on fourteen Australian novels, several of which are canonical works that have been analyzed extensively by other scholars. My work should lead to a reassessment of the novels and authors under discussion and prompt further research into suburbia in Australian literature. There are a number of novels that I could not include in this project due to space limitations that other scholars may choose to examine or re-examine after reading my work. I wish to reinvigorate the debate regarding suburbia in Australian literature and move it beyond Gerster, Kinnane and Wetherell's calls for Australian authors to engage more closely with suburbia. While I agree with their position and share their belief that Australian novelists are neglecting a great deal of interesting material, I show that the authors who have explored suburbia since 1961 have already moved Australian literature in a new direction, away from the traditional focus on the bush and the city, demonstrating that the literal and theoretical space between the city and the bush contains the most interesting and important engagements with contemporary Australian culture.

Endnotes

1. Search conducted on July 9, 2012 at http://www.austlit.edu.au/. In fact, AustLit lists 1450 poems and 669 short stories about the "suburbs," while there are only 284 novels categorized as dealing with "suburbs," of which some are extracts, and genre fiction is included, such as romance, mystery, crime, young adult, humor, and science fiction. A narrower search for novels about "suburban life" returns just forty-eight entries. A wider search for all works regarding "suburban life" generates 477 entries, including poetry, short stories, novels, plays, columns, autobiographies, criticism and screenplays. Likewise, searches for "suburban" novels and novels about "suburbia" both returned just forty-eight results, as opposed to 1777 "bush" novels, 362 "outback" novels, 672 "country" novels, 181 "rural" novels, 920 "urban" novels and 539 "city" novels. (Of course, there is some overlap between the novels listed under the "bush," "outback," "country" and "rural" categories, as well as the "city" and "suburban" categories).
2. WorldCat search conducted on July 9, 2012.
3. According to Lynn Spigel, in 1993, 86% of white residents of suburbia in the United States lived in areas with a black population below 1% (236).
4. Australia now has the least affordable housing of all developed, English-speaking nations. Prices in Melbourne have more than doubled in the past decade and mortgage interest rates are higher than in the U.S., Britain and most of the EU. Australians pay "6.6 times the median household income for a median-priced home," while "in New Zealand, Ireland and Britain a median-priced home cost[s] between 5.5 and six times the median yearly household income" and in the US and Canada buyers pay between three and four times the median household income (Schneiders).
5. In the first two chapters of this book, I argue against the claim that Patrick White is anti-suburban.
6. Architects have long been opposed to suburbia. The architecture critic Deyan Sudjic notes that in the early twentieth century architects were "horrified" by the "monotony" of New York and London's suburbs, and later by the suburbs of Los Angeles. Le Corbusier argued that suburbia created an "enslaved individualism," while Lewis Mumford attacked suburbia for being what he termed "a multitude of uniform, unidentifiable houses, lined up inflexibly at uniform distances" (Sudjic 197).

7. Searches conducted on July 9, 2012.
8. AustLit searches conducted on July 9, 2012. AustLit lists 1472 works about White, including 1066 works of criticism and 564 reviews. It is important to note that AustLit is not totally comprehensive and may not index some works published outside Australia.

Exploring Suburbia

CHAPTER 1

PATRICK WHITE'S *RIDERS IN THE CHARIOT* (1961)

AN ANTI-SUBURBAN NOVEL?

A detailed examination of suburbia in the Australian novel must address the work of Patrick White (1912-1990), Australia's only winner of the Nobel Prize for Literature, who published two novels in the 1960s that are widely considered classic examples of anti-suburbanism in Australian literature: *Riders in the Chariot* (1961) and *The Solid Mandala* (1966). Both novels have achieved canonical status. The body of work that I term "Australian suburban fiction" begins with White's novels; indeed, White was the first prominent Australian novelist to use a suburban setting. White has often been labeled "anti-suburban," and *Riders in the Chariot* and *The Solid Mandala* (which I address in the next chapter), both set in fictional western suburbs of Sydney, have been considered evidence of White's alleged disdain for suburbia and its inhabitants. To cite a number of examples, Joseph Dewey argues that White "caustically satirized ... [Australia's] suburban culture" (752); the authors of *The Oxford Companion to Australian Literature* claim that White "deplores" "suburban ugliness" and that White's fictional suburb Sarsaparilla "represents the materialism, ugliness and 'exaltation of the average' that he deplores" (Wilde et al 72; 608); McCann argues that White sometimes demonstrates a "paranoid fear of suburbia" and is "often vehemently anti-suburban" ("Ethics" 145; "Decomposing" 59); Powell concludes that White's suburban novels "confirm rather than question the images of the suburbs as places of boredom, prejudice and vulgarity" (127-28); Elizabeth Webby argues that *Riders in the Chariot* and *The Solid Mandala* "are particularly critical of the closed minds and averted eyes of those living respectably in suburbia" (11-12); Gerster insists that White displays "sniggering contempt for suburban (usually female) philistinism" in *Riders in the Chariot* (567); Kinnane labels White "anti-suburban" and groups him with other anti-suburban writers and artists ("Shopping" 41-42); and Simon During states unequivocally, "White hated the suburbs" (16).

Moreover, critics often repeat claims that White is anti-suburban, seemingly without questioning the accuracy of such claims. As McCann notes, "It is now customary to place White's fiction in a modernist literary culture that spurned the vapidity of suburbia" ("Decomposing" 70). For example, Veronica Brady begins her essay "God, History, and Patrick White" by stating, "White has usually been seen as a ferocious critic of Australian suburban life" (172). She provides a footnote citing "two excellent articles by Andrew McCann ... [that] point to White's reputation as a hater of suburbia" and notes that McCann's articles "proceed to question this interpretation" (176), but she does not provide any other evidence to support her opening claim, nor does she engage with McCann's questioning of White's anti-suburban reputation.[1] Towards the conclusion of her article, Brady claims the novel "directs" "disgust ... against the citizens of Sarsaparilla" (176); however, she does not provide examples of the alleged "disgust" and overlooks the fact that indisputably "good" characters also reside in Sarsaparilla. For far too long, critics have erroneously labeled both White and his work "anti-suburban." In the following discussion I provide a new, detailed interpretation of White's relationship with suburbia and demonstrate that *Riders in the Chariot* presents a much more ambivalent and nuanced representation of suburbia than critics have previously acknowledged.

WHITE'S REPUTATION AND CRITICAL RECEPTION

The mass of published criticism on White's work clearly demonstrates his central importance within Australian literary studies. According to the AustLit database, more criticism has been published on White's work than on that of any other Australian writer.[2] Although two decades have passed since White's death, his work continues to inspire critical debates and new interpretations. Kerryn Goldsworthy argues that White's reputation "was made by, and rests on, his novels," claiming that his work "dominated Australian literature for three decades" and that "his influence continues to go wide and deep in the work of contemporary Australian writers" (126). Similarly, Michael Ackland argues that White's novels "continue to haunt Australian intellectual life, to shock, inspire and tantalize" (415). White's immense influence on Australian authors was demonstrated clearly in 2003 when the nearly three thousand members of the Australian Society of Author's voted for their Top Forty Australian Books; their list included five novels by White (including two in the top ten), as well as David Marr's biography of White. White was the only author with more than three books on the list ("Top Forty").

Analysts of White's work place him among the great twentieth-century writers, elevating him to the status of a global figure. In a review of *Voss* published in 1958 in *Australian Letters*, Robert Fry notes that reviewers had already compared White to D.H. Lawrence, William Faulkner, Leo Tolstoy, Thomas Hardy, Joseph Conrad and Jane Austen (40). Although White's central place in Australian literature is unquestionable, his critical reception has engendered much debate. Alan Lawson and Wenzhong Hu debate the extent to which White has allegedly been lauded overseas while disparaged in Australia. In 1973, Lawson countered those who claimed Australian critics had treated White harshly. In a detailed analysis of reviews and criticism of White's work, Lawson argued that John Thompson, in his 1958 article "Australia's White Policy," presents

> [a] bleak review of the treatment accorded Patrick White by Australian critics ... [that] has been simplified and exaggerated

> many times ... and the 'anti-White-ism' of Australian reviewers seems to have become one of the unexamined truisms of our literary culture ... it needs to be insisted that White's Australian reception has been very much better, the overseas reviews often less favourable, and the general critical standard of the response higher, than the accepted account would suggest. ("Unmerciful" 379)

In 1994, Wenzhong Hu revisited the debate over White's critical reception. Like Lawson, Hu notes Thompson's 1958 argument and shows that in 1961 Geoffrey Dutton essentially repeated Thompson's claim when he wrote, "Australian critics had never approved of White, and their reactions were mostly hostile" (qtd. in Hu 8). Dutton, an editor of *Australian Letters*, which published "The Prodigal Son" and other works by White, was White's close friend for twenty years; the men often talked on the telephone, corresponded, and stayed at each other's homes: Marr claims Dutton "became like a son to White" (Marr 303, 327, 348, 371-373, 640). Thus, Dutton's repetition of Thompson's claim and his championing of White are unsurprising.[3] Hu claims that no one openly disputed Thompson or Dutton, but when Maurice Dunlevy repeated their claims in the *Canberra Times* after White won the Nobel Prize, Lawson responded with two articles and six letters in the *Canberra Times*, in addition to the aforementioned essay. Hu argues, however, that the debate over White's critical reception in Australia is "far from over" (333). Indeed, as recently as 2004, Dewey repeated the claims of Thompson, Dutton and Dunlevy (752).

After White won the Nobel Prize, his novels were canonized and White himself "was almost transformed into a kind of literary icon" (Hu 338). Hu points out that upon White's death, Prime Minister Bob Hawke "paid tribute to him and obituaries all praised him highly," and argues, "There is not a single Australian writer, except for Christina Stead perhaps, who enjoyed a reputation anywhere near White's during his lifetime" (338). Hu claims that although White "was heralded [in America] as a significant writer in the early years, his prestige did not last," and notes that upon his death *The Guardian* newspaper in Britain declared, "'He was almost a forgotten writer as far as most Western critics were concerned'" (339). In During's controversial 1996 monograph, he acknowledges White's "extraordinary status in the national culture," which he argues would only be preserved

> so long as the country needs critiques of ordinariness and his readers can overlook how, in his novels, the primary figure of that ordinariness and the object of his exorcisms is, again and again, the middle-aged, middle-class, not highly educated, suburban woman. (100)

During went so far as to claim that White is "doomed to be increasingly neglected, or, at any rate, celebrated only in lip-service" (100).

In 2001, Charles Lock described White's reputation as being "in that mysterious slump to which most writers are, for a while, posthumously consigned" (72). In 2007, Birns and McNeer described White as "the stranded behemoth of Australian literature," noting that he is "always a point of reference," but "curiously external to contemporary literary discourse and to the shelves of contemporary bookstores, inside or outside of Australia" ("Introduction" 11). However, new critical work on White continues to appear and he remains a prominent figure in global literary studies.[4] During's prediction that White's reputation in Australia is doomed to demise has so far proved empty.[5] Within Australia, studies of White's work underwent a resurgence due to a hoax perpetrated in 2006 by *The Australian* newspaper, which sent a chapter of White's novel *The Eye of the Storm* to twelve of Australia's leading publishers and agents under the name Wraith Picket (an anagram of Patrick White); ten rejected the manuscript, deeming it unpublishable, while two did not respond (Malouf, "Patrick White Reappraised").

In response to the hoax, White's fans established websites and reading groups; prominent writers, critics and academics responded with articles in the mainstream media; and academics organized a symposium entitled Remembering Patrick White, which was held in Sydney in May

2007, featuring many of Australia's most prominent literary scholars. An international conference on White's work held in London in 2010 attracted many prominent critics, including Simon During, and a conference commemorating the centenary of White's birth scheduled to be held in Hyderabad, India, in November 2012 will feature critics from around the world, demonstrating the ongoing vitality of White studies.

"The Prodigal Son" and White's Life in Suburbia

In 1958, White published an essay entitled "The Prodigal Son" that became his most famous work of non-fiction prose. Marr claims the essay contains White's "most devastating attack ... against Australia. He wrote nothing like it again, and nothing he has written is so often quoted" (328). In the essay, White explains his reasons for returning to Australia from abroad and provides criticisms of Australian society that have been used as evidence by critics who argue that White is elitist, anti-suburban and anti-Australian. As Bernadette Brennan notes, critics have dismissed "White's ongoing relevance ... by labelling him and his writing 'elitist'" (34). The oft-quoted passage from "The Prodigal Son" follows:

> In all directions stretched the Great Australian Emptiness, in which the mind is the least of possessions, in which the rich man is the important man, in which the schoolmaster and the journalist rule what intellectual roost there is, in which beautiful youths and girls stare at life through blind blue eyes, in which human teeth fall like autumn leaves, the buttocks of cars grow hourly glassier, food means cake and steak, muscles prevail, and the march of material ugliness does not raise a quiver from the average nerves. (White 38-39)

White does not mention suburbia at all, and the phrase "in all directions" implies that the "Great Australian Emptiness" exists in all parts of Australian society, whether urban, rural or suburban. Moreover, White specifically refers to a mindset rather than a physical location. While White sees architecture that he does not find aesthetically pleasing and consumer goods as symptoms of widespread anti-intellectualism, it takes a leap of logic to read the passage as proof of the author's anti-suburbanism.

Moreover, White refers to the state of Australian society as he perceived it upon his return to Australia, not at the time he wrote the article, more than a decade later. Interestingly, White presented a contrary perspective in 1947 while corresponding with his American publisher: "The people are beginning to develop, and take an interest in books, and painting, and music, to an extent that surprises me, knowing them fourteen years ago. One gets the impression that a great deal is about to happen" (qtd. in Ackland 405). In the same year, White wrote to another friend, "Even the uglier aspects of the place have their significance and rightness, to me" (qtd. in Marr 245). And in 1956, two years before the publication of "The Prodigal Son," White wrote to his American publisher claiming, "Quite a lot of them [Australians] are beginning to look for works of art, and will accept *Voss*, and even exalt it" (qtd. in Marr 320). These brief examples reveal that White's attitudes towards Australian culture were more complex than "The Prodigal Son" suggests. The frequent quotation of the above passage from "The Prodigal Son" has created a distorted view of White's attitudes towards Australian society.

In "The Prodigal Son," White points out that in the ten years between his purchase of "Dogwoods" at Castle Hill, and the time of writing the essay, he had "hardly stirred" from his outer-suburban home (37). White lived at Castle Hill for another eight years after composing "The Prodigal Son," bringing his residence in the suburb to a total of eighteen years (White, *Flaws* 138). If White really hated suburbia, he surely would not have voluntarily lived there for almost two decades. Moreover, White based his fictional suburbs of Sarsaparilla, Barranugli and Paradise East on Castle Hill and used them as the settings for two novels, a novella, two plays and several short stories, indicating a fascination with suburban life. Elizabeth Salter argues that White's return to Australia after the Second World War "gave him the stimulus needed for the full development of his talent" (232). In addition to providing the inspiration, setting and background material for many of his works, Marr argues that suburban life provided White and his homosexual partner Manoly Lascaris with a degree of freedom to live together (246). Although White's sexual orientation was well-known among his friends and the literary community, he was not publicly "out" and suburbia afforded him and Lascaris more privacy than they would have had if they lived in the city.

In "The Prodigal Son," White declares that what he perceived to be "the exaltation of the 'average'" in Australian society was what made him "panic most" upon his return to Australia (39). However, rather than find other subject matter, White chose to focus on the average, writing *The Tree of Man*, in which he sought "to discover the extraordinary behind the ordinary, the mystery and the poetry which alone could make bearable the lives of ... [average] people" (39). In another frequently quoted passage from "The Prodigal Son," White declares, "Above all I was determined to prove that the Australian novel is not necessarily the dreary, dun-coloured offspring of journalistic realism" (39). Thus, not only did White seek to push the Australian novel in new directions through Modernist experimentation, he chose to do so using suburbia as his setting. White admits that after several years at Castle Hill he "began to see things for the first time. Even the boredom and frustration presented avenues for endless exploration; even the ugliness, the bags and iron of Australian life, acquired a meaning" ("The Prodigal Son" 39). Hence, rather than being a site unworthy of the artist's attention, suburbia is for White a locale in which experimentation, insight and discovery are both a possibility and a reality.

Although White's home at Castle Hill was not typically suburban, being a six-acre farm rather than a quarter-acre block, it was not completely rural either, and became increasingly suburban as Sydney expanded. A map in Marr's biography shows Dogwoods close to a police station, banks, a cinema, and the post office. Marr describes Dogwoods as "not really a country house but a bungalow," while White described it as "'a bit of Strathfield in a paddock,'" referring to a more central Sydney suburb

(Marr 262). In *Flaws in the Glass*, White describes Dogwoods as "a suburban villa" (137). In 1955, White planned to move to a more typically suburban home. Due to ill health, he decided to sell Dogwoods and find "a modern house in an acre of garden bush"; however, he received no offers (Marr 302-303). In 1959, White wrote, "My so-called farm has now been swallowed up by suburbia," and Marr states that by that time Castle Hill "had grown into a suburban shopping centre" (350).

Writing to James Stern regarding rumors that the Housing Commission had purchased land adjacent to Dogwoods, White stated, "we don't know how much of their horrible boxes will be visible through the trees ... I should hate to leave here, and wouldn't know where to go next" (Qtd. in Marr 350). In a letter composed in 1963, White indicates that he viewed Dogwoods as located in suburbia. Stating that he had written to the *Sunday Telegraph* in response to a piece on his play *The Season at Sarsaparilla* in which the reviewer asked how "a rich bachelor [could] know anything about suburbia," White noted that he had "spent the last seventeen years in Sarsaparilla" (Qtd. in Marr 420). When White won the Nobel Prize in 1973, the subdivision of Dogwoods had begun; two of the streets were named Patrick White Place and Nobel Avenue. At one point in *Flaws in the Glass*, White writes, "I hated the years spent at Castle Hill"; however, his hatred was not caused by Castle Hill's suburban location or neighbors, but was due to White being "constantly ill with asthma" due to negative reactions to the vegetation (139). Writing of his decision to leave Castle Hill after his mother died in 1963 and he inherited half of his father's substantial wealth, White states, "it was impossible to continue living in what had become a suburb, when our interests – music, theatre, film, friends – were concentrated in the city. But to make the break was hard" (*Flaws* 146). White and Lascaris moved to Centennial Park in inner Sydney in October 1963, an area which White described as "a middle-class suburban precinct" (*Flaws* 147, 149). At no point in his autobiography does White express explicitly negative sentiments about suburbia.

Riders in the Chariot

The majority of *Riders in the Chariot* is set in Sarsaparilla, the fictional suburb White based on Castle Hill; portions of the novel are also set in England and Germany. Like H.G. Wells and George Orwell before him, White proved with *Riders in the Chariot* that a serious work of art can draw on suburbia and its inhabitants for both its subject matter and inspiration. White uses the suburban setting to explore a multiplicity of themes, including immigration, the legacy of colonialism, spirituality, religion, the role of the artist in society, the relationship between humans and nature, family relationships, class, consumerism, racism, intolerance, bigotry, suffering and redemption. Ackland describes *Riders in the Chariot* as "immensely ambitious" (403), while Jacqueline Banerjee deems the novel "the most impressive, coherent and inspiring expression of White's unique qualities as a novelist" (92). Webby argues that White's choice of "a Jewish refugee, an Aboriginal artist and two women" as his four riders anticipated "three of the major future challenges to old ideas of Australian literature and the 'Australian tradition': from multiculturalism, the women's movement and Aboriginal activism" ("Introduction" 12). Likewise, Goldsworthy reads the novel as "an early model for the ideals of multiculturalism" that was "extraordinary" for its time and claims that upon its publication, "White began to be seen as one of the country's great artists, constructing a nation and its social history in his writing" (127).

Marr views *Riders in the Chariot* as essentially "a study of ... good people pitted against evil" (361). Likewise, Salter sums up the novel's theme as "redemption through suffering" (236). However, critics arguing that the novel is primarily concerned with a single theme ignore the complexity of the work and many of the issues White tackles. To date, no critic has undertaken a thorough study of White's engagement with suburbia in the novel. However, suburbia is not the only aspect of the novel critics neglect. Webby notes that White's representation of Australian society in his fiction "has not been much studied": she argues that Patricia Morley's *The Mystery of Unity: Theme and Technique in Patrick White's Fiction* (1972), "The first intensive critical study of themes and preoccupations in White's fiction," inspired the approach of much of the subsequent criticism, so that Morley's "emphasis on the metaphysical, the mystical, the spiritual and the symbolic aspects of White's work became the critical orthodoxy" ("Our Invisible"). Moreover, Webby suggests that even though White's work has been the subject of more scholarship than "any other Australian author, it is clear that many aspects of his work remain largely unexplored, including the political, the comedic, the ways he represented Australian society and the relationship of his works to Australian and international literary traditions" (Webby, "Our Invisible").

However, the critical tide may have turned, and scholars are both re-examining White's oeuvre and analyzing certain aspects of his work for the first time. In 2007, Brennan published an excellent article on *Riders in the Chariot* in which she argues that the novel and White's "message of the need for loving-kindness in the face of difference, and fear of that difference" is as relevant today as it was when the novel was first published in 1961 (32). Brennan argues that White's engagement with Australian society in *Riders in the Chariot* can guide readers toward strategies for countering the prevalent "climate of fear being fuelled by false assertions about the threat difference poses to 'ordinary Australians' and their way of life" (40). Brennan concludes that White's writing helps readers "understand the absolutely ordinary fears and insecurities of the suburban Australian consciousness" (43-44). In 2009, Cynthia vanden Driesen published *Writing the Nation: Patrick White and the Indigene*, in which she provides a detailed examination of White's representations of Indigenous Australians in *Riders in the Chariot*, *Voss* and *A Fringe of Leaves*, and argues that White's "contribution to the general debate on postcolonial issues and the politics of black/white relations within postcolonial Australia" has not previously been explored in detail (xxvi).

Riders in the Chariot focuses on the spiritual journeys of four characters: Miss Hare, an elderly spinster and only child of wealthy parents; Mrs. Godbold, a poor English immigrant who survives by taking in laundry; Mordecai Himmelfarb, a Jewish Holocaust-survivor refugee immigrant;

and Alf Dubbo, a diseased Aboriginal artist. Other characters who play important roles are Mrs. Jolley and Mrs. Flack, both representatives of middle-class suburban values. It is apparent from just a brief description of White's cast of characters, even before engaging closely with the novel's themes, that *Riders in the Chariot* reveals the richness, complexity and variety of life in suburbia. In the following close readings of White's characters and themes, I demonstrate White's complex exploration of suburbia and Australian society, proving that White was not an anti-suburban writer and that his representations of suburbia are complex and ambivalent.

Miss Hare, Nature and the Colonial Legacy

Miss Mary Hare, the first character White introduces, is an elderly spinster living in a decaying colonial mansion named Xanadu,[6] surrounded by suburban development. Mary Hare's father, Norbert, used his inherited wealth to live a life devoted to pleasure on an estate containing "exotic, deciduous trees, the rose garden which his senses craved, [and] pasture for … pedigree Jersey cows" (24). Norbert is a descendant of the class of English gentry whose experiences replicate those of White's own family, especially their efforts to recreate England in Australia, both culturally and physically, by planting English vegetation, importing English livestock, and replicating English architecture. McCann notes that White's portrayal of suburbia is also a portrayal "of a settler society actively engaged in the colonisation of territory and the appropriation of apparently untamed space" and argues that White situates "the genesis of the Australian suburb in an unmistakable colonial context" ("Ethics" 146, 147). White presents the conflict between the natural environment and Norbert's attempts to impose English ideals upon it as one the colonizers must lose. After Norbert's workers attempt to clear and "tame" the landscape, the indigenous vegetation "which had been pushed back, immediately began to tangle with Norbert Hare's willfully created park" and began the process of reclamation (17). McCann argues that White depicts Xanadu "as an ultimately grotesque attempt to consolidate an image of

European civility and gentility in the alien and subtly resistant landscape of the Australian bush" ("Ethics" 147).

Rather than perpetuating her father's imposition of English vegetation and landscaping, Miss Hare allows the indigenous vegetation to defeat the colonizing species and attempts to commune with nature. Rodney Stenning Edgecombe argues that "There is no discrimination in Miss Hare, no fixities of hierarchy and order that might otherwise invite her to exalt European trees above Australian scrub" ("Weeds" 26). Her land is described as belonging to her "over and above actual rights," indicating an unusual intimacy (13). Miss Hare's relationship with nature is emphasized by her refusal to enter her property through the front gates, choosing instead to enter on her hands and knees through a tunnel in the vegetation (14). Edgecombe describes Miss Hare's relationship with nature as an "intimate symbiosis ... a mode of perfect receptivity and quietude" (*Vision* 36). Likewise, Chapman claims that Miss Hare "has come as close to identify with nature ... as White can imagine is humanly possible" (92).

Mary Hare begins communing with nature as a child. In an incident clearly indicating her intent, Mary throws herself on the ground and hollows "out a nest in the grass, with little feverish jerks of her body, and foolish grunts, curling round in the shape of a bean, or position of a foetus" (28). As an elderly woman, Miss Hare retreats into the bush, "always listening and expecting until receiving" (46). Conversing with Himmelfarb, Miss Hare declares, "'the earth is wonderful. It is all we have. It has bought me back when, otherwise, I should have died'" (199) and goes on to claim that when she dies, she "'shall sink into it ... and the grass will grow out of me'" (200).[7] Silvia Gzell argues that Miss Hare "scorns behaviour which is merely conventional and meaningless," living alone by choice, "aware of her difference from other people" (183). Likewise, Chapman posits that Miss Hare's "indifference to ordinary standards of comfort makes her the target of sneers from commonplace minds like Mrs. Jolley" (198). Miss Hare's rejection of conventional behavior can be interpreted as a criticism of suburban values; conversely, she can be viewed as evidence that suburbia contains a variety of people following diverse lifestyles, and that suburbia is not homogenous, nor is it necessarily "plastic" and in conflict with nature.

Miss Hare and her housekeeper Mrs. Jolley clash repeatedly during the latter's tenure at Xanadu. The conflicts climax when Mrs. Jolley kills a snake Miss Hare has been feeding. Mrs. Jolley declares, "'That is not killing ... That is ridding the world of something bad,'" to which Miss Hare replies, "'Who is to decide what is bad?'" (105). After each of her conflicts with Mrs. Jolley, Miss Hare escapes into the bush "to revive" (77). Werner Arens argues that Miss Hare's excursions into the bush are attempts to restore "her faith in the goodness of the earth" (134). Miss Hare's retreats into the bush also serve to emphasize the difference between her spirituality, which focuses on nature, and Mrs. Jolley's, which is confined to the built environment, namely the church and home. On one of her bushwalks, Miss Hare encounters the Indigenous artist Alf Dubbo. Although she has seen Dubbo before "on the roads round Sarsaparilla," on this occasion Dubbo speaks to her in a voice "agreeable, direct and unexpected" (78, 79). Significantly, the two riders first meet in the bush, the environment in which they are both at home.

Edgecombe argues that Miss Hare's love for the natural environment "is above all disinterested – it expects no return" (*Vision* 41). Iris Ralph dubs Mary Hare an "ecological avatar," arguing that she is "a *green* interloper in the 'glass house' of Xanadu" (original emphasis) (32). Ralph notes that "The ecocritical content of *Riders in the Chariot* ... hardly has been spoken to by scholars" and claims the ecocritical content of White's writing "is central to any discussion of White and, further, that this content is central to White's metaphysical themes" (32).[8] Edgecombe views Miss Hare as possessing a "complete" sympathy with "the natural world" ("No Gift" 53); this characteristic prompts Ralph to claim Miss Hare as "a model for ecocentric as opposed to anthropocentric values" (36). Despite Miss Hare's oneness with the natural environment, when she leaves Xanadu near the end of the novel "she does not make any environmental provisions for the land or the flora and fauna that have been slowly reclaiming the estate. Instead, some years before her disappearance she bequeaths Xanadu to a cousin she hardly knows" (Ralph 36). At the end of the novel, Miss Hare's cousin sells the estate, Xanadu is bulldozed, the land subdivided, and new houses are erected.

Mrs. Jolley and Mrs. Flack: "Evil" Guardians of Suburban Values

Although Miss Hare prefers to be alone, her "increasing infirmity" requires her to employ a housekeeper, Mrs. Jolley, a widow from suburban Melbourne (22). When Mrs. Jolley arrives in Sarsaparilla and Miss Hare meets her at the bus stop, Mrs. Jolley asks, "'You haven't a car, then?'" signaling the importance of modern consumer goods in her life and contrasting her to the nature-loving Miss Hare. Mrs. Jolley reacts with despair upon learning that Miss Hare does not own a vehicle: "Mrs Jolley could not believe any of this ... she could have cried" (51). Mrs. Jolley declares that in her family, "everybody has their own car" (52). Thus, White establishes the women as opposites from the outset and sets up the conflict that inevitably ensues. Upon entering Xanadu, Mrs. Jolley comments, "'it is easy to see that it is a long time since you had a lady here,'" indicating the mansion's neglected state and her own prejudices regarding how "ladies" should live (53). When Miss Hare later expresses her fear that Mrs. Jolley is unhappy at Xanadu, Mrs. Jolley replies, "a lady does expect something different," specifying "a home, and a Hoover, and kiddies' voices" (67). Here White aligns Mrs. Jolley with stereotypical suburban values such as domesticity, cleanliness, motherhood and consumerism.

White uses the contentious relationship between Miss Hare and Mrs. Jolley to explore spirituality and religion, subjects rarely associated with Australian suburbia. When Mrs. Jolley inquires if Miss Hare is a Christian, Miss Hare replies, "'It would not be for me to say, even if I understood exactly what that means'" (73-74). Mrs. Jolley, in contrast, boldly declares, "'I am ... I attended the C. of E. [Church of England] ever since I was a kiddy'" (74). Mrs. Jolley's certainty and adherence to mainstream Christian views are juxtaposed to Miss Hare, who admits, upon being pressed, "'I believe. I cannot tell you what I believe in, any more than what I am ... Oh, yes, I believe! I believe in what I see, and what I cannot see. I believe in a thunderstorm, and wet grass, and patches of light, and stillness" (74). Unable to understand Miss Hare's transcendentalism, Mrs. Jolley asks, "'But what is over it?'", a question Miss Hare refuses to answer (74). Mrs. Jolley is both unable to understand or accept a spiritual position different from her own, so much so that she is enraged. The narrator notes that Mrs. Jolley "hated" Miss Hare's face, and when Miss Hare leaves the room, Mrs. Jolley hopes "she might hear a body fall. She hoped Miss Hare might die, even" (74). Mrs. Jolley bakes a cake, her way of restoring order to the household, on which she writes in icing, "FOR A BAD GIRL" (76). She sings as she bakes, in her mind celebrating and populating "square brick homes" with "ladies and the kiddies" (75). Thus, while Miss Hare represents a spirituality and communion with nature unbound by either religion or structures built by humans, Mrs. Jolley takes refuge in a religion with clear boundaries and a suburban ethos that is similarly defined and solid.

Miss Hare dreads conversations with Mrs. Jolley, which the narrator describes as "the piles of brick that Mrs Jolley built to house her family in, the red brick boxes increasing and encroaching" (77). Although White's narrator employs images of suburbia in a negative manner in this passage, it would be a mistake to read it as an attack on suburbia by White or evidence of his alleged anti-suburbanism, since such a reading relies on conflating White and his narrator. Even if White conveys some of his own attitudes and prejudices, either through his narrator or his characters, his narrative technique employs numerous points of view and his characters present a variety of attitudes, making it impossible to identify any one position as White's. Thus, while White's work contains sentiments that are hallmarks of the anti-suburban tradition, it is impossible to prove that White shares those sentiments. In an essay on recurring problems in White criticism, Lawson notes that White is "often said to be a dogmatic, intrusive, too-knowing author," but argues that "there are grounds ... for affirming the opposite or at least insisting that the effect is the opposite to authorial certitude and interpretive limitation" ("Meaning" 286). Lawson goes so far as to claim that "White's sympathies are widely engaged but always qualified: he endorses none, is totally detached from none" and concludes, "White is clearly less interested in absolutes than many of his critics have been" ("Meaning" 286, 287).

Upon Miss Hare's return to Xanadu after her encounter with Dubbo, Mrs. Jolley expresses shock that her employer has been in the bush "'on a Sunday!'" before launching into a diatribe revealing her racism and fear of nature, "'Pooh! Some dirty abo[9] bloke! I would not have an abo come near me. And in the bush! They are all undesirable persons. And in the bush! You will run into trouble, my lady'" (80, 81). Edgecombe argues that for Mrs. Jolley the bush is "a place of evil, contradistinguished from the brick boxes of suburbia of which she is the celebrant" ("No Gift" 60). For Mrs. Jolley, the bush is evil because it represents the unknown and the uncontained, and because it is the native abode of Indigenous Australians.

Although Mrs. Jolley is not one of the riders of the novel's title, she is the subject of much discussion in the criticism, along with her friend Mrs. Flack, because they are vivid, memorable characters often read as representing suburban values. Both women are widows whose husbands died in suspicious circumstances. As During notes, "in White's novels the truly typical suburban middle-class person is the wife rather than the husband" (48). Indeed, the minor characters Harry Rosetree and Tom Godbold are the only suburban husbands in the novel. Miss Hare refers to Mrs. Jolley as "'one of the evil ones! ... [who] has entered into a conspiracy with another devil, and will bring suffering to many before it destroys them both'" (201). Marr claims that Mrs. Jolley and Mrs. Flack are "creations of pure hate" (370). White described the women as "devils" when writing to his publisher; they are based on a pair of widows in the United States who poisoned their husbands in an attempt to collect life insurance (Marr 370).[10] Like White and his characters, critics often describe Mrs. Jolley and Mrs. Flack as evil.[11] Mrs. Jolley is characterized repeatedly by her fondness for material possessions, machines, and the built environment, such as cars, trams and houses. Mrs. Jolley is described from Miss Hare's point of view as "The woman whose three daughters' husbands had built with bricks, boxes in which to live" (58). Later in the novel, Miss Hare concludes, "'I do not think Mrs. Jolley sees beyond texture-brick and plastic'" (392). Mrs. Jolley likes to gossip, holds fixed standards for human behavior, and is intolerant of those who do not share her opinions and beliefs.

Some critics argue that Mrs. Jolley and Mrs. Flack are merely caricatures, rather than developed characters. For example, Salter claims, "White's ferocity sacrifices characterization for caricature, as exampled by those two harpies Mrs Jolley and Mrs Flack" (238), while Gzell claims White satirically distorts "most members of society" in order to make his riders heroic and exaggerate "their separation from other people" (181). Gerster argues that "Most of White's suburbanites are caricatures, or to be more precise grotesques, rather than fully realized characters. His particular fondness is for creating inane, spiritually shriveled suburban women" (567). However, Brennan argues that "to label Mrs Flack and Mrs Jolley as simply caricatures is to dismiss their potent power" (37). During goes so far as to claim that White is "under-read" because "he simplified and scapegoated ordinary life and people," especially "heterosexual, middle-class women" (57). However, Webby argues that White did not attack the "ordinariness" of Mrs. Jolley and Mrs. Flack, as During claims, "but their materialism and their black-and-white view of the world, especially their lack of tolerance for anything or anyone perceived as different. What he was attacking was their assumption of the high moral ground, their belief in themselves as 'good Australians'" ("Our Invisible"). Likewise, Brennan posits that White rails against "the suburban mindset," rather than suburbia as a whole, critiquing the "fear of stepping outside prescribed boundaries, of appearing to be ... anything other than 'ordinary' Australians," and the unquestioning acceptance of "labels or codes of appropriate conduct" (38).

Mrs. Jolley and Mrs. Flack meet on the bus and soon the former is in the habit of visiting the latter's home in Sarsaparilla, which she greatly admires:

> Mrs Jolley loved the latch at Mrs Flack's. She loved the rustic picket gate. She loved the hedge of Orange Triumph. To run her glove along the surface of Mrs Flack's brick home gave her shivers. The sound of its convenience swept her head over heels into the caverns of envy. (92)

As their relationship develops, the women "produce their knives and try them for sharpness on weaker mortals" (95). Later in the novel, Mrs. Flack instigates the events that lead to the death of Himmelfarb and the disappearance of Miss Hare. White's narrator introduces a passage in which Mrs. Flack and Mrs. Jolley espouse racist anti-immigrant sentiments by declaring, "The voice of Sarsaparilla ... took for granted its right to pass judgement on the human soul" (273). Mrs. Flack bemoans the recent arrival of refugees from Europe and positions them as displacing Australian soldiers serving overseas: "'I would not of thought it would come to this ... a stream of foreign migrants pouring into the country, and our Boys many of them not yet returned ... Who will feed us, when we are so many mouths over, and foreign mouths" (273). Mrs. Flack soon directs the conversation from the general to the specific, focusing on Himmelfarb: "'They say,' she said, 'there is a foreign Jew, living ... below the post-office, in Montebello Avenue, in a weatherboard home'" (274). Not content to discuss Himmelfarb from afar, the women walk to his home, hoping to catch a glimpse of him, gossiping cruelly about their neighbors along the way.

The women hide behind a bush while watching Himmelfarb's house, which the narrator describes as "suitably, obscenely poor" (276). White's narrator reveals that Mrs. Flack and Mrs. Jolley longed "for something that would rend their souls – a foetus say, or a mutilated corpse" (277). Rather than evidence of evil or violence, the women are stunned to see Mrs. Godbold emerge from Himmelfarb's door, followed by the Jew himself:

"They had never seen anything so yellow or so strange. Strange? Why, dreadful, dreadful!" (277). Rather than something disgraceful or evil, Mrs. Flack and Mrs. Jolley witness an act of kindness and friendship. Mrs. Godbold has bandaged Himmelfarb's hand, which he injured at work: "How private, and mysterious, and beautiful it was, even the intruders suspected, and were deterred momentarily from hating" (279). The actions of Mrs. Godbold, herself a suburban housewife, demonstrate that Mrs. Jolley and Mrs. Flack are not necessarily representative of suburban women. In fact, they may well be anomalies. However, their xenophobia soon returns, and as Mrs. Jolley walks back to Xanadu, she fantasizes about killing an animal and "drifted dreamily through the series of possible ways in which she might continue to harry the human soul" (279-80).

During her final confrontation with Miss Hare, Mrs. Jolley quits her job (381). Miss Hare reveals she is aware of much more than she is usually given credit for, commenting, "'You will go, I suppose, to Mrs Flack ... For life, I expect'" (382). Miss Hare proceeds to declare, "'The two of you will sit in Mrs Flack's *lounge*, watching us behave. Even directing us'" (382, original emphasis). When Mrs. Jolley refers to Himmelfarb as "'a dirty Jew,'" Miss Hare is enraged,

> "My *what* Jew?" The words were choking. "'Dirty'? What is true, then? My kind man! My good! Then I am offal, offal! Green, putrefying, out of old, starved sheep. Worse, worse! Though not as bad as some. Offal is cleaner than dishonest women. What is lowest of all? You could tell me! Some women! Lower, even. Some women's shit!" (384, original emphasis).

Mrs. Jolley retorts with a standard anti-Semitic line, "'Who did the Jews crucify?'" to which Miss Hare responds, "'The Jew! ... It was horrible ... I have never allowed myself to think about it'" (385). Mrs. Jolley departs, and the two do not see each other again, "except from a distance" (386).

Mrs. Godbold: The Immigrant Saint

Ruth Joyner emigrates from England to Australia after the accidental death of her brother and her widowed father's decision to remarry (312). Upon arriving in Sydney, she goes into domestic service, working in a number of houses before taking a position with Mrs. Chalmers-Robinson, where she meets Tom Godbold, who delivers ice to the household, and soon marries him (314, 330). The couple move to Sarsaparilla, "to live in a shed, temporary like" where Mrs. Godbold "began to bear children, and take in washing" (351). However, the shed which "started temporary ... ended up permanent" (351). Mrs. Godbold endears herself to her neighbors through her kindness and generosity. She nurses Miss Hare through an illness, prompting Miss Hare to declare "'she is the best of women,'" bandages Himmelfarb's injured hand, offers to do his laundry, and bakes bread for him (81, 279, 283, 285). Mrs. Godbold is a cheerful character who sings as she irons and smells of "scones and clean laundry" (299, 302). Moreover, Mrs. Godbold is a devout Christian who believes in service, sacrifice, suffering and humility.

However, Mr. Godbold does not share her religious convictions: "What he had time for could be very quickly specified. It was beer, sex, and the trots, in that order" (300). Mr. Godbold flies into a rage when one of his daughters declares, "I am saved for Jesus!" He exclaims, "You are saved for Crap!" before beating his wife repeatedly with a newspaper. As his rage escalates, he shouts, "'This is what I think of all caterwaulin' Christians!'" backhanding his wife across her ear. He punches his wife in the stomach and kicks her while she crumples to the floor, announcing he is going out to get drunk: "It had all happened before, of course" (303). The narrator states that Mrs. Godbold's nature "denied her the opportunity of flight. She had to suffer" (301).

When Alf Dubbo collapses at Mrs. Khalil's brothel, where Mrs. Godbold has gone in search of Tom, she ministers to him and treats him "as if he was a human being," even while the other people present utter racist epithets (367). After finding Tom at Mrs. Khalil's, Mrs. Godbold declares, "'I will follow you to hell if need be'" (372). However, he leaves permanently and dies alone in poverty several years later (372). Walking away from the hospital after viewing Tom's body, Mrs. Godbold weeps, not for herself, but "for the condition of men, for all those she had loved … for her fellow initiates, the madwoman and the Jew of Sarsaparilla, even for the blackfellow she had met at Mrs. Khalil's" (374). Edgecombe argues that even though Mrs. Godbold's religion "bears some superficial resemblance to Mrs Jolley's in its naïve Evangelical cast," it is "a creed of extraordinary dignity and finds embodiment in ideals of humility and service" (*Vision* 47). Mrs. Godbold's former employer, Mrs. Chalmers-Robinson, describes her as "'a kind of saint,'" "'a rock to which we clung,'" and "'the rock of love'" (635). Bliss argues that Mrs. Godbold is "undeniably good and a force for good in the novel. Hers, in fact, is the most unalloyed good the novel offers" (*Patrick White's Fiction* 92).

White's characterization of Mrs. Godbold allows him to deal with issues common in suburban fiction, such as domestic violence and immigration. While the domestic violence can be read as a negative depiction of suburbia (or simply a realistic depiction), Mrs. Godbold is unlike the other immigrants in the novel in that she is not discriminated against or pressured to assimilate, undoubtedly because she is English. White thus demonstrates that immigrants are ill-treated due to racism and xenophobia, rather than because they are not Australian-born. Mrs. Godbold also serves as evidence that suburbia is not solely populated by evil suburban housewives like Mrs. Jolley and Mrs. Flack, but also by morally upright women who are more concerned with helping others than acquiring the latest consumer products and gossiping about their neighbors.

Mordecai Himmelfarb: The Immigrant in Suburbia
During a dispute White experienced with a Sydney taxi driver over a fare, the driver repeatedly screamed, "Go back to Germany!" (Marr 248). The incident inspired White to write *Riders in the Chariot*, as it gave him a sense of what it was like to be an immigrant in Australia (Marr 248). White

Patrick White's *Riders in the Chariot* (1961)

also perceived his sexuality as helping him to understand the immigrant's life: "As a homosexual I have always known what it is to be an outsider. It has given me added insight into the plight of the immigrant – the hate and contempt with which he is often received" (qtd. in Marr 248). Of course, White's partner, Manoly Lascaris, was both an immigrant and a homosexual. When Lascaris obtained Australian citizenship in a ceremony amongst a crowd of Greeks and Italians, the magistrate "warned them not to speak foreign languages in public and urged them to read the poetry of Henry Lawson" (Marr 269). When constructing the character of Mordecai Himmelfarb, White drew upon his own experiences and Lascaris's in Australia, his time in Germany before the Second World War, and the lives of a number of Jewish immigrant friends in Sydney.

Himmelfarb is born and raised in the fictional German town Holunderthal, "to a family of well-to-do merchants, some time during the eighteen-eighties" (123). A brilliant young scholar, he embarks on a career as an English professor, receiving a doctorate before continuing his studies at Oxford (142). Himmelfarb returns to Germany shortly before the First World War. Being "a good German," he volunteers for the infantry, is wounded twice, and wins a medal (153). After the war, Himmelfarb is appointed to the University of Bienenstadt and marries Reha Liebmann (155). Himmelfarb's publications lead to his appointment as the Chair of English at his hometown university (178). When the Nazis gain power, Himmelfarb loses his job (186). Soon after, Reha is captured by the Nazis while he is away (196). Himmelfarb's friends hide him in a rural mansion, but he surrenders during a British bombing raid (221). He is transported to a concentration camp, escapes during an uprising, and makes his way to Palestine. However, disenchanted with the Zionists, Himmelfarb immigrates to Australia (249).

Once in Sydney, Himmelfarb does not attempt to re-enter academia, claiming, "'The intellect has failed us'" (257). Gzell argues that Himmelfarb

> rejects the shelter of academic life in favour of the unprotected life at Sarsaparilla. In his desire for atonement for his sins he denies himself any course which is familiar or easy, preferring to submit himself to the strains which will tax his resources of integrity and survival. (184)

Himmelfarb works a series of menial jobs: at a piggery, as a janitor in a hospital, and as a dishwasher (258). After the war ends, Himmelfarb moves to Sarsaparilla in search of seclusion (258). He buys a derelict house, which he is able to afford due to "dry rot, inadequate plumbing and a leaky roof" (258). Himmelfarb takes the bus to his factory job in Barranugli, living in many respects a typical working-class suburban existence (266). However, in contrast to representative suburbanites such as Mrs. Flack and the Rosetrees, the family of Jewish immigrants who attempt total assimilation, Himmelfarb lives in an "almost empty house" that is poorly maintained and lacks a carefully tended garden (283).

When Himmelfarb is offered a job at Brighta Bicycle Lamps, his new employer, Mr. Rosetree, declares, "'But it will be monotonous. I warn you. Bloody monotonous. It will kill you,'" to which Himmelfarb replies, "'I have been killed several times already'" (265). Himmelfarb's workmates do not joke with him as they do with other coworkers, since they perceive "something strange" and "Nothing like his face had ever been seen by any of them" (267). His difference ensures continual rejection: "If sometimes the foreigner found it necessary to speak, it was as though something preposterous had taken place" (267). Despite numerous attempts, Himmelfarb does not make any male friends in Australia, a fact he is reminded of by his foreman, Ernie Theobalds, who declares, "'a man stands a better chance of a fair go if he's got a mate'" (401). Reflecting on his lack of a mate, Himmelfarb "remembered the blackfellow with whom he had not yet spoken" (402). Himmelfarb and Alf Dubbo have exchanged glances and reached a kind of understanding: "with this fellow flotsam, the Jew had formed ... an extraordinary non-relationship ... he would sense the abo's approach. How he went to meet his silence. How they would lay balm on wounds every time they passed each other" (403). Dubbo and Himmelfarb finally converse after Himmelfarb discovers a Bible that Dubbo had been reading in the washroom (405).

As Himmelfarb prepares for Passover and sets the Seder table, he yearns for Jewish companionship and travels uninvited to Paradise East to visit the Rosetrees. However, the Rosetrees are unwilling to acknowledge their Jewish heritage and refuse to extend hospitality. When Himmelfarb arrives home, he is met by Mrs. Godbold, who brings him some leftover lamb (513). When he takes the leg of lamb to his table, he finds that it is "almost the twin of the one he had laid that afternoon on his own Seder table" (515). Thus, Himmelfarb finds acceptance and love from a woman who is both a Christian and an outcast, rather than amongst his fellow Jews, or the average suburbanites. Salter claims, "No Australian who lived an urban life after the war could pretend that the 'reffo,' the New Australian, was other than an outsider in the community" (236). The mock-crucifixion of Himmelfarb at the factory is the climax of the novel and I devote a later section of this chapter to it.

The Rosetrees: Victims of Assimilation?
White deals with issues of immigration, assimilation, religion, racism and consumerism in suburbia through the Rosetree family, Jewish immigrants who have changed their names from Shulamith and Haim Rosenbaum to Shirl and Harry Rosetree, abandoned Judaism, and adopted Catholicism. White introduces Harry Rosetree into the narrative when Himmelfarb applies for a job in his factory. During the interview, Himmelfarb asks Rosetree, "'You are not from here?'" to which Rosetree replies, "'I am an Australian'" (262). However, Rosetree soon admits to being from Vienna, but declares that speaking German is forbidden on the premises, "'Not on no account … We are Australians now'" (262). When Himmelfarb indirectly asks Rosetree if he is Jewish, Rosetree replies, "'If it is religion you mean, after so much beating in the bush – and religion in these countries, Mr Himmelfarb, is not an issue of first importance – I can plainly tell you I attend the Catholic Church of Saint Aloysius '" (263).[12]

In addition to changing their names and religion and refraining from using their first language, the Rosetrees adopt a thoroughly suburban lifestyle in Paradise East, dwelling in a "texture-brick home" at "quite a good address" (268). The suburb is still growing, and the sound of falling trees and construction is heard from the Rosetree's home (268-69). Edgecombe notes that White presents "suburbia in process of asserting itself against the scrub" ("Weeds" 30).

Harry Rosetree takes pride is his suburban home and material success. On Sundays, he stands "outside his apricot, texture-brick home, amongst all the advanced shrubs he had planted ... Who wouldn't feel satisfied?" (269). Edgecombe posits that "the paraphernalia of a suburban garden serves to advertise the completeness of his assimilation" ("Weeds" 30). Harry is also proud of his children, who are models of assimilation: "they had learnt to speak worse Australian than any of the Australian kids, they had learnt to crave for ice cream, and potato chips and could shoot tomato sauce out of the bottle even when the old black sauce was blocking the hole" (269). The Rosetree children are so thoroughly assimilated that Steve refers to traditional Jewish meals as "'bloody foreign food'" (271). Harry Rosetree hates Himmelfarb because he is a constant reminder of his religion and ancestors and his betrayal of them; "How repellent he found all miserable reffo Jews" (494). When Himmelfarb travels uninvited to Paradise East on Passover, Harry brushes him off with the excuse that he must "water a few shrubs before it is dark" (505). Harry believes that watering one's garden is one of the most important activities in suburbia and is thus a convenient excuse for dismissing unwanted guests.

Shirl has assimilated more than any other member of the family and possesses the authority to declare "What is not Australian" (269). She is described as having a "gift for assimilation," speaking the language "better than anyone" (269). Even though Shirl is more thoroughly assimilated than Harry, she compromises "her quest for Australian conformity by extrapolating from her Central European experience" in her eagerness to assimilate, as is evidenced by the Rosetrees' mistaken choice of Catholicism for their new religion (Edgecombe, "Weeds" 30). In their ignorance, the Rosetrees choose the wrong denomination of Christianity for their class and suburb. One of Shirl's friends, Marge Pendlebury, states, "'I would never ever of suspected you of being tykes. Only the civil servants are Roman Catholics here, and the politicians, if they are anything at all ... Arch and me are Methoes, except we don't go; life is too short'" (270). White presents Shirl as the real owner of the home, the car, the shrubs, the grandfather clock, the radio,

> the washing-machine, and the Mixmaster ... because when she asked the neighbours in to morning tea and scones, she would refer to: *my* home, *my* children, *my* Ford Customline. There was a fur coat, too, still only one, but she was out to get a second while the going was good. (269, original emphasis)

Shirl's materialism is emphasized again two hundred pages later when the narrator states: "Sometimes she thought she was happiest with her own furniture. So now she began to run the shammy leather over the rosewood and maple veneer, until wood was exalted to a state of almost pure reflection" (577).

Obviously, Shirl's materialism can be read as a criticism of suburban values. Malouf adopts a typical anti-suburban position, arguing that the "Rosetrees and others, out of terminal anxiety at their own emptiness and inauthenticity, fill the void of their days" with material possessions ("Introduction" vii). Gzell argues that the Rosetrees "live a lie, concealing their Jewish origin by change of name, religion, speech and diet in order to escape the strain and probable loss of status which a true living out of their identity would entail" (185). Similarly, McCann argues that the Rosetrees "experience their own Jewish-European past as contamination, and accordingly need to banish it from their own 'Home Beautiful' ... [yet they] cannot completely repress their past, and as a result their domestic space is continually threatened by the traces of their contaminating history" ("Ethics" 151). Brady goes further, claiming that the Rosetrees "are seen as figures of evil" (174). However, when Himmelfarb dies,

Harry expresses extreme remorse and attempts to arrange a traditional Jewish burial for Himmelfarb, but arrives at Mrs. Godbold's too late, finding that Himmelfarb has already been buried (580). Devastated, Harry returns home and commits suicide (584, 586). Harry's suicide indicates both his inability to connect with his fellow Jews and to assimilate fully into Australian society. He is trapped in an interstitial space from which he sees death as the only escape.

The Role of the Indigenous Artist in Society
Through the character Alf Dubbo, White simultaneously addresses two major issues: the status of Indigenous Australians and the role of the artist in Australian society. White perceived artists, himself included, to be marginal figures in Australian culture. In *Flaws in the Glass*, White argues that until "the beginning of the Whitlam era ... artists ... [were] a downtrodden minority" (226). Indigenous Australians were also a "downtrodden minority," to say the least, and thus Dubbo is doubly marginalized. White's Indigenous character is born

> on a reserve, to an old gin named Maggie, by which one of the whites she had never been able to decide. There he would have remained probably, until work or cunning rescued him. That he was removed earlier, while he was ... a leggy, awkward little boy, was thanks to the Reverend Timothy Calderon, at that time Anglican rector of Numburra. (408).

Calderon and Mrs Pask, his widowed sister, take Dubbo in and treat him as "their Great Experiment" (408). Dubbo's adoption by Reverend Calderon, "a cultured man, of birth even, whose ideals had brought him from the Old Country" (409), allows White to engage with religion and colonialism, in addition to indigeneity and the role of the artist in society. Like Norbert Hare and Mrs. Chalmers-Robinson, Reverend Calderon represents the legacy and demise of British colonialism in Australia.

White wastes no time broaching the issue of racism, his narrator noting that "the most skeptical of the rector's parishioners" view Dubbo as lazy and conclude that only "the rector would not have expected laziness from the bastard of an old black gin" (409). However, while highlighting the racism of the townspeople, White's narrator simultaneously makes a racist remark about another marginalized group within Australian society and perpetuates a stereotype, stating, "It did not occur to the critics, of course, that the boy might have inherited his vice from some Irish ancestor" (409). Despite being a half-caste, born of a white father and an Indigenous mother, Dubbo is treated as if he is entirely black and referred to as "the blackfellow" or "the abo"; "Officially, of course, he was not a man, but a blackfellow" (533). Cynthia vanden Driesen argues that Dubbo's "tragic experiences stem simply from the fact of his blackness," claims that his "loneliness" is "a comment on the destructiveness ... of white colonialism," and views Dubbo as a character who is "adrift in a world" that has been "completely taken over by the whites" (117).

From an early age, Dubbo shows artistic talent and intellect: "Those who were interested in him were soon convinced that he might grasp almost anything, provided he wanted to" (409). Mrs. Pask teaches Dubbo to paint in watercolors, declaring, "'art is first and foremost a moral force'" and claiming, "'there is something miraculous in the creative act'" (411). She tries to prevent Alf from using oil paints, her reason being that "'Oil paints lead to so much that is sensual, so much that is undesirable in art'" (420). Mrs. Pask's fear of Alf discovering sensuality through art is a manifestation of her fear and loathing of homosexuality. Alf is forced to leave Reverend Calderon and Mrs. Pask after the latter discovers her brother and Alf engaging in consensual sex (432). After weeks of travel on foot, Alf ends up at the Mungindribble town rubbish dump, where he enters into a sexual relationship with a woman named Mrs. Spice who survives by prostitution and selling used bottles. After living with Mrs. Spice and contracting a venereal disease, Alf wanders from town to town in the outback performing odd-jobs, but never staying anywhere long, because

> there was always the possibility that he might be collected for some crime he began to suspect he had committed, or confined to a reserve, or shut up at a mission, to satisfy the social conscience, or to ensure the salvation of souls that were in the running for it. (443)

Dubbo's artistic talent is described by the narrator as "his secret gift" and compared to his disease. Together, his talent and his disease are "the two poles, the negative and positive of his being; the furtive, destroying sickness, and the almost as furtive, but regenerating, creative act" (444). Once Dubbo has physically matured, he develops "the courage and curiosity to make for Sydney," where he sleeps in parks before discovering "a house sufficiently dilapidated, a landlady sufficiently low, and hopeful, and predatory, to accept an abo" (445). White presents Dubbo as constantly disparaged and discriminated against in matters of employment and housing, and existing on the margins of society. As vanden Driesen notes, "Every 'home'" that Dubbo occupies "is only courtesy of the forbearance of the whites" (127). After his arrival in Sydney, Dubbo meets a prostitute named Hannah who recognizes that he has syphilis and offers to let him rent a spare room in her suburban home (450-51). Dubbo accepts her offer and moves into the house in an unnamed suburb with a view of wires and aerials above slate roofs (452). With Hannah's assistance, Dubbo receives treatment for his venereal disease and is eventually cured (454). Dubbo continues to paint after arriving in Sydney, but possesses

> little desire to learn from the achievements of other artists ... But once he came across the painting by a Frenchman of the Apollonian chariot on its trajectory across the sky ... He realized how differently he saw this painting since his first acquaintance with it, and how he would transcribe the Frenchman's limited composition into his own terms of motion, and forms partly transcendental, partly evolved from his struggle with daily becoming, and experience of suffering. (445-446)

Art becomes Dubbo's vocation to such an extent that he is "sufficiently sustained both physically and mentally" and is able "to ignore for the most part what people called life" (448). While living in Hannah's house, Dubbo creates

> the skeletons of several works which he did not have the strength or knowledge to paint. 'The Chariot,' for instance. Ezekiel's vision superimposed upon that of the French painter in the art book, was not yet his own ... The picture he did paint now was 'The Fiery Furnace,' almost the whole of it one Friday. (460)

During a party at Hannah's, Dubbo is persuaded to show his paintings to a guest, Humphrey Mortimer, who offers to buy several of them for a large sum, an offer Dubbo declines (465-69). Weeks later, Dubbo discovers that several of his paintings are missing, including "The Fiery Furnace" and the work-in-progress of the Chariot (476). After Dubbo attempts to choke Hannah in his rage, she admits selling the paintings to Mortimer (479). Mourning his loss, Dubbo destroys his remaining paintings and leaves, taking a room at Mrs. Noonan's house in Barranugli (481-82). At Barranugli, Dubbo takes to reading the Bible, and although he "could accept God because of the spirit that would work in him at times," he is unable to accept Christ as anything more than "an ambitious abstraction, or realistically, as a man," due to "the duplicity of the white men" (482-83). When Mrs. Godbold asks Dubbo if he is a Christian, he replies,

> "No ... I was educated up to it. But gave it away ... When I found I could do better ... There is no point putting on a pair of boots to walk to town, if you can do it better in your bare feet." (370)

Edgecombe argues that Dubbo's spiritual quest "finds consummation in his handling of paint, in the incarnation of aesthetic rather than overtly religious truths" (*Vision* 59).

Dubbo takes a job at Harry Rosetree's factory, where he meets Himmelfarb. At the factory, Dubbo's non-Indigenous coworkers do not associate with him. However, he prefers to be left alone, as it allows him to "travel quicker, deeper, into the hunting grounds of his imagination" (483). Watching the events leading up to Himmelfarb's crucifixion unfold, "Dubbo was stationed as if upon an eminence, watching what he alone was gifted or fated enough to see. Neither the actor nor the spectator, he was that most miserable of human beings, the artist" (531). Dubbo does not try to save Himmelfarb: "Now Dubbo knew that he would never, ever act, that he would dream, and suffer, and express some of that suffering in paint – but was, in the end, powerless" (536). However, the mock-crucifixion of Himmelfarb has a profound effect on Dubbo: "Because he was as solitary in the crowd as the man they had crucified, it was again the abo who saw most. All that he had ever suffered, all that he had ever failed to understand, rose to the surface in Dubbo" (538). Vanden Driesen argues that Dubbo "is untouched by the guilt shared by all the whites" over the mock-crucifixion (131); however, while he is not guilty of instigating or encouraging the torture, his passivity and failure to intervene renders him complicit in the atrocity. Dubbo partially expiates his guilt by helping Himmelfarb when he is cut down from the tree. Alf does not return to the factory after Himmelfarb's death, but instead immerses himself in painting to such an extent that he is "unaware how many days he had been at work" (592). As he paints, Dubbo's tuberculosis worsens, and the blood he coughs up mingles with the paint on the canvas (592). After finishing "The Deposition," Dubbo sets to work on his Chariot painting (597). Dubbo dies of a tubercular hemorrhage after finishing "The Chariot" and his paintings are sold cheaply at auction by his landlady (601-02).

Although White knew several painters well, was an avid art collector, and frequented exhibitions in Sydney, at the time of writing *Riders in the Chariot* he had never met an Indigenous Australian.[13] As Marr puts it,

> Dubbo the black painter is entirely White's invention ... For the portrait of Dubbo he drew on books, newspapers and the Withycombe's grim stories of the blacks around Barwon Vale. In

Australian fiction, the Aboriginal had been shown as artist/mystic or squalid fringe dweller. Dubbo was both. (360)

Dewey argues that Dubbo is the "heroic center" of the novel (756), while Malouf claims Dubbo "is at this point embarrassing" ("Patrick White Reappraised"). Webby and Goldsworthy both argue that White was ahead of his time in his inclusion of an Indigenous man as one of the four main characters ("Introduction" 12; 127). While Malouf's assessment may point to aspects of Dubbo's characterization such as his drunkenness and venereal disease, White's sympathetic depiction of Dubbo's marginalization, both from mainstream Australian society and his traditional culture, reveals important truths about Australia's treatment of its Indigenous peoples, and once again demonstrates that depictions of diversity are not the exclusive province of the urban landscape, and that suburbia is the location in which many of the most important issues in Australian society are situated.

The Mock-Crucifixion of Himmelfarb
The climax of White's massive, ambitious novel is the mock-crucifixion of Himmelfarb, which is performed by Mrs. Flack's illegitimate son Blue, who works at Harry Rosetree's Brighta Bicycle Lamps with Himmelfarb and Dubbo. Mrs. Flack declares she is in control of Blue, and he will carry out her instructions: "'Blue will act upon an idea, if you know what I mean, Mrs Jolley, and no harm done, of course, if it is the right idea and the right person in control'" (294). On the morning of the day Himmelfarb is attacked, Blue calls his mother from the pub near the factory to tell her of his lottery win. She informs him that Mrs. Godbold visited Himmelfarb the previous evening, "'Forgetting, it would seem, the time of year. It was *them* that crucified Our Saviour. Tomorrow. Think of it'" (518). Immediately before instigating the crucifixion, the drunken Blue remembers the conversation with his mother, especially her words, "*suffer every Easter to know the Jews have crucified Our Lord*" (532, original emphasis), and as his mood darkens, "All the injustices to which he had ever been subjected grew appreciably sadder. But for all the injustices he had committed,

somebody had committed worse. Not to say the worst, so he had been told, the very worst. And must not go unpunished" (532).

Himmelfarb reports to work the day before Good Friday, even though Rosetree has excused him (523). Himmelfarb's co-workers are not in a working mood due to the impending holiday and the lottery win by Blue and his mates: "In the circumstances, his concentration was distasteful, abominable to many, who could not prevent themselves glancing, however, at the bloody foreign Jew" (524). Foreshadowing the crucifixion, a circus passes in the street outside, with a clown acting out a public hanging on the back of a truck (527). The circus procession is followed by an actual funeral procession. Sensing the momentum and confluence of events, and fearing for Himmelfarb's safety, Rosetree orders Himmelfarb home, but he refuses, declaring, "'You will not be blamed'" (529). When the crucifixion begins, Blue approaches Himmelfarb "whimsically ... Because Blue the vindicator was also Blue the mate. It was possible to practice all manner of cruelties provided the majority might laugh them off as practical jokes" (532). Himmelfarb does not resist; "His expression remained one almost of contentment" (533).

As the mob pushes Himmelfarb into the factory yard towards the tree, young girls chant, "'Go home! Go Home!'" while older women sing "'Go home to Germany!'" and men chant "'Go home to hell!'" (534). Himmelfarb falls down and is kicked in the ribs (534). The narrator comments, "Some of the men would have taken a hammer, or plunged a knife, if either weapon had been at hand. Into the Jew, of course" (535). Blue obtains rope and hoists Himmelfarb into a tree, where he hangs bleeding: "... he had been grazed by nail or tin, so that blood, quite a lot of it, did flow. At least one of his hands was pierced. Through the torn shirt, it could be seen that the disgraceful ribs were gashed" (535). As Himmelfarb hangs, he appears dead, but his eyes are "visionary rather than fixed" (538). The crowd of onlookers are frustrated and unnerved by Himmelfarb's refusal to speak or protest (539). Although Rosetree hides in his office during the crucifixion, his secretaries eventually persuade him to act, so he orders his

Patrick White's *Riders in the Chariot* (1961)   35

foreman Ernie Theobalds to intervene (542). Theobalds takes Himmelfarb down from the tree and advises him to go home (543-44). Himmelfarb quietly leaves "the factory in which it had not been accorded to him to expiate the sins of the world" (545).

However, Himmelfarb's suffering is not over, as he is a victim of arson later the same day. As Mrs. Flack gleefully relates the tale to Mrs. Jolley,

> "It is a bunch of young fellers ... whose sense of decency was outraged by a certain person ... Only to give warning, they say. They was flicking little balls of paper, soaked in somethink, into the Jew's place, to put the wind up him like. When matters got out of hand. In a weatherboard home." (547-48)

Miss Hare sees the fire from Xanadu and runs to help. Ignoring the protests of the onlookers, she rushes into the burning house, thinking Himmelfarb is within (551). She emerges "a blackened thing ... Her wicker hat ... turned to a fizzy Catherine wheel, wings of flame ... sprouting from the shoulders of her cardigan, her worsted heels ... spurred with fire" (552). Thinking Himmelfarb is dead and seeing Mrs. Jolley and Mrs. Flack in the crowd, Miss Hare cries, "'You ... are the devils!'" (553). However, Mrs. Godbold and Bob Tanner, her eldest daughter's suitor, had rescued Himmelfarb earlier and taken him to the Godbolds' shack (555, 559). Dubbo watches through the window as Mrs. Godbold and Miss Hare tend to Himmelfarb (568). As he observes, he mentally composes his painting "The Deposition" (569). After midnight, Himmelfarb dies, like Christ, on a Friday (572). As Brennan puts it, Himmelfarb is "destroyed for his failure to become an ordinary Aussie bloke" (32).

Critics disagree about whether or not the mock-crucifixion scene is plausible. During, characteristically, claims that the mock-crucifixion is "wildly improbable" (26). In contrast, arguing that the mock-crucifixion is plausible, Webby compares it to the 2005 Cronulla riots, arguing that both events "are fuelled by alcohol, mateship, religious and racial intolerance and ... [the] sense of being morally superior" ("Our Invisible"). Malouf argues that the mock-crucifixion is driven by "the same mob fury and resentment of what is different that is behind every pogrom or massacre or ritual killing" ("Introduction" viii). Brennan argues that recent events, including the firebombing of a mosque in Brisbane "in retaliation for the September 11 attacks in America"; incidents in which Muslim girls have had their headscarves torn off; the Cronulla riots, in which Anglo-Celtic gangs wrapped themselves in Australian flags, wore t-shirts proclaiming "wog free zone," and chanted slogans including "Lebs go home" and "ethnic cleansing unit"; and an attack in 2007 in suburban Melbourne on orthodox Jews walking home from Synagogue by "a minibus full of drunken football fans," all confirm that the mock-crucifixion of Himmelfarb is not "beyond the realm of possibility" (32, 40).

The examples Brennan provides strongly support Graeme Huggan's claim that racism is deeply embedded within Australian society, despite Australia's "official commitment to multiculturalism and social egalitarianism" and the "public revulsion of the mob violence and ideological extremism" that periodically resurface (*Australian Literature* v). McCann argues that "the Australian racists," including Blue, his mates, Mrs. Jolley and Mrs. Flack, "are not so much representations of actual Australians ... as they are representations of the performativity of normality" ("Ethics" 146). McCann's point is that White's characters are performing the roles that they believe "normal" citizens of their community should play. In a text prepared for the Nobel Foundation, White argues that he "learned from personal experience" that acts like the mock-crucifixion of Himmelfarb occur in Australia "in all quarters, in many infinitely humiliating ways" (qtd. in Bliss, *Patrick White's Fiction* 86). White obviously believed that the crucifixion scene accurately depicts the racism, violence, intolerance and xenophobia present in Australian society.

The Destruction of Xanadu
Near the end of the novel, after the deaths of Himmelfarb and Dubbo and the disappearance of Miss Hare, Xanadu is demolished. The residents of Sarsaparilla, including Mrs. Jolley and Mrs. Flack, gather to watch the

Patrick White's *Riders in the Chariot* (1961)   37

destruction, which they find entertaining (605; 611-13). Not only is the house razed, but the native bush that Miss Hare loved is also destroyed. In a passage similar to those found in many suburban novels, White describes the destruction of the natural environment by suburban development: "the bulldozers went into the scrub at Xanadu. The steel caterpillars mounted the rise, to say nothing of any sapling, or scrubby growth that stood in their way, and down went resistance" (624). After Xanadu is demolished, the site is "shaved right down to a bald, red, rudimentary hill" and the developers erect pre-fabricated homes (624). In the novel's clearest anti-suburban passage, which Malouf describes as "one of ... [White's] most savage sermons on the ugly, characterless fibro homes that have replaced the grand folly of Xanadu" ("Introduction" ix-x), White depicts the lives of the residents of the new development as fragile, conformist, lacking in meaning and boring. The new homes cling to "bare earth," where

> the wafer-walls of the new homes ... rub together at night, and sleepers might have been encouraged to enter into one another's dreams, if these had not been similar. Some times the rats of anxiety could be heard gnawing already at Bakelite, or plastic ... So that, in the circumstances, it was not unusual for people to run outside and jump into their cars. All of Sunday they would visit, or be visited ... Then, on finding nothing at the end, they would drive around, or around. They would drive and look for something to look at. (636)

However, the unmistakably anti-suburban sentiments of the passage are countered five pages later. Several years after the construction of the new homes, Mrs. Godbold visits the site where Xanadu once stood (636). Upon arriving at

> the new settlement of Xanadu ... Mrs Godbold could not help admiring the houses for their signs of life: for the children coming home from school, for a row of young cauliflowers, for a convalescent woman, who had stepped outside in a dressing gown to gather a late rose. (640)

Unlike White's narrator, Mrs. Godbold sees the suburban development as full of vitality, rather than conformity, boredom and meaningless lives. Mrs. Godbold begins visiting the new development frequently, "where the new homes rocked and shouted with life" (641).

In *Patrick White's Fiction*, Bliss espouses a typically anti-suburban attitude when she claims, "the reader wonders how she [Mrs. Godbold] can condone and even celebrate the supplanting of magnificent Xanadu by a jerry-built suburb" (96). Malouf provides a less judgmental and more receptive reading, describing the passage as a "beautiful coda to the book," claiming, "Only the greatest masters can stand aside and allow themselves to be admonished by one of their creations whose vision, by some miracle of autonomy, is larger than their own" ("Introduction" ix-x). However, Malouf's suggestion that White is being admonished by Mrs. Godbold rests on the assumption that the anti-suburbanism in the aforementioned passage represents White's own attitude towards suburbia. In fact, White's inclusion of an opposing viewpoint (Mrs. Godbold's) is evidence that he is not necessarily anti-suburban. We must not assume that the narrator, or a certain character, speaks for the author.[14] White presents a number of conflicting attitudes towards suburbia - all, some or none of which may represent the author's personal views.

Is *Riders in the Chariot* Anti-Suburban?

Riders in the Chariot undoubtedly contains anti-suburban material; however, claims that the novel and its author are anti-suburban are suspect. Such claims rely on a reductive interpretation of the novel that conflates White and his narrator and ignores material that either celebrates suburbia or fails to fit into a pro-suburban/anti-suburban binary. During argues that White was part of a Modernist literary movement "that can only be understood in terms of its critique of contemporary culture," and claims White made his reputation through novels "profoundly critical ... of contemporary Australian ways of life, such as suburbia, middle-class affluence and love of sport" (36, 11). However, being critical of contemporary culture does not make one anti-suburban, since, as the second quotation from

Patrick White's *Riders in the Chariot* (1961) 39

During acknowledges, suburbia is only one facet of Australian society. During offers no proof that either White or *Riders in the Chariot* are anti-suburban.

Gerster acknowledges that White depicts suburbia as a location in which artistic creation occurs, even while arguing that White hates the suburbs and views them as aesthetically barren and ugly (573); he claims White turns suburbia "into a geographic hell ruled by female demons" and argues that White displayed "sniggering contempt for suburban (usually female) philistinism" (567). Even if Gerster's depiction of White's characterization of Mrs. Jolley, Mrs. Flack and Shirl Rosetree as "sniggering contempt" were accurate, an author's contempt for the behavior of a group of characters by no means equates to contempt or hatred for suburbia. Gerster goes on to accuse White of possessing a "waspish preoccupation" with "suburban materialism" and posits that he "employs the Shirl Rosetrees of this world as the most common denominators against which the few spiritually rich suburbanites are celebrated for their difference" (567). Again, even if one accepts Gerster's assessment of White's attitude towards suburbia and its residents, the fact remains that White celebrates residents of suburbia, and that, as Gerster himself phrases it, suburbanites can be "spiritually rich" (567).

Powell claims White is "a partial exception" to the anti-suburban tradition, arguing that "there is warmth in some of the characters and relationships," yet suggests White's suburban novels "confirm rather than question the images of the suburbs as places of boredom, prejudice and vulgarity" (127-28). Likewise, Andrew Taylor provided what Lawson describes as "an unusually sympathetic description of White's fundamental attitudes towards suburbia" ("Unmerciful" 388) when he argued,

> "For barren and ugly or sweet and sickly though it may be, it [suburbia] is still the breeding ground of human lives. And where human lives are being bred, there are always some who

will, perhaps only part-consciously, grope towards the fullness of living." (Qtd. in Lawson, "Unmerciful" 388)

Despite being sympathetic to suburban lives, Taylor's rhetoric, especially the use of "part-consciously" and "grope," suggests that suburban lives are less fully lived than those in other locales and that the inhabitants of suburbia are not intellectually aware.

Writing in 1979, Banerjee notes that critics view White as being "too concerned with the faults in contemporary Australian society," arguing that such a concern "does not need to be taken seriously" (110). However, Banerjee contends that White's criticisms of Australian society have "stuck in the throats of his Australian critics," citing R.F. Brissenden's claim that White "'cannot convince us that the people who live in Sarsaparilla are so thoroughly and inhumanly evil as to deserve the unmitigated disgust with which he finally presents them'" (Qtd. in Banerjee 110). When critics like Brissenden make such claims, they conflate White with his narrator and interpret the narrator's descriptions of suburban residents in an overly sensitive manner. Banerjee notes that after White's Nobel Prize triumph, there was "an inevitable increase in the amount of critical attention paid to him" and argues that some of the post-1973 scholarship "constitutes a critical back-lash against the earlier works, in particular, against *Riders in the Chariot*" (91). Banerjee claims *Riders in the Chariot* has received "more than its fair share of criticism" and that White "has been most consistently attacked" for his perceived "harsh treatment of Australian suburbia," for which "he has been accused of downright misanthropy" (91). Brady also argues that *Riders in the Chariot* "has been largely misunderstood as misanthropic" (172).

Regarding the riders, often viewed by critics as outsiders in suburbia, Banerjee argues,

> Surely the point is that *no* society can admit such people. The herd instinct, the instinct for survival – call it what you will – self-interest under some guise or another will close the ranks against those who are born or made too sensitive to life's sufferings,

too earnest in their search for truth through them. (111, original emphasis)

Thus, Banerjee views White's depiction of the rejection of the riders by the citizens of Sarsaparilla as a criticism of the "herd instinct" or mob mentality, rather than a criticism of suburbia. Indeed, the mock-crucifixion of Himmelfarb could have occurred anywhere, not just in suburbia, as White has argued.[15] Likewise, Goldsworthy argues that rather than criticizing a specific community, such as the suburban community of Sarsaparilla, the target of White's critique is "an *absence* of any coherent sense of community in ordinary Australian life" (128, original emphasis). Bliss acknowledges that *Riders in the Chariot* "ends by celebrating more than it questions or condemns. Even the virulent satire ... is tempered by Mrs. Godbold's final awareness that life in any form is precious" (*Patrick White's Fiction* 98). Even *if* White does convey some of his own attitudes and prejudices through his narrator and characters, his narrative technique makes it impossible to identify any one position as White's. Clearly, *Riders in the Chariot* presents an ambivalent attitude toward suburbia, containing both celebration and condemnation, and thus previous assertions by critics that White and his fiction are anti-suburban have failed to take into account the nuances and complexity of White's representations of suburbia. I continue my argument that White is not an anti-suburban writer in the next chapter, which examines White's 1966 novel, *The Solid Mandala*.

Endnotes

1. Nicholas Birns, editor of *Antipodes*, informed me that Brady added the footnoted reference to McCann after suggestions by himself and the anonymous referees of the article. Thus, to be fair, it was not Brady's purpose or original intention to engage with McCann.
2. See note 8.
3. White and Dutton had a famous falling-out in 1982 (see Marr 612-15).
4. According to the MLA Bibliography, eighty-six peer-reviewed journal articles, thirty-three chapters and essays in edited collections, and five monographs were published on White's work between 1990 and 2010; the criticism was published in Australia, the United States, Britain, Canada, Germany, France, the Netherlands, India, Singapore, Poland, South Africa and New Zealand, demonstrating the global nature of White studies. Interestingly, the number of works published on White since his death is more than triple the total number that the MLA database lists for Tim Winton, arguably Australia's most popular living writer. Search conducted on August 28, 2010.
5. Cynthia vanden Driesen describes During's monograph on White as "threaded through with contradictions," argues that his analyses "remain thinly substantiated, if at all" (156), and claims that During's work contains a "proliferation of irrelevant speculation and unverified assumptions" (158).
6. White's description of Xanadu and its owner contains a number of allusions to Samuel Taylor Coleridge's poem "Kubla Khan."
7. This image recalls Walt Whitman's *Leaves of Grass*.
8. The natural environment was undoubtedly important to White; he overcame his distaste for public speaking to serve as "an important spokesman for the anti-nuclear and environmental movements" (During 14).
9. The frequent use of "abo" by the narrator and characters in the novel is jarring to the contemporary reader, for whom "abo" is highly pejorative.
10. Mrs. Jolley is also based on Mrs. Lumsden, White and Lascaris' housekeeper for several months, who "grew in memory to become the detestable Mrs Jolley of Sarsaparilla" (Marr 257).
11. Werner Arens labels both Mrs. Jolley and Mrs. Flack as "evil" (134, 135); Brady claims White presents "suburban ladies" "like Mrs. Jolley and Mrs. Flack ... as figures of unmitigated evil" (173); Bliss calls them

"satanic" (*Patrick White's Fiction* 85); Edgecombe labels the women "venomous" (*Vision* 55); and Brennan dubs them "ignorant and inadequate suburban witches" (33). Malouf describes Mrs. Jolley and Mrs. Flack as "the upholders of the average" in the novel, and considers Mrs. Jolley to be "one of the great comic monsters of modern fiction" ("Introduction" vi, viii).
12. Aloysius was James Joyce's middle name and the name of his patron saint (Ellmann 30). *Riders in the Chariot* contains several allusions to Joyce and his work. In fact, White was heavily influenced by Joyce and took the title of his second novel, *The Living and The Dead*, from Joyce's story "The Dead."
13. White's lack of contact with Aborigines was not unusual for a person of his class, especially during his lifetime. According to Marr, White's first meeting with a person of Aboriginal descent took place while he was researching Fraser Island for *A Fringe of Leaves* (1976) (cited in vanden Driesen 157).
14. See Wimsatt and Beardsley's "The Intentional Fallacy."
15. See Bliss, *Patrick White's Fiction,* 86.

Chapter 2

Patrick White's *The Solid Mandala* (1966)

Seven Decades in Suburbia

Despite the fact that *Riders in the Chariot* is over six hundred pages long and engages with a plethora of issues central to Australian suburban life, it did not satiate White's desire to write about suburbia. His next novel, *The Solid Mandala*, which Nicholas Birns describes as the "hidden twin" of *Riders in the Chariot*, is also set in the fictional suburbs of Sarsaparilla and Barranugli ("*The Solid Mandala*"). Moreover, in the interim between the novels, White published short fiction and drama set in suburbia: the short story collection *The Burnt Ones* (1964) and the plays *The Season at Sarsaparilla* (1965) and *A Cheery Soul* (1965). Although *The Solid Mandala* is roughly half the length of *Riders in the Chariot* and focuses on fewer characters, White again uses the suburban setting to address important social issues, including the role of the artist in society, immigration, family relationships, religion, conformity, consumerism, and class. The novel establishes the suburban setting from the outset, opening with a section in which Mrs. Dun and Mrs. Poulter ride the bus from Sarsaparilla to Barranugli.[1]

The Solid Mandala focuses on the lives of twin brothers Arthur and Waldo Brown; the action spans approximately seventy years of their lives, from their birth in England until shortly after Waldo's death in Sarsaparilla. Other important characters include Mrs. Poulter and Dulcie Feinstein, the daughter of Jewish immigrants, who becomes the love interest for both Waldo and Arthur. The other characters in the novel are all minor, including the twins' parents George and Anne Brown; Mrs. Poulter's husband Bill; Mrs. Dun; Dulcie Feinstein's parents, and the man who becomes her husband, Leonard Saporta; Mr. and Mrs. Allwright, Arthur's employers; Mrs. Musto, the wealthy socialite; and Waldo's library colleagues. Even though the cast of characters is small, half of them are immigrants and several are Jewish. Thus, White once again creates characters who reveal the diversity within suburbia.

White divides *The Solid Mandala* into four sections, mirroring the marble of the novel's title. The first section, "In the Bus," presents Mrs. Poulter and Mrs. Dun riding the bus from Sarsaparilla to Barranugli. In this short, eleven-page section, White's third-person narrator utilizes dialogue extensively, along with short passages of description. The second section, "Waldo," is by far the longest at one hundred and ninety pages; here White presents the lives of the Brown brothers from Waldo's perspective, relaying his thoughts through indirect discourse. The third section, "Arthur," covers seventy-nine pages and presents Arthur's perspective on the brothers' lives, often contradicting, correcting or adding depth to Waldo's accounts. The fourth and final section, "Mrs. Poulter and the Zeitgeist," spans twenty-two pages, adopting Mrs. Poulter's point of view and relating events in her life and the aftermath of Waldo's death. Bliss notes that White's use of indirect discourse in the "Waldo" and "Arthur" sections is almost uninterrupted (*Patrick White's Fiction* 102).

White's narrative technique in *The Solid Mandala*, namely his use of multiple points of view and indirect discourse, makes it impossible for readers to attribute any anti-suburban sentiments in the novel conclusively to White. Moreover, as Bliss points out, "the unmarked shift from autho-

Patrick White's *The Solid Mandala* (1966)

rially endorsed narrative to Woolfian indirect discourse sometimes causes confusion over whose point of view is in force" (*Patrick White's Fiction* 102). Although *The Solid Mandala* has been labeled an anti-suburban novel and an example of White's alleged hatred of suburbia,[2] the novel, like *Riders in the Chariot*, actually presents a nuanced, ambivalent and at times celebratory representation of suburbia. The characters, relationships and physical settings in the novel reveal White's complex representation of suburban life and his close engagement with important social issues, demonstrating that anti-suburban readings of the novel fail to recognize White's subtlety.

Mrs. Poulter and Mrs. Dun: Representative Suburban Housewives?

From the first page of *The Solid Mandala*, White establishes Mrs. Poulter and Mrs. Dun as suburban domestic consumers. While traveling from Sarsaparilla to Barranugli on the bus, Mrs. Poulter declares, "'There's more life up this end ... It's the shops that gives it life'" (3). However, Mrs. Poulter's contention also serves as a counterpoint to the claims of vehement proponents of the anti-suburban intellectual tradition, such as Esson, who contend that suburbia lacks vitality. Although Mrs. Poulter and Mrs. Dun both live on Terminus Road in Sarsaparilla, they first meet on the bus (4). Their friendship is quite new when the action of the novel begins (3). White uses the dialogue between Mrs. Poulter and Mrs. Dun to provide exposition, frame his narrative, and indicate their status as uneducated working class characters through their use of informal vernacular language.

Mrs. Dun is concerned about the threat of violence in suburbia and expresses her fear to Mrs. Poulter, declaring, "'They could come and murder you in broad daylight'" (6) and "'there are times when you'll wanter be [seen by one's neighbors]. When someone's got you by the throat'" (7). At the end of the novel, when Mrs. Poulter discovers Waldo dead and runs to Mrs. Dun's house for assistance, Mrs. Dun is so afraid that she refuses to let Mrs. Poulter inside and tells her to go away and call the police (299). On her way from the Browns to Mrs. Dun's, shocked by her gruesome discovery, Mrs. Poulter recalls,

> The flat faces of all those Chinese guerillas or Indonesians ... dragged out across the dreadful screen. All those Jews in ovens, that was long ago, but still burning, lying in heaps. Lone women bashed up in Mosman. Maroubra, Randwick, places you went only in your sleep. (298)[3]

Mrs. Poulter's television viewing links genocide, domestic violence and suburbia in her mind, and Waldo's death appears to be the realization of her fears.

While riding the bus in the opening section, Mrs. Dun and Mrs. Poulter discuss the Browns and their custom-built verandah. Mrs. Dun expresses surprise that anyone would depart from suburban architectural norms, and when Mrs. Poulter describes the late Mr. Brown as a white-collar worker, Mrs. Dun does not know the meaning of the term; moreover, when Mrs. Poulter states that Mr. Brown worked in a bank and read in his spare time, Mrs. Dun shrivels (7). Hearing that the Browns are English immigrants, Mrs. Dun complains about the influx of foreigners, but admits, "'the English is different'" (7). Mrs. Poulter attributes the Browns giving their son the strange name Waldo to Mr. and Mrs. Brown's penchant for reading, a trait she also sees as causing Waldo to become a reader and work in libraries. In response, "Mrs. Dun hissed. She was terrified" (9). Gerster describes this incident as "one of several moments of unintended comedy" in the novel (567); however, like many White critics, Gerster makes the mistake of trying to determine White's intent. Nevertheless, White clearly presents Mrs. Dun as afraid of education and the educated. Pierre Francois argues that White uses the respectable suburban "bourgeoisie" to cloak "absolute evil" so frequently that it constitutes a "widespread motif in White's fiction" (115). Furthermore, Francois notes that in White's fiction old ladies "often harbour in their innermost hearts the most horrendous, lethal drives" and claims Mrs. Dun "is another suburban devil" (115). However, despite sharing qualities with Mrs. Jolley and Mrs.

Flack from *Riders in the Chariot*, such as narrow-mindedness, ignorance and fear of immigrants, Mrs. Dun is far from a "suburban devil" and lacks the malice necessary to instigate violence. Furthermore, Francois' inclusion of Mrs. Dun amongst the bourgeoisie indicates a serious misreading of her class.

The reader's first impression of the twin protagonists Waldo and Arthur is filtered through the perspective of Mrs. Poulter and Mrs. Dun, who observe the brothers from the bus. From Mrs. Dun's perspective, the old men are "stumping, trudging" along the footpath between Barranugli and Sarsaparilla, "blotting out the suburban landscape, filling the box of Mrs. Dun's shuddering mind ... she almost smelled those old men ... they were holding each other by the hand " (10-11). Mrs. Dun is particularly shocked that the men hold hands, even though they are brothers: she "hated what she saw" (11). In the closing section of the novel, Mrs. Poulter reflects on Mrs. Dun and concludes that she is "cold" and "something of a disappointment" (291). Nevertheless, Mrs. Poulter continues to associate with her out of habit and enjoys having company on the bus and during visits to David Jones[4] or the cinema.

Although White's technique of using a pair of suburban women as characters in *The Solid Mandala* mirrors *Riders in the Chariot*, the similarities are superficial. While Mrs. Dun shares some characteristics with Mrs. Jolley and Mrs. Flack, Mrs. Poulter is more akin to Mrs. Godbold, the suburban saint. White's narrator initially presents both women negatively, declaring it is "perhaps doubtful whether anyone would notice Mrs. Poulter or Mrs. Dun unless life took its cleaver to them" (4); however, numerous positive descriptions of Mrs. Poulter appear as the novel progresses, so that the overall characterization is overwhelmingly positive. Herring argues that the character development of Mrs. Poulter throughout the novel "is one of its chief surprises and an essential part of its meaning" (181). Likewise, A.A. Phillips posits that Mrs. Poulter seems at first to be "one of those suburban Old Ducks whom White can pencil in with light mastery, but she becomes a more significant and a more deeply imagined personality. She is the hinge which connects the central figures" (33). Furthermore, Beston claims that Mrs. Poulter is elevated in the novel's final scenes "as a comforting madonna and a kind earth mother" and "endowed with a vibrant life spirit" (110).

Mrs. Poulter and her husband Bill move from the country to the developing suburb of Sarsaparilla seeking peace and quiet. Moreover, Bill considers land in the suburb a good investment, since he expects the area to undergo further development (4-5). The "Waldo" section reveals that the Poulters settled in Terminus Road opposite the Browns around 1920 (133). When the Browns discuss the Poulters' arrival, Arthur provides his family with information gleaned from talking with the new neighbors, revealing that in the country Mr. Poulter worked as a rouseabout and Mrs. Poulter worked in the homestead (134). Bill constructs the couple's new suburban home with the help of a local lad while the couple lives in a shed on their block of land and Mrs. Poulter acquaints herself with the Browns by borrowing cups of sugar and rice (134). Soon after arriving in Sarsaparilla, Mrs. Poulter confides in Mrs. Brown regarding the reasons for their move to suburbia, including the fact that Bill's nerves are damaged because of time he spent "in a camp" during the First World War (135).[5] Before her death, Mrs. Brown often described Mrs. Poulter as "a thoroughly good-hearted, reliable young woman" (21).

Characteristically, Arthur and Waldo hold opposing views of Mrs. Poulter. Waldo views her as an "inalterably stupid creature" with a "too stupid" face and "stupid-looking calves" (54; 134); she is "one of the fifty-seven things and persons Waldo hated" (51). In contrast, Arthur views Mrs. Poulter as an excellent neighbor and an attractive woman (21; 251). Indeed, Arthur loves Mrs. Poulter and develops a relationship with her that attains such a degree of intimacy that she allows him to touch her hair (258). Because Arthur suffers from an unspecified mental disability (he is often referred to as slow, simple or dumb), Mrs. Poulter believes she can have an intimate friendship with him without appearing unfaithful to her husband (253). Mrs. Poulter often beckons Arthur from across the street (253), and the pair spends a great deal of time together, either in the Poulters' home or walking the suburban streets. When Mrs. Poulter tires of Arthur, who lacks the social skills to recognize that he has overstayed his welcome, she dismisses him by taking up a book and declaring that she is going to settle down alone (253). However, Mrs. Poulter is not well read; her reading matter is limited to the obituaries and advertisements in the local newspaper, the Bible and an Encyclopedia (254).

Like Mrs. Godbold in *Riders in the Chariot*, Mrs. Poulter is a devout Christian married to an unbeliever (294). Mrs. Poulter's relationship with Arthur is tested by a discussion she initiates concerning Christianity. Mrs. Poulter declares it is strange that the Browns have never attended church; Arthur replies that his parents attended until they learnt "'they could do without it'" (255). Arthur goes on to explain that his parents "'began to feel it wasn't true,'" and when prompted by Mrs. Poulter, elaborates, "'About virgins. About Him'" (255). Shocked, Mrs. Poulter exclaims, "'Don't tell me ... that *you* don't believe in Our Lord Jesus Christ?'" (255, original emphasis). Arthur replies that he does not know much about Jesus and turns the question back on Mrs. Poulter: "'How do *you* know, anyway?'" (255, original emphasis). Mrs. Poulter asserts, "'It's what everyone has always known,'" and claims, "'I couldn't exist without Our Lord'" (255). Arthur intensifies the debate and angers Mrs. Poulter by revealing that his mother claims Christians constantly gloat over the blood of Christ (255). When Mrs. Poulter asks, "'Don't you believe they crucified Our Lord?,'" Arthur responds, "'I reckon they'd crucify a man ... Yes ... From what you read. And what we know. Christians ... are cruel'" (255). As he did in *Riders in the Chariot*, White uses suburbia in *The Solid Mandala* to explore the contested place of religion in Australian society.

When Arthur dances his mandala,[6] his most expressive and intimate act of the novel, he dances it for Mrs. Poulter (259). Despite the fact that Mrs. Poulter breaks off her relationship with Arthur due to local gossip and her husband's complaints, she often thinks of him fondly, especially the day he danced for her: "the bonfire of Arthur's head had never quite gone out for Mrs. Poulter" (296). Mrs. Poulter is childless, although she was once pregnant and suffered a miscarriage (294). Despite her obvious sorrow over her miscarriage, and her husband's lack of religious beliefs, Mrs. Poulter seems content with her life in suburbia:

> You couldn't say she wasn't comfortable. He kept the home painted up ... Took a few jobs on the side ... For the few extra luxuries. You had to keep up with the times ... She had the electricity, she had the phone ... Bill said people in history had never had it so good ... You couldn't complain. Not with the electric frying-pan ... not with the phone, and two doctors. And the telly. (291)

In addition to the enjoyment she derives from her consumer goods, Mrs. Poulter enjoys gardening and knitting, stereotypical domestic pursuits for a suburban housewife (252; 292). However, she derives the greatest pleasure from her television, especially the news programs:

> She loved the telly. It made her sit forward ... waiting, most of all for the *real* programmes, when they let off one of the bombs, or an aeroplane caught fire at the moment of crashing, or those guerillas they'd collared, of course they were only Orientals, and once it showed you the bodies they'd shot ... All the while they were firing on a mob of squealing Orientals, in Singapore, or some such place. (295, original emphasis)

Earlier, I referred to the effect on Mrs. Poulter of watching violent episodes on television, namely the association of genocide with violence in suburbia. However, it is also important to acknowledge Mrs. Poulter's excitement over watching "real" violence, her ignorance concerning foreign affairs, and her lack of compassion for the foreign victims of violence, whom she views as "only Orientals" (295).

Beston argues that White is ambivalent towards his characters, and claims that White's ambivalence towards Mrs. Poulter does not fully emerge until the final section of the novel (110). Furthermore, Beston claims that White uses the passages about Mrs. Poulter's consumer goods and television viewing to mock her, portray her "as a representative of the spirit of the times," and satirize "Australian suburbia with its ugliness and emotional emptiness and concern for material comforts" (110). Beston posits that because Waldo is dead in Part Four, "any slur on her [Mrs. Poulter] is White's own" (108), rather than Waldo's, and claims that Mrs. Poulter's acceptance of suburbia, "which White rejects so disdainfully, considerably undercuts his elevation of her to the sainthood at the end" (110). However, Beston's contention that White satirizes suburbia conflates Mrs. Poulter with suburbia, and he makes the mistake of interpreting a single example of what he perceives to be anti-suburban sentiment as representative of White's own attitudes. Overall, White characterizes the suburban homemaker positively, while acknowledging her flaws, and she shares much in common with Mrs. Godbold, the saint of *Riders in the Chariot*.

Waldo: The Immigrant "Artist" in Suburbia
Whereas White used Alf Dubbo to explore the role of the artist in society in *Riders in the Chariot*, in *The Solid Mandala* the artist character is an aloof English immigrant. Readers first encounter Waldo Brown as an elderly, retired man, but as the novel progresses, they gain knowledge of Waldo's life from childhood until his death in his suburban home approximately seventy years later. Waldo is the younger of the twin brothers by a few hours, although he plays the role of "the elder by years" due to Arthur's unspecified mental condition (20). Through Waldo, White uses the suburban setting to address the role of the artist in society, immigration, family relationships, conformity and class. Once again, White reveals the richness of suburbia as a setting for fiction. Waldo is an immigrant who aspires to be a writer, struggles in his relationships with his brother and parents, shuns religion, and conforms to deeply held convictions regarding how a person of his class should behave. Although Waldo does not possess a university education, having entered the work force after high school, he perceives himself as an intellectual belonging to the cultural elite and

looks down on those whom he deems uneducated or unintelligent. Waldo views himself as middle class, despite lacking the economic and educational status necessary to be a member of that class; however, the only characteristics he shares with the working class are a low economic status and a modest home in an outer suburb. Thus, Waldo is best described as lower-middle-class, which Rita Felski labels "a singularly boring identity" that intellectuals have typically viewed with scorn (34).

John Hartley argues that the lower middle class have "the lowest reputation in the entire history of class theory," and that the lower middle class "attracts no love, support, advocacy or self-conscious organization" (186). In her article "Nothing to Declare: Identity, Shame and the Lower Middle Class," Felski argues that individuals who meet the sociological criteria for the lower middle class "do not usually form a group consciousness around that status," preferring to perceive themselves as middle class because being lower middle class is a negative identity "usually applied from outside" (41). Felski claims, "The lower middle class often feels itself to be culturally superior to the working class ... while lacking the cultural capital and earning power of the professional-managerial class" (35); her description perfectly describes Waldo's attitude and economic status. Moreover, Felski identifies "status anxiety" and shame as hallmarks of the lower middle class (36, 39). Waldo displays both attributes frequently, especially status anxiety concerning his desire to be an intellectual and artist, and shame regarding Arthur's behavior and his perceptions of how other members of the community view his family.

Waldo is obsessed with keeping up appearances, both with regard to his physical appearance and the behaviors he perceives society to deem acceptable. He is a meticulous dresser who always wears a suit in public and believes he has a duty to uphold high sartorial standards (63). Arthur's relationship with Mrs. Poulter enrages Waldo due to the effect Waldo perceives the relationship has on his family's reputation. Waldo appeals to Arthur to stop seeing Mrs. Poulter, accusing him of degrading the family, declaring "'it's us, it's us too, ought to be considered, if you did you wouldn't traipse through the scrub, or in the street, the *street*, holding hands with Mrs. Poulter!'" (141, original emphasis). Felski identifies additional important attributes of the lower middle class that are reflected by Waldo's character, namely the association of the lower middle class with domesticity, "feminine gentility" and "the triumph of suburban values and the symbolic castration of men" (43). Waldo does not engage in any stereotypical masculine activities and other characters frequently perceive him as feminine, a trait emphasized by his use of his mother's dress-box to hide his literary endeavors and, especially, by the scene in which Waldo, in his old age, "obsessed" and "possessed," tries on his dead mother's dress (184-5).

The Browns emigrate from England to Australia while the twins are quite young, although old enough to have started school, acquired English accents and begun developing a sense of national identity. Upon their arrival in Sydney, the Browns lodge with the Thompson family in Barranugli, close to Mr. Brown's job at the bank and a few blocks from the twins' school. The brothers' English accents cause problems for them at school, where their speech is not understood until they learn to speak Australian English (212). Waldo reveals his elitism by preferring to speak "English" rather than "Australian," arguing that the former has a larger vocabulary (212). Arthur, on the other hand, quickly learns to speak Australian English most of the time because he wants to be trusted and understood (212). Waldo is "suspicious" of the locals and "inclined to call them Australians" (213). Like the protagonists of *Riders in the Chariot*, Waldo is indisputably an outsider; however, unlike Miss Hare, Mrs. Godbold, Mordecai Himmelfarb and Alf Dubbo, Waldo is clearly not a heroic character.

Although Arthur is mentally deficient, he is physically stronger. Waldo is the weaker and smaller twin during childhood. Waldo's father tells visitors that Arthur "got a start" on Waldo because Waldo "'was born with his innards twisted'" and the doctor had to sort them out (26). Waldo's physical weakness leads his parents to shelter him as a child (26). However,

Waldo's weakness is short-lived and he grows taller and better built than his parents expected (68). Waldo decides early in life to emulate his mother rather than his father (52) and identifies strongly with her aristocratic English lineage and her superior attitude towards native Australians and their speech: "Nothing annoyed their mother more than what she called a 'sloppy Australian vocabulary'" (92). Mrs. Brown returns Waldo's favor, and "Waldo was officially her favorite, Arthur her duty" (22).

Waldo exhibits literary tendencies and ambitions from an early age. He stays up late reading and copies "extracts into notebooks" (74-75). In keeping with the anti-intellectualism of mainstream Australian society, in which creative pursuits have traditionally been viewed with suspicion and the masculinity and heterosexuality of artistic boys questioned, Waldo sees his interest in literature and his writing as activities that must be hidden and is ashamed if his passions are publicized. Visitors to the Brown home "inquired about Waldo's Writing as though it had been an illness" (23) and Waldo's parents "scarcely mentioned" his literary ambitions "through shame or fear, or simply because they didn't believe" (68). Waldo is so ashamed of his literary ambitions that when his mother asks about the book he is writing, he "feel[s] the flesh shrivel on his bones" (154). Waldo is a voracious reader, tackling Tennyson and Tacitus as a child, "but because Dad was the reader in the family he did most of it furtively" (74). Waldo's ambitions and his parents' reactions are displayed clearly in a scene in which Waldo, while still a child, declares he is going to write and perform a Greek tragedy (32).

Waldo's desire to write is not solely the product of egotism or a desire for fame. On a basic psychological level, Waldo is driven to express himself and to be recognized as special:

> Other people continued to reduce Waldo's intentions and make them appear foolishly capricious, if not downright idiotic. They did not grasp the extent of his need to express some *thing*. Otherwise how could he truly say: I exist. The prospect of remaining a nonen-

tity like the schoolteachers or his parents made him sweat behind the knees. (76, original emphasis)

Waldo is particularly critical of people he perceives as ordinary, such as the Poulters, his teachers and his parents. When Arthur suggests that Waldo write about Leonard Saporta, the Jewish carpet merchant who marries Dulcie Feinstein, Waldo protests that Saporta is "'such a very *ordinary* man. I have nothing against him. But why I should *write* about him! … There is nothing in Leonard Saporta … that anyone could possibly *write* about'" (23, original emphasis). Of course, it is evident to the reader that the Jewish immigrant Saporta is an interesting and unusual character;[7] moreover, White expressed his intention to find the extraordinary in the ordinary in his essay "The Prodigal Son" (39), and thus Waldo's comment on ordinariness is an ironic metafictional comment by White. Waldo's frequent inability to find a subject he deems worthy stems from his elitism and narrow conception of literature.

Additionally, Waldo fears being unable to perform artistically and of running out of time. At one point he cries, "'Oh … but I have not expressed half of what is in me to express!'" (24), echoing John Keats' fear of dying before fulfilling his literary ambitions.[8] Waldo struggles with various manifestations of writer's block, often doubting his abilities (63). Being a writer is central to Waldo's self-perception. When he first meets Dulcie, he declares, "'What I really want to do … is write'" (87), and when she asks for specifics he replies, "'Sometimes I think novels, sometimes plays. It might even be some kind of philosophical work' …It would have been so much easier if he had been able to tell her: I want to, and am going to, write about *myself*" (87, original emphasis). Beston argues that Waldo is "driven to excel intellectually" because he is "denied the possibility of shining physically" and is "impaired emotionally" and interprets Waldo's lack of creative ability as "tragic" (111). Indeed, Waldo's lack of the abilities necessary to fulfill his artistic ambitions is one of the few aspects of his character that may elicit readers' sympathy.

After his retirement, Waldo attempts to increase his artistic productivity, flinging himself at the dress-box in which he keeps his work "with such passion he had torn off one of the cardboard sides ... Mostly he corrected, though sometimes ... he would also write" (203). However, Waldo is unable to convert his ambitions into reality, and his literary output consists chiefly of notebooks and an unpublished fragment of a novel entitled *Tiresias a Youngish Man* (111; 166).[9] Although Waldo somewhat presumptuously joins the Fellowship of Australian Writers, his sole literary achievement is to present a paper on Barron Field to the Beecroft Literary Society (63; 166).[10] After a climactic encounter with Arthur over a poem Arthur composes, Waldo concedes defeat and burns his unfinished manuscripts in his suburban backyard:

> About four o'clock he went down, Tiresias a thinnish man, the dress-box under his arm, towards the pit where they had been accustomed to burn only those things from which they could bear to be parted. ... Then crouched, to pitch a paper tent ... got it to burn ... He began to throw his papers by handfuls ... It was both a sowing and a scattering of seed. When he finished he felt lighter, but always had been, he suspected while walking away. (205)

Edgecombe argues that "Arthur has forced Waldo to confess that he is writing about nothing" (*Vision* 77), and thus Waldo recognizes the futility of his literary ambitions and abandons them.

Waldo's failure as a writer is emphasized by his fifty-year career working in libraries, first at the Sydney Municipal Library and later at the Public Library (63; 174). He spends his days surrounded by books, the physical evidence of other people's ability to realize their literary ambitions, yet his own work is unpublished and he is unable to enter fully into the literary life.[11] Waldo's desire to be a writer is accompanied by a sense of superiority and a desire for intellectual companions. Waldo develops his sense of superiority while at Barranugli High (92): he does not "'like to ask favours'" or "'be beholden to anybody'" (19). He seems himself as "only marking time" before creating "the work of art he was intended to create," but believes that his first priority must be to "create detachment" (139). Phillips interprets Waldo's cultivated superiority and detachment as a defense mechanism, describing Waldo as "the cold intellectual who dabbles a toe in the water of life and withdraws in fear of committing himself to the depths" (32). Other critics interpret Waldo's behavior less sympathetically. Herring describes Waldo as an "arch-egoist" (182) and Francois argues that Waldo's "ego inflation is suggested by his overbearing propensity to dub himself a genius, [and] compare himself favourably with Goethe and Beethoven whom he patronizes as though they were second-rate artists" (104).

While waiting to hear if he will receive a job at the library, Waldo envisions himself arriving at the Feinstein's suburban villa, announcing, "Here I am, an intellectual, working at Sydney Municipal Library ... you must respect, not my genius exactly, but at least my Australian-literary ambitions" (104). However, Waldo is disappointed in his quest to find intellectual companions "with whom to exchange the Everyman classics and play Schubert after tea" (24) or to swap books and "letters written in the kind of literary style which went with such relationships" (85). He finds intellectual companions of sorts with his library colleagues; however, he prevents the friendships from becoming intimate and does not invite anyone to his home, "Because Mr. Brown of the intellectual breathers in the Botanic Gardens must never be confused with the subfusc, almost abstract figure, living on top of a clogged grease-trap ... under the arches of yellow grass, down Terminus Road" (175). Waldo reveals his lower middle class status anxiety through his need to prevent other "intellectuals" from viewing his living conditions in outer suburbia.

Waldo prevents his friendship with his colleague Walter Pugh from becoming close because he views Walter's literary ambitions as "ridiculous," despite harboring his own (136). Consequently, Waldo "never really had a friend of his own sex" (136). Waldo's desire for an intellectual companion is so strong, however, that he tries unsuccessfully to befriend Bill Poulter, even though "the material wasn't promising" (136). Waldo's inability to develop close relationships with other people is not entirely due to his pretensions and lower middle class anxieties; it is the result of a more basic problem: although he "would have confessed it only to himself, he did not understand people" (92). In contrast, even though he is "simple," Arthur makes friends easily and inspires affection.

Although Waldo is in many ways not a typical suburbanite, declaring, "'I am not one to mow the lawn on Sunday'" (149), he expresses affection for suburbia on several occasions. While walking through Sarsaparilla, "the world in which people lived ... [populated by] families in advertised clothes, who belonged to Fellowships and attended Lodges and were not afraid of electrical gadgets," Waldo secretly yearned "for the brick boxes to an extent where his love had become hatred" (24). Waldo admires the vitality, community and human progress evidenced by suburbia. Edgecombe argues that Waldo goes so far as to place "faith" in "regimented suburbia as an instance of rational order" (*Vision* 69). As the narrator states in the "Waldo" section, even though Waldo is "appalled" by "steel and concrete" constructions, such as service stations, "he would never have admitted [it] in public, he would never have rejected any usable evidence of human progress" (53).

Waldo's alleged distaste for concrete and steel is partially contradicted by a passage in which he counts and names cars, an activity described as his "secret vice": "He began to count, to name the passing cars: the Chev the Renault the Holden two more three Holdens the Morris Minor the Bentley" (108). Therefore, although Waldo does not engage in stereotypical suburban pursuits such as mowing the lawn, he finds much to admire in suburbia and spends almost seven decades there. White goes so far as to present suburbia as a site of inspiration for the artist. Some of the most "satisfying moments" of Waldo's life occur when he returns to Sarsaparilla after a day of work in the city, "by exhausted summer light, or breathtaking winter dark, his thought so lucid, so pointed, so independent, he could have started ... there and then at the Barranugli bus stop to rough out something really important" (139-140).

In addition to lacking the ability to make friends and develop intimate relationships, Waldo hates most people, including his own family (74). Waldo views Arthur as a burden he has been "saddled with" since birth, building his hatred over the years to such an extent that Arthur fears Waldo "was preparing to die of the hatred he had bred in him" (19; 288). Bliss compares Waldo to Arthur's solid mandala marble, "Tense, rigid, involuted, and self-enclosed," argues that it is "only by seeing through his own eyes and those of his always loving brother ... [that] the reader [can] approach Waldo at all, for the very essence of his being is to repel others," and claims Waldo is incapable of either "imaginative work" or "real love" (*Patrick White's Fiction* 102; 103). Waldo's hatred becomes so intense that he decides Arthur should die and hopes the strenuous daily walks will cause Arthur to have a heart attack (198). David Tacey views the twins' walk along the Barranugli Road, "which is woven throughout the scenes of the first half of the novel" as "The final and almost epic event in the life of the twins" (131).

Waldo's death is precipitated by his discovery of a poem composed by Arthur, which Bliss characterizes as a "clumsy but terrifying" composition "which celebrates mankind's common pain" (*Patrick White's Fiction* 103). The discovery of the poem, which contains a "sense of connection and community ... brings forcibly home to Waldo his own sterility and anomie" and "drives Waldo to jealous fury" (Bliss, *Patrick White's Fiction* 105-106; 103). Tacey argues that Waldo's rage is caused "not merely because ... [the poem] activates his psychic complex, but because it is a literary form ... which threatens his own role as the secret poet of the Brown family" (135-36). Waldo is so enraged that he tries to choke Arthur to death; however, in the attempt, he dies of a paroxysm, thus killing himself (Tacey 136). Believing he is responsible for Waldo's death, Arthur panics and flees, wandering Sydney's streets for three days and nights. Waldo's body is mutilated by the twins' dogs before being discovered by Mrs. Poulter.

There is some disagreement amongst critics over the meaning and appropriateness of Waldo's death. Francois argues, "No death could be more grimly appropriate for Waldo ... whose existence was bogged down in negation from the cradle to the grave" (117). Herring claims that Waldo's death represents White's judgment of him, and that White's judgment, "conveyed through the dog's symbolic mutilation of his corpse, could not be harsher" (183). Furthermore, Herring contends, "White clearly invites us to make" the harshest judgment of Waldo and argues, "he alone is denied the author's compassion" (183; 184). In contrast, Beston believes Waldo "is treated more cruelly than any other important character in White's novels," arguing that White lacks compassion by denying Waldo "any achievement in life" and having him "die in such damning circumstances" (112). According to Beston's reading, "Waldo dies in murderous hatred" before being eaten by the dogs, which rip his throat open and tear his penis off (112). Beston interprets the circumstances of Waldo's death as "disturbing in themselves," but even more so, "when we consider that immediately before his death Waldo has his defenses shattered by Arthur ... [and] understandably turns in hatred upon the truthbringer. For this hatred, White damns him irretrievably" (112).

Beston argues that throughout *The Solid Mandala* White provides material allowing for "a sympathetic interpretation of Waldo" and "makes his damnation dubious" (111). He contends that a sympathetic reading of Waldo allows readers to "see where White departs from his early compassion and attempts to manipulate" readers "into adopting his growing antipathy for Waldo" (Beston 111). Furthermore, Beston claims that White himself "shows sympathy for Waldo" early in the novel, "but soon comes to abandon it," injecting "sarcastic comments intended to make the reader dislike and even condemn Waldo ... A number of incidents, too, suggest in White an enjoyment of Waldo's distress" (111). While Waldo obviously contains characteristics that readers may find both sympathetic and unsympathetic, individual readers may interpret Waldo's character in conflicting ways, and no reader or critic can know White's intention and incontrovertibly claim that White dislikes one of his characters or intends to manipulate his readers.

Arthur: The Saint of Suburbia

The "Arthur" section, which begins with the Brown family aboard ship en route from England to Australia, presents the events of the novel from Arthur's point of view and conveys his thoughts through indirect discourse. Many of Waldo's depictions of events are corrected, further developed or re-interpreted when viewed from Arthur's perspective, often radically altering the readers' knowledge. Herring argues that Arthur's version of events serves as a check on Waldo's, "showing how his apparent blunders are deliberate" (182). Thus, the "Arthur" section provides a new understanding not just of Arthur himself, but also of Waldo, Mrs. Poulter, the Feinsteins, and the twins' parents. Whereas Waldo's primary concerns are his writing, class anxiety and finding intellectual companions, Arthur focuses on religion and spirituality, love and enjoying life. While Waldo presents himself as an intellectual, holds a respectable job, and outwardly appears to be a successful member of society, Arthur is the saint of suburbia, a simple character like Mrs. Godbold in *Riders in the Chariot* who lacks the trappings of material success and does not conform to societal norms, yet through his actions reveals himself to be humble, loving and primarily concerned with helping others.

Throughout the novel, White constantly presents the twins as opposites. Thus, Waldo is a sickly child favored by his mother, while Arthur is strong, good-looking and his father's favorite (27; 26; 22). Arthur exhibits such strength as a child that his father predicts he will become a wrestler or an athlete (27). Although Arthur is mentally slow, he is born with a gift for figures that is "found growing in him, as naturally as hair," while mathematics is Waldo's great intellectual weakness (29, 225). In contrast to Waldo's early development of a passion for intellectual pursuits, Arthur learns to bake bread from his mother and derives great joy from the domestic activity, despite the disapproval of his father, who is "disgusted" and views baking as "nothing for a boy" (29). The description in the

"Arthur" section of Arthur and his mother baking together calls in to question Waldo's assertion that he is his mother's favorite. Arthur and Mrs. Brown are described as a "closed circle" entering into a "conspiracy of butter and bread," which is a "mystery they had to celebrate" and one that only "she and Arthur were to understand" (226). Arthur's baking relationship with his mother gives him the most intense satisfaction he ever experiences before his relationship with Mrs. Poulter (226).

Despite his mental slowness, Arthur's gift for numbers leads him to be "in some demand" at school, where he helps other boys with their homework in exchange for marbles (222). Arthur regards himself as immune to the physical and emotional bullying prevalent amongst schoolboys, but he fears for Waldo, whom he sees as vulnerable because he is "too clever by half," likes books, and is "said to be their mother's darling. Because of it all, Waldo needed defending from himself and others ... poor Waldo was so different, and so frail" (222; 223). Arthur's alleged mental slowness is called into question by the fact that he is often more perceptive than other characters and even as a child understands that Waldo's intellectual pursuits, penchant for speaking British English and physical appearance will not be accepted by the schoolboys who maintain the societal status quo. When Waldo is bullied at school, Arthur comes to his rescue, bellowing, "'I'll kill ... the pair of you buggers if you touch ... my brother'" (39).

After the twins complete primary school, Waldo begins attending Barranugli High School, but Mr. and Mrs. Brown decide Arthur is unsuitable for further schooling and arrange an apprenticeship for him with the local shopkeeper, Mr. Allwright (226). In addition to serving customers and stocking shelves, Arthur drives a horse and buggy around the suburb delivering groceries, an activity that gives him a sense of independence and allows him to befriend many members of the community, including the Feinsteins and Mrs. Musto, the wealthy owner of Fairy Flour whose influence later secures Waldo's first library job (228). Arthur spends his entire working life with the Allwrights, making him a well-known figure in the suburb for more than half a century, and retires at the same time as Waldo (280).

Arthur repeatedly demonstrates a great fondness for the physical structures of suburbia; he loves the houses and the Speedex Service Station, which is built on the site where Allwright's General Store once stood (52; 53). He is particularly fond of "the classical facade" of his family's brown weatherboard house (217). Moreover, Arthur likes to spend his mornings checking prices in the local Woolworth's supermarket (48). Indeed, it is Arthur, the most saint-like of all the characters in the novel, who most clearly celebrates suburbia and does not express any anti-suburban sentiments. It would certainly be a mistake to contend that Arthur's love for suburbia is evidence that White also celebrates suburbia; however, Arthur's attitude towards suburbia serves as weighty evidence against claims that *The Solid Mandala* is an anti-suburban novel.

Despite Arthur's "slowness" and shabby physical appearance, which often disturbs strangers (67) and situates him as an outsider, he is far more socially aware and integrated into society than Waldo. Arthur's five decades working for the Allwrights give him extensive experience observing, listening to and interacting with the residents of his suburb. As a result, Arthur knows much more about the lives of his neighbors, and indeed about human behavior, than Waldo. Moreover, unlike Waldo, Arthur rarely cares what other people think and say about him (197), a trait that allows him a great deal of freedom and independence. When Waldo urges Arthur to take pride in himself and value what others say about him, wondering whether Arthur even cares if people like him, Arthur is able to confidently retort, "'No ... Because they mostly do'" (198).

Arthur's wealth of social interaction enhances his perceptiveness, which he demonstrates on numerous occasions. For example, he knows that the raincoat he habitually wears makes him look "like a real old faggot" (275), senses that "only the very clever and the very stupid can dare to be dishonest" (244), and, most significantly, perceives during the Second World War that the Holocaust is not a unique or isolated event.

When Waldo asks how the Holocaust is relevant to their suburban existence in Australia and asserts, "'We don't put people in ovens here,'" Arthur replies, "'We didn't think of it'" (166). This episode echoes White's argument regarding the mock-crucifixion of Himmelfarb in *Riders in the Chariot*, namely that such acts occur in Australia "in all quarters, in many infinitely humiliating ways" (Qtd. in Bliss, *Patrick White's Fiction* 86). One of the reasons Waldo hates Arthur is because he recognizes that Arthur is unusually perceptive "and might even be the core of truth" (179).

Arthur's "slowness" is also belied by his lifelong interest in reading. As a child, Arthur repeatedly begs his father to read the Greek myths to him and Waldo (217). After retiring, Arthur spends much of his time reading at the library. As Waldo's colleague Miss Glasson puts it, "'He asks for the most extraordinary things ... The *Bhagavad Gita*, the *Upanishads*! He's interested in Japanese zen'" (188). Arthur also reads Western classics, including *The Brothers Karamazov* and *Through the Looking-Glass* (189). Like Waldo, Arthur also writes, attempting to create his own literary works. During the twins' childhood, when Waldo declares that Arthur cannot perform in his proposed play, Arthur says he will write his own Greek tragedy and act all the parts. When questioned about the play's subject, Arthur says it is about a cow that gives birth to a stillborn calf, revealing both his empathy and humility (33). Arthur also writes poetry about "the daughter he had never had" and "the wives he carried inside him" (284). Arthur's poems are the only part of him that he keeps hidden from Waldo, because some of them contain "a kind of blasphemy against life" (287).

Indeed, it is Waldo's discovery of one of Arthur's poems that causes the rage that leads to Waldo's death. Thus, although Waldo perceives himself as an artist and his brother as an "imbecile" (23), Arthur is the twin with the ability to create powerful art. In addition to reading and writing, Arthur gives Waldo writing advice. Arthur argues that "simple people" are more transparent and that one can "'see right into them, right into the part that matters. Then you can write about them'" (23). Most significantly, Arthur proclaims, "'it doesn't matter what you write about, provided you tell the truth about it'" (23). Waldo is unable to write truthfully in his own works, and the brutal truth of Arthur's poem is one of the main causes of Waldo's rage.

Although Waldo and Arthur's parents raise them as atheists, Arthur expresses a deep interest in religion and spirituality. As Herring notes, in his old age Arthur "becomes perplexed by the problem of pain" and the emphasis on suffering in Christianity (185). Arthur declares that he does not understand cruelty and is particularly troubled by the crucifixion (51). Arthur becomes obsessed with suffering and Christianity, and his library visits to read *The Brothers Karamazov* are an attempt to understand the relationship between them, as well as a quest to make sense of his relationship with Waldo (277). While Arthur is at the library reading *The Brothers Karamazov*, he is confronted by Waldo, who is ashamed and outraged by Arthur's presence and afraid that Arthur will embarrass him in front of his colleagues and the patrons (277). Waldo loudly commands Arthur to leave the library and addresses him as "Sir," "Indicating that he, Arthur, his brother, his flesh, his breath, was a total stranger" (278-79). David Coad interprets Arthur's reading of *The Brothers Karamazov* as evidence of "his interest in the *other world*, the moral, spiritual world inside man" (114, original emphasis) and argues that it is significant that Arthur's "quest for the sacred" does not involve the Christian church, whether represented by a congregation or a building (113). Coad sees the fact that Arthur does not consider joining a church as consistent with White's own "mistrust and reservations about institutionalised religion" (113).

Arthur comes to perceive himself as possessing spiritual knowledge that both Waldo and their father will never acquire, and thinks of himself as "the keeper of mandalas, who must guess their final secret through touch and light" (234). The mandala dance that Arthur spontaneously performs for Mrs. Poulter is his most intimate, expressive, and spiritual act of the novel. Through his dance, Arthur attempts to express his love for the important people in his life, including Mrs. Poulter, Dulcie and Waldo. However, he is unable to "dance his brother out of him, not fully. They were too close for it to work" (260). Additionally, the mandala dance is an expression of suffering: "in the centre of their mandala he danced the passion of all their lives, the blood running out of the backs of his hands, water out of the hole in his ribs" (260). Afterwards, Arthur comes to see the dance as a perfect moment in his life that can never be repeated and is therefore cause for sadness (261). Although Waldo refers to Arthur as a "'big fat helpless female'" and his "club foot" (36; 41), Arthur sees himself as Waldo's protector, rather than as a burdensome dependent. Arthur believes that he is strong and Waldo is weak, and that he thus has a duty to protect Waldo (209). At one point, Arthur decides that he cannot afford to die because of his duty to Waldo, which includes performing "the humblest tasks" and allowing Waldo to believe that he is superior (285). The parallels between Arthur and Mrs. Godbold, both suburban saints, are abundantly clear.

When Waldo dies while attempting to choke Arthur to death, Arthur believes he has committed fratricide and in his despair stampedes "through the house ... It was a wonder the cries torn out of him didn't bring the structure down" (288). When compared to Waldo's cold decision to attempt to drive Arthur to a heart attack through strenuous walks, Arthur's genuine grief over Waldo's death provides yet another example of the numerous contrasting behaviors of the twins. Despite Arthur's many positive qualities, critics disagree over whether or not he is an admirable character. Herring views Arthur as the protector of his family (181), Bliss claims that he achieves sainthood (*Patrick White's Fiction* 113) and Edgecombe sees him as an empathetic visionary mystic (*Vision* 64, 68). However, Beston argues that two main factors prevent readers from viewing Arthur as a saint: first, "he is presented as physically repulsive right through the book," and second, there is not enough evidence to support the claims regarding "his inspirational effect upon others" (108). Furthermore, Beston contends that White's language describing Arthur's appearance and actions "are so evenly disdainful in all three Parts that one comes to suspect a repugnance in White himself for his own creation" (108). Furthermore, Beston argues that White manipulates his readers into sharing "his distaste for his character" (109). Beston's assertion that Arthur is consistently presented as physically repulsive is incorrect; in fact, Arthur is repeatedly described in positive terms, such as strong, athletic and handsome (22; 26; 27). Additionally, there is ample evidence that Arthur inspires others, especially Mrs. Poulter and Dulcie Feinstein, who names one of her children after Arthur. Beston's contention that White possesses disdain and repugnance for Arthur simply cannot be proven, nor can his claim that readers share White's alleged distaste for Arthur.

Mr. and Mrs. Brown and Their House in the Suburbs
Although Waldo, Arthur and Mrs. Poulter are the central characters in the novel, the twins' parents, George and Anne Brown, play significant roles and allow White to address important issues in suburban life, including immigration, religion and non-conformity. Superficially, Mr. and Mrs. Brown may seem like a typical suburban couple, since he commutes by train to his job at the bank and she is a housewife raising children in a modest detached home; however, White demonstrates that a great deal of complexity exists beneath outward appearances conforming with societal norms. Although the Browns are English, and thus more acceptable than immigrants from other nations, they are still perceived as being foreign and strange by the Australian-born residents of Sarsaparilla. Mrs. Brown is referred to as "vague" or "English" by other citizens of Sarsaparilla because she maintains her English manners and keeps to herself emotionally, "which was a Bad Thing in a new country" (25), especially one in which openness and informality are valued. When Mrs. Brown entertains visitors, she serves tea in elegant porcelain "which they had brought out with them from Home" (67). White's capitalization of the word "home" functions on one level to emphasize the Browns' retention of their English national identity, but also works on another as a realistic portrayal of the manner in which English immigrants referred to their homeland.[12]

George Brown also keeps to himself and does not engage in everyday practices common to Australian men, such as playing and watching sport, drinking and gambling. Instead, he spends the majority of his free time reading, and passes on his love of literature to his sons, to whom he reads Greek and Roman myths and recites Shakespeare (27, 70). Mr. Brown is rarely seen without a book; as a child, Waldo thinks that his father must be solely responsible for keeping the pocket editions in business (73). Throughout the novel, Mr. Brown is depicted reading a variety of texts, including *Thus Spake Tharathustra*, *The Autocrat of the Breakfast Table*, *Religio Medici*, *Sesame and Lillies*, *Essays in the Study of Folk-Songs* and *The Brothers Karamazov* (73, 76, 191). While Waldo is a high school student, his father begins teaching himself Norwegian with the intention of reading Ibsen in his original language, and jokes that learning Norwegian will allow him to "translate his thoughts into a language which could not be read" (70, 264).

Significantly, Mr. Brown is never shown reading an Australian book. Indeed, all of his reading matter is European, indicating that he considers Europe his intellectual home. Mr. Brown's reading habits and failure to engage in typical activities for an Australian adult male indicate that he is an immigrant who has made no attempt to assimilate. Although he lives and works in Australia, Mr. Brown does not participate in Australian culture in any way. Essentially, he lives in the same manner that he would have if he had remained in England. Mr. Brown's retention of his English culture and habits are closely linked to the reasons for the Browns' emigration to Australia. Unlike many immigrants, who leave their homelands to escape war and poverty, or, at the least, in pursuit of greater economic opportunities, the Browns leave England to escape from Anne Brown's family and their restrictive traditions and religious beliefs. Thus, the Browns primarily leave England to escape the Quantrells, not to escape English culture.

However, there is some evidence that the Browns perceive English culture as restrictive. After his retirement, Mr. Brown occasionally discusses his escape, which he credits to intellectual enlightenment, but recounting his physical and intellectual journey causes his mood to darken and his breathing to thicken, "clogged with the recurring suspicion that he might be chained still" (139). At one point, Mr. Brown tells Waldo and Arthur that they have been "'reared in the light in an empty country'" in which there are no shadows or discipline, and a great deal of freedom, and as a result there is much they will never understand (153). In a brief discussion of their emigration, George and Anne Brown refer to it as an escape, and Anne calls her family "'intolerable,'" "'beastly'" and "'warped by tradition,'" "'Sitting in their pews ... Sunday after Sunday. Keeping in with God and society. Then going home to sharpen their knives for the week'" (42). Mr. Brown declares that in Australia they are free and the children have opportunity (42). In the first years after settling in Sarsaparilla, the Browns enjoy a peaceful and pleasant life, spending evenings sitting on the front verandah as a family. When the southerly wind blows, bringing relief from the heat, Mr. Brown refers to it as "'Just about the cheapest fulfillment of anybody's expectations'"; such comments please Mrs. Brown, who had "married beneath her" partly because of her husband's subtle wit (29).

Mr. and Mrs. Brown's rejection of religion plays a large part in the manner in which they raise their sons, setting them apart from their community. Unlike Mrs. Poulter, who is a devout Christian, and Mr. Poulter, who is an apathetic unbeliever, the Browns are actively atheistic, raising their sons as rationalists and demanding that they be excused from religious instruction at school. Mr. Brown teaches his sons that "everything ignorant people referred to as the supernatural" does not exist (40), and the twins are not taught to pray, being instructed instead that everything depends on their own will and that they can achieve their ambitions if they are determined and confident (71). Edgecombe argues that the Browns are rationalists because they are afraid of "risking their dignity" and "appearing vulnerable" (*Vision* 85). However, the Browns' rationalism and rejection of religion is more likely caused by their association of religion with the hypocrisy and repressive traditions of the

Quantrell family and the Baptist congregation George attended before rejecting Christianity.

In addition to being an immigrant who continues to dress in English styles (35), Mr. Brown has a club foot that sets him apart and draws the attention of strangers, especially children (27). Waldo is ashamed of his father's physical deformity, dislikes walking with him to the railway station, and resents riding the train with him to Barranugli, where his father works and he attends high school (28, 35, 69). At times Waldo would rather die than travel in his father's company (70). Despite Waldo's negative feelings towards his father, Mr. Brown remains fond of Waldo and treats him justly (27). Mr. Brown insists on treating others with respect, as evidenced in a discussion between Waldo and his parents about buying his first razor, and a discussion regarding the Feinsteins. When Waldo claims that shaving will not cause him to grow a five-o'clock-shadow and declares, "'I'm not a dago,'" his father immediately corrects him and insists that such derogatory language is forbidden in their home (73-74). On another occasion, when Waldo declares, laughing, that the "'Trouble with [the] Feinsteins is they're so damn Jewish. That's usually the trouble with Jews,'" his father rebukes him and states, "'Mr. Feinstein's a fine man'" (118). To Waldo's great surprise, his father is a respected member of the community. When Waldo first meets Mr. Feinstein, the cultured immigrant and successful businessman declares, "'I have heard about your father. He is, they say, a fine man ... A man of independent ideas ... [possessing] The courage of his own convictions'" (97).

George Brown's job at the bank in Barranugli is the primary element of his characterization as a typical suburban husband and father. His job is portrayed as unsatisfactory and lacking opportunity for advancement. When Arthur is a child and asks his father if he will be promoted to the Head Office, Mr. Brown replies, "'On their day of judgement'" (46). Mr. Brown's assessment of his career prospects is correct, and he works in the same position in the Barranugli branch until he retires. Upon his retirement, George Brown is presented with an engraved watch and "other considerations," presumably a pension, but from Waldo's perspective, his father seems haunted by indignity and spends most of his time in retirement simply sitting in a chair (151). When the twins are young, their mother occasionally takes them to visit their father while he is working in the bank. Waldo describes the building as solemn and cool inside, and is disappointed when their father puts a stop to their calls, since visiting the bank increases Waldo's sense of importance (46). During their final outing to the bank, the twins see their father counting money in a "cage" (47). The sight of his father standing in a cage looking out at him leaves such an impression on Waldo that he remembers the event even more distinctly than the morning in 1922 when he finds his father dead (47-48, 114). White's depiction of white-collar work as imprisonment may be interpreted as an anti-suburban sentiment; however, it would be more accurate to read the scene as a criticism of capitalism and white-collar employment.

After George Brown dies, his wife becomes dependent upon her sons financially, and later, physically. The elderly Mrs. Brown and her adult sons live a quiet, simple life. She rarely leaves the house and spends most of her time reading catalogues and prospectuses (156). The Browns decide not to modernize and never obtain a telephone or have electricity connected to their house, preferring to spend their evenings reading by lamplight (155). As the years pass and Mrs. Brown's health diminishes, she becomes an alcoholic confined to her room. Anne Brown finally dies in 1932, ten years after her husband.

The Browns' suburban bungalow on Terminus Road in Sarsaparilla plays a significant role in *The Solid Mandala*, since Waldo and Arthur live in it for more than sixty years and much of the action of the novel takes place within its walls. In his autobiography, White reveals that he based the Browns' house on Dogwoods, his house in Castle Hill (*Flaws* 153). While lodging with the Thompsons in Barranugli after their arrival from England, the Browns buy a vacant block of land on Terminus Road, named for its proximity to the railway station (215, 216). Mr. Brown visits Sarsaparilla looking for a suitable locale in which to raise his family and meets the storekeeper, Mr. Allwright, who claims the developing suburb is on the ascendancy, but will retain some quiet backwaters (215). Seeking privacy and a quiet life, the Browns buy their land from Mr. Allwright, despite protests from Mrs. Brown, who thinks her husband's commute to Barranugli will be too long (216). Once the local builders begin constructing the Browns' weatherboard home, the family travels to Sarsaparilla from Barranugli each Sunday to observe the progress (217). George Brown decides to express his difference from other suburbanites and his fondness for Greek civilization by having the builders construct a Greek pediment above the front verandah (30). However, the builders do not fully understand Mr. Brown's vision and are not able to properly execute his design, with the result that the finished house has the appearance "of a little, apologetic, not quite proportionate temple" (31). Later, once the family saves enough money, their house is painted brown and "accepted by the landscape," since all the surrounding houses are brown, and the classical pediment becomes less noticeable (32).

When the house is new, it stands squarely, smells of timber, and is clearly visible from the street (31). However, as time passes, the house slowly decays and becomes camouflaged by trees and long grass. Herring argues that *The Solid Mandala* is "a chronicle of senescence and decay," since three of the four family members die, the house slowly disintegrates, the quince trees "become wormy and woody," and "the sea of grass encroaches more and more" (182). The physical decay of the Browns' home, "a disintegrating wooden box," is emphasized by the "irregular bricks" of the path from the gate to the verandah, the "fragile" front gate itself, which is decomposing, and the waves of grass, which is chest-high by novel's end (167, 20, 21, 166, 111).

However, the changes over time to the house and the yard are not necessarily negative. In fact, they can be interpreted positively as part of the process of establishing a home. The sixty-plus years that Waldo and Arthur spend living in their house make them part of the suburban landscape and allow them to develop a deep sense of belonging that can only be acquired over time. Arthur feels possessed by Terminus Road, since that is where his life is lived. Although the brothers leave the house each day to go to their places of employment, "their actual life was the one which continued knotting itself behind the classical weatherboard facade" (276). Arthur feels that despite the "timber thin as paper, fretting iron, [and] sinking foundations," the house will "continue to fulfill its purpose" and survive (285).

Suburban Immigrants and Others: The Feinsteins and the Chinese

In *The Solid Mandala*, the Browns are not the only immigrants in suburbia. White's cast of characters includes the Feinsteins, a family of European Jewish immigrants, and an unnamed Chinese family. The Feinsteins own two residences: a townhouse near Mr. Feinstein's music store in the city, and a suburban villa in Sarsaparilla (117). When Waldo meets Dulcie Feinstein, she explains that her family resides in their suburban home "'on and off ... When Daddy feels he wants a change of air'" (84). Waldo is unable to understand why anyone would choose to spend time in Sarsaparilla if they had other options, but Dulcie views the arrangement as normal (84). Inside the Feinstein's house, the piano is "the dominant object" (94), indicating their upper-middle-class status, which is also signaled by other accoutrements, such as a "walking-stick made from rhinoceros hide ... [a] signed photo of Sarah Bernhardt, a ship in a bottle, and ... [a] gold clock on the mantelpiece" (98). Like Waldo's father, Mr. Feinstein no longer practices the religion of his youth, and he refers to his prayer-cap as something people wore in the days when they were superstitious (102). Waldo perceives the Feinsteins to be remarkably foreign and pays particular attention to their accents. Mr. Feinstein possesses "a fairly strong Australian accent," which Waldo interprets as an attempt to make up for his foreignness, while Mrs. Feinstein, "of doubtful syntax," pronounces the letter R in a manner that "made you wonder," and her use of tenses sometimes seem to "have been lifted out of a bad translation" (99, 97, 94). Waldo views the Feinsteins as so different that he "grew guilty for their own foreignness" (99). Herring describes the Feinstein scenes as "superb social comedy" (184). The humor of the scenes is largely generated by Waldo's reactions to the Feinsteins' difference and the ways in which his interactions with them reveal his own ignorance and elitism.

The Feinsteins are not the only family of immigrants in the suburb apart from the Browns. An unnamed Chinese family live on a hill behind the Poulter's house, where they run a market garden. The Chinese are first mentioned early in the novel during the conversation between Mrs. Poulter and Mrs. Dun, and make several brief appearances. Mrs. Poulter tells Mrs. Dun that she never knew the Chinese woman, even though she lived behind the Poulters, and reports that according to local gossip, the Chinese family is wealthy. According to Mrs. Poulter, the Chinese woman is not without refinement, "'But a Chinese is never the same'" (5). Mrs. Poulter's racism, discussed earlier with reference to her television viewing, is highlighted by her emphasis of the Chinese' difference and her suggestion that they are inferior to the white residents of Sarsaparilla.

On several occasions, Arthur sees the Chinese woman on the hillside standing beneath a flowering wheel-tree (257, 138, 281). During their first encounter, Arthur and the Chinese woman stand looking at each other for a few moments before she turns away and walks behind some sheds. The narrator describes the Chinese woman as "so little connected with them [Arthur and Mrs. Poulter] or their other surroundings" (257). Herring argues that the Chinese woman standing beneath the flowering wheel tree is an "exquisite image" (187). However, White's inclusion of the Chinese family is remarkably vague. Readers never learn whether the Chinese are immigrants or descendants of immigrants.[13] The age of the Chinese woman is not revealed, nor is the size of her family. In fact, she is little more than a memorable image. White's inclusion of the Chinese in Sarsaparilla and his representation of them as marginalized others serves to highlight the racism of Australian society. Simultaneously, the inclusion of the Chinese is a reminder that suburbia is not a homogenous white zone;

rather, it is a locale in which a diverse array of people live in close proximity.

Portrayals of Sarsaparilla's Infrastructure

In addition to using the lives of his characters and the Browns' house to explore suburban life, White includes numerous physical descriptions of the suburb of Sarsaparilla. White's depiction of his fictional outer-Sydney suburb cannot accurately be characterized as negative; rather, White provides a blend of celebratory, ambivalent and negative portrayals. Mrs. Poulter, one of White's suburban saints, takes pride in "the glossier side" of Sarsaparilla, especially "the picture windows and the textured brick" (5), however, she feels that the suburb does not possess as much community spirit as the rural area where she previously lived (153). White includes a number of positive references to Sarsaparilla's ongoing suburban development. The houses built after the Second World War on O'Halloran Road, where the Feinsteins live, are depicted as "flaunting" signs of life (125). When Waldo and Arthur walk along the main street of Sarsaparilla, they are fascinated and overwhelmed by their intimate knowledge of their suburb, which they know so well that they could dismantle their surroundings "brick by brick, tile by tile" and then put the pieces back together (48). Woolworth's grocery store, one of the primary landmarks of the suburb and a hub of activity, is presented on several occasions as the object of Arthur's love (48).

Waldo views the shops, houses and streets of his suburb as proof of humans' rationality, which he prizes above all else (52). Waldo enjoys looking into the houses of Sarsaparilla, although not too closely, for occasionally his observations revealed "displays of perversity to damage temporarily his faith in reason" (52). Waldo prefers to view the houses from a detached distance that allows him to view them as "labeled boxes" containing furniture, rather than passions (52). Such passages simultaneously reveal the vitality and variety of life in suburbia, and Waldo's inability to deal with other humans on an emotional level. Waldo is interested in the history of Sarsaparilla, especially the remnants of early settlement, such as the Allwright's store, the market gardens, and the few colonial houses; however, he is "particularly sensitive" to people he thinks of as "failures who had been dumped in the long grass" of Sarsaparilla (76-77).

Waldo frequently projects his self-loathing, elitism and disdain for people whom he perceives as inferior to himself onto the suburban infrastructure. During the "Waldo" section, Sarsaparilla is described as having "ramparts" that are "erected laboriously brick by brick, to withstand some hostile thing, by those who had not yet died: the infallible ones with professions and offspring" (112). Waldo is clearly jealous of other peoples' professions and children, and decides that it is pathetic to even think about them (112). The road to Barranugli is depicted as "a replica of itself at many other points," such that Waldo often forgets which sections he has already passed (54). The narrator posits that if Waldo "had not been a superior man, of intellectual tastes, it might have become intolerable, or perhaps had, because of that" (54). Clearly, Waldo's prejudices cause his negative reactions, rather than any inherent characteristics of suburbia.

On one occasion, Waldo expresses dissatisfaction about the distance between Sarsaparilla and the library where he works in Sydney's city centre. He claims it is too far to travel and that the lengthy commute causes him to return home exhausted (119). Waldo comes to think of Terminus Road as too far from "everywhere," and occasionally resents Sarsaparilla's perceived isolation and considers renting a room in the city, where he hopes "his thoughts might take infinite shape instead of remaining the blurred mess he could never sort out" (119). Here Waldo mistakenly places the blame for his lack of creative output on his physical location, failing to realize that the problem lies within and that moving into the city will not necessarily help his writing. However, Waldo also considers the possibility that living in suburbia "allowed his thoughts their flowing line" and moving into the city might "tighten" and extinguish them (119-120). Nevertheless, his focus on the importance of the location in which one tries to create is misguided. Moreover, Waldo does not attempt to rent a room in the city and remains in Sarsaparilla until his death.

Conclusion: *The Solid Mandala* is Not an Anti-Suburban Novel

The novel contains little material that could be construed as anti-suburban: such readings of the novel rely on highlighting White's portrayal of Mrs. Dun and Mrs. Poulter and interpreting them as both satirical and representative of White's own attitudes. Arguably, the most blatant example of an anti-suburban sentiment is the following line from the opening "In the Bus" section: "In High Street the overstuffed bus began to spew out its coloured gobbetts" (12). The description of citizens of suburbia as "coloured gobbetts" (chunks of raw meat) that are spewed out is an incontrovertibly negative depiction. However, it should be noted that it is people who are described as "gobbetts," thus the description targets residents of suburbia, rather than suburbia as a whole. Moreover, the line is by far the most negative in the novel and does not necessarily represent White's views. The multitude of celebratory and ambivalent depictions of suburbia in the novel far outweigh the impact of the "gobbetts" line.

Although critics such as Beston and Herring repeatedly attempt to discern White's intent, claiming that White hates and mocks his characters and that the novel "is tainted with a distaste for human beings" (Beston 106; Herring 103; Beston 113), Lawson recognizes that White's narrative technique makes such assertions impossible to prove and requires critics to tread carefully. Lawson argues that White creates characters in whom his viewpoint "is only apparently invested"; this technique "leaves readers uneasy and uncertain" ("Meaning" 287). Lawson argues that rather than limiting interpretation, White's "cryptic, enigmatic, ironic, and satiric elements" require "interpretative pluralism" ("Meaning" 287). As a result, White's work "frequently evokes … radically contradictory interpretations" and the body of criticism on White's work contains many "utterly opposite, mutually exclusive thematic readings" (Lawson, "Meaning" 291).

As mentioned earlier in this chapter and in the previous chapter, the majority of critics who have written about White have labeled the author and his novels *Riders in the Chariot* and *The Solid Mandala* anti-suburban. My analysis of both novels and "The Prodigal Son" reveals that White's work is not anti-suburban; in fact, it contains a nuanced, complex, sometimes celebratory and often ambivalent representation of suburbia. Hopefully, future analysis of White's suburban novels will acknowledge White's complex and detailed engagement with suburbia and the many important social issues that he addresses through his use of the suburban setting. My next chapter analyzes three canonical novels set in suburbia, which, unlike White's novels, are unquestionably anti-suburban and serve to establish and then perpetuate the anti-suburban tradition in the Australian novel.

Endnotes

1. White based the episode on his own experiences. In order to reach Sydney's CBD by public transport, White made an eight-mile bus journey from Castle Hill to Parramatta, where he boarded a train into the city (Marr 267).
2. See Dewey (752), Wilde et al (72; 608), McCann ("Ethics" 145; "Decomposing" 59), Powell (127-28), Webby (11-12), Kinnane ("Shopping" 41-42), and During (16).
3. Mosman, Maroubra and Randwick are suburbs of Sydney.
4. David Jones is an Australian department store.
5. Bill's time in the camp during the First World War is not explained. It is unclear whether he was an internee of German descent, a guard, or some other kind of worker in the camp. However, Beston notes that the surname Poulter "is very like the German *Polter*, an objectionable, noisy sort of person" (107), so perhaps Bill Poulter could be read as an Australian of German descent.
6. The *OED* defines "mandala" thus: "a. A symbolic circular figure, usually with symmetrical divisions and figures of deities, etc., in the centre, used in Buddhism and other religions as a representation of the universe, and serving esp. as an object of meditation. b. In Jungian psychology: an image or archetype ... of a similar circle visualized in dreams, held to symbolize a striving for unity of self and completeness." In *The Solid Mandala*, the title refers to Arthur's cherished marble, as well as the dance he performs for Mrs. Poulter.
7. Leonard Saporta shares some characteristics with Leopold Bloom in Joyce's *Ulysses*.
8. See "Sleep and Poetry."
9. The title of Waldo's fragment recalls T.S. Eliot's *The Waste Land*, in which Tiresias is invoked. Moreover, the physical descriptions of Waldo may remind some readers of Eliot. In his notes on *The Waste Land*, Eliot writes that despite being "a mere spectator," Tiresias is "the most important personage in the poem, uniting all the rest ... the two sexes meet in Tiresias" (70). Thus, the title of Waldo's fragment of a novel suggests his sexual/gender ambiguity.
10. Although the name Barron Field may appear to be another example of White's fondness for creating satirical proper nouns, such as Barranugli

and Mungindribble, Barron Field was an English poet and literary critic who arrived in New South Wales in 1816 and wrote *First Fruits of Australian Poetry*, considered to be the first book of poetry published in Australia.

11. In his excellent recent article on *The Solid Mandala*, Birns argues against reading Waldo's library work as part of White's characterization of Waldo as a failed artist.
12. English immigrants to Australia and their descendants have traditionally referred to England as "Home," even if they have never been there. The practice was common from the European settlement of Australia in 1788 until at least the 1950s and is frequently reflected in Australian literature. Richard White notes that a number of critics observed the practice of calling England "Home" continuing in the 1950s (47). Although the media focuses on Asian immigration and asylum seekers from Africa and the Middle East, distorting public perceptions of immigration, the English still comprise the largest percentage of immigrants to Australia each year. White was born just over a decade after Federation into a wealthy family of English descent: he once described himself as "an anachronism, something left over from that period when people were no longer English and not yet indigenous" (Qtd. in Ackland 401).
13. Chinese immigration to Australia began during the goldrush of the 1850s. In response, the Australian colonies introduced anti-Chinese immigration restriction acts (Collins 103). The White Australia Policy was implemented in 1901 and not repealed until 1972. Thus, Chinese immigration to Australia virtually ceased during the period the novel covers. Therefore, it is logical to assume that the Chinese residents of Sarsaparilla are native-born Australians, descendants of Chinese immigrants who came to Australia during the goldrush.

CHAPTER 3

ESTABLISHING AND PERPETUATING THE ANTI-SUBURBAN TRADITION

GEORGE JOHNSTON'S *MY BROTHER JACK* (1964), DAVID MALOUF'S *JOHNNO* (1975) AND TIM WINTON'S *CLOUDSTREET* (1991)

In the previous two chapters, I argued that Patrick White's *Riders in the Chariot* and *The Solid Mandala* have erroneously been labeled anti-suburban novels.[1] In this chapter, I contend that George Johnston's *My Brother Jack* is the first indisputably anti-suburban Australian novel, and that subsequent canonical novels, namely David Malouf's *Johnno* (1975) and Tim Winton's *Cloudstreet* (1991), are also thoroughly anti-suburban. Moreover, as a group of highly influential novels published over a period of almost thirty years, *My Brother Jack*, *Johnno* and *Cloudstreet* illustrate the trajectory of the anti-suburban tradition in the Australian novel, which is established by Johnston and subsequently perpetuated by Malouf and Winton.

George Johnston was born in 1912 in the Melbourne suburb of Malvern, the same year White was born in London. Although both men wrote canonical novels, their lives and reputations were markedly different. White was born into upper-class privilege, received an exclusive private education, and earned worldwide literary acclaim, while Johnston was born into a working-class family, attended public schools, entered the workforce at fourteen, and failed to establish a reputation anywhere near that of White's. In fact, Johnston is now largely remembered for just one novel, *My Brother Jack*. Johnston's family moved from Bendigo, in central Victoria, to the Melbourne suburb Elsternwick, where Johnston was raised, just before World War One. During the 1920s, while still a teenager, Johnston began working as a journalist for *The Argus* newspaper. In 1938, Johnston married Elsie Taylor and settled with her in the new suburb of Glen Iris (J. Kinnane 170).[2] During the Second World War, Johnston served as a war correspondent and published books during and after the war based on his experiences in New Guinea, China, Burma and Italy. In 1951, he moved to London to work as the European correspondent for Sydney's *Sun* newspaper, accompanied by his second wife, the writer Charmian Clift. Johnston gave up journalism in 1954 and settled on the Greek island Hydra to write fiction.[3] Johnston returned to Australia a decade later, following the success of *My Brother Jack*, which won the Miles Franklin Award in 1964, and lived in Sydney until his early death in 1970, a consequence of contracting tuberculosis in Greece. *My Brother Jack* became the first volume of a trilogy: the second installment, *Clean Straw for Nothing* (1969), also won the Miles Franklin Award; Johnston died before completing the final volume, *A Cartload of Clay* (1971). In 1970, two months before his death, Johnson was awarded the Order of the British Empire for his services to literature.[4]

Numerous critics have described *My Brother Jack* as canonical, and the novel has sold in large numbers.[5] In 2002, Josephine Jill Kinnane noted that *My Brother Jack* had not been out of print since its initial publication almost four decades earlier (177). The canonical status of *My Brother Jack* and its continuing appeal was also demonstrated by a new television adaptation in 2001. In 2003, *My Brother Jack* was voted number ten on the Australian Society of Authors Top Forty Books list, ahead of White's *Riders in the Chariot* ("Top Forty Australian Books"), and in early 2010 *My Brother Jack* was voted number six in the "Favourite Australian Novels" readers' poll conducted by *Australian Book Review*. Despite its canonical status and ongoing popularity, *My Brother Jack* has received little critical attention, especially when compared to White's work. Many of Johnston's eighteen novels, such as *Death Takes Small Bites* (1948), *The Cyprian Woman* (1955) and *The Saracen Shadow* (1957), are classified as crime and detective novels; some were published under the pseudonym Martin Shane; and most are set outside Australia: all of these factors may explain why little criticism has been devoted to Johnston's novels.

In 1974, Geoffrey Thurley claimed Johnston was the victim of "academic disdain" in Australia and argued that Australian academics were "as contemptuous of Johnston ... [as they were] proud of the more intellectually impressive White" (62). More than two decades later, in 1998, Jennifer Rutherford stated that she lacks sympathy for *My Brother Jack* and sought to understand why "such an ostentatiously masochistic novel should be given the privileged status it has received in Australia" (125). Thurley takes up Johnston's case and argues that with *My Brother Jack* he "takes his place confidently within the great classical tradition of the novel that leads back through *The Great Gatsby* and *Great Expectations* to *Don Quixote*" (62). Thurley repeatedly claims that Johnston is a better novelist than White (64, 65, 67) and declares Johnston is "the pick of the mid-century Australian novelists" (71). Moreover, Thurley argues that *My Brother Jack* is "among the better novels written in English since the death of D.H. Lawrence" (76).

My Brother Jack: Establishing the Anti-Suburban Tradition in Australian Fiction

My Brother Jack, Johnston's fifteenth novel, is an autobiographical novel and a Bildungsroman (Scheckter 115, 119). Moreover, it is a canonical example of "typically anti-suburban writing" (McCann, "Decomposing" 59). From the first page of the novel, Johnston presents an overwhelmingly negative depiction of suburbia, which he sustains throughout the text. The novel traces the development of the first-person narrator David Meredith from his working-class childhood in Elsternwick through his adolescence, entry into the workforce, first marriage, relocation to a newly developed suburb, ascent of the career ladder, and overseas exploits as a war correspondent, ending with the narrator in his early thirties courting the woman who becomes his second wife. Johnston begins the novel by declaring, "a person doesn't begin to exist without parents and an environment and legendary tales told about ancestors" (1). On the first page, Johnston establishes the suburban setting (and his negative attitude towards it) through a description of his childhood home in Elsternwick,[6] which his narrator and alter-ego, David Meredith, describes as an "undistinguished" weatherboard house with "a corrugated iron roof" located "behind a wire fence, privet hedge, [and] small square lawn of buffalo grass," with "the name *Avalon* in gilt letters on a blackwood panel in a flat and dreary suburb far away in Melbourne, Australia" (1). Although the phrase "far away" refers to the spatial and temporal distance between Johnston's childhood home and the time and location from which he writes the novel (the Greek island Hydra, in the early 1960s), it also situates Elsternwick as remote and marginal.

Lee Brotherson argues that Johnston's decision to describe the Meredith home on the first page of the novel and to emphasize its suburban setting accords "a primordial status" to place "in the presentation of character" (2). Thus, for Johnston, setting and character are inextricably intertwined, and David and the rest of the Meredith family are products of suburbia. Gerster claims that Johnston's decision to rename his childhood home "Avalon" in the novel serves to highlight the "comic pretentiousness" of suburban house-naming practices and argues that the romantic allusion to the mythical British isle highlights David's frustration with his status as "a cultural outsider who craves escape from the 'shabby suburban squalor' into which he was born" (566). Furthermore, Gerster argues that the "appearance of 'Avalon' on the first page of the novel alerts its readers to the central theme of suburban Australia as a land of the living dead" (566). Indeed, both actual death and "living death" are omnipresent in the Meredith's *Avalon* due to the First World War.

David's parents both serve overseas during the war; his mother as a nurse in France and his father as a sapper, first in Gallipoli and later in Europe (2). After David's parents return home in 1919, his mother works in the operating theatre of a military hospital, and his father as a tram mechanic (2-3). Due to his parents' wartime absence and his mother's decision to care for disabled veterans in their home for years afterwards, "every corner" of the Meredith's "little suburban house" is "impregnated … with the very essence of some gigantic and somber experience that had taken place thousands of miles away" (11). David describes the war and its legacy as moving in "behind the privet hedge to occupy every room and every cranny of our mundane little house" (12). The deaths inside the house of David's grandmother and a number of older relatives, combined with the presence of amputees, lend the house a constant aura of decay, sorrow and stymied vitality.

In an attempt to imbue his family with importance and a legacy stretching back to the European settlement of Australia, David emphasizes the exploits of a number of ancestors, several of whom were allegedly involved in some of the most iconic events in Australian history. David improbably writes of a Scottish ancestor "in the naval landing party which first hoisted the British flag over the new settlement at Botany Bay in 1788" (18). He claims that his paternal grandfather "made quite a name for himself" after traveling to Australia "as second mate on a smart Liverpool clipper" which he abandoned in order to join the goldrush (18-19). According to David, his grandfather "later became an officer of the Mounted Constabulary in the man-hunt after Ned Kelly and his gang, and later still prospered enough to own a goldmine and two news- papers" (19). In addition to providing David's family with a somewhat glorious past, the exploits of his ancestors serve to establish a link between the family's suburban present and the colonial past, connecting them to what David sees as a more exciting and important era, and providing the Merediths with bona fides as true-blue Australians. As Maryanne Dever points out, David's relationship with his homeland "is marked by a deep, on-going division ... between his overt disaffection for the world of suburban Australia and his ... admiration of the subtler significances of his heritage" ("Artist" 19).

As David progresses through childhood towards adolescence, his awareness of suburbia and his dissatisfaction with it increases. David describes the suburban world of his childhood in the 1920s as one that "spread forever, flat and diffuse, monotonous yet inimical, pieced together in a dull geometry of dull houses behind silver-painted fences of wire or splintery palings or picket fences and hedges" (29). David notes that the "sad, tidy habitations" of suburbia all

> had names like *Sans Souci* and *The Gables* and *Emoh Ruo* ["our home" spelt backwards]... and *The Rest* and *Nirvana* and, of course, other *Avalons* beside ours ... All the way through to the city proper there was nothing to break the drab flatness of this unadventurous repetition. (29, original emphasis).

Rather than contemplating the complexities of the vast numbers of lives lived in suburbia and all the dreams, joys and achievements of his fellow suburbanites, David focuses solely on the physical features of suburbia, especially the flatness and the repetition. He states that upon returning to visit "A lifetime later ... the horrible flatness of it all was just as real as ever, but far more depressing" (29). The negative depiction of suburbia presented here by Johnston is created primarily through David's judgmental use of language, especially "monotonous," "dull," "sad," "nothing," "drab," "unadventurous" and "horrible" (29). The physical environment is itself neutral; it is David's interpretation of it that is biased.

Due to what he perceives as the dullness and predictably of suburbia, David states that he and his older brother Jack are only "very occasionally" able to "experience a true adventure" (30). Apart from a freak cyclone that he and Jack are caught up in at the waterfront (30), the only excitement David describes as part of his suburban life is the presence of "feuding gangs" with as many as eighty members each that roam the suburbs and fight with sticks, stones and razors (33-34). David declares that the most terrifying thing about the suburbs is not the gangs, but that the suburbs and their inhabitants "accepted their mediocrity" (35). In a passage reminiscent of Esson, David argues that the suburbs are

> worse than slums ... [because] They betrayed nothing of anger or revolt or resentment; they lacked the grim adventure of true poverty; they had no suffering, because they had mortgaged this right simply to secure a sad acceptance of a suburban respectability that ranked them socially a step or two higher than the true, dangerous slums of Fitzroy or Collingwood. (35)

However, David's assertion that the suburbs lack suffering is greatly contradicted by his own experiences, especially of the domestic violence perpetrated by his father, calling into question his self-awareness and reliability as a narrator.

Johnston's inclusion of domestic violence in *My Brother Jack* is one of the earliest examples of authorial engagement with the issue in suburban fiction.[7] David claims that his father's "failure to have made anything of his life ... made him morose, intolerant, bitter and violently-tempered" (37). Jack Meredith Senior's "displeasure and resentment" are mostly taken out on his wife (37). Johnston's narrator depicts verbal and physical fights between his parents as an almost nightly occurrence, claiming, "I can hardly recall a night when I was not wakened in panic by the stormy violence of my parents' quarrels. Often Mother would run from the house in the dead of night, swearing never to return" (37). David focuses in detail on "one specially terrible occasion" when he and Jack are "awakened in the sleep-out by the sound of Mother, who was outside in the rain and darkness, whimpering like an animal as she tried to crawl into hiding" (37). In response to the domestic violence, David develops a habit of hiding in a sea chest, where he tries to work out ways of murdering his father "without being found out or getting Mother into trouble," since he is terrified that his mother will run away and leave her children "unprotected against his [father's] ragings and injustices" (39, 40).

However, the domestic violence does not remain confined to the husband-wife relationship. Mr. Meredith begins inflicting violence upon his sons and institutes a system of monthly punishments. Although Jack and David are routinely punished with "a cuffing around the ears or a slash with a stick or a strap" if caught breaking any household rules (42), their father decides to also punish his sons once a month by thrashing them "for the offences which *escaped* his attention," since he reasoned that the boys must be lying and getting away with some offences (42, original emphasis). David declares that the monthly beatings "went on for several years" and speculates that they must have caused him a great deal of psychological damage (42). As Jack matures physically and becomes a prize-winning boxer, he confronts his father and tells him that he will not accept any more beatings; however, David's beatings continue "more ferociously than ever" and only cease because his father eventually beats him so severely that he has to be treated by a doctor, who threatens to report Mr. Meredith to the police (47).

Although *My Brother Jack* is an autobiographical novel and closely follows the facts of Johnston's life, the domestic violence in the novel seems to be fictional. Garry Kinnane, Johnston's biographer, states that Johnston "appalled the whole family by the way in which he represented his father ... The most disturbing thing about this brutal portrait is its fabrication" ("The Reconstruction" 436). According to Brian Matthews, Johnston's siblings Jack and Marjorie insist their father was not physically violent ("Notes" 368). Matthews speculates that Johnston created Mr. Meredith's tyranny "in order to provide an element of conflict" and "a harsh environment in which to gain sympathy for young Davy" ("Notes" 368). In addition to providing conflict and eliciting sympathy for the protagonist, Johnston's characterization of Mr. Meredith presents him "as an embodiment of all the ills which suburban male is heir to" (Eagle 38-39), adding another dimension to the anti-suburban stance of the novel. Johnston conflates the ugly behavior of Mr. Meredith with the ugliness of suburbia in an attempt to draw a grotesque portrait of the suburban male.

David's anti-suburban attitudes are strengthened once he enters the workforce and spends more time in the city. Like his brother Jack before him, David leaves school at fourteen to take up an apprenticeship. Whereas Jack is apprenticed to a suburban plumber, David's parents recognize his artistic sensibilities and apprentice him to a lithographic firm in the city, a position that requires him to take art classes in the evening at the National Gallery (49, 48, 20). Like millions of other suburbanites around the world, David commutes to work by train. In order to qualify for a cheaper ticket and save more of his wages, David takes an early train to work that arrives an hour before his workday begins, and uses the time to explore the city. He gravitates to the wharves on the Yarra, where "for the first time," he becomes "aware of the existence of true beauty, of an opalescent world of infinite promise that had nothing whatever to do with the shabby suburbs" (70). David's wanderings in the city and fascination with the shipping industry indicate the genesis of his romanticization of travel. In keeping with the anti-suburban intellectual tradition, Johnston presents urban space as the location of beauty and vitality, qualities that do not exist in suburbia according to those who subscribe to anti-suburban prejudices. However, beauty is clearly in the eye of the beholder in David's case, since many residents of suburbia in the 1920s would have viewed Melbourne's wharves as dirty, ugly and dangerous.

Although Jack does not express the anti-suburban attitudes frequently voiced by David, he also sees the city as the location for adventure and excitement. Jack spends almost every night in the city seeking sexual conquests (54). David claims that the city "was fiercely generating a life of its own" and declares

> The Jazz Age had reached its crescendo: the wail and boop of saxophones … and the mad jumping of the Charleston had even

> begun to invade the hitherto inviolate stuffiness of our suburbs. Beyond our neat hedged perimeters, the world suddenly seemed transformed into a jungle of iniquities, of violence, sex, flaunted revolt, alarming uncertainties. (54)

In addition to hearing tales of Jack's nocturnal urban exploits, David encounters inner-city bohemians and artists through his art classes and "begins to move out of the suburban culture of his childhood" (Rutherford 110).

David's entrance into the workforce, discovery of the shipping world, and encounters with cosmopolitan and bohemian youth at his art classes converge to set him on a path towards becoming a writer. David's desire to write springs from his passion for reading, a pastime his father vehemently disapproves of in stereotypical hyper-masculine working-class style: "'You and your blasted books!' he would snarl. 'All you're doing, my lad, is muddling your mind and ruining your eyesight. Why the devil don't you get out and *do* something'" (56, original emphasis). Likewise, Jack, the prototypical Aussie male, disapproves of David's three male friends, who are all bookish, fearing that their companionship will turn David into a homosexual (56-57). Andy Medhurst argues that homophobia is a central suburban value, and claims, "sexual dissidents ... are the most vigorously policed victims of the suburban cult of conformity. Of all the hegemonies of suburbia, it is the hegemony of heterosexuality that cuts deepest" (266). Jack's fears are unfounded, as David is heterosexual and claims that at the time he did not even know the meaning of the word "homosexual" (57).

Lacking formal education in literature, David and his friends compete with each other to "discover" important authors, such as Ibsen, Chekhov, Tolstoy, Balzac, Flaubert, Gibbon and Defoe (57).[8] Despite the fact that they understand little of their reading, David and his friends are excited by their encounters with the literary world and soon "a secret desire" forms in David's mind: "I wanted to write. It began with poems, but they were very strange poems to emerge out of the Melbourne suburbs, because I had read *Heimskringla* and become obsessed by the Viking sagas" (57). Like Waldo in White's *The Solid Mandala*, David understands that reading and writing literature are activities treated with suspicion in Australia. Just as Waldo hides his writing in his mother's dress-box, David keeps his notebooks hidden in his mattress, "in case Jack should find them," even though he describes his own poetry as "worthless" (57-58). David soon becomes a published writer and embarks on a successful career, although as a journalist, rather than as a poet or fiction writer. While still a teenager, David writes an article about the shipping industry and sends it under the pseudonym "Stunsail" to the *Morning Post*, where it is published; his reaction is to be "torn between a lofty exultation and a blushing shame" (74). David secretly cashes his payment check (the equivalent of seven weeks' pay), tells nobody about his publication, and spends his small fortune on used books (74).

David realizes that the countless hours reading in his bedroom, the notebook full of poems hidden inside his mattress, and his rejection of Jack's attempts to turn him into a "normal" adolescent have all converged "into the semblance of a path that would lead somewhere" (75). He states, "I was fifteen. And I was a writer. Lonely and secretive, and desperately anonymous, but still a writer" (75). The *Morning Post* accepts every piece David submits, and he quickly establishes the reputation on which he later builds his successful journalism career (81). However, the conflict between David and his father over his reading and writing soon reaches a climax. David receives a gift of five pounds from his mother and grandmother for his sixteenth birthday, which he is expected to spend on oil paints (87). However, he sees a secondhand typewriter for sale and instinctively buys it (87). When David arrives home with the typewriter, his father is outraged, forbids him from bringing it into the house, and demands that he either return without the typewriter or not come home at all (89, 91, 92). David chooses the typewriter and all it represents over his family home. Thus, for the first time in the novel, David physically rejects suburbia.

Not knowing where else to go, David makes his way to the city studio of his artist friend Sam Burlington, who takes him in (92-94). At Sam's, David is exposed to a bohemian urban subculture that is presented as infinitely more exciting that suburbia. David begins his stay with Sam early in the autumn of 1928 and remains away from his family's home until winter settles in (96). Although David usually sleeps on Sam's sofa, Sam requires him to leave whenever he throws a party or wants to entertain a girl; on such occasions, David sleeps on a bench in Fitzroy Gardens (108). Despite his initial excitement at being exposed to urban bohemian culture, David soon tires of "the discomfort and inconvenience" and becomes homesick (108). In a ploy designed to facilitate his return home, David suggests that Jack pursue his dream of working in the bush and declares that it is his turn to protect their mother (115). He helps Jack find a job in the bush, but admits that "the whole thing had been done on a kind of false basis … I could no longer face a continuance of discomfort and inconvenience and cold and loneliness" (116). Thus, David returns to *Avalon* and finds comfort and security in the suburbia he long despised.

However, rather than settling into a quiet life in suburbia, David's world is soon shaken by a series of events involving his urban bohemian friends, a murder in suburbia, and the expatriation of an artist. Jessica Wray, Sam's girlfriend, is found murdered "in a desolate area of suburban parkland" (124). Sam is accused of the murder and the case becomes a media sensation. David learns of the murder and the accusation of Sam while reading the newspaper at a tram stop. Soon after, he boards a train into the city; during the journey his shock and dismay are conflated with his hatred of suburbia:

> I began to feel the thing turning in and beginning to invade me. An infinite distress possessed me. The carriage rocked and clattered through the flat suburbs; the shouting of the porters was echoed by the wheels and the name of every station seemed to clang from the steel rails along which we were rushing headlong into horror … Elsternwick, Ripponlea, Balaclava, Windsor, Prahran, South Yarra … I was in a second-class smoking compartment. Women

> never rode in smokers in those days, and at each station more men would get in, and they were all discussing the murder, some of them with gravity, but mostly with coarse jokes and comments, and with lechery ... The train clattered on through the grimy deserts of suburban rectitude. (123)

In addition to David's attitudes towards suburbia being influenced by his distress over the murder, he is also disgusted by the coarse comments of the suburban male commuters, many of whom lecherously comment that they would have liked to have had sex with Jessica and suggest that she was "asking for it" by posing nude for portraits and being sexually active. David views the comments of the suburban commuters as further evidence of the narrow-mindedness, philistinism and conformity of suburbia, especially as the commuters express disapproval of the bohemian lifestyle, which is set up in binary opposition to the suburban lifestyle.

Jessica's killer soon strikes again, and Sam is exonerated (141); however, the public scandal fanned by the media damages his reputation and spirits so severely that he feels compelled to leave Australia (142). Not only does Sam never return to Australia, he ceases painting and spends his life growing rosebushes in the south of France (142-43). As Eagle states, Sam "carries his suburban stigmata to the end of his days" (39). Garry Kinnane argues that suburban "prejudice against ... bohemianism" forces Burlington to expatriate himself and claims that David perceives "the disease" of philistinism to be "widespread, infecting the whole culture," noting that the theme "emerges frequently throughout the trilogy, especially as a factor in [David] Meredith's expatriatism" ("The Reconstruction" 437-38). Eagle posits that Jessica's murder and Sam's expatriation occupy a "dominant position in the novel" because the episode depicts "an artist destroyed by suburban values and falsehoods" (39). It seems unlikely that such a scandal experienced during youth could crush the creativity and bohemianism of an artist so totally; Johnston exaggerates both the supposed philistinism of suburbia and the affect of the scandal on the artist in order to provide more evidence for his indictment of suburbia and his justification for expatriation.

Jessica's murder and Sam's expatriation are followed by the arrival of the Great Depression, which David depicts as "the insidious creeping movement of dark, strong, unpredictable forces … It was out in the suburbs mostly that one gradually came to see it" (152). David describes unemployed citizens "shambling along the suburban streets" (153). In Elsternwick, the unemployed are a constant "unnerving" presence of "pathetic and yet somehow oddly sinister figures" who knock on the door and ask "for an hour's work to cut the hedge or to mow the lawn or to stack firewood or even to run errands … or sometimes more bluntly just to ask for a handout of food or money" (154). David's father demands that David paint a sign stating, "BEGGARS, HAWKERS, AND CANVASSERS WILL BE PROSECUTED" and attach it to the front gate; similar signs are soon seen "on gates all over the suburbs" (154). David's description of the victims of the depression and of the attempts of the more fortunate to keep the unemployed away presents suburbia as an inhospitable, unsympathetic environment.

During the Depression, Jack, the "honest Aussie battler at times inflated to impossibly heroic proportions" (G. Kinnane, "The Reconstruction" 438), struggles to find consistent employment and lives with Sheila, his future wife, in the suburb of Windsor. Describing a visit to Jack and Sheila's house, David claims that they live on "an even sadder street" than the one he grew up on (160). For David, the physical manifestations of sadness are "facing rows of identical little duplexes, sitting behind picket fences and small desiccated garden plots filled with geraniums … All the houses had door-knobs that were brightly polished, and coloured glass leadlights, and names on their gates" (160). Interestingly, the very physical features of the suburb and the houses that David interprets negatively are now highlighted as selling points by real estate agents who sell homes in Melbourne's formerly-working-class suburbs for small fortunes to affluent professionals.

As the Depression worsens and the employees at the lithographic studio are forced to take alternating two week periods off work without pay,

David tells his boss that he can support himself by writing and asks the firm to release him from his apprenticeship (159). The firm and David's parents agree, and soon he is working full-time for the *Morning Post*, publishing under his own name (160). While Jack struggles to find work, David prospers financially and pays for his parents to redecorate their house (171). While helping with the renovations and hammering up new paneling in the hallway, David realizes that his motivations are not altruistic. Rather than generously sharing his money with his family, he is "trying to hammer out the past, trying to seal it off forever behind a skin of polished veneer" (171). As he hammers, he attempts to batter away "at childhood and boyhood and youth, desperately driving nail after nail after nail through the treacherous emotions of a tiny suburban history" (171-72). David views the home improvements as marking a major turning point in his life and declares that even though he still lives at home, the renovations and Jack's return have combined to dislodge him from *Avalon* (174).

David's burial of his suburban childhood under layers of paneling is soon followed by the beginning of his relationship with Helen Midgely, who becomes his first wife. David presents the genesis of their relationship in the context of resistance to the Depression, stating that the Depression had caused an "enormous 'escape' thing ... a yearning desire among people to be distracted from the miseries and fears of the times," one of the manifestations of which is "a fantastic flourishing all through the suburbs of the threepenny lending-libraries ... Along the main street in our suburb there must have been at least a score of these libraries at that time" (175-76). David visits one of the libraries and discovers that the employee on duty is Helen, a young woman he once met at a party who tremendously impressed him (176, 84-86). David writes of "being startled at the improbability of her smartness and her obvious self-confidence in that rather dreary suburban setting," claiming that he "was too naïve then to realize that the great suburban artifice is to be smart on nothing" (178). David soon calls regularly on Helen at the library and stays after closing time, first to talk, but soon to have sex (181, 183-84). The couple conducts a sexual relationship for almost four years before Helen decides they should marry (186, 192, 210).

Since he plans to marry Helen, David decides that his mother's sixtieth birthday party would be a good time to introduce her to his family (210). However, Helen finds the Merediths' working-class manners too rough and is uncomfortable with the presence of David's nieces and nephews (213-221).

When the conversation shifts to politics and the Spanish Civil War, Helen and Jack get into an intense argument, which prompts Jack and David to go into the backyard to talk (222-226). The Merediths' suburban backyard is described as "squalid" and "scruffy," containing broken fence palings, "messy thickets" of "untrimmed shrubs," "patchy unkempt lawn," and "the tangled wire of the ruined fowl-house and the old wood-shed with the chassis of some ancient invalid wheel-chair rusting on its roof" (226). Jack becomes nostalgic for his childhood and yearns "to just stand there on the cracked brick path looking at this shabby suburban squalor that surrounded him, this sad and pointless world confined within the patched palings of the dividing fences and the red, ribbed rooftops" (227). The birthday party ends badly, and David's negative attitudes to suburbia are emphasized again when he drives Helen home along a road that is "grey and flat and treeless, like a dead drain running through a dead landscape" (232).

David and Helen marry two months after the birthday party debacle (233). Despite David's hatred for suburbia, the couple begins their married life by moving into a newly constructed house in a freshly developed suburb.[9] When the couple marries, David is twenty-six and Helen thirty (233). Describing the events in retrospect, David speculates that the age disparity led him to entrust the majority of "the material construction" of their life together to Helen: she

> naturally assumed leadership on matters of taste and sophistication ... It was she who decided on the house in Beverley Grove, in a new

'garden' subdivision in what at the time was considered a 'good' suburb, and which placed almost half suburban Melbourne between us and the two old, shabby, antiquated houses where we had separately grown up. (237)

The new house that Helen chooses is an iconic "double-fronted, ultra-modern, red brick, three-bedroom villa" located on a block with a "sixty-foot frontage behind a low brick fence ... beside a concrete drive leading to a separate fibro-plaster garage" (237). David notes that the new house in Beverley Grove was a token and symbol "of social progression. Of an advancement of caste, even" (238). Foreshadowing his later rejection of the Beverley Grove house, David describes the new subdivision in terms frequently used by suburbia's critics, noting that there were only three basic floor plans "for all the hundreds of houses in the subdivision" (238). However, since David is not yet ready to reject the new manifestation of suburbia, he claims that despite the lack of floor plan choices,

> there were still no two houses in any one street, grove, crescent, drive, or avenue which could be said to really look alike. Each front elevation had its own distinct difference, in the design of the porch, in the placement of the picture-window, the run of the paths ... the position of the drive, the design of the chimney, the style of the front door, and so on, and even further permutations were possible, because there were three distinct ways in which the roofs of flat terracotta tiles could be pitched. (238)

Although the above passage reads more like an apology for suburbia than a criticism of it, and gives a glimpse into the variety present within suburban architecture (not to mention the lives lived within the houses), David's extended diatribe later in the novel totally nullifies and contradicts the rare positive claims he makes for suburbia here.

By the time David and Helen move into their Beverley Grove home, he is firmly established in his career, earns a good salary, has money in the bank, and possesses an "unshakable self-confidence" (239). Feeling optimistic about the future, David and Helen purchase consumer goods on credit: David "extravagantly" buys a flashy red MG sports car, while Helen bargains and shuns "excessive extravagances," being "a dedicated home-builder in the best practical sense," although she does have "her heart set" on decorating and furnishing the home according to her precise wishes (239). Helen also takes control of the couple's social life, choosing companions "as conscientiously and with as much attention to taste and suitability as she would select the picture for a wall, the guest-towels for the bathroom, the mats for the dining-table, the tapestry covering for a lounge chair" (240). David notes that Helen considers it a great success that within weeks of their arrival in Beverley Grove they are "on the friendliest visiting terms with Wally and Sandra Solomons," a couple David describes as occupying "a rather special little niche in ... [his] memory as perhaps the two must stupid human beings ... [he has] ever known" (241).

Soon after moving to Beverley Grove and beginning to socialize with other middle-class suburbanites, David realizes that the Turleys (David's colleague Gavin and his wife Peggy) are the only couple that interests him (251). A small dinner party that the Turleys hold for the Merediths exposes David to a different lifestyle and instigates his rejection of suburbia. In his article on *My Brother Jack*, Thurley argues that the visit to the Turley's "is decisive in crystallizing David's own disgust with the life he and Helen have set up" (73).The Turleys, importantly, do not live in working-class or middle-class suburbia. Rather, they live in a huge dilapidated mansion in Toorak,[10] "which had been built some seventy years before when old Sir Luke Turley ... decided on something a little more substantial than the Colonial residences which, in various pink sections of the Imperial map, he had for decades inhabited" (252). The Turley mansion, named *Bangalore*, emphasizing its colonial provenance, is described as being "quite a walk" up a long driveway, and possesses a "massive old entrance with the name of the house ... chiseled in stone above a heavy, paneled door" (252). David describes the Turley mansion as possessing "solidity and dignity ... and even a sense of some continuing splendour in its decay" (253).

Despite their address and aristocratic lineage, the Turleys live simply in a wing of the mansion amidst "extraordinary" clutter, and serve their guests a basic meal (253, 255). Matthews describes the Turleys as stereotypes of "the moderately affluent, cultured class who are above the need for outward show, and whose very casualness, untidiness and apologetic disorder are marks of their inherent and inimitable style" (xv). After dinner, the men retire to Gavin's study for brandy, where David is exceedingly impressed by the disarray of the room, which is furnished with old leather armchairs, a long trestle table and jerrybuilt bookshelves (256-58). David admiringly describes the room as one that "no woman was ever allowed to clean up" (256). While David and Helen are driving home later, Helen begins laughing and exclaims, "'And there I was thinking the Turleys would probably have a butler! David, how *can* people like Gavin and Peggy live in such a shambles! In that *midden*! Goodness! wouldn't you just love to put a vacuum-cleaner through it?'" (262, original emphasis). Helen's adherence to suburban standards of cleanliness serves to emphasize the importance she places on appearance and consumer goods.

David turns against his new suburban home on the "despondent morning" after the visit to the Turleys (263). He sees the disorder of the Turleys' house as evidence of vibrant life and views the Turleys' lifestyle as "delightful, illuminating and enviable" (Matthews xiv). Standing in his study contemplating the differences between his life and Gavin's, "tense and wary as a trapped animal," David hears

> the Sunday morning sounds drifting ... through the thin brick walls ... Beverley Grove awakening to the active pursuits of its day – the snarling chirrup of its lawn-mowers and the hiss of garden hoses ... and the idling cough of the cars coming out of their fibro-plaster garages for the ritual washings. (263)

This passage draws heavily on the anti-suburban intellectual tradition and is remarkably similar to Allan Ashbolt's critique of suburbia. Ashbolt's article was published two years after *My Brother Jack* and may be influenced by Johnston's anti-suburban tirades. David notes that looking out his study window he has a view of "the top of a paling fence, part of a red brick wall, and the plumbing outlets from the Phylands' bathroom" (264). In contrast, Gavin would be able to look out from his study and "dwell on the rank vegetation and broken statuary of his 'splendid' old garden" (Gerster 568). The privileging of the older, established inner suburb over the new outer suburb that Johnston presents is a trope that is repeated in subsequent suburban novels, namely Malouf's *Johnno*, Winton's *Cloudstreet* and McCann's *Subtopia*.

When Helen asks David if he will wash the car, as he usually does on Sunday mornings, he says he is busy (264). As an act of rebellion against the suburban order Helen has imposed, David re-arranges his study and destroys some of the decorations Helen purchased for him (265-68). The following Sunday, David washes the car as usual and notes that there are seven others being washed on his street (270). David's hatred for suburbia continues to grow, and he declares that the next Sunday is the worst yet (271). David has to climb onto his roof to install a mast to hold the aerial for a new radio (271). After completing the installation, David remains on the roof surveying the Beverley Park Gardens Estate, and declares that as far as he can see there is

> nothing ... but a plain of dull red rooftops in their three forms of pitching ... and the green squares and rectangles of lawns intersected by ribbons of asphalt and cement, and I counted nine cars out ... being washed and polished. (271)

David's use of the word "nothing" reflects his dismissal of the presence in suburbia of anything other than the physical, whether houses, lawns, streets, driveways or cars. Johnston's narrator consistently refuses to consider the lives of the residents of suburbia, let alone admit that they may have value. When David does refer to his fellow suburbanites, it is to pronounce them lower than slum-dwellers and slaves to conformity.

Establishing and Perpetuating the Anti-Suburban Tradition 103

Repeating in a modified form his earlier claim that the suburbs are worse than the slums, and echoing Esson's claims regarding vitality, David posits that the slum-dwellers "might be a worthier tribe ... because they still grappled with existence where audacities were possible, and even adventure" (272). In other words, audacity and adventure are not possible in suburbia. Still sitting on the roof, David reflects that while the slum-dwellers have "a fetish about keeping front door-knobs polished," the fetish is applied to cars and gardens in the "'good' respectable suburbs" to such an extent that suburbanites will follow their suburban car-washing and gardening rituals "no matter what desolation or anxiety or connubial treacheries" are "practiced behind the blind neat concealment of their thin red-brick walls ..." (271-72). David takes a pro-working-class, anti-middle-class stance and draws on the anti-suburban tradition of representing the inner-city slums as more vital and non-conformist than suburbia.

David's rooftop reverie, which Paul Carter describes as one of the most memorable passages of the novel (291), eventually develops into an epiphany: "I stayed up on the roof because once I had worked this out a great many other things began to follow. Strange things. Terrifying things. Wondering things" (272). David realizes that he does not love Helen and never has (272). In one of the most anti-suburban passages in all Australian fiction, David concludes that many of the problems in the world have "nothing whatever to do with 'downtrodden masses,'" but are caused by "half the world" residing "in mental deserts very much like the Beverly Park Gardens Estate" (272). David goes further, claiming that "the real enemy was not the obvious embodiment of evil, like Hitler or his persecution of the Jews or the Russian purges or the bombs on Guernica," rather, it is suburbia and its

> awful fetish of respectability that would rather look the other way than cause a fuss ... I stared around over the whole of the sterile desolation, and I realized with a start of panic that I had got myself

into the middle of this red and arid desert, and there was nobody to bring me water. (272- 273)

Gerster describes David's epiphany as a "terrible vision of the tedium and complacency of suburban life and ritual," and argues that David's vision instigates his separation "from both his enthusiastically suburban wife and his country" (568). Eagle notes that a full twenty pages of the novel are devoted to David's "realisation that he hates his suburban existence in Beverly Grove, to the hatred he feels for everything he sees as he sits on the roof of his house" (37). The "savage attack" reaches a climax with an "extraordinary passage" in which suburbia is described as "a mental desert" (Eagle 37). However, David's anti-suburban rant does not end with his claim that suburbia is a desert; in fact, it continues for another ten pages, prompted by the realization that "There was not one tree on the whole estate" (274). David speculates that trees must have been present before the development of the suburb and declares that upon close examination of the landscape

> there were little folds to it and faint graceful rises and declivities ... The place would have been really beautiful at one time ... before ... bulldozers and graders grubbed out all the trees ... And now there was nothing but a great red scab grown over the wound the bulldozers had made, and not a single tree remaining. (274)[11]

David's response to his realization that suburbanization has destroyed the natural environment is to climb down the ladder, jump in his car, and drive straight to the local nursery (275).

At the nursery, David insists on purchasing a tree that will grow quickly and chooses a sugar-gum that should grow thirty or forty feet within a few years (276). Unsurprisingly, Helen does not approve of planting a gum tree in the middle of the front lawn: "'I personally think they're rather *ordinary*. They're so drab ... I'd honestly prefer something decorative ... some nice flowering shrub, or camellia ... What would look lovely would be one of those Japanese dwarf-maples'" (277, original emphasis).

Establishing and Perpetuating the Anti-Suburban Tradition 105

Just as White did in *Riders in the Chariot*, Johnston presents the issue of indigenous versus native vegetation and depicts the indigenous trees as superior to foreign imposters. Intent on reclaiming a tiny piece of the natural environment from suburbia, David resists Helen's preference for a foreign tree, exclaiming, "'No dwarf anythings! I want a tree. A proper bloody tree!'" (278). Attempting to explain his vision to Helen, David shouts,

> "... there's not one tree growing in this whole damned street ... on the whole estate ... And this is a *grove* we live in, darling ... We've been letting them pull the wool over our eyes. The Beverley – Park – Gardens – Estate ... It isn't a park and it isn't a garden and this isn't a grove" (278, original emphasis)

As his marriage disintegrates, David derives "spiteful comfort" from the sugar-gum, which grows remarkably quickly and becomes "much more than merely a symbol of protest against suburban values" (280). In addition to being a narrative device that allows Johnston's narrator to fight and eventually flee suburbia, the sugar-gum provides Johnston with a means by which he can depict David's neighbors as narrow-minded conformists. David's neighbor, Mr. Treadwell, complains to Helen that the sugar-gum's roots are getting under his driveway, which they might damage, and where they might extract nutrients from the soil near his dahlias. David refuses to act and exclaims,

> "... what's wrong with some upended cement slabs? The place is too damned neat as it is ... I'd like to have two whacking great Moreton Bay figs like those at the Turleys,' and then we could tip the slabs up the whole length of the street! Which might be a bloody good thing!" (281, original emphasis)

Several weeks later, Mr. Phyland, another neighbor, also complains about the sugar-gum. David's response is to fertilize the tree (282). Eventually, the neighbors threaten to make an official complaint to the council, and since Mr. Treadwell is a retired magistrate, David concedes defeat to "the forces of conformity" and agrees to remove the tree (282, 283). He takes his anger out on Helen, exclaiming, "'God! you just can't afford to be different, can you? You always have to conform to their rotten dreary suburban sameness ... let's go the whole hog, shall we, and give a name to the house?'" (283).

Soon after the sugar-gum incident, World War Two begins and David is swamped with work at the newspaper, leading him to lead a life apart from Helen. David is chosen to be the war correspondent for the *Morning Post* and sent to New Guinea, where he is stationed for over a year and emerges with "a greatly enhanced reputation" (313, 319). After New Guinea, David's employers send him abroad again, first to the United States, where he has two books published, then to London, Rome, Athens, Cairo, Iran, India, Burma, Ceylon, China, Afghanistan and Romania (333-34). David's articles are "admired, syndicated, [and] published abroad" (320). His overseas adventures allow him to meet "Prime Ministers and Presidents and great generals and admirals and statesmen and leaders" (334). David's adventures and successes overseas starkly contrast with his former life in Beverley Grove and further serve to present suburban life as boring, mundane and routine. As Eagle argues, "the Australian needs adventure, a *man* needs adventure. Suburban life, domestic life, cannot give it to him ... so the great, the necessary *adventure* must be sought elsewhere" (37, original emphasis). David expects Helen to end their marriage while he is abroad covering the war and dreads returning to "drop back again into the mundane horrors of the Beverley Park Gardens Estate" (344-45).

Returning to Melbourne at the end of the novel for a week's leave after two years away, David nostalgically revisits the haunts of his childhood and youth, spending all of his time in the city and by the waterfront, avoiding the suburbs completely. In addition to avoiding suburbia, he begins an affair with a much younger woman, Cressida Morley. Not only is Cressida much younger than Helen, she is decidedly not suburban; she was raised in a rural area by the ocean and "would never have known a suburban street in her life, or a garden subdivision" (354). Cressida repre-

Establishing and Perpetuating the Anti-Suburban Tradition 107

sents virgin nature, especially the ocean and the bush. Brotherson interprets David's decision to "abandon the bourgeois values of suburbia" as finding "its supreme expression in his love affair and eventual marriage with Cressida" (7). Likewise, Matthews reads David's union with Cressida as the culmination of a journey that began with his rejection "of the melancholy suburbs and the empty marriage" (xiv).

David Meredith, as both narrator and protagonist, is undeniably and overwhelmingly anti-suburban. Superficially, Helen may seem pro-suburban, since she chooses to live in suburbia and both conforms to and maintains suburban values. However, Helen can certainly be read as a character created by an author as an attack on suburbia. Helen is materialistic, selfish, shallow and domestic. Rutherford argues that Helen is "entirely vapid and lacking" and that her "interest in aesthetics and art is a social pretence" (112). Although *My Brother Jack* is an autobiographical novel, Helen is a fictional character. Matthews states that Helen "is not a portrait of Johnston's first wife, Elsie" ("Notes" 369), while Garry Kinnane notes that "Helen bears more resemblance to Johnston himself than to his first wife" ("The Reconstruction" 441). Johnston's overwhelmingly negative depiction of suburbia and suburbanites such as Helen can be read as self-loathing and a repudiation of his former suburban self. Both Matthews and Kinnane interpret Johnston's characterization of Helen as an attack on suburbia ("Notes" 369; G. Kinnane, "The Reconstruction" 441), while Eagle suggests that the negative characterization of Helen is the result of Johnston's "need to blame women for the feeling of imprisonment he felt in suburbia" (38). Helen is certainly not a sympathetic character and her suburban values and desires are presented by Johnston in an entirely negative manner.

Although many suburban novels deal with a wide range of social issues, Johnston's novel has a narrower focus. He does not engage in any detail with issues common in suburban fiction, such as immigration, multiculturalism and religion, referring only briefly to an influx of Jewish immigrants and refugees before World War Two (153). Unlike White's suburban novels, which present a multiplicity of voices and attitudes towards suburbia, making it impossible to identify a dominant message, Johnston's narrative is dominated by David's voice and presentation of events, characters and settings. David's portrayal of suburbia is overwhelmingly negative, and other characters that might defend suburbia, or at least present it more neutrally, are not given a voice. *My Brother Jack* is the first anti-suburban canonical Australian novel; as such, it establishes the anti-suburban tradition in the Australian novel.

Johnno: Perpetuating the Anti-Suburban Tradition

A generation younger than White and Johnston, David Malouf was born in Brisbane in 1934 to parents of Lebanese and English descent. Malouf enjoys an international readership and reputation perhaps greater than any Australian writer since White; Peter Carey is the only Australian writer with a comparable or greater international standing.[12] Andrew Taylor notes that Malouf is one of Australia's "most celebrated and rewarded" authors ("Bread" 715).[13] Within Australia, Malouf's work is widely read and highly respected, and a number of his novels have attained canonical status, including *An Imaginary Life* (1978), *Remembering Babylon* (1993) and *Fly Away Peter* (1982).[14] Malouf graduated from the University of Queensland with an Honours degree in language and literature in 1954. He left Australia in 1959 for Europe and worked in England as a secondary school teacher for a number of years before returning to Australia in 1968. Malouf taught in the English Department at the University of Sydney from 1968 to 1977, when he turned to writing full-time, and for many years thereafter divided his time between Australia and Italy. Although his current reputation rests primarily on his novels, Malouf published two volumes of poetry before publishing his first novel, *Johnno* (1975), and has continued to publish poetry, as well as short fiction, an autobiography, a play, numerous essays, and two opera libretti, one of them based on White's *Voss* (Rooney 214-15; Randall xv-xvii).

Published eleven years after *My Brother Jack*, Malouf's *Johnno* contains many echoes of Johnston's work, depicts the suburbs in an overwhelmingly negative manner, and perpetuates the anti-suburban attitudes presented by Johnston, thereby becoming the second canonical novel in a developing body of anti-suburban Australian novels. Malouf claims that *Johnno*, set largely in Brisbane during the 1940s and 1950s, broke new ground by engaging with the urban environment, stating that "no one else had got [Brisbane] into fiction" (Willbanks, *Australian* 145). In his Neustadt Lecture, Malouf states that he "wanted to put [Brisbane] on the map; to make it, in all its particularity, a place that would exist powerfully in the lives of readers in the same way that Dickens's London does, or Dostoevsky's Petersburg" ("A Writing Life" 702). Although Malouf sees himself as an innovator (and has certainly produced innovative work), in *Johnno* he approaches the urban and suburban environments in a conservative manner, utilizing traditional anti-suburban strategies and consistently presenting Australian culture as inferior to European culture; as a result, the novel is an extended postcolonial manifestation of the cultural cringe. As Edward Said argues in *Culture and Imperialism*, "the extraordinary global reach" of European imperialism "still casts a considerable shadow over our own times" (5) and contemporary Australians, like Malouf, remain heavily influenced by European culture. In his study of Malouf's work, Don Randall argues that Malouf uses European culture as a resource from which he derives his "principal standards of style" (190). Likewise, Delys Bird partially attributes Malouf's international reputation and sales to his "transnational style," which she describes as "urbane, poetic and classically allusive" (184-85), while other critics claim Malouf is "thoroughly European in his interests and attitudes" (Wilde et al 455).

However, Malouf's privileging of European culture is not confined to his prose style or the novel's content; the circumstances of the novel's composition and other texts produced by Malouf situate *Johnno* in a European context. In a preface written twenty-five years after the novel's initial publication, Malouf describes his composition of *Johnno* in Florence in an apartment adjacent to the one in which Dostoevsky wrote *The Idiot*, placing himself within the European intellectual tradition ("Preface" vii). In Malouf's Neustadt Lecture, delivered in 2000, he states that he sought to emulate Dickens and Dostoevsky when writing *Johnno* ("A Writing Life" 702). Malouf does not refer to any Australian writers in his preface, in the Neustadt Lecture, or in *Johnno*, which contains numerous references to European literature. Moreover, since *Johnno* is an autobiographical novel that closely adheres to the details of Malouf's life and Dante is more like Malouf than any other Malouf character (Randall 30-31), the attitudes presented in the novel regarding suburbia, Australia and Europe may mirror Malouf's own.

Although setting *Johnno* in Brisbane is logical in that *Johnno* is an autobiographical novel and Brisbane is Malouf's hometown, using Brisbane as the setting also allows Malouf to emphasize the city's marginality (Antor 513). Brisbane is doubly marginalized, since it is far from Europe and outside the cultural and political triangle of Melbourne, Sydney and Canberra. Australia's two largest cities and former national capitals, Melbourne and Sydney, have always overshadowed Brisbane, which, in comparison, was for many years perceived as "a big country town," rather than a city (Winter 46). Moreover, if Australian cities are marginal in relation to Europe, and Brisbane is marginal in relationship to Sydney and Melbourne, then Brisbane's suburbs are even further displaced, and, perhaps, inferior. Randall considers Malouf a "writer of place," arguing that his career is shaped by a desire "to discover and delineate the specific places in which experience unfolds" (15-16). Thus, it is entirely in character for Malouf to use his first novel as a vehicle to explore the location of his childhood, which he describes as "poor, shabby, [and] unromantic" in his 1997 preface (xii).

Much like *My Brother Jack*, *Johnno* is a hybrid novel that contains elements of the Bildungsroman and autobiographical writing (Antor 509). The novel begins with a prologue in which Dante, the "somewhat conventional" first-person narrator returns to Brisbane from London (Daniel 184). Dante's father suffers a heart attack, triggering his return. While Dante is en route from London to Brisbane, his father suffers a series of strokes and dies. Sorting through his father's possessions after the funeral, Dante discovers his school magazine from 1949, which contains a photograph of his friend Johnno. At this point, the narrative reverts to Dante's childhood, and the story of Dante and Johnno's mysterious relationship begins. Both Dante and Johnno consider Australia to be a cultural desert and look to Europe as the source of culture. Dante's English mother "imposes" English manners and morals on him (3), and from an early age he immerses himself in European literature and history. Dante is uninterested in Australian history, preferring to read about the Plantagenets and the Wars of the Roses (20); he considers Australia to be "familiar and boring" (20). The narrator, whose real name is never revealed, is dubbed "Dante" by Johnno after he publishes a poem entitled "To Beatrice." The constant repetition of the name "Dante" serves as a reminder that both the narrator and Johnno privilege European culture.

Throughout *Johnno*, depictions of Brisbane and its suburbs range from negative to nostalgic, although the depictions are mostly disparaging and Malouf never engages closely with the outer suburbs. Dante initially resides with his family in a large, upper-middle-class home in South Brisbane. Later, Dante's family moves to a new house in the new suburb of Hamilton; however, he states that his memories "were all of our old house in South Brisbane, with its wide latticed verandahs ... [and] its vast garden that ran right through to the street behind" (4). In fact, Dante's family only decides to relocate from South Brisbane to Hamilton after the arrival of the Second World War in Australia's theater, which profoundly affects Brisbane and its inhabitants. The arrival of the American military in 1942 turns Brisbane from a provincial backwater lacking in culture into a city of importance:

> Brisbane was suddenly at the centre of things. Though we hardly knew it at the time, our city was having its moment of greatness, its encounter with History: General MacArthur had arrived and the whole Pacific campaign was being directed from his office at St. Lucia. (27)

However, the war that awakens Dante's "sleepy sub-tropical town" (28) also causes "the sudden fall from grace" (30) of several local girls and the relocation of "the negroes" to the south side of the river, giving Dante's old-fashioned suburb "a 'bad name'" (31); as Dante comments, "South Brisbane, with its big rambling mansions, each one with a tennis court ... was finally done for; no-one respectable would ever live there again" (31). Here, Malouf depicts Brisbane as unimportant until the foreign influence of the Americans lends it prestige and transforms the social landscape; the inner suburbs are subsequently depicted as a haven for the "less desirables" (Aboriginals, prostitutes and the homeless) who are forced out of the urban area. Dante's concern with status and class distinctions permeates the novel.

Believing that South Brisbane is no longer good enough for them, Dante's family relocates to Hamilton, where Dante's father has built a three-storey brick house, paid for by profits earned from "buying and selling houses in the suburbs" (6). Although Dante describes Hamilton negatively, he also refers to it as "one of the best suburbs in Brisbane" (49). South Brisbane may no longer be respectable enough for a family who send their son to Brisbane Grammar, but Hamilton makes the grade. Dante describes the new house at Arran Avenue as "huge, ugly, show-offish," (4) "grim" (49), and "depressingly modern" (4); Hamilton has none of South Brisbane's old-world charm. Here Malouf follows the Australian literary tradition of privileging the old over the new (Gerster 569) and presents the old house in the inner suburb as superior to the new house in the outer suburb, a strategy Johnston previously employed in *My Brother Jack*, and which Winton mimics in *Cloudstreet*. Malouf alludes to the destruction of the natural environment that occurred in order to create Arran Avenue, describing Dante's new address as "a narrow dead-end street that runs straight into the hillside" with "bush beginning where the bitumen peters out into a track" (49). However, Malouf does not address the issue of environmental degradation in detail.

Establishing and Perpetuating the Anti-Suburban Tradition 113

Despite Malouf's stated aim of creating a fictional Brisbane as important and realistic as Dickens' London or Dostoevsky's Petersburg, both Dante and Johnno disparage Brisbane repeatedly. Dante describes Brisbane as "so sleepy, so slatternly, so sprawlingly unlovely!" and declares, "I have taken to wandering about ... looking for one simple object in it that might be romantic, or appalling even, but there is nothing. It is simply the most ordinary place in the world" (51-2). Compared to European cities, Brisbane does not stand a chance; romance and loveliness are qualities found in the old world, not the new. In an echo of Stephen Dedalus in Joyce's *Ulysses*, Dante recoils from the idea that he may have been shaped by his hometown, a place so backward that "Kids, even in this well-to-do suburb [Hamilton], go to school all the year round with bare feet" (52).

In contrast to the established European cities to which Dante and Johnno fantasize about escaping, Brisbane is "shabby and makeshift," full of "wooden houses perched high on tar-black stilts ... Nothing seemed permanent ... Brisbane was a huge shanty-town, set down in the middle of nowhere" (83). During one of his most negative rants, reminiscent of David Meredith's in *My Brother Jack*, Dante dismisses Brisbane as

> nothing: a city that blew neither hot nor cold, a place where nothing happened, and where nothing ever would happen, because it had no soul. People suffered here without significance. It was too mediocre even to be a province of hell. It would have defeated even Baudelaire! A place where poetry could never occur. (84)

According to Dante's way of thinking, European cities have souls, important events happen in them, suffering is significant, and poetry is abundant; the Australian city and its suburbs are unworthy of art. Malouf's inclusion of tirades against Brisbane and its suburbs perpetuates the anti-suburban tradition established by Johnston, especially when one considers the fact that, unlike White's novels, they are not countered by neutral or celebratory descriptions of suburbia.

During their years as university students, Dante and Johnno frequent the Greek Club in the city and cause trouble at brothels in an attempt to live the kind of life they have read about in novels by Dostoevsky, Tolstoy and Balzac, and to discover the adventure and excitement that they perceive suburbia to lack. However, no amount of alcohol or recklessness can alter their conception of Brisbane, which Johnno describes as "the ugliest place in the world" (82) and "the bloody arsehole of the universe" (83). Heinz Antor argues that Malouf depicts Brisbane as "a backwater of boring homogeneity" (513-14); however, the presence in the novel of Aboriginals and immigrants provides clear evidence of difference, even though they are not depicted in any detail. Upon graduation from university, Johnno secures a job at a copper mine in the Congo (98).[15] Before departing and making his break "into perfect freedom" (98), Johnno delivers his most virulent diatribe against Australia:

> "I'm going to shit this bitch of a country right out of my system ... How long will it take me, do you think, to shit out every last trace of it? ... I'll say to myself every morning as I squat on the dunny, there goes another bit of Australia ... And at the end of seven years I'll have squeezed the whole fucking continent out through my arsehole." (98)

Ken Gelder and Paul Salzman argue that "Johnno's scatological rejection of Australia is the most forceful" in all the Australian literature of exile and alienation (*Diversity* 86).

Johnno spends three years in the Congo as an anti-Kurtz, reading works by Schopenhauer, Wittgenstein, and Bonhoffer in an attempt to acquire "civilization" before moving to Europe (107). After educating himself, Johnno declares he is "no longer a barbarian" and possesses "the capacity for living ... among civilized men"; he urges Dante to "give up shadow boxing in the suburbs of limbo" and join him in Europe (107). Although almost everyone he knows has left Brisbane, Dante lingers for two years, traversing the suburbs on his motorbike, learning nothing and achieving nothing (109-110). Eventually, Dante travels to Europe, where Johnno has already spent a year in Paris, which Dante finds "grey" and "smog-ridden" (111). When Dante arrives, Johnno fails to meet him at the railway station, and Dante declares he is "more miserable" than ever before in his life (112). Clearly, Europe is not the antidote to suburban boredom and despair that Dante imagined it to be, nor has it met Johnno's expectations. In order to secure work teaching English, Johnno must pass as Scottish, since the French detest the Australian accent (114). Dante soon learns that Johnno hoped Dante would arrive with enough money to help him escape (115). As Randall notes, Johnno's only place in Europe is that of the outsider who drifts unenlightened from one cultural site to the next (36).

Dante stays in Paris with Johnno for a month, during which time he sees little of the city and Johnno spends most of his time reading (116). Disappointed, Dante travels to England and takes a teaching position "in a bleak industrial town" where he is soon living "a life as suburban and ordinary in its way as anything ... [he] might have settled for at home" (127). Dante discovers that even Europe contains suburbs and ordinariness, and he pursues a suburban existence devoid of exoticism for several years, although the details are not provided (129). Three years pass and people in Australia consider Dante an expatriate, a term he considers "too grand" to describe his situation (128). Meanwhile, Johnno leads a nomadic existence, moving from Paris to Vienna to Bucharest and finally Athens, where Dante reunites with Johnno and finds him living a squalid, aimless life, far removed from the European glamour the pair imagined in Australia (130). After four years away, Dante returns from the centre to the margins, disappointed in Europe and himself, and discovers that Johnno returned to Australia three months earlier (145). Johnno drowns under suspicious circumstances before Dante is able to learn whether Johnno returned to Australia due to defeated expectations (148).

Gerster claims that Dante makes a "qualified reconciliation" (573) with the previously rejected suburbia at the end of *Johnno*, arguing that the novel "allows for some final acceptance of [suburbia's] limitations and recognition of its potentialities" (573). Despite the "qualified reconciliation" Gerster identifies, *Johnno* closely conforms to the anti-suburban tradition by including many negative depictions of Brisbane's suburbs. Significantly, Malouf's positive descriptions of Brisbane are of the urban core and South Brisbane. Moreover, Malouf largely ignores the new, outer suburbs where most of Brisbane's population resides. Malouf's characters are rarely seen at home in the suburbs, which are referred to disparagingly in passing. Gelder and Salzman argue that Malouf's Brisbane is "the archetype of the supposedly arid Australia of the post-war period" (*Diversity* 85). The Australian actor David Tredinnick states in typical anti-suburban fashion that he first read *Johnno* while being "tortured ... by the living death that passed for adolescence in an Australian outer suburb of the early 1980s" and claims that the novel accurately depicts suburbia (165).

Johnno is remarkably similar to *My Brother Jack* in that it is an overwhelmingly anti-suburban novel that contains numerous negative depictions of suburbia; it is also a tightly focused novel that does not address many social issues. Whereas White's *Riders in the Chariot* and *The Solid Mandala* engage with issues such as immigration, religion, racism, multiculturalism, environmental degradation and the role of the artist in society, *Johnno* largely ignores these aspects of suburban life. The primary concerns of the novel are death; guilt; adolescence; memory; expatriation and exile; marginalization and belonging; and male relationships. Critics including Ivor Indyk and Stephen Kirby argue that a homosexual connection exists between Dante and Johnno;[16] however, Malouf asserts in his 1997 preface that *Johnno* is not a "gay novel in disguise," although he acknowledges that his characters have homosexual experiences (x). Moreover, Patrick White, who considered *Johnno* one of the best Australian novels, complimented Malouf for "finding the 'only way' to write a book about the love of two men for one another. Malouf took this to mean that he had the emotions right in *Johnno* but saved everyone from the difficulties" (Marr 583).

Randall considers White to be the Australian writer most like Malouf, notes that both writers adopt "an international style and perspective" and claims that Malouf's work re-examines "topics and concerns inaugurated by White" (7). According to Randall, Malouf shares with White a "multi-sited imagination and a perspective upon Australia that is not quite inside and not quite outside the place" (7-8). Discussing the postcolonial character of Malouf's work, Randall situates it in a body of writing from settler colonies that includes Timothy Findley, Michael Ondaatje and J.M. Coetzee, with whom Randall perceives Malouf to share "a deep-seated insecurity about belonging to one's place" (8). Randall argues that Malouf and Coetzee share "an intense and abiding concern with the marginalization, disenfranchisement, and exclusion that are at work in the social order of the postcolony" (9). Dante's rejection of suburbia and subsequent expatriation are a manifestation of a postcolonial anxiety regarding belonging. The degree to which Malouf himself belongs in Australia has been debated, partly due to his periods of residency in England and Italy, but also because his Lebanese ancestry has made him "susceptible to construction as an other in the society of his birth" (Randall 11). In *Cloudstreet*, Tim Winton provides a thorough engagement with the postcolonial quest for belonging while following Malouf's example of perpetuating the anti-suburban tradition established by Johnston.

Cloudstreet: Anti-Suburbanism, Indigenous Australians and non-Indigenous Belonging

In 1991, sixteen years after the publication of Malouf's *Johnno*, Tim Winton's *Cloudstreet* was published and quickly became a highly influential canonical novel. Almost thirty years younger than Malouf, and approximately fifty years younger than White and Johnston, Winton can be seen as a third-generation member of a group of anti-suburban writers. Born in 1960, Winton is the most popular and critically acclaimed Australian novelist of his generation. Robert Dixon notes that Winton has won "a staggering number of national and international literary awards" ("Tim Winton" 248).[17] Winton was declared an Australian

National Living Treasure in 1997 and listed in the *Bulletin* magazine in 2006 as one of the "100 Most Influential Australians."[18] He is known for his description of West Australian coastlines and landscapes, vivid depictions of working class Australian life, and a remarkable prose style that makes extensive use of the vernacular. In her study of Winton's work, Salhia Ben-Messahel notes that Winton defines himself as an "author of the working classes" and argues that his work "reflects a strong commitment to political and cultural issues, such as Aboriginal rights and reconciliation, the protection of the environment, and cultural heritage" (8).

Cloudstreet was an instant success and the recipient of a number of prestigious awards, including the Miles Franklin Award, the NBC Banjo Award and the Western Australian Premier's Book Award. By 1995, less than four years after its initial publication, *Cloudstreet* had already sold 130,000 copies in hardcover alone (Field 63). *Cloudstreet* is often required reading in secondary and tertiary courses, and less than ten years after publication was already established as a "Great Australian Novel" (Dixon, "Tim Winton" 247, 258). Moreover, *Cloudstreet* has become *the* most popular Australian novel; it was voted number one on the Australian Society of Authors' Top Forty Australian Books list in 2003 ("Top Forty"), and number one, by a margin of three to one, in the "Favourite Australian Novels" readers' poll conducted by *Australian Book Review* in 2010. Gelder and Salzman argue that the "sheer popularity" of *Cloudstreet* "has turned it into something of a national treasure, making it iconic" (*Celebration* 17). Due to its tremendous popularity, influence and critical acclaim, *Cloudstreet* plays a significant role in perpetuating the anti-suburban tradition in Australian literature, although it does so in a much more complex manner than *My Brother Jack* and *Johnno*.

Winton was born in the Perth seaside suburb of Scarborough and spent most of his first twenty years in Karrinyup, "a suburb freshly carved out of thick scrub on the outskirts of Perth" (Bennett 282; Flanagan 12). However, Winton rarely writes about the suburbia of his youth, choosing

Establishing and Perpetuating the Anti-Suburban Tradition 119

instead to set the majority of his work in coastal towns and rural areas. Thus, *Cloudstreet* is an anomaly within Winton's body of work, since most of the action of the novel takes place in West Leederville, an inner suburb of Perth, from the middle of the Second World War through to the early 1960s. Winton depicts suburbia negatively in *Cloudstreet* and has frequently expressed his dislike for the suburbs, which he has described in interviews as "a pretty narrow world" (Rossiter, "The Writer" 30) that is "bland" and produces "a kind of autism" (Taylor "Interview" 376); moreover, Winton has stated that he is uninterested in writing about "people who have no real existential questions and are purely hedonistic consumers" (Qtd. in Rossiter, "In His Own" 3).

Dixon argues that the many strengths of *Cloudstreet*, including the elevation of the regional to national significance, the re-creation of colloquial speech, and the location of the spiritual in the everyday, combine to make Winton "seem like an anti-modern, anti-metropolitan, even anti-intellectual writer" ("Tim Winton" 257). Likewise, Gelder and Salzman note that Winton's "literary persona" can "seem just a little old-fashioned" (*Celebration* 30). Although Winton has a reputation as a champion of the working class, frequently touts his working class credentials, and is not usually viewed as an intellectual, his attitudes towards suburbia mirror those of anti-suburban intellectuals. Winton also follows Malouf's method of privileging the older, inner suburb over the newer, outer suburb. Despite the novel's suburban setting, all of the central characters are involuntary transplants from the bush, forced to move into the city due to tragedy, death, and poverty, perhaps because of Winton's stated disinterest in writing about suburban characters. Although *Cloudstreet* is often described as a family saga and a novel about suffering (Watt 62), Winton addresses numerous other issues, including tragedy, faith, doubt, religion, work, violence, nationalism, community, belonging, European settlement and the treatment of Indigenous Australians. While *My Brother Jack* and *Johnno* are narrowly-focused novels, *Cloudstreet* is epic in its scope. Rather than attempting to address all of the aforementioned issues, my analysis focuses on the ways in which Winton perpetuates the anti-suburban tradition, his representation of Indigenous Australians, and the struggle of non-Indigenous Australians to establish a legitimate claim to belong on a stolen continent.

Suburbia, colonialism, Indigenous land rights and non-Indigenous belonging are fundamentally intertwined, since all Australian suburbs occupy land stolen from Indigenous Australians. Huggan argues that Australian literature "is thoroughly if not always explicitly racialized" (*Australian Literature* 151), and thus it is not uncommon for Australian suburban fiction to address racial issues. Marilyn Anthony attributes *Cloudstreet*'s greatness to the way it confronts readers with difficult issues (93). Indeed, Winton's engagement with Indigenous issues and settler colonialism makes the novel far more than a beautifully written nostalgic family saga: it is a narrative about the past, present and future of the Australian continent and the peoples who claim it as their home.

David Crouch views *Cloudstreet* as a novel "concerned with the continuity and legitimacy of settlement" ("National" 102). At the beginning of the novel, the Pickles and Lamb families are forced by a pair of tragedies to leave their respective rural, coastal homes in Geraldton and Margaret River and settle in Perth. When Sam Pickles' brother dies suddenly, Sam inherits the house on Cloud Street in the inner suburb of West Leederville and moves his family there. Sam soon realizes that he can earn money by renting out half the house, which is an "enormous, flaking mansion" (47). The Lambs find the house through a newspaper advertisement, and soon the two families begin sharing the structure that eventually becomes their home. As Gelder and Salzman argue, the once empty house is quickly "filled up with characters" and the emphasis "is on possession," which "means two things in this novel: the characters' occupation and ultimate ownership of the house, and a vague sense that the house is haunted, that it is already occupied by others" (*Celebration* 28). Bill Ashcroft argues that *Cloudstreet* is "squarely grounded on its central metaphor," which he identifies as the house on Cloud Street "that stands for the nation itself: irascible, hybrid, haunted by its past, myth ridden but ultimately redeemable" (148). In interviews, Winton has acknowledged that the house is a metaphor for Australia, and that the Lamb and Pickles families are forced to move into it, rather than choosing it for themselves, just as the convicts were taken from Britain to Australia against their will (Shore 44). Winton has stated that the house "'doesn't want the Lambs and the Pickles; it wants to shrug them off ... It's strange and scary, and totally alien to them and resistant, and the continent is that way and in lots of ways remains that way for us'" (Shore 44). Thus, *Cloudstreet* is a novel about the displacement of Indigenous peoples through urban and suburban development and the settlers' struggle to establish a legitimate claim to belong.

Like Australia, the house on Cloud Street has a tragic, shameful history. Before Sam's brother Joel purchased the house, which had stood uninhabited for over twenty years, it was owned by an elderly widow who trained Indigenous girls to become domestic servants (36). The girls had been forcibly removed from their families. One of the girls committed suicide in the library; in response, the widow evicted the others. Soon afterwards, the widow died of a heart attack in the library while playing the piano (36). When the widow died, she fell forward and her nose hit middle C; the echoing note is heard decades later by Fish Lamb. Stuart Murray argues that the house is "a palimpsest of the nation even as it is the domestic space that contains individual struggles. The note from the piano rings throughout the house in an echo of the barbarity of racial prejudice" (87). The ghosts of the Indigenous girl and the widow haunt the house for almost half a century, and they are not exorcised until Rose gives birth to her son in the room where the Indigenous girl and the widow died. Thus, Winton situates the brutal treatment of the Indigenous people by the settler-invaders in the suburbs, rather than presenting the issue as one that only possesses relevance in the bush.

Crouch argues that the haunted house on Cloud Street "seems to draw its animation and potency from its own unpleasant history" and suggests that Winton explores "uncomfortable regions" lurking "beneath the surface of dwelling and dwellings in Australia" ("Writing" 44). Crouch claims that Winton "only conjures the indigenous past, the prior occupation of the house or the country, as something shadily other, suppressed, and belonging to some unearthly haunted realm" ("National" 99), points out that the Lambs and the Pickles are haunted by "the ghost of the stolen Aboriginal girl," and speculates that the characters "perhaps suffer the unease of dwelling upon *her* land, and the greater massacres and injustices standing in the shadows" ("National" 100, original emphasis). Crouch is correct to assert that Winton's engagement with Indigenous issues occurs "beneath the surface"; it is not the primary focus of the novel, yet it is ever-present and repeatedly resurfaces. Gelder and Salzman contend that the haunting lends *Cloudstreet* a "Gothic sensibility" that connects it with the dispossession of the Indigenous people, but note that it is "a subdued theme" (*Celebration* 31). Moreover, Gelder and Salzman view the primary focus as being on "the occupation of the house" and the notion that the Lambs and the Pickles "are destined ultimately to belong there" (*Celebration* 29).

Winton's presentation of the Cloud Street house as a metaphor for Australia also operates on the level of landscape. Crouch argues that when the Pickles first move in to the "great continent of a house" that "doesn't belong to them" (Winton 41) they explore it "like fearful first settlers" and "The expanses of space and unyielding alien surfaces ... paralyse the inhabitants in a way that echoes the same sense of primal unease, a sense of not belonging," which "plagued settlers as they initially encountered the 'vast outdoors' of Australia" ("Writing" 48-49). Ben-Messahel claims that the house provides "material form to the history of the country and of British colonization" (167). Crouch suggests that the tension between non-Indigenous possession and the quest for belonging are "crucial": he points out that the Lambs and Pickles are homeless and uprooted before arriving at Cloudstreet, then "unsettled in their occupation of the new place" ("National" 99). By settling in an inner suburb, which is an alien environment to them, the Lambs and the Pickles begin the process of establishing belonging and unconsciously participate in the ongoing displacement of the Indigenous peoples.

One of the major themes of *Cloudstreet* is the characters' struggle to adapt to the suburban environment, which also functions as a metaphor for the struggle of non-Indigenous Australians to adapt to life on a new continent. The refugees from the bush find themselves dwelling in a house so close to a railway line that the windowpanes rattle when trains pass. The fact that the residents of Cloudstreet are transplants from the country is emphasized soon after the Lambs arrive, when they convert their half of the backyard into a semi-rural environment (51). Just as English settlers in the colonial period introduced non-Indigenous species and created English gardens, the Lambs modify their environment to suit their tastes, since they are unwilling to abandon their rural traditions and embrace suburban life. Meanwhile, the Pickles' half of the yard is neglected: "The grass is shin high out in their half of the yard. Bits of busted billycarts and boxes litter the place beneath the sagging clothesline" (78). Although the Pickles do not convert their portion of the backyard into a mini-farm, neither do they embrace the suburban lifestyle and create a garden with flowerbeds and carefully mown lawns. The refusal of both families to abide by suburban conventions is consistent with the anti-suburban sentiment that climaxes at the end of the novel.

The process of establishing a sense of belonging is largely achieved through the development of community. Suburbia is often criticized for lacking a sense of community and opportunities for social interaction. According to the stereotype, suburbanites live separate lives in separate houses. However, Winton presents West Leederville as being more akin to a village than a stereotypical impersonal suburb, and thus worthy of celebration. The shop that the Lambs open in their front room creates a sense of community, becoming important enough to be a tram stop, and soon "the shop was Cloud Street, and people said it, Cloudstreet, in one word" (60). Both Cloudstreet and its residents are known throughout the suburb and the shop serves as a meeting place and focal point. Winton's

Cloudstreet has much more in common with Malouf's South Brisbane than with White's Sarsaparilla and Barranugli or Johnston's Beverley Park Gardens Estate, as both Cloudstreet and South Brisbane are in close proximity to the city center, whereas White and Johnston's fictional suburbs are many miles from the centre of the cities in which they are located.

Like many other authors of suburban fiction, Winton addresses the relationship between the suburbs and the natural environment. Winton, a "passionate environmentalist" (Jacobs 311), depicts the new suburban developments on the margins of the city as destructive, since they are built on bushland cleared with bulldozers, while in the inner suburbs, which the Swan River flows through, the natural environment and the built environment enjoy a more symbiotic relationship. Winton presents characters that prefer the remnants of the natural environment to the built environment. *Cloudstreet* both begins and ends with Fish Lamb returning to nature by drowning himself in the Swan River in central Perth, an act Winton presents as joyful and liberating. The Lamb and Pickles children frequently swim in the river, many of the characters fish on the river, and when the families hold a celebratory picnic, they do so at the river. Throughout the novel, the natural environment, particularly bodies of water, is depicted as a source of life, comfort, escape and joy, in stark contrast to the built environment, especially the new outer suburbs. Ashcroft argues that water is "a constant presence on the horizon of the novel" and serves as "the element of ambivalence and transition" (148). More specifically, Ashcroft posits, "Virtually everything of importance in people's lives, every major change, self-discovery, or shift" occurs "on, or in relation to, the river" (149), rather than in suburbia.

Winton does not depict the city center and the inner suburbs as active destroyers of the natural environment, even though they are built upon land that was once undeveloped. However, he does use the binary construction common in Australian literature to set the city and its suburbs in opposition to nature: "From the river you could be in the city but not on or of it. You could be back from it out there on the water and see everything go by you, around you, leaving you untouched" (138). Similarly, when Lester Lamb converses with his son Quick as they fish from their boat on the river, he emphasizes the difference between rural and urban/suburban life: "Easy to be a good man out here [on the river] ... Lester pointed to the lights above Perth water where the city hung and the suburbs began their outward roll. But up there, that's the test" (304). Life in the city and suburbs makes being "a good man" difficult, as Lester learns first hand when he commits adultery with Dolly Pickles, a spontaneous act resulting from the economic pressures of the urban/suburban environment, which cause the Lambs and Pickles to share a house. Here Winton depicts both the city and the suburbs as morally degrading environments, suggesting that moral standards are more easily maintained in the natural environment.

Winton's perpetuation of the anti-suburban tradition is achieved in part through Toby Raven, an ambitious, cosmopolitan young journalist whom Rose Pickles meets while working in the city and with whom she has her first romance. In a passage reminiscent of *Johnno*, Toby describes Perth as

> "the biggest country town in the world trying to be a city. The most isolated country town in the world trying to be the most cut-off city in the world, trying desperately to hit the big time ... There's something nesting here, something horrible waiting. Ambition, Rose. It squeezes us into corners and turns out ugly shapes." (289)[19]

Despite Toby's disdain for Perth, he revels in introducing Rose to the world of the cosmopolitan urban intellectual. He presents Perth as a place where culture resides, a far cry from Geraldton, Rose's childhood hometown. Even though Perth contains some culture, it is far too provincial for Toby, who, like Dante and Johnno in Malouf's novel and Waldo in *The Solid Mandala*, sees himself as a cosmopolitan intellectual: "Toby read the London newspapers and talked of escaping Perth for a real culture: Bloomsbury, the Left Bank, or Sydney at a pinch" (290-1). Toby represents urban culture, which he sees as superior to suburban culture. Despite the fact that Toby treats Rose poorly and ultimately rejects her, and is certainly a poor ambassador for cosmopolitanism, Rose also eventually rejects suburbia.

During her relationship with Toby, Rose nurtures dreams of middle-class suburban bliss, imagining herself "married with children, with a house in the clean new suburbs" (291). Later, once Rose marries Quick, she renews her suburban dreams, imagining the kind of house millions of Australians aspire to own: "I want to live in a new house ... In a new suburb in a new street. I want a car out the front and some mowed lawn" (326). In order to pay for the new house in the suburbs, Quick joins the police force, where he becomes involved in the hunt for The Nedlands Monster, Perth's first serial killer. Eventually the killer is caught and revealed to be a suburban husband and father. Winton's inclusion of the Nedlands Monster supports the notion, also present in Carey's *The Tax Inspector*, that suburbia is an environment where evil develops and resides.

Quick and Rose both work hard to achieve their suburban dream; their new home is located on land freshly carved out of the bush by bulldozers (just like David's new house in Beverley Grove and Dante's new house in Hamilton). Rose and Quick's new suburban home is clearly modeled on the house in which Winton was raised, located in the Perth suburb of Karinyup on a street inhabited by Dutch, English and Yugoslav immigrants who lived in "little boxy" houses (Field 62).[20] Winton cites one of his major influences as

> living a suburban life when the suburb itself was a work in progress. When I was a kid in Karrinyup there was bush on one side of the fence and civilization on the other and it was all just happening before our eyes, the pushing back of the bush, the domestication of the landscape.(Rossiter, "The Writer" 35)

Winton states that the destruction of the natural environment by suburban development "had an impact" on him, which he describes as "a sense of loss from early on" (Rossiter, "The Writer" 35).

Quick is dissatisfied with the suburban accommodation he and Rose rent while awaiting the construction of their house, which he sees as "orderly, calm suburbia ... merely a list of things missing" (339). Significantly, when Quick escapes the stresses of family life earlier in the novel and transitions from childhood to adulthood, rather than moving to another suburb of Perth he flees to the bush where he finds freedom outside the confines of suburbia and comes to terms with his traumatic childhood. Murray argues that Quick fails as a bushman, and that his failure reveals that meaningful identity is not necessarily "informed by an engagement with the land and settler values" (86). However, Quick certainly does not find meaningful identity in suburbia either; rather, it is within his extended family and their atypical living arrangement that Quick finds belonging.

Not only does suburban life dissatisfy Quick, he eventually loses all interest in moving to the new suburb:

> And the new house, their dream? Well, it went up bit by bit and Quick sometimes went out just to look at it, the brick box with its red tile roof same as all the other half-finished houses in the street. It looked empty and he'd lost his way with it somewhere. He couldn't imagine them living in it. (339)

Here Winton's description of the new suburb echoes the anti-suburban rants in *My Brother Jack* and the critiques of anti-suburban intellectuals such as Robin Boyd. Meanwhile, Rose holds on to her suburban dream: "'We're getting somewhere,' Rose thought. 'Our own house, a baby, money in the bank'" (360). To Rose, suburbia represents safety, security, and privacy, a place where she and Quick can raise a family away from the intrusions of their parents; for Quick, the new suburbs represent conformity and isolation from "real life," which takes place in the inner suburbs or the bush. Winton's negative depiction of suburbia echoes that of Johnston and Malouf; all three authors portray the new brick houses as empty, depressing, and lacking in character and history.

During a visit to the new house, Quick encounters the Indigenous man who repeatedly appears to him and other characters throughout *Cloudstreet*, often as a guardian angel or black Jesus. The Aborigine tells Quick to go home and declares, "This isn't your home. Go home to your home, mate" (362). Ben-Messahel claims that the Indigenous man is "the mystical holder of the truth about the community," who "bears testimony to colonial deeds and ... reminds White Australians of the power and importance of place" (214). Winton has stated that "the black man serves as the conscience of the people," describing him as "a 'guardian angel' who is rejected ... the guy is saying: Learn to belong, don't break community" (Rossiter, "In His" 12-13). Not only does the Indigenous man's appearance and command serve to remind Quick of his feelings about suburbia, it also reminds readers that the European settlers stole the land. Thus, in addition to being the site where the suburban and natural environments collide, the suburbs are the site where the issue of Indigenous land rights, one of the central issues in Australian society, must be addressed. The question of who owns the land in Australia and who can legitimately lay claim to belong to the land is central to *Cloudstreet*. Moreover, it is an issue that Winton has addressed repeatedly in interviews.

Winton has made it clear that he believes "White Australia" should value Indigenous culture highly. He has stated that "we live with a contradiction in Australia: one of the most anti-religious European cultures on the most spiritual and religious of continents" (Qtd. in Rossiter, "In His Own" 4). Winton's position regarding Indigenous ownership and belonging is complicated, however, by his statements regarding his sense of belonging and identity as a non-Indigenous Australian:

> When I got to Europe I knew the moment I set my foot down that I wasn't European. I'd been brought up all my life to think that I was a European ... I felt torn, almost, like torn out of the soil from home ... I knew that if I stayed away too long I'd be adrift, and I felt like I was going to wither up and die. I know this is where I belong. I know my continent, I know my country ... No-one's really going to be able to convince me that I don't belong here ... I wouldn't

> say it's a kind of new Aboriginality, I wouldn't even feel that I had to even chase after the term, but it's a feeling of belonging ... I'm not embarrassed about coming from here, although I'm ashamed of the way my forebears have brought me into the country ... I'm not ashamed to be here as a white Australian. (Qtd. in Rossiter, "In His Own" 13)

Winton's position is certainly not unique; in fact, it is typical of many non-Indigenous Australians who recognize and acknowledge that the continent was stolen from its original inhabitants, yet feel a deep sense of belonging for the country in which they were born and raised. Crouch notes that Winton's work reveals the complex sentiment described by Peter Read in his book *Belonging: Australians, Place and Aboriginal Ownership*: "I want to feel I belong here while respecting Aboriginality, neither appropriating it nor being absorbed by it" (Qtd. in Crouch, "Writing" 51).

In an interview with Ben-Messahel in which she asks Winton if he feels closer to Aboriginality than to Western culture, he replies,

> I have learnt to be closer to the land, but this hardly compares to genuine Aboriginal belonging. I wouldn't make too bold a claim for myself here. I envy Aborigines for their oneness with the land and the spirit of the country but I don't envy them their confusion and irredeemable loss. (107)

Elsewhere, Winton speaks of Indigenous attitudes to the land, claiming, "The notion of knowing your ground and your country is almost a religious thing," and indicates an awareness of the complexities of his position by positing, "I suppose if my skin were dark this would have more credibility" (Guy 128). Crouch suggests that Winton may possess a "latent guilt ... which undermines a sense of belonging" ("Writing" 50). Huggan argues that "the continuing struggle for cultural ownership in Australia" contains "a fundamental dissonance between what we might call the politics of ownership and the poetics of belonging ... belonging might somehow provide the moral grounds for illegitimate ownership" (viii-ix). Likewise, Anna Johnston and Alan Lawson argue that the European settler/invaders "referred to themselves as indigenous" in order to establish their legitimacy and express "their own increasingly secure sense of moral, spiritual, and cultural belonging" on the Australian continent (363). Furthermore, in order to establish a nation, settler/invaders need to "write the epic of the nation's origin" (Johnston and Lawson 365). Winton's claims regarding belonging are clearly a part of the process that Huggan, Johnston and Lawson identify. Moreover, *Cloudstreet* reveals characters attempting to establish themselves as Indigenous. Furthermore, as a national narrative, the novel itself plays an important role in establishing claims to belonging by non-Indigenous Australians.

While Quick and Rose's new house is under construction, the inner suburbs undergo redevelopment. In the inner suburbs, "All the old houses were coming down and salmon pink duplexes were going up in their place" (363). Sam considers joining the development boom, discusses his intentions with Dolly, and suggests selling Cloudstreet and moving to a new suburb. Significantly, the Indigenous man who commanded Quick to go home also appears to Sam, and when Sam tells him of his plan, the Aborigine states, "You shouldn't break a place ... Too many places busted ... You better be the strongest man" (406). After a combined family dinner with the Lambs, Sam decides to stay in the established inner suburb rather than move out to the new suburbs. Winton's inclusion of the Indigenous man's assertion that Sam should not break a place is problematic, since it suggests that the Indigenous man does not have a problem with Sam occupying land that once belonged to Indigenous people. Moreover, it also implies that Sam is already at home in Cloudstreet, even though the house (and the inner suburb in which it is located) occupies stolen land and is haunted by Indigenous ghosts. Gelder and Salzman argue that the Indigenous man, whom they refer to as an "apparition," symbolically hands "over property to the non-Aboriginal characters ... giving them his blessing into the bargain"; they contend that "Native title isn't even an issue here, as the novel leaves its Aboriginal characters behind in order to chart a fully realised *non-Aboriginal* form of belonging" (*Celebration* 31, original emphasis). Winton seems to be suggesting that non-

Establishing and Perpetuating the Anti-Suburban Tradition 131

Indigenous Australians can legitimately claim to belong on the Australian continent, whilst simultaneously arguing that further suburban development/occupation should not take place and that Indigenous cultures should be respected.

During a spontaneous bush holiday, Quick and Rose discuss their parents' decision to remain at Cloudstreet. Rose admits that she cannot bear to leave either: "I don't want our new house. I want the life I have" (419). Rose and Quick decide not to move into their new house in the new suburb, rejecting suburbia as an isolated site where they do not belong. Murray argues that Rose and Quick's decision to stay at Cloudstreet and participate in the establishment of a "new tribe" represents a "reformed national space ... a world that is more supportive and just" and indicates that Winton is making a point about European settlement (88). The "new tribe" created at Cloudstreet is a non-Indigenous tribe, convinced that it belongs on land stolen from the former owners. All of Winton's characters reject the suburbs: thus, the novel perpetuates the anti-suburban tradition and presents suburbia as an inferior locale in comparison to both the bush and inner urban areas. However, the manner in which suburbia is rejected also serves as a reminder that the suburbs are built upon stolen land.

Discussing the composition of *Cloudstreet*, Winton tells Andrew Taylor, "'I was writing Perth for myself. I was re-imagining it. In a civilized city the city of your parents exists, the city of your grandparents exists, the city of their parents and their grandparents exists'" ("Interview" 376). Winton's belief that age and history are essential elements of a "civilized city" strongly echoes Dante's views about Brisbane in *Johnno*. In both *Johnno* and *Cloudstreet*, the inner, older suburbs are more authentic and worthy locations as settings for fiction because they have history and permanence, whereas the newer, outer suburbs are rejected due to a perceived isolation, emptiness, and lack of culture. Moreover, Winton's claim that a "civilized city" is one that is unchanged for many generations reveals a belief that belonging can be established over time, regardless of the circumstances of the initial settlement/invasion, and points to a nostalgic attitude towards urban space. Dixon argues that "nostalgia is by its very nature conservative: it prefers the past to the future; it is at best ambivalent about modernity; it prefers the local and the traditional to the global" ("Tim Winton" 257). *Cloudstreet* is certainly a nostalgic novel; it is also in many ways inherently conservative and reactionary.[21]

Critics present conflicting assessments of Winton's use of Indigenous characters and his engagement with Indigenous issues, such as the stolen generations, land rights and belonging. George Watt argues that the presence of Indigenous characters "helps to reinforce Winton's view of existence as fluid ... [and] interconnected" (65). Watt suggests that Winton's inclusion of ghosts in the house makes "the past part of the present" and reveals that even a single Aboriginal death leaves "an indelible mark on the white Australian community" (66). Winton's use of Indigenous characters also contains a positive element, according to Watt, since non-Indigenous characters "experience something approaching enlightenment" when they "open themselves to the spirit of Aboriginal presence" (66). However, other critics take issue with Winton's use of Indigenous characters. Crouch argues that the "ghostly, or otherworldly, status given to indigenous people in the novel becomes a way of erasing, objectifying and othering them" ("National" 100). Similarly, Gelder and Salzman argue that Indigenous "histories are removed from the novel" and point out that the only Indigenous characters who appear "are cast as non-real, spectral, ethereal" (*Celebration* 31).

Crouch questions Winton's method of resolving "the evils of the past," namely the exorcism of the ghost of the Indigenous girl by the birth of a white child; he argues that the issue of possession is not resolved in *Cloudstreet* and that the novel "offers a fantasy of perfect reconciliation that denies any further need to negotiate with either the past or the other" ("National" 100; 102). Furthermore, the removal of the fence dividing the backyard of Cloudstreet, the joint folding of the tent by Oriel and Dolly, and the symmetrical ending of the novel, which concludes

Establishing and Perpetuating the Anti-Suburban Tradition 133

in the same moment where it began, all serve to indicate closure and suggest that resolution has been achieved, even though issues such as belonging and Indigenous land rights are clearly unresolved. Gelder and Salzman contend that in order for non-Indigenous Australians "to occupy an empty place, to settle and belong," they need to forget "what was there before" (Gelder and Salzman, *Celebration* 32). Although they acknowledge that "It is probably impossible" to determine how common such forgetting is in contemporary Australian society, Gelder and Salzman suggest that "the popularity of *Cloudstreet*" is due in part to the ubiquity of such forgetting (*Celebration* 32).

Although *Cloudstreet* deals with Indigenous issues in a problematic manner, it does so in a far more detailed and complex manner than any other novel set in suburbia by a non-Indigenous author. Moreover, despite the presence of conservative attitudes, *Cloudstreet* is a remarkably innovative novel, especially with regard to style, structure and theme. Nevertheless, *Cloudstreet* contains numerous negative depictions of suburbia and perpetuates the anti-suburban tradition established by Johnston and Malouf. Since *Cloudstreet* is the most popular Australian novel, it plays a crucial role in perpetuating the anti-suburban tradition and has probably disseminated anti-suburban sentiments to more readers than any other Australian novel, with the possible exception of *My Brother Jack*. My next chapter examines two more recent novels that further perpetuate the anti-suburban tradition: *Steam Pigs*, by the Indigenous author Melissa Lucashenko, and *Subtopia*, by the academic and novelist A.L. McCann. I use the novels by Lucashenko and McCann to demonstrate that contemporary, non-canonical novels published since *Cloudstreet* draw heavily upon the anti-suburban tradition established and perpetuated by the novels discussed in this chapter.

Endnotes

1. Small portions of this chapter appeared in a different form in my article "Rejecting and Perpetuating the Anti-Suburban Tradition: Representations of the Suburbs in *The Tax Inspector*, *Johnno* and *Cloudstreet*."
2. Glen Iris is approximately nine kilometers east-northeast of Elsternwick, where Johnston grew up.
3. Johnston wrote *My Brother Jack* while living with Clift and their children on Hydra (G. Kinnane, "The Reconstruction" 439).
4. Much of the biographical and publication information in this and the previous paragraph draws from the entry for George Johnston in the AustLit database: http://www.austlit.edu.au.
5. In 1984, Chester Arthur Eagle described *My Brother Jack* as "one of the best known and most widely accepted portrayals of Australian life," noting that it had sold 284,000 copies by 1981 (35). Eagle predicted that the regular inclusion of *My Brother Jack* on reading lists for English and Australian Studies courses would ensure the novel's continued influence (35). In 1985, Laurie Hergenhan declared that *My Brother Jack* was currently the most popular Australian novel (Brotherson 7). Four years later, Dorothy Jones pronounced, "*My Brother Jack* has attained canonical status" (72), and in 1990, Brian Matthews claimed the novel "thoroughly and securely warrants its status as a contemporary Australian classic" (xv).
6. Elsternwick is approximately ten kilometers south-southeast of Melbourne's central business district. Traveling to Elsternwick from the CBD, one passes through five or six suburbs, depending on the mode of transport. Whereas Elsternwick was a working-class and relatively outer suburb in Johnston's youth, the proliferation and spread of Melbourne's suburbs in the past seventy years and the gentrification of older suburbs have led to Elsternwick now being considered an upper-middle-class inner suburb.
7. White tackled the issue five years previously in *Riders in the Chariot*, and domestic violence also appears in later suburban novels, including Tim Winton's *Cloudstreet*, Peter Carey's *The Tax Inspector*, and Melissa Lucashenko's *Steam Pigs*.
8. Like the characters in Malouf's *Johnno*, David and his friends only read works by European authors.

Establishing and Perpetuating the Anti-Suburban Tradition 135

9. Johnston based the Beverley Park Gardens Estate on Glen Iris, where he lived with his first wife. Although Johnston describes Beverley Grove as having half of suburban Melbourne between it and Elsternwick (237), Glen Iris is less than nine kilometers from Elsternwick. Although Glen Iris was an outer suburb when first developed, it could now be described as located on the inner edge of the middle belt of eastern suburbs and considered relatively close to the CBD, especially when compared to the newest suburban developments in the south-east at Cranbourne, fifty kilometers from the CBD.
10. Toorak is an inner suburb approximately two kilometers from the CBD that is perhaps the most expensive and exclusive suburb in Melbourne. Toorak contains many multi-million-dollar mansions and is synonymous with wealth, exclusivity and "old money."
11. Johnston's depiction of the role of bulldozers in the destruction of the natural environment and the construction of the suburb echoes White's reference to bulldozers in *Riders in the Chariot*. Bulldozers are also used as emblems of suburbanization and environmental degradation in Tim Winton's *Cloudstreet* and his short story "Aquifer," A.L. McCann's *Subtopia* and Peter Carey's *The Tax Inspector*. See also Adam Rome's *The Bulldozer in the Countryside: Suburban Sprawl and the Rise of American Environmentalism*.
12. Bliss argues that Carey is "increasingly seen as the heir and successor to Patrick White" ("Peter Carey" 291).
13. Malouf's many awards include the Grace Leven Prize, the Australian Literature Society's Gold Medal, the New South Wales Premier's Literary Award, the *Age* Book of the Year Award, the Friends of the National Library of Australia Celebration Award, the Neustadt International Prize for Literature, the Lannan Foundation Literary Award, the Geraldine Pascall Prize for Critical Writing, the International IMPAC Dublin Literary Award, the Prix Baudelaire, the Commonwealth Writers Prize, the Prix Femina, and the Victorian Premier's Literary Award. Malouf has also been short-listed for the Booker Prize and many other awards. He was awarded the Order of Australia in 1987 and declared an Australian National Living Treasure in 1997.
14. *An Imaginary Life, Remembering Babylon* and *Fly Away Peter* were all voted into the Australian Society of Authors' Top Forty Australian Books list in 2003, at number eight, twelve and thirty-five, respectively.
15. Martin Leer interprets *Johnno* as "a study in the title character's attempt to escape his 'fate' … Australia, and particularly Brisbane" (10).

16. See page 7 of Indyk's monograph *David Malouf*, and Kirby's article "Homosocial Desire and Homosexual Panic in the Fiction of David Malouf and Frank Moorhouse."
17. For an excellent analysis of Winton's career and the conditions that enabled it, see Robert Dixon's "Tim Winton, *Cloudstreet* and the Field of Australian Literature."
18. For a complete list of Winton's awards, see http://www.austlit.edu.au/run?ex = ShowAgent&agentId = A)i8.
19. Toby's contention that there is "something horrible waiting" foreshadows The Nedlands Monster.
20. Winton provides a detailed examination of his childhood suburb in his short story "Aquifer," which is included in his collection *The Turning*. For an analysis of "Aquifer," see my article "Environmental Degradation, Indigenous Displacement, and Non-Indigenous Belonging: Suburbia in Tim Winton's 'Aquifer' and Liam Davison's 'Neary's Horse.'"
21. Gelder and Salzman also conclude that *Cloudstreet* is "a conservative novel" (*Celebration* 30).

CHAPTER 4

A NEW GENERATION PERPETUATES THE ANTI-SUBURBAN TRADITION

MELISSA LUCASHENKO'S STEAM PIGS (1997) AND A.L. MCCANN'S SUBTOPIA (2005)[1]

Melissa Lucashenko's debut novel, *Steam Pigs*, published six years after Winton's *Cloudstreet*, addresses in detail issues that Winton explored, especially suburbia, Indigenous identity and belonging. However, unlike *Cloudstreet*, *Steam Pigs* examines the issues from the perspective of an Indigenous writer and protagonist. Melissa Lucashenko was born in 1967 in Brisbane; she is of European and Indigenous Yugambeh and Bundjalung descent. Lucashenko grew up in Brisbane's southernmost suburbs, the primary setting of *Steam Pigs*, which won the Dobbie Award for women's fiction and was shortlisted for the New South Wales Premier's Literary Awards and the Commonwealth Writers Prize.[2] Lucashenko is firmly established as one of Australia's leading Indigenous authors.

In the same tradition as Johnston's *My Brother Jack* and Malouf's *Johnno*, *Steam Pigs* is a combination of a Bildungsroman and an autobiographical novel. Like her protagonist, Sue Wilson, Lucashenko lived on the southern outskirts of Brisbane, worked as a barmaid and delivery driver, practiced karate, and attended Griffith University. The autobiographical aspect of the novel is emphasized by its final line: "A person should write a book" (245). However, unlike many autobiographical Bildungsromane, the protagonist does not tell her story through a first-person narrative. Rather, Lucashenko utilizes a third-person narrative, albeit a limited one, written almost exclusively from the protagonist's point of view, which frequently employs the second-person voice and occasionally slips into a first-person authorial commentary. Although the novel is ostensibly written in the past tense, a number of passages are written in the present tense. Lucashenko's shifts in voice and tense do not appear to follow any discernable logic; however, they may deliberately eschew traditional narrative techniques.

At the beginning of the novel, seventeen-year-old Sue lives with her brother Dave in the working-class suburb of Eagleby on Brisbane's southern outskirts. Sue seeks sanctuary in Eagleby after fleeing Townsville when an accidental pregnancy and subsequent abortion damages her relationship with her family. However, after a few months, Dave kicks Sue out following an argument over money, and she moves in with Roger, her boyfriend. The couple initially shares a flat with Roger's cousin Maureen and her kids, and later move into their own flat in the neighboring suburb of Beenleigh. Sue soon becomes the victim of domestic violence, and after several months of abuse, summons the courage to leave Roger. She discovers that the suburbs cannot provide the sanctuary she seeks, and by the end of the novel escapes suburbia and re-settles in the inner-city neighborhood of West End. *Steam Pigs* is a bold and innovative novel that utilizes a working class outer suburban setting to address crucial social issues such as Indigenous identity, racism, belonging, domestic violence, gender and sexuality, and alcohol and drug abuse. However, the novel ultimately presents suburbia as a destructive site that needs to be rejected in favor of the life-affirming inner city, serving to perpetuate the anti-suburban tradition in Australian fiction, and calling into question the novel's radical power.

Lucashenko depicts the working-class suburb in an overwhelmingly negative manner with regard to the physical environment, the residents' lifestyles, and the suburb's relationship to the city, the bush, and other suburbs. Eagleby is flat, hot, ugly, boring and isolated. Sue lives with her brother Dave in a "tiny brick box" on Slammer Street (6). The street name suggests both a prison and violence, emphasizing the isolation of the suburb, the residents' lack of mobility, and one of the many social problems within the community. The suburb's residents engage in a range of destructive behaviors, including substance abuse, domestic violence, sexual abuse, child abuse, racism, assault and theft. In her article on *Steam Pigs*, Margaret Henderson argues that Lucashenko "positions class as critical and unavoidable in her suburban geography" (79). Not only are the social problems depicted in the novel presented as working-class issues, Lucashenko places Eagleby in opposition to Brisbane's middle and upper-class suburbs.

Eagleby is one of approximately thirty suburbs comprising Logan City, a local government area located on the southern edge of Brisbane, home to approximately 170,000 people. *Steam Pigs* contains numerous criticisms and negative depictions of Logan City as a whole, and of individual suburbs within the region. Eagleby is described as "that death of outer suburbia" in which passive unthinking suburbanites "slumped and sweated it out in their pokey rooms ... melded into limpid living rooms, tranced by the flicker of [television] screens" (5). Sue thinks of Eagleby as a "'fucken dump'" (43), and she and Dave disdainfully refer to the "snarling locals" as "Argles" in an attempt to differentiate themselves from their neighbors (5-6). Sue's life in Eagleby is "flavoured" by sweat and beer, and despite her "mockery of the 'fat fucks' smoking dope next door," she knows she belongs and worries that she will "drown" (6). Life in Eagleby is a life without hope or progress; the sole goal is survival. Moreover, Eagleby is a parochial and isolating community. When Sue is hired as a delivery driver, she desperately seeks to share the news with someone, but Maureen is at bingo, Roger is taking an exam, and Dave is at work (60). She cannot think of a single person she can visit, even though she has lived in Eagleby for nearly eighteen months, since the outer suburb provides few social opportunities (60).

Lucashenko presents the working-class suburb as an isolated site lacking in opportunities for economic advancement. Some of the youth of Eagleby move into Brisbane hoping to "make their million," lured by images of the city and "big money" on television (7). However, they do not realize that wealth cannot be acquired with hard work, that it is "bred on town ridges that look to the mountains" (7). Lucashenko's narrator claims that "Very little [money] trickles down the gullies onto the stinking frying plains, for those who hold it take very good care not to let it go" (7). Lukashenko presents the affluent middle and upper class suburbs in Brisbane as a closed world to which the working class are denied access. Although Sue lacks analytical skills, she instinctively knows enough to avoid wasting her time and energy trying to improve her social and economic position, choosing instead "to withdraw gracefully" and receive "an honourable discharge in the race to be Working Class Hero of 1998" (7).

One of the many negative aspects of Eagleby is the suburb's lack of entertainment options. Since the suburb does not have a public swimming pool, and only one family can afford a private pool (17), Eagleby residents must leave their suburb to swim. Eagleby's closest swimming spot is located in the neighboring suburb of Beenleigh, where "six pipes took Cedar Creek under the country road," creating "a free waterslide" (12). On weekends, "nearly two hundred people" would travel to Beenleigh to swim (12). Suburbanites with a car and money can drive thirty minutes south to the beaches of the Gold Coast, or drive north to the Hyperdome at Loganholme to see a movie or go shopping. Within Eagleby, entertainment options outside the home are limited to the video store, a few shops, and the pub (8).

A New Generation Perpetuates the Anti-Suburban Tradition   141

Domestic entertainment in the outer suburb largely consists of watching television, drinking copious amounts of alcohol, and taking drugs. Lucashenko presents Eagleby as a community in which alcohol and drug abuse is rampant. Alcohol and drugs are used as an escape from the brutal realities of suburban working class life, although they frequently exacerbate problems such as violence and poverty. The narrator notes that Sue and Dave drink excessively and that "Sue drank negatively sometimes, slugged it down till she spewed" (6). Sue's attitude towards marijuana is summed up in the following passage: "Ah fuck what's the difference, stoned once a week, once a day, or all day every day, life goes on pretty much the same. Not as if we're bloody brain surgeons, is it? Then it might matter" (103). Lucashenko's narrator reveals that the average Eagleby resident views drugs as a cure for all problems: "Too fat? Have a cone. Too poor? Have a cone. Lonely, bored, unemployed, sick of yer family or yerself? Have a cone" (104). The negative effects of drugs, such as Roger's short-term memory loss, are only occasionally acknowledged (137).

Teenage pregnancy is common in Lucashenko's Eagleby, and since Sue spends a lot of time looking after her nephews, people often mistake her for their mother, even though she is only seventeen and the boys are six and four: "that made her a mother at eleven, but give or take a couple of years on their part and she was just another teenage mum, and the colouring matched" (11). The narrator declares that puberty begins at eleven in Eagleby and "middle age hits hard at twenty-five" (57). Roger lives with his cousin Maureen, who is thirty-six and will become a grandmother once her pregnant fifteen-year-old daughter gives birth. Sue thinks of teenage pregnancy as "the first step on the road to poverty for all us blackfellas" (57). Lucashenko depicts the children of Eagleby as mistreated and neglected. The kids are "treated as subhuman until they hit puberty and start demanding otherwise with voices, fists and occasionally, the law" (45). Maureen's kids spend most of their time playing video games or watching television and horror movies (36). In Lucashenko's version of suburbia, life is a struggle, and new lives are usually unplanned, unwanted and neglected.

One of the numerous anti-suburban passages in the novel begins when Sue drops her nephews off at their mother's unit in the nearby suburb of Woodridge. As Sue leaves the treeless and litter-strewn Housing Commission flats, she is thankful that she is childless: "There but for the graceagod go I, she thinks, and who woulda been surprised if I *had* ended up at twenty or so, down here with two or three or four kids in a shitty little box" (116, original emphasis). Sue thinks of the mothers on welfare as "bloody bludgers" and considers herself to have broken free of her economic and family background, "conveniently forgetting the months of abuse" she had received from relatives and friends once they learned of her abortion (116). However, on another occasion, Sue considers the possibility that she may end up as "an Eagleby housewife, dodging Roger's crunching fists and crying into pillows over a life lost to screaming children" (46). In an anti-suburban rant prompted by a trip to the local shopping centre to buy Christmas presents, Sue

> ... looks around in teenage contempt ... [at] Fat women in cotton skirts that showed their pooltable legs bearing crap presents ... Straggly kids crying being dragged by one outstretched arm, fathers walking ahead cursing them. Whole families of beergutted twenty-five year-old men in T-shirts proclaiming that 'Holdens Shit On Falcons' ... O they're an attractive lot, alright, Sue told herself, the poor white trash that looks down on us Murries as ignorant and drunken, while they piss their own lives away at the pub and the video store. All of a sudden she feels a surge of anger at the dull, pale, acned faces that surround her. These are the bastards that put us on Palm, she thought, the ones who voted for that cunt Joh. Ah, go get rooted, ya braindead lotta cunts. (101)

Sue's disgust is initially driven by aesthetic concerns, but she quickly conflates ugliness with whiteness and blames working-class suburbanites for the racism and forced removal from their native lands that her fellow Indigenous Australians have suffered, as well as blaming them for

A New Generation Perpetuates the Anti-Suburban Tradition 143

the election and repeated re-election of Queensland's notoriously corrupt longest-serving Premier, Sir Joh Bjelke-Petersen. Suburbia, class, race and violence continually intersect in such ways throughout the novel.

Lucashenko depicts crime as an aspect of suburban working-class life that is ever-present, condoned and taken for granted. Kids in Eagleby siphon petrol from neighbors' cars at night to refuel their trail bikes (vii); the possession and use of illegal drugs is so common that "every second backyard" contains "a black plastic potted plant" (104); assaults and domestic violence are almost daily events; and drink-driving is considered normal behavior. Although Sue does not approve of Roger dealing marijuana (50), she does not ask him to stop and frequently partakes of his supply. Furthermore, Sue is not averse to breaking the law herself. She steals a bottle of rum from a drive-in bottle shop simply because she has the opportunity. Moreover, her brother, who is with her when she commits the crime, expresses approval, and later the same evening she returns and steals three more bottles (65, 66). While discussing with Roger the details of her new job delivering auto parts, Sue declares that she could easily steal some merchandise and declares that she will do so before she quits the job (74).

Lucashenko presents violence as an ever-present component of life in the working-class outer suburb. The violence is prevalent in both the domestic and public spheres; in the former, most of the violence is perpetrated by males against women and children, while in the later, violence erupts in the form of fights at the pub and in a controlled sporting arena, namely karate. However, the violence of both the public and domestic spheres is linked, as the narrator reveals during an explanation of the Eagleby residents' motivations for taking karate lessons at the community centre:

> Survive ... without a jarred head or winded gut and you know you're well on the way to hardheaded Logan City competence in the carpark and the pub ... that's what they're all there for, every one of them, avenging their father's beatings, their mother's

sarcasms, building themselves painful ladders into new worlds where they're the biggest, the strongest, the least vulnerable, where nothing can get them again. (4)

The children of the suburb are frequently the victims of violence, which is often inflicted upon them as punishment. Kirk and Lucky are described as "good kids by Eagleby standards, meaning they didn't whinge and did what they were told automatically for fear of being hit – hard" (11). After Sue moves in with Roger, he spends a lot of time with her nephews and does not hesitate to beat them when he thinks they deserve it. After Roger belts Kirk for almost scratching his Ute, Sue expresses her disapproval: "'You didn't have to belt him, Rog. It's not as if he's yours, you know, and he didn't scratch the car anyway'" (32). However, as the novel progresses, Sue is less inclined to defend her nephews: "a childhood of floggings has conditioned her to be cautious with men's anger. What to do, what to do? See the child picked on, or speak up and maybe cop it herself?" (53). Lucashenko presents domestic violence as being passed down through the generations by males who are beaten as children then repeat the behavior as adults.

The primary type of violence Lucashenko deals with in *Steam Pigs* is male-on-female domestic violence. Henderson argues that the houses in Eagleby rarely contain "a sense of comfort or permanency," since the domestic spaces "are temporary accommodations within an environment that may suddenly erupt into violence" (75-76). Lucashenko addresses domestic violence in detail through Roger's abuse of Sue. Even before Sue moves in with Roger, it is apparent to the reader that he is violent, since Roger's reaction to the news that Dave has kicked Sue out is to offer to beat him up (41). Throughout their relationship, Roger repeatedly beats Sue. She comes to live in constant fear of triggering another attack through her words or actions. In the aftermath of the pub fight in which Roger is injured, Sue wonders how he will "react to being stripped of his dignity" and decides that men are "temperamental buggers" who may flip at any time and "start throwing punches around or screaming abuse" (87). Sue's

A New Generation Perpetuates the Anti-Suburban Tradition

generalization about men and violence indicates that her only experience with men has been with violent and abusive men. Sue believes that her nephews do not have appropriate male role models and need to be around "strong, proud, gentle men, not the shells of violent adolescent-minded bastards they encountered in Eagleby" (54). She contemplates taking her nephews up north to the bush to show them "how their people used to live," since they have "only the vaguest hint of an idea" that they are black (54).

After a verbal fight on Christmas morning, Sue contemplates her relationship with Roger and wonders if it will always be violent: "She loves Rog, and he's supposed to love her, but they fight so much all the time, and each time's getting worse. She can't work him out, one minute everything's fine, the next he's exploded into rage over absolutely nothing" (110). Having left the flat in a rage and gone drinking with his mates, Roger's feelings about the fight are presented in one of the rare passages of the novel presented from his perspective:

> His anger is quick to come, quick to go, only problem was, when it went there is usually a fucken pile of guilt a mile high ... But I didn't hit her, he reminded himself continually, I didn't, even if she was asking for it I didn't, that's something isn't it, I didn't. (111)

By thinking "she was asking for it," Roger reveals that he believes domestic violence is justified in certain situations. His attitude is the exact opposite of that held by Kerry, Sue's social worker friend and eventual savior, who insists there are "no excuses for domestic violence" (139).

After being beaten yet again by Roger, Sue visits Kerry's house with a black eye (141). While comforting Sue, Kerry insists that she repeat the mantra, "It's not my fault" (143). When Sue tries to defend Roger, Kerry declares, "'I don't care if it's Roger or fucking Adolf Hitler who done that to you, it's not *your* fault, okay? No woman ever deserves to be bashed, ever. No excuses'" (145, original emphasis). Later in the novel, on the morning after Roger gives Sue the worst beating she has ever suffered and then rapes her, she calls Dave in tears begging him to provide her with a safe haven (195). However, Dave refuses, so she turns to Kerry and her partner Rachel for help. The women are out of town for the day, so Sue has to wander the hot, empty suburban streets until they return (196-98). When Rachel collects Sue from a phone box, she declares she will not return to Roger (200).

Kerry lives in an old Queenslander in Beenleigh (63).[3] The house serves to set Kerry apart from the other residents of the southern suburbs, since most of them live in small brick houses or flats. Kerry's big white wooden house has a jacaranda tree in full bloom in the front yard, and "The whole place with its wraparound verandahs has an inviting feel to it that the local brick boxes can never attain" (67). Like Johnston, Malouf and Winton, Lucashenko privileges the old wooden house over the newer brick houses. Inside, Kerry's walls "are adorned with posters and geegaws from around the world. The pictures are full of women, lots of them black women – talking, laughing, marching, working" (68). Sue describes Kerry's house as "'amazing'" and declares, "'You've got so much stuff – it's really different to our place'" (68). While giving Sue a tour of the house, Kerry shows Sue

> her artefacts from the Northern Territory, painted birds from Ramingining, [and] clothes from the Tiwi islands ... Kerry's been in enough Eagleby homes to know that tiny fishbowls with miserable orange inmates, posters of Elvis, and pride-of-place family photos are as great a gesture towards aesthetics as Sue's likely to have seen. (68)

The interior decorations serve to emphasize the difference between middle class and working class domestic spaces and the absence of foreign and high cultures from the lives of the working class. Sue begins visiting Kerry and Rachel weekly and describes their house as "a feast of words, [with] books in every room, a motley assortment of paperbacks, women's studies texts, tattoo mags, ancient orange Penguins ... and a whole library of poetry" (188). Kerry and Rachel's Queenslander shows Sue an alternative lifestyle that she may be able to attain if she can escape her class and environment.

Lucashenko writes about Queenslander houses in her essay "Not Quite White in the Head." She reads the Queenslander, especially in its contemporary manifestation as a signifier of middle class affluence, as representative of a "lifestyle [that] is meant to convey a mood of summer indolence, perhaps by the pool but certainly taking in a verandah and an open plan weekend in which cold drinks and friends replace the claustrophobia and TV of the brick bungalow" (Lucashenko, "Not Quite" 29). Similarly, in *12 Edmondstone Street,* Malouf presents the Queenslander house in positive and nostalgic terms as a cultured middle-class sanctuary. The Queenslander in *Steam Pigs* serves as an example of a superior alternative to the typical suburban existence in Eagleby, not merely in terms of architecture, interior decoration and class, but also in a more literal sense. Kerry and Rachel are university-educated lesbian feminists and the house serves as a physical manifestation of their identity, often in very literal ways: no men are allowed to enter the house, which has been declared "women's space." It is by emulating Kerry and Rachel's lifestyle that Sue escapes the restrictions of her working class suburb.

Lucashenko also uses the working class suburban setting of her novel to examine issues of gender and sexuality, which are intertwined with class, race and socioeconomic status. Sue grows up in a highly patriarchal culture and is expected to conform to traditional gender roles. Sue begins cooking during childhood, since her father leaves when she is quite young and her mother is usually too drunk to cook, and, as a female, Sue is expected to fulfill the role her mother neglects (226-27). After moving to Eagleby, Sue becomes a surrogate mother for her nephews, providing childcare, cooking and cleaning, and collecting the kids from school (16). Once Sue begins seeing Roger, she takes over the cooking and cleaning, even when visiting friends (32). Moreover, Sue attempts to conform to mainstream standards for female beauty, having "absorbed the lessons of hundreds of *Dolly*'s and *Cosmo*'s only too well" (39). Likewise,

Roger holds fixed, narrow views of both male and female gender roles. He expects women to cook, clean, obey and provide sex on demand. Roger is openly homophobic and misogynistic and frequently expresses disapproval of Sue's friendship with Kerry and Rachel.

Lucashenko uses Kerry and Rachel to present alternative performances of gender and sexuality, and both women constantly encourage Sue to become more open-minded and enlightened regarding such issues. Kerry is a social worker with an office in the community centre where Sue takes karate lessons. Sue sees a flyer at the shopping centre advertising one of Kerry's courses in self-esteem for women and is particularly interested in learning about "negotiating skills and conflict resolution" (60-61). Sue has seen Kerry around the suburb and considers her "deadly cool," remembering that she rides a Harley and "doesn't take shit from no-one" (60-61). Sue visits Kerry and finds that the tattooed blond woman possesses "an openness and friendliness that puts her at ease" (62). When Sue learns that Kerry's house is "women's space," she is "a bit stunned by the idea of women telling men they weren't allowed to go somewhere ... *Wild*. Most of the men she'd grown up with would give you a flogging for less. Wow" (63, original emphasis). Lucashenko's narrator notes that during Sue's first meeting with Kerry, the "seeds of revolution" are sown, although Sue is oblivious to the fact that she has begun the process of enlightenment and escape (64).

Sue soon meets Kerry's partner Rachel, but due to her naiveté takes a while to realize the women are lesbians (69, 70). Sue holds conflicting views on lesbianism; she is disgusted by the thought of lesbian sex, but otherwise considers it a great idea: "No muss, no fuss, no fucken blokes being heroes or beltin ya up all over the place" (114). When Sue finally leaves Roger, she embraces life as an independent woman, thinking, "I never want another man fucking me over, ever ever again! Just peace and quiet, and a little place of me own. Bitta freedom, no hassles" (216). Lucashenko has written about gender and sexuality in several essays, stating that she views Australia as "a deeply misogynistic society" that "has a deep terror of powerful women" ("Many Prisons" 141). Lucashenko argues that non-Indigenous people can learn a lot about gender from Indigenous culture and claims that "Not many non-Indigenous people know much about gender … To the extent that most white Australians, for example, have thought about gender, it's to support or mock the idea of female equality" ("Gender" 50).

In addition to introducing Sue to new ideas about gender and sexuality, Lucashenko uses Kerry and Rachel, and, to a lesser extent, Roger, to introduce Sue to higher education. Although Roger is a university student, he is by no means typical or representative of Eagleby's residents, and Lucashenko presents higher education as an unusual pursuit in the working class outer suburbs. Rachel attends university, where she is studying to be a history teacher (71). Kerry suggests that Sue can also attend university if she wants and suggests that she go in for a day with Rachel (72). Kerry delights in prodding Sue to break out of her comfort zone, declaring, "'don't sit in Eagleby on yer black arse whingin about how dumb you are when we both know it's bullshit'" (72). During one of Sue's visits, Kerry and Rachel engage in a heated intellectual debate about the causes of poverty and oppression, leaving Sue astonished and confused, since "there wasn't a hint of violence or even fear" and she had never witnessed an intellectual debate before (72).

When Rachel takes Sue to visit the university, she is intimidated by the concrete and glass buildings. Rachel explains that university is "'not like outside. You can do whatever you want, practically, and say what you think, you don't haveta hide it. No-one gives a damn what you do or why you do it'" (121). Sue is confused and unconvinced: "'… as for not minding what you said, she's never heard of anything so bloody silly. Everywhere she's ever been there's been a boss or father or uncle or *someone* to flog ya into line, bugger saying what ya think!'" (121, original emphasis). Rachel tries to convince Sue to apply to the university and sees herself "melodramatically" as "a guardian angel standing at a crossroads, urging Sue to go on to the great God of Higher Education and Future. The other signpost said (in code) poverty, racism, patriarchal bullshit, getting fucked over all your life" (121-22). Sue tells Rachel that Roger does not approve of her attending university, since her wages pay the rent, and they would have to find cheaper accommodation (122-23). After Rachel informs Sue that she will be eligible for Abstudy and the degree will only take three years, Sue agrees to let Rachel fill out an application form for her (123).

Much to Sue's surprise, Roger is delighted by her acceptance into university, proclaiming, "'We're gonna be rich'" (192), and they then discuss how much money they will be able to make after graduation. Roger has heard about a job opening for a research officer with the student union, which he describes as

> "Thirty grand a year for sitting on yer arse! That's enough to pay off a house, and everything." Rog couldn't believe it, he was twenty-six and in a position to buy a place of his own, well, assuming he got the job, that is ... Pretty good for a blackfella. (193)

Sue suggests that they buy a weatherboard house in the suburb of Mt. Gravatt, near the campus, and the couple spend the next half hour

> planning where to buy their dream house ... the years ahead positively gushing with money, cos everyone knew that uni graduates got the good jobs, the government jobs on big money where you could flex on and off and no-one cared if you were gone for two hours at lunch, and they paid you heaps for doing fuck-all. (193)

Sue and Roger's discussion of money and white-collar careers vividly reveals their ignorance of the realities of white-collar work and middle class life. Throughout *Steam Pigs*, Lucashenko repeatedly examines the attitudes towards employment and money held by the residents of working class suburbia. Most of the working class suburbanites who are employed work in menial, low paying and unrewarding jobs. When Sue first arrives in Eagleby, she has not yet discovered "the tedium of bluecollar employment" and "would have gone to extraordinary lengths to be admitted to the mythic world of Work" (2). Driven by "an urgent need for cash," Sue lies about her age and experience and obtains a job as a barmaid (2, 10). Before she even starts work, Sue celebrates by spending money on new clothes for herself and dinner for Dave and her nephews (10).

Sue's decision to spend money she has not yet earned is indicative of the working class attitudes and behaviors depicted throughout the novel. The working class characters constantly struggle to meet rent, mortgage and car payments, partly due to unemployment and low wages, but largely because of their habit of spending large portions of their income on alcohol and drugs. Moreover, whenever a character receives an unexpected financial windfall or a new job, his or her first instinct is to spend the money on a night out on the town, clothing, or a new vehicle, rather than paying off debts or saving the money. Sue perceives money as providing her with the ability to "stay away indefinitely from the claustrophobia of her too-large, too-poor family in a too-small town," although even in Eagleby she is "tied to them by the umbilical cord of the phone, the line that rang like a cash-register when her social security money arrived" (2). While Sue lives with Dave, she gives most of her income to him for board and the rest goes towards car payments (14, 28). Dave struggles to meet his mortgage payments after his wife leaves him, and Sue manages to buy groceries for the household of four with just fifty dollars per week; however, half of the money is spent on Dave's beer (8-9).

Sue loses her job at the pub when it goes out of business, but realizes that she is much better off than her co-worker Helen, who has mortgage payments and an unemployed husband who is "liable to bash her head in when she told him" (49). Sue dreads going to the dole office, where she will have to "stand in a humiliating queue with forty other people who can't look each other in the eye" (50). However, Sue soon gets over the disappointment of losing her income, telling herself that something will come up, and decides that in the meantime she will "spend a few days in a pleasant blur of beers and sunshine between home and the pool" (51). When Sue visits the CES (Commonwealth Employment Service) office, she learns that a high school education is an adequate qualification to obtain office or factory work, but "good jobs" in the area are "few and far between" without "a trade, or specific training" (57). In *Steam Pigs*, Lucashenko never depicts work as fulfilling or as part of a career with an upward trajectory; it is merely a means to make money, which is valued solely for its acquisitive power.

Eventually, Sue finds a job driving a van delivering auto parts to service stations around Brisbane and immediately dreams of a better life (58). She calculates how much money she will make and decides that it will be enough for her and Roger to rent a townhouse, "Maybe even a flash one in a complex with a pool" (59-60). Henderson argues that a job such as Sue's is "highly valued" in Eagleby, since it is full-time and involves driving a new vehicle (76). While driving her delivery van, Sue sees a used car for sale for eight thousand dollars, decides that Roger will co-sign the loan, and imagines herself taking the car for weekend trips to the Gold Coast (77). Sue performs well at her job and receives a twenty dollar per week raise, which prompts her and Roger to visit a real estate agent and start searching for their own flat with a pool (77). Sue and Roger never consider saving money; they are solely interested in the power of money to buy material goods that will supposedly improve their situation. Lucashenko's depiction of suburban consumerism is consistent with critiques of suburban materialism in the anti-suburban tradition.

Sue's first exposure to the inner-urban environment occurs when Kerry and Rachel arrange a surprise eighteenth-birthday-party for her at a café in Brisbane's West End, an area Sue associates with hippies, yuppies and Murries (134).[4] Sue arrives before Kerry and Rachel and is met by their friend Louise, "A dark-haired, pasty-faced woman ... in black combat boots and a vomitous-coloured dress, a Murri bracelet dangling from her wrist, but Sue can tell from the way she talks and stands that she's white" (133). While waiting for Kerry and Rachel, Sue and Louise discuss Eagleby, which Sue admits is a long way from the CBD and has lots of unemployment and domestic violence. However, Sue becomes tired

A New Generation Perpetuates the Anti-Suburban Tradition 153

of "hearing about Logan City's faults" and thinks "what about the bush being close? and we're only twenty minutes from the surf?" (134). Sue has acknowledged Logan City's faults before, and even claimed to hate suburbia, but does not enjoy discussing suburban social problems with a cosmopolitan inner-urban resident. Sue's suburban lack of sophistication is emphasized during lunch when she has foccaccia and thinks of it as "fancy wog sandwiches" (134).

After Sue leaves Roger and temporarily moves in with Kerry and Rachel, the women devise a plan to help Sue reclaim her possessions and locate a new place for her to live (205, 206). The women's friend Bianca seeks to rent out her flat for six months while she is in Europe; the flat is located on the top floor of a building in West End with a view over the city (206). Sue decides that fleeing north out of the suburbs will "keep [her] out of trouble and Roger's grasp" and gratefully accepts the offer (206, 209). Kerry arranges for Louise to look after Sue and introduce her "to the feminist scene," since she lives around the corner from Sue's new flat (209, 210). Sue and Kerry successfully retrieve Sue's possessions and car while Roger is absent (213-216) and Sue moves into her new home in West End, located less than a kilometer from the location of Dante's South Brisbane home in Malouf's *Johnno* (and Malouf's own childhood home at 12 Edmonstone Street).

Once Sue is settled in her West End flat, which she shares with a fellow student, Melinda, she learns that her brother Mick is incarcerated and starts writing to him. In her letters, Sue informs Mick that she often goes to movies and libraries in the city, which is home to many yuppies, Asians and Indians (221). Sue describes West End as being full of "ethnics" and Murries (221). After a couple of months in West End, Sue is amazed that six months previously she had not been able to recognize immediately that Kerry and Rachel are lesbians (235). Sue's newfound ability to decipher cultural and sexual signifiers reveals her increasing cosmopolitanism. Living in the inner suburb exposes Sue to a diverse range of ethnic and cultural groups, makes her aware of sexual diversity, and provides her with easy access to cultural experiences (such as libraries, galleries, museums and theatres) which are unavailable in Eagleby.

When Rachel and Kerry visit Sue they jokingly refer to her as a "city girl" and discuss her new life, which is the polar opposite of her suburban life and includes "The discovery of a political world on the edge of the city, a complex feast of groups, arts festivals, anarchists, Murri organizations, [and] bookshops" (236). Kerry mockingly refers to the residents of West End as "'The liberal elite' and 'Champagne socialists,'" to which Sue replies, "'whatever ya call it, it's like another fucking planet ... I can't work out why youse live down in Yobsville'" (236). Rachel admits that some of the residents of the southern working class suburbs are "'pretty neanderthal,'" but argues that "'there's *something* down there'" and there are "'people in Logan City that are *alive*, not just existing'" (237, original emphasis).[5]

The narrator reveals that Kerry would "move north in an instant herself, if the job wasn't in Eagleby. Fucking working-class heroes were all bullshit as far as she was concerned, and so-called working-class vitality was more often than not fuelled by booze or borderline mental illness" (237). Sue is intrigued by Rachel's somewhat positive view of Logan City, since she had "spent the last couple of months congratulating herself on her narrow escape ... and had successfully persuaded herself she didn't miss a thing about 'Slumsville,'" but now wonders if she really feels that way (237). Kerry states that she and Rachel live in Logan City "'cos that's where all the social welfare work is. Eagleby's just the place for the poor, and the uneducated, and the marginal ... but those people (surprise, surprise) are also the bashers and the drinkers" (238). Sue claims she hated Eagleby when she lived there and really likes West End, but admits she sometimes thinks "'about moving back down to Dave's or just a flat by myself in Eagleby'" (238). However, Sue does not express such feelings on any other occasion and when the novel concludes she is residing happily in West End, far from her previous suburban life.

Living in West End not only provides Sue with safety and freedom and allows her to become more culturally sophisticated, it also precipitates a physical transformation. Before going out for lunch in Chinatown with Kerry and Rachel, Sue changes into "long army pants, a dark blue T-shirt and genuine secondhand Doc Martens" and fastens "a necklace of tiny Murri beads around her neck" (238-39). Kerry and Rachel make a fuss over her outfit, declare that she looks "fantastic," and ask, "'What have ya done with Sue Wilson?'" (239). Sue feels that she finally blends in with her friends and strides out to the car "on top of the world" thinking, "Maybe I can leave Railway Estate and Eagleby behind ... as she felt the red, black and yellow beads around her neck" (239). On one of the final pages of the novel Kerry half-ironically declares, "'So Sue ... you've done it! Thrown off the shackles of patriarchy! Vindicated your race and sex! Well done'" (241). Henderson argues that Sue's "contact with feminist politics and alternative ways of living," combined with her "gradual uncovering of her Aboriginality," eventually culminate "in her rejection of the white masculinist values of Eagleby and its destructive culture," choosing instead "the more plural and feminised habitat of West End" (77).

Along with class and gender, Indigenous identity is one of the primary issues Lucashenko addresses in *Steam Pigs*. Tanya Dalziell argues that the novel refuses "any ethnographic notion of Aboriginality as a fixed and entirely knowable identity" and claims, "Lucashenko deliberately introduces the complexities that the shifting intersections of class, gender, race, and sexuality across cultural differences can precipitate in postcolonial Australia" (144). Sue gradually learns to embrace her Indigenous identity as the narrative progresses. Early in the novel, when Dave mocks her for building a fire in the backyard, the narrator states that Sue considers having "a bit of Aboriginal blood" as "largely an irrelevance"(9). However, by the end of the novel Sue identifies primarily as Indigenous.[6]

When Roger watches Sue arrive at his flat for their first date, he approvingly notices her athletic body and attributes it to her being Murri (19).

Roger has red hair, freckles and fair skin, but has an Aboriginal father and identifies as Indigenous. Since Roger does not possess outward markers of Aboriginality, Sue initially thinks he is white. When Sue asks Roger if he has "black blood," he replies, "'Where I come from we just say we're all Aboriginal, eh? None of that half-caste, quarter-caste bullshit. Like, I've got Scots and Irish too, I won't deny that, but my heart's with the blackfellas. Waka Waka I am'" (20-21). Roger's father is a member of the stolen generations (21). Sue decides to accept Roger's claims about his heritage, but thinks that it will take an effort for her to accept him as Indigenous, since she is "used to the northern omnipresent dark faces ... Together the two of them might add up to a real Aboriginal, she thought briefly" (21). Roger is sensitive about his fair skin and does not like to be reminded "that he's freckly and pale" (27, 130).

Roger attends Griffith University, where he takes classes in economics, law, politics and Aboriginal studies, and Sue learns a lot from him about Indigenous history and culture, such as the "Gurindjii fight of the sixties" (43, 52).[7] Roger is highly political and forbids Sue from watching the news on the commercial television station, labeling it "ruling class propaganda" (138). Sue reflects that she "had no clue" about her Indigenous identity "until talking to Roger woke her up" (54). By midway through the novel, Sue thinks of herself primarily as Indigenous. When Sue and Roger bargain with a farmer over a used car she wants to buy and the farmer complains about the drought and times being tough, she thinks, "Times're tough all round, buddy ... try being a Murri and broke yer whole life and not just when there's a drought on, then you'll know what tough times are" (119). Sue embraces her Indigeneity to such an extent that she wishes her skin were darker. While looking at a *Dolly* magazine, Sue resents "the dark skin of the beautiful Maori girl modeling sarongs" and thinks

> poorfella me, black inside but looking like a wog all me life. Unreal innit, years ago when Annette [her mother] was a girl all she got for being a bit dark was abuse and running away from the welfare

with her babies, and now of course it's trendy, (so long as you're not "too" dark that is) and here's me with me pale skin. (127)

While talking with Kerry and Rachel, Sue claims that being a victim of domestic violence is "'part of being Murri, you know, you expect it'" (145). Kerry will not let Sue make excuses for domestic violence and challenges her, asking, "'If Roger was white, would you put up with this? ... Kerry stares Sue down ... angry with a system that could do this to people, fucked up Murries all over the damn country. Land – *gone*, families – *gone*, dignity – *gone*, culture – *gone*" (146, original emphasis). Kerry argues that Sue confuses "colonisation with culture, and blackness with oppression," declaring,

> It's manipulative bullshit that whites use to fuck minorities all the time, internalised oppression, letting us define what makes you who you are, and till you get over this hurdle, your whole life is going to revolve around being fucked up one way or another. What you've more or less said is what most whites think too, that there's nothing more to being Aboriginal than drinking and fighting and being poor. (147)

Throughout the novel, Lucashenko uses the suburban setting to confront questions of Indigenous identity and racism in similarly direct language.

Sue claims she does not have "'some big identity crisis,'" but had previously told Kerry and Rachel she was raised white and was deeply hurt when other Murries "reminded her she had a family of coconuts" (145). When Sue visits her family in Townsville and takes Kirk with her, she points out Palm Island from the window of the plane and wonders "whether she'd ever know her true family story, ever know why her mother wouldn't talk about growing up, and which was her tribe" (149). Sue thinks of Dave as a "coconut" and decides he does not understand assimilation and reclaiming Indigenous identity:

> It was all too complicated for Sue to try and explain to him, he'd just mock her and ask her when she was going to put in for land

rights, like she had no right to and it was all a bit of a joke. The whites had done a real good job on him. (166)

Sue's mother does not view herself as Indigenous at all: Sue attributes this to shame caused by "being brought up like a whitefella ... they'd brainwashed the old people so well that it wasn't a matter of denying their Aboriginality, more a matter of them really thinking they *were* white" (166, original emphasis). While in Townsville visiting her family, Sue tries to pay attention to a news story on television about land rights, but cannot hear the report because her family members want to talk instead (156).

Once Sue returns to suburbia from Townsville, Kerry continues to push her to develop her Indigenous identity and take responsibility for her life. Kerry declares that "a person can only blame society while they're still ignorant" and argues that people who know that they have to live with racism and sexism every day have to decide how to live:

> "You want to be a victim, fine, go ahead ... Just don't expect any help from me to do it. There's enough white wankers out there who are more than happy to see blacks as the downtrodden sufferers, and you know why? ... Cos victims are *safe*, sister. No-one ever got challenged by a victim." (189, original emphasis)

After Sue is accepted into Griffith University and decides to major in Aboriginal studies (191), Kerry warns her that the other Murries will disapprove if she speaks out and projects strength, since it "challenges their own way of thinking" (190).

While Rachel helps Sue move into her flat in West End, Sue learns that Bianca, the owner, an "ordinary old British Aussie ... another West End feminist, heavy on the ideology," has been discussing Murri issues with Kerry for years and was eager to help an Indigenous woman (220). Sue is annoyed, but thinks, "yeah, okay Bian*kah* I'll be your huddled masses if it makes you feel better. Just don't think we're even ... rent on a continent don't come cheap" (220, original emphasis). Once in West

End, Sue begins reading a collection of stories by an unnamed Indigenous author and starts contemplating issues of land ownership and belonging. Lucashenko includes five pages of a piece entitled "Anyday Story," which is written from the point of view of an Indigenous narrator. The narrator of "Anyday Story" claims, "*in the white places of Australia,*" such as Brisbane, "*the Europeans walk arrogantly, and exhibit none of the fear they bring to Alice Springs or Kakadu. They drive to work up Brunswick Street, or take the train home to Yeerongpilly without pausing to think*" (229, original emphasis).[8]

After reading "Anyday Story," Sue reflects on information Roger relayed to her from Aboriginal studies lectures:

> Queensland coppers issued licenses to shoot blacks ... they used native police to track and betray tribes not their own ... they came swooping in at dawn and [within] half an hour it was all over, for the Bundjalung, the Kamiloroi, the Yugambeh, the Yuggera ... and the coastal nations have had to rebuild from splinters and remnants ... A slow growing back of the clan over the years, decades, centuries. Children stolen. Men sacrificed to the prisons and the drink. Women raped then discarded by anyone white with the inclination and opportunity. And now with so much white blood in us, the darker inland people despise us as white, for all that none of us ever asked for the white man's coming, for all that it was an accident of history that saw the colonisation start in the east and not the west or north. (234)

After reading about Indigenous history, Sue goes to sleep without the aid of a bedtime drink for the first time in weeks (234). Lucashenko presents Indigenous history as a cure for Sue's nightmares, a positive substitute for alcohol or marijuana, and the knowledge that will allow Sue to fully embrace and understand her Indigenous identity. In her essay "A Lighter Shade of Pale: Being Aboriginal in 2002," Lucashenko argues, "there's more than one way to be a blackfella" and points out that

> blackfellas still live all over Australia … Murries in Queensland. Koories in New South Wales and Victoria. Other words in other places. Some of us still dark, still black looking. Some of us with fair skin and blonde hair, only inside we could be real black. (1)

Lucashenko insists that skin color is unimportant: "its about what's under the skin. Your heart, and your mind. Your spirit" ("Lighter" 1).

Nevertheless, to a great extent, skin color dictates the manner in which Indigenous characters in *Steam Pigs* perceive themselves and are treated by others. The novel contains numerous instances of racism, most of them linked to perceptions of skin color. Roger's cousin's kids have "their father's dark skin" and Sue realizes that "it won't be long … before the local shop owners and coppers'll have them pegged as Trouble" (27). While Sue is in Townsville, she witnesses the harassment and arrest of an Indigenous man by the police, which enrages her: "'Geez, don't it make yer fucken wild! They get away with murder, I hate them, I just hate them!'" (182). When her friends console her and suggest that the man will soon be out on bail, Sue exclaims,

> "But he didn't do anything in the first place! He's gotta go to the watch-house, why? Cos he's black, that's why. And if they killed him, who'd fucken care? Just a bunch of poor hopeless blackfellas …" Sue spoke bitterly, thinking of little black Oliver who'd been in her class in grade eight, and who'd died in the cell over two years ago now. (182)

The issue of Aboriginal deaths in custody is referenced a number of times in *Steam Pigs*, and Sue sometimes wears a T-shirt declaring, "Stop Black Deaths in Custody" (135).

At the end of the novel, Sue walks through Brisbane's Fortitude Valley and observes a group of Murries hanging out on some steps,

> one of them begging with a weather eye open for the law, the rest passing a bottle around and laughing at their countryman's lack of success … Sue found herself wondering morbidly which of

them would die next, would it be another "accident" in the park, a drunken brawl that got "out of hand" ... another suspicious death in custody. (243)

Remembering the lack of opportunity in Eagleby, Sue thinks, "And now I'm a million miles away from all that ... living in luxury in my flat that the government's paying for, and half me life spent listening to people at uni talk about blackfella's problems or poor people's problems" (243). Thanks to being "saved" by Kerry and Rachel, Sue occupies a liminal space in society somewhere between the Indigenous people begging on the streets and the privileged whites who are her peers at university.

In her autobiographical essay "Black on Black," Lucashenko declares, "Racism isn't in the past" (114). While counseling Sue regarding what to expect once she starts university, Kerry claims that whites will dismiss Sue as "just angry, or politically naïve, or a thousand other things, before they'll admit that Murries can be as smart and capable as them. The racism's engrained into us Sue, and it takes constant weeding-out" (190). Sue considers the fact that just up the road from her new flat, the notorious Boggo Road jail is "full of black women and poor women and addicted women and women who snapped from being bashed one time too many" (243). Reflecting angrily on a debate at university over a case in which an Indigenous woman was released after serving six years of a life sentence, Sue wonders how she refrained "from slamming this white bitch's teeth down her throat" and thinks how easy it is for outsiders to argue that being released after serving just six years of a life sentence is a miscarriage of justice: "Try living it from inside those white walls of time. Try being black and being in jail when you walk out the gate, born jailed, live jailed, die jailed" (243-44). In another of her essays, "Many Prisons," Lucashenko argues that mainstream Australian society "does not understand Aboriginal people. White people and most non-Aboriginal people of colour in Australia have almost no idea what it is to be Aboriginal" (140).

Although Lucashenko presents the treatment of Indigenous people by non-Indigenous Australians extremely negatively, she is not afraid to address problems within the Indigenous community, such as domestic violence, child abuse, alcohol and drug abuse, and racism against whites and other groups. During a brawl in a pub car park, Roger calls Sue's conquest, Carlos, a "'wog,'" and moments later, when Sue fights the woman Roger has been flirting with, she calls her a "'fucken ugly old white slut'" (83). Thus, although Roger and Sue are often the victims of racism, they are racist themselves. Sue's racism is revealed during the Townsville section of the novel, when she refers to her brother's girlfriend as a "'dirty white slut'" and during a confrontation with a trucker, who she calls a "fucken ugly white cunt" (175, 177). After moving to West End, Sue thinks of her flat-mate Melinda as "a stiff whitey" (223).

Like other Australian suburban novels, *Steam Pigs* contains references to the bush and the natural environment. Although Lucashenko does not directly address the environmental degradation caused by suburban development, she depicts the bush as the true site of Indigenous culture and a place to which characters long to escape. During her early days in Eagleby, Sue creates a garden outside Dave's house, in a "largely futile" attempt "to coax greenery into the Eagleby dust and rocks" (16). However, Sue does not create a traditional suburban garden consisting of English-style flowerbeds; rather, she plants indigenous species and experiences "solace and serenity" as she waters her garden: "When she looked after her bottle-brush trees it was like she was in another world, earthspeaking" (16-17). After Sue moves in with Roger, she worries that her indigenous plants are not being watered and wonders if they will survive the summer (54). Here, the indigenous plants clearly represent both Sue's own plight and the future of Australia's Indigenous people.

Lucashenko presents the bush as a site of escape and renewal, especially for the suburban Indigenous characters. While contemplating Dave's sorrow over being abandoned by his wife of eight years, Sue thinks, "Man, you wanna take a trip out bush, get your head clear again" (25). Similarly, Sue thinks that if Roger "spends some time out of the city he'll settle down ... stop having these periodic fits of depression that come over him, stop smoking [marijuana] so much and ease up on Kirk too" (55). The narrator reveals that Sue possesses "great faith in the recuperative powers of the bush" and believes that if a person can "listen to the early morning magpies, or see the sun dawning on dew-wet grass without feeling something holy," they may as well shoot themselves in the head (55). After fighting with Sue, Roger thinks he should "head out west away from the bloody cities and drama, go bush" (112). Although Lucashenko does not directly address the destruction of the bush due to the construction of suburban streets and houses, she explicitly addresses the issue of land ownership and Indigenous history.

During a scene in which Roger drives into the city from Beenleigh, past the suburbs of Springwood, Rochedale, Eight Mile Plains, and Mt. Gravatt, the narrator notes that the region is Yuggera country (111-112).[9] Lucashenko explicitly depicts suburbia as occupying Indigenous land; however, she does not depict suburbia as having replaced Yuggera country, but as existing on top of it, as an overlay, so that the true history and identity of the land exists underneath, visible to those who possess Indigenous knowledge. Lucashenko has obviously thought deeply about the relationship between suburbia and Indigenous ownership and belonging. In her essay "Gender, Genre and Geography," Lucashenko claims that "the vast majority" of Australians "are still struggling with the concept of the land of the quarter-acre block and the great Australian dream" (50). Lucashenko argues that Indigenous people who "know the land and sea" allow it to "enter into" them and possess "the potential to experience healing and wholeness"; moreover, they

> don't need to know about quarter acre blocks because geography doesn't come in that, it comes in whacking great slabs and plateaus and beaches. It comes in valleys and ranges. It comes with responsibilities attached and it comes with the ability to teach us how to live correctly if we are humble enough to recognise our true significance in relation to it. (50)

Here, Lucashenko clearly argues that suburbia divides Indigenous land into discrete pieces that makes it difficult for people to appreciate the scale of the natural environment and to forge strong connections with it. Moreover, she rejects the iconic suburban quarter-acre block as an artificial division of land.

Throughout *Steam Pigs*, Sue struggles with issues of belonging in several senses: namely, belonging to her family, belonging in working class suburbia, belonging to the Indigenous community, and belonging to Indigenous land. Near the beginning of the novel, Sue admits she belongs in Eagleby, but later adopts inner-Brisbane as home. Walking through the inner suburbs of Brisbane, Sue remembers "Anyday Story" and sees the city "through different, more confident eyes," realizing "for the first time" that she can claim it "as her own, [as] a part of her life and her psyche" (239-40). Sue remembers that the land Brisbane occupies is Murri land,

> whatever they'd done to it or put on it. It was Yuggera country ... and that meant she had a connection to work from. No matter what monied artifacts they put on the surface, her belonging roots reached deep into the soil, anchoring her like an old rivergum. (240)

Gelder and Salzman argue that Sue's evolving Indigenous identity is itself "a form of belonging" that is manifested as "a land claim on the city itself, as if it is both her destination and her traditional home" (*Celebration* 60). Sue's efforts to establish belonging in Yuggera country, which has been invaded, stolen and developed by the dominant non-Indigenous society, reflect what Baker and Worby identify as the contemporary, post-Mabo struggles in Australian society "over land and its meanings and values" (19). However, since Sue grew up in Townsville and does not know which country her Indigenous ancestors belonged to, her claim to belong in Yuggera country is questionable. By Sue's logic, any Indigenous person can belong to any land that was occupied before 1788 by Indigenous people. However, the reality is much more complicated, since each Indigenous group, such as the Waka Waka or Bundjalung, had their own country, and members of other Indigenous groups did not belong to that country. Yuggera country is not Sue's "traditional home," to use Gelder and Salzman's phrase. Sue chooses to adopt Yuggera country as her country since she needs a place to which she can anchor herself.

Henderson argues that Sue's escape from outer suburbia to "'bohemian' inner-city West End" resembles "a classic bourgeois trajectory of self-improvement" and "the feminist quest for personal liberation away from the deserts of the outer-suburbs" (78). However, Henderson suggests that the narrative is complicated by "Sue's growing awareness of her Aboriginal identity and its specific history of space," since she simultaneously occupies Yuggera country and the Brisbane of the white feminists and yuppies (78). In "Black on Black," Lucashenko addresses colonialism and Indigenous land ownership, arguing that labeling Australia "post-colonial" is "the biggest crock of shit I've been asked to swallow in a long time," since two years before the publication of her article, the government of Queensland "used its legislative powers to put 12 percent of the state off-limits to native title claims … is that post-colonialism? Cos, if it is, it feels a lot like colonialism to the Indigenous owners" (115). Likewise, Huggan states that even though Australia is "postcolonial with respect to its former British colonizers, it remains very much colonial or, perhaps more accurately, *neo*-colonial it its treatment of its own indigenous peoples" (*Australian Literature* 27, original emphasis).

Steam Pigs is an innovative and confrontational novel that addresses many of the most pressing issues in contemporary Australian society, including Indigenous identity, land ownership and belonging; domestic violence; gender and sexuality; alcohol and drug abuse; and racism. However, the novel ultimately adopts a traditional approach by presenting suburbia as a locale that should be rejected in favor of the inner city, which serves to perpetuate the anti-suburban tradition and detracts from the novel's potential to provide a new model for engagement with suburbia. Moreover, the fact that Sue is "saved" and enlightened by urban whites, rather than her fellow Indigenous Australians, sends a troubling message about the relationship between Indigenous and non-Indigenous Australians, echoing the banishment of the Indigenous girl's ghost in *Cloudstreet* by the birth of a white child. *Steam Pigs* suggests that the solutions for Indigenous working-class, suburban social problems are to be provided by white university-educated residents of the inner city, a relationship that perpetuates the colonial relationship between white and Indigenous Australians.

Subtopia: Suburbia, Radicalism, Terrorism and Expatriation

A.L. McCann's novel *Subtopia* (2005) is one of the most recently published examples of suburban fiction addressed in this study.[10] Like Lucashenko's *Steam Pigs*, published eight years earlier, McCann's novel combines innovative and provocative subject matter with an overwhelmingly negative depiction of suburbia. However, unlike Lucashenko, McCann does not address issues of Indigenous identity or the struggle for both Indigenous and non-Indigenous Australians to develop a strong sense of belonging, ignoring several of the most important contemporary issues in Australian society. Nevertheless, as Peter Pierce argues, McCann's novel is a groundbreaking addition to Australian literature, a "bold and adventurous" novel that possesses a range that "makes most contemporary Australian fiction seem parochial" ("*Subtopia*" 1). In his article on *Subtopia*, Wetherell argues that the novel deserves high praise (175). Despite its fascinating engagement with radicalism, terrorism and expatriation, *Subtopia* is yet another addition to the body of anti-suburban fiction, drawing from and perpetuating an anti-suburban tradition that is now more than four decades old. Moreover, given McCann's extensive knowledge of Australian literature, especially suburban fiction, the anti-suburbanism of the novel is probably not accidental.

Andrew McCann was born in Adelaide in 1966 and grew up in the Melbourne suburb of East Brighton. McCann earned an arts degree from the University of Melbourne, followed by a Ph.D. in English at Cornell University. McCann returned to Australia in 1996 and taught at the University of Queensland and the University of Melbourne before accepting his current position at Dartmouth College, where he is Associate Professor of English.[11] He has published extensively on Australian and British literature and is the leading critic on suburbia in Australian literature, and thus is often cited in this book. He publishes fiction as A.L. McCann, partly to distinguish himself from fellow Australian novelist Andrew McGahan (Griffin 1).[12]

McCann's debut novel, *The White Body of Evening* (2002), won the 2002 Aurealis Award for Excellence in Horror Fiction. McCann's decision to publish his second novel, *Subtopia*, with Melbourne's independent Vulgar Press, after publishing his first novel with HarperCollins, reflects his disenchantment with the mainstream Australian publishing industry. On its website, the Vulgar Press prominently declares that it is "dedicated to the publication of working-class and other radical forms of writing."[13] McCann has expressed his views on the publishing industry in interviews, and, most memorably, in his essay entitled "How To Fuck a Tuscan Garden." In response to a question from Kara Nicholson regarding his intended audience for *Subtopia*, McCann claims that the novel

> will appeal to disgruntled Generation-X types and to everyone else bored with national allegories, happy endings and the idea that we have to feel good about crap. It is also a novel about radical experience (or its impossibility) and the ghosts of the late sixties and early seventies. So it is pitched at the left more generally. (1)

As an academic who grew up in Melbourne's suburbs and has written extensively about suburbia in Australian fiction, McCann possesses a deep knowledge of his material. The novel's themes, including suburbia, expatriation, male friendship, consumerism, radical politics, music, terrorism, and the gothic, overlap McCann's academic expertise. Michelle Griffin notes that Subtopia draws heavily from an honors seminar McCann taught at the University of Melbourne entitled "*Suburbia in Post-War Fiction*," and McCann has stated that fiction allows him to explore his ideas "in a way that is liberated from the narrowness of academic writing" (Griffin 1). When asked about the novel's setting, McCann states that he has spent most of his life in cities (Nicholson 1). Thus, the suburban setting of the novel reflects both McCann's life experience and his academic interests and expertise. It is fitting that McCann has been mistaken for McGahan, as *Subtopia* could easily have been marketed as grunge fiction due to the characters' drug and alcohol abuse, the urban settings, and the graphic descriptions of sexual acts and organs.[14]

McCann is clearly uninterested in pleasing nationalists and satisfying mainstream literary tastes. Not only does *Subtopia* avoid common themes for Australian novels, such as first contact, exploration, the bush, and national identity, McCann mocks celebrity authors such as David Malouf, Thomas Keneally and Peter Carey through the figure of David Murray-Merry.[15] McCann takes many risks in *Subtopia*, not just in terms of subject matter and setting, but also with his narrator and plot. The protagonist and first-person narrator, Julian Farrell, is not likeable or worthy of admiration; he is sarcastic, passive, and lacks ambition. Wetherell describes Julian as an "exceptionally humourless young man" and "a melancholy, colourless type who somehow manages to be engaging" (175). *Subtopia* begins in 1977 in Moorabbin, a south-eastern suburb of Melbourne, after a brief prologue set in Berlin reveals that Martin Bernhard, one of the central characters, is dead, and that Julian is "Sick, angry, unattractive" and "pushing thirty" (10).

In his article "Subtopia or Sunnyside?," Wetherell describes Moorabbin as located in

> Melbourne's vast sandbelt, a score or more of suburbs straddling the Nepean Highway from, say, Brighton down towards Frankston. Moorabbin is flat, relatively featureless, and bisected by a multi-lane highway. Like much of suburbia throughout the Western world, it looks unsurprising though not unpleasant. It is neither posh nor down-at-heel. (174)

Eleven-year-old Julian meets Martin, a rebel from a broken family, moments before witnessing a symbolic auto accident. Martin quickly becomes the most important person in Julian's life and their relationship

A New Generation Perpetuates the Anti-Suburban Tradition 169

unites the novel, despite its tenuous nature. The novel is divided into four sections, each carrying titles indicating the major themes: "Notes from Suburbia," "Free Radicals," "Your Sickness is a Weapon," and "Dislocations." Within these sections, the action moves from Melbourne to Berlin, then to New York and back to Melbourne, before concluding with a return to Berlin.

Discussing the international movements within the novel, McCann states: "The novel's movement from Melbourne to Berlin is partly about an interest in this fantasy of a radical, politicized city that is sharply juxtaposed to suburbia" (Nicholson 1). About half of the novel is set in suburbia, including the Melbourne suburbs Moorabbin, Elwood, Brighton, St. Kilda, Malvern, Fitzroy and Carlton, and an unnamed suburb of New York City located in Queens, all of which McCann depicts in an overwhelmingly negative manner. Like Johnston's *My Brother Jack* and Lucashenko's *Steam Pigs*, *Subtopia* contains many explicitly anti-suburban passages and presents suburbia in a one-dimensional manner. Almost half of the novel takes place in Germany, while a little less than a third is set in the USA. In addition to covering a lot of ground geographically, the novel spans three decades, from the late seventies in Moorabbin, to the early eighties in St. Kilda, the late eighties in Berlin, and the early nineties in Queens.

Both the plot and subject matter of *Subtopia* reveal the influence of Malouf's *Johnno* and Johnston's *My Brother Jack*; all three novels are explicitly anti-suburban and feature protagonists who reject suburbia and escape to Europe. Additionally, the relationship between Julian and Martin is remarkably similar to that of Johnno and Dante in *Johnno* and David and Jack in *My Brother Jack*. Julian receives a copy of *My Brother Jack* from his father and strongly identifies with the novel's "near-hysterical hatred" of suburbia, states that he had not previously realized one could write a book about hating suburbia, and credits the novel with consolidating his dreams of escape (56). Pierce argues that the novel is partly "a grunge version" of *Johnno* ("*Subtopia*" 1). Although McCann's direct, gritty and often-graphic prose style is unlike that of Malouf, *Subtopia*, like *Johnno*, is packed with references to European writers, including Dostoevsky, Ibsen, Camus, Dickens, Fielding, Trollope, Kant, Hesse and Adorno. Like Dante and Johnno, Julian's intellectual life revolves around European texts. Since only a third of the novel takes place in Australia and the narrator is ambivalent about his nationality, lacks a strong desire to return home, and rejects mainstream Australian society, the novel is more transnational than Australian.

The anti-suburbanism of *Subtopia* is already evident in the brief prologue, which, despite being set in Berlin, refers to the "wide, flat suburbs of Melbourne's south," where one has to "concentrate hard to effect even the most minimal kind of transformation" (10). The first chapter begins with Julian recounting an act he witnessed at the age of ten beside the swimming pool in a suburban backyard: his uncle, nicknamed the Silver Fox, molests Julian's nine-year-old sister Connie by slipping his hand inside her bathing suit (13). Not only does McCann associate suburbia with child sexual abuse from the outset, he also associates suburbia with the Silver Fox: a lecherous, egocentric character who works in "real estate and development," races a yacht named *Moby Dick*, keeps a stash of pornography, and evokes an "easy, leisured lifestyle," replete with a "house in Hampton, the pool, a pine sauna, a big Ford Fairlane" (14, 17). The narrator encourages the reader to despise the Silver Fox, who is conflated with suburban ideals, and thus despise suburbia too.

Julian describes his childhood home in Moorabbin as "a brick-veneer box with paper-thin fibro walls" (20), a description echoing the anti-suburban description of brick-veneer houses in White's *Riders in the Chariot*, Johnston's *My Brother Jack*, Malouf's *Johnno*, Winton's *Cloudstreet*, and Lucashenko's *Steam Pigs*. Martin also lives in "a brown brick box," although his home has "fallen into disrepair" and is "surrounded by giant weeds" that have "taken over the lawn ... The backyard was worse. Waist-high grass concealed all sorts of junk ... The yard looked like the ruins of an ancient society reclaimed by wild, untamed vegetation" (24-25). McCann's description of Martin's backyard hints at the presence of indigenous vegetation and suggests the bush; it reveals a suburban backyard that is not controlled and does not conform to suburban norms and ideals, thus symbolizing Martin's radicalism.Although Julian, unlike Martin, is not a radical, he does not meet the standards of behavior expected of a suburban male and refuses to conform to suburban ideals. His Aunt Lois makes fun of his pale complexion and urges him to spend more time in the sun. Julian's cousin Danny confides that his father, the Silver Fox, thinks Julian is physically unfit and a negative influence:

> These assumptions of healthy, Australian boyhood, against which I so manifestly failed, wormed their way into me without much resistance. I had a vision of myself skulking away into the darkness of my room like a cockroach, hiding from the sun, hiding from the vistas of health and vitality that populated the world beyond me. (28)

Julian gives in to expectations for a time and distances himself from Martin, whom Julian describes as "the one person more physically unfit for life than I was. He was uglier, more awkward and much worse at sport" (28).

Julian thinks of Australian suburban life in the late 1970s as "an organized culture of distraction" in which his uncle presides "over groups of revelers glued to the TV set, obsessed with epic Davis Cup ties, fifth sets that never ended, or the high drama of the centenary test match" (30). Julian recalls that Martin "was already living in a world that was so much broader ... In his midst everything else started to seem trivial, ephemeral or childish" (30). Martin is Julian's window to the wider world and constantly introduces him to ideas and behaviors that he would not have encountered within the confines of his own sheltered middle class suburban existence. Towards the end of 1977, Julian and Martin start spending as much time as possible away from home, wandering the streets of Moorabbin. However, they find the "deserted" suburban streets "every bit as claustrophobic as the houses" they try to escape (36).

In one of the novel's many anti-suburban passages, Julian describes Moorabbin as populated by "Red-brick dumps along the highway, [and] filthy snotty kids in the commission houses," prompting "the intolerable feeling of being stuck in some sort of corpseworld – an intractable and obstinate suburban expanse that could survive any aspiration pitted against it" (36). Wetherell notes that here Julian recalls his view of Moorabbin in 1977, when he was eleven years old, and argues that at such an age "boredom with one's environs is probably endemic, and neither driver's licence nor wider opportunities have come along to lift it" (174-75). However, Wetherell also points out that Julian's "later impressions of the suburb are no more positive" and questions whether Moorabbin is "really as bad as it is described" in *Subtopia*, stating, "I live in the sand-belt myself, in an equally flat and featureless suburb only a few kilometers from Moorabbin, and had not, till I read *Subtopia*, considered that I might be living in corpseworld or near it" (175, 174). Jay Thompson, also a Melbourne resident, provides an alternative interpretation, writing that he finds McCann's descriptions of suburbia "enthralling," "because they really capture the sense of banality, repetition and emptiness that characterises many a suburban existence" (279). However, although Thompson subscribes to the anti-suburban intellectual tradition here, he later admits, "the portrait of suburban life offered in *Subtopia* might ultimately be *too* bleak" (279, original emphasis). McCann's narrator occasionally slips into an academic tone and comments on suburbia in a manner more appropriate for an essay than a novel. During one of Julian's diatribes against suburbia, he declares:

> Events in suburbia seldom generate the dynamism that can propel us on to something else. Rather, they tend to stasis, like a boring, plotless movie in which the camera seems to limp from one moment to the next, without being able to establish any meaningful or vital connection between scenes. I guess this lack of dynamism is part of the point of the suburb. Despite the multitude of little traumas that cluster around it, suburban experience is exactly the opposite of historical experience, which is big on making connec-

tions, big on building narratives out of whatever events it can lay its hands on. The suburb is history at a standstill. (40-41)

Passages such as these, written in a more formal style than the rest of the novel, suggest to the reader that Julian's views on suburbia are really McCann's views. McCann certainly does not give the reader any reason to believe otherwise, and there are no passages celebrating suburbia to offset Julian's constant negativity. Julian's repeated description of suburbia as a "corpseworld" perpetuates the anti-suburban tradition, and, given his knowledge of both the fiction and criticism of suburbia, McCann probably does so deliberately.

Martin is the first of the main characters to escape Moorabbin. At the end of 1977, his mother remarries and the reconfigured family moves to the inner suburb of Elwood, adjacent to Elsternwick, Johnston's childhood suburb and the setting for *My Brother Jack*. Martin's mother Carol and her new husband Jeff purchase "a large but dilapidated Federation-style house" (41). Julian notes that within twenty years the Elwood house would be "worth a small fortune," once Elwood became "another key location in the Antipodean fantasy of 'cosmopolitan' living," but argues that "in the late seventies Elwood was just eccentric, a place that jarred against the suburban desire for neat, well-organised spaces" (42). Thus, Julian characterizes the move from Moorabbin into Elwood as a move out of suburbia into a more exciting and liberated space.

Martin's house in Elwood is reminiscent of the Turleys' Toorak mansion in *My Brother Jack*. When Julian first visits Martin's Elwood house, he expresses a delight and enthusiasm for its difference to the suburban norm, echoing David's sentiments regarding the Turleys' mansion:

> It was a wonderful, ramshackle place, quickly filling up with Carol's flourishing penchant for *objets d'art* ... bronze statuettes, tinted glass, antique wood, cut crystal and elaborate chandeliers ...

> But it was a shambles as well. Martin left food all over the place. No one seemed to notice. (42)

Martin's Elwood house, just like the Turley mansion in *My Brother Jack*, Dante's South Brisbane childhood home in *Johnno*, the Cloud Street house in Winton's novel, and Kerry and Rachel's Queenslander in *Steam Pigs*, serves as a signifier of cosmopolitan difference, in opposition to the brick-veneer "boxes" of suburbia. In *Subtopia* and the aforementioned novels, the larger, older home, usually located close to the city centre, is presented as superior to the newer brick-veneer homes of outer suburbia.

Julian's escape from suburbia begins when he starts attending Melbourne High in third form; "a boys-only school that was a longish train-ride away in South Yarra" (like Toorak, an exclusive inner suburb) (48). Once at Melbourne High, Julian finds a new group of friends who are "all equally dislocated, all travelling in from equally far-flung suburbs" (48). After school, Julian and his friends meet in the city and watch movies or play video games (48). Thus, Julian spends most of his leisure time in the city, only returning to suburbia at night. However, Julian's escape from suburbia is incomplete, and during the school holidays he hangs out with Martin in Moorabbin. The pair find themselves back where they were three years earlier, "wandering through the empty streets" with their "furtive longings … virtually crushed … by the world of mute, inexpressive detail spreading out from the highway, ossified in the bitumen, the gutters, the little fences, the red-brick tedium" (51). Both Julian and Martin view Australian culture as inferior, derivative and oppressive. Julian is disgusted by the consumerism and hedonism that he sees as representative of Australian culture. Julian and Martin despise the Australian obsession with sport and Martin declares, "'Australia is a fucking hole … the most vacuous place on the planet'" (142), echoing Johnno's criticisms of Australia in Malouf's novel.

Having noticed Julian reading Ibsen, Camus and Graham Greene, Julian's father gives him a copy of *My Brother Jack* before he begins university. During the summer between high school and university, Julian reads *The Brothers Karamazov* instead of going to the beach, and looking back on that time, states,

> Even then it was clear that reading these books had become a way of evading the narrowness of my surroundings, a refuge, a means of escape, a flightpath into a purely individualised world that sheltered me from the outside ... it was *My Brother Jack* and Johnston's love affair with Greece that consolidated my fantasy of flight and gave it tangible coordinates. (56)

Julian's hopes of escape centre on Carlton and Fitzroy, inner suburbs which he associates with "cafes, bohemia, [and] counter-culture" (57). Julian enrolls at the University of Melbourne, in Carlton, and thus spends his days in one of the hubs of the counter-culture.

Walking through the city towards Flinders Street station during his first week of university, Julian reflects that he will soon "be back in the void of the suburbs, [amongst] miles of brick veneer, asbestos and scalloped roof-tiles spreading to the bay on one side, and to swampy, semi-rural wastelands and landfills on the other" (65). In a passage describing a train journey that echoes (in reverse) the section of *My Brother Jack* where David takes the train into the city after learning of Jessica Wray's murder, and which contains some of *Subtopia*'s most anti-suburban sentiments, Julian describes traveling past

> the railyards, the MCG, the platforms of Richmond station ... Old factories, graffiti, the Rosella sign, sawtooth visions of industrial decay leading over the river to South Yarra. Then Toorak, Hawksburn, Armadale, Malvern, the Caulfield racecourse, shopping strips, speeding automobiles, one house after another ... the ghosts of tired commuters dozing off with their newspapers and their paperback novels. Lassitude, boredom, a multitude of obstinate details crowding out thought at the arse-end of the working day, lonely wage-slaves trudging home to the sluggish rhythms of commerce, goods and services, professional intercourse, mass transport, furtive cravings, gross domestic product and a leisurely game of golf on the weekend ... For a moment I felt lost, utterly

lost, a fragile bit of biology in a huge system of roads and rail and random associations, about to vanish altogether with the compulsive shuddering of the train, about to wake up on the other side of the darkened glass, a transparent reflection of myself. A ghost. (65-66)

In typical anti-suburban fashion, Julian associates the physical infrastructure of suburbia, capitalism, and industry with slavery, thwarted desires, disintegration, the loss of agency, and, ultimately, death. For Julian, a fulfilling, healthy and interesting life is impossible in suburbia. He constantly depicts capitalism and consumerism as a disease, conflating them with his fear of cancer, and repeatedly refers to suburbia as the "corpseworld."

In an attempt to transcend what he perceives to be his mundane suburban existence, Julian develops a fascination with radicalism and terrorism. *Subtopia* incorporates radicals and terrorists from the 1970s as heroes and objects of desire. McCann's depiction of radicalism and terrorism opposes the dominant rhetoric of post-9/11 Western culture, which overwhelmingly portrays terrorism as an evil perpetrated by Muslim, Middle-Eastern, anti-Western males. In contrast, McCann's radicals and terrorists are European or of European descent, the majority are female, and none of them are motivated by religious extremism. McCann's terrorists resist the dominant ideology, rather than trying to impose an ideology on others. Julian is seduced by radicalism and terrorism during his adolescence. He recalls memories of "West German terrorists, women mostly," whom he associates with a story he hears "about kidnappers in Europe cutting off the ear of a boy they were holding for ransom" (29).

Over the next two decades, Julian becomes obsessed with half a dozen characters who are either radicals or terrorists, including Martin, Ulrike Meinhof, Ingrid Gutmann, Anja and Penny Gibson. Additionally, Julian continually fantasizes about terrorism, either in the form of large-scale terrorist attacks on Melbourne and New York, or small-scale attacks that he perpetrates. Julian's fascination with radicalism and terrorism is inher-

A New Generation Perpetuates the Anti-Suburban Tradition 177

ently anti-suburban; it is driven by a desire to transcend his suburban existence and transform himself into a person who is decidedly *not* suburban, middle-class, passive, law-abiding and responsible. Moreover, as David Sornig argues, Julian conflates his desire for transcendence through radicalism and terrorism with his sexual desires for Ulrike Meinhof, Ingrid, Penny, Anja and Martin (68).

Julian's first contact with a radical occurs in 1977 when he meets Martin moments before they witness a car accident. McCann's description of the accident could easily be that of a terrorist attack: "The sound of crushed metal and broken glass exploded through the lethargy of the afternoon, hit us like a shock wave, and then jangled away into eerie silence" (21). Martin's reaction is to comment that the spectacle is "Just like a film" before proceeding to assist the victim, while Julian remains mute and idle (22). From the dramatic beginning of the friendship through to Martin's death in Berlin nearly two decades later, Julian and Martin occupy opposite positions of passivity and activity. Pierce argues that Julian is drawn to Martin by his own "melancholy and obsessive" personality (1). Similarly, Sornig argues that Martin is Julian's "romanticized, ghosted Other" and that their friendship gives Julian the opportunity to vicariously live dangerously without having to "move beyond his own conventionality and safety" (68).

McCann constructs Martin's status as a radical through a series of actions that consistently contradict, oppose or actively resist cultural norms. Soon after they meet, Julian and Martin discuss military history while shooting toy tanks with an air rifle in Martin's suburban backyard. Martin claims that the single biggest death toll in World War Two was inflicted by the Allied bombing of Dresden, adopting a position sympathetic to the traditional enemy (26). Julian states that prior to meeting Martin, who shoots and melts toy U.S. Marines, he was unaware that America could be the subject of animosity (26). Martin's radical ideas and sympathies are constantly paired with real and threatened violence. When Julian's cousin physically confronts Martin during a game of backyard cricket, Martin threatens to burn his father's yacht (27). On another occasion, angry with Julian for ignoring him, Martin grabs a beer bottle, smashes the base against a gutter, and chases Julian with his improvised weapon (30). Martin goes so far as to imitate actual terrorist tactics when he makes a Molotov cocktail. Claiming that he is practicing to bomb the Silver Fox's yacht, he ignites the weapon and hurls it against the back wall of a suburban milk bar, where it explodes.

Julian and Martin's paths diverge when Julian transfers to Melbourne High and Martin moves to Elwood. Once Julian starts university, the two are reacquainted through mutual friends in St. Kilda, where Martin shares a flat with his German girlfriend, Anja, lives off the dole, and spends his time drinking and taking drugs. Julian is drawn to St. Kilda by the presence of political radicals, punks, goths, prostitutes and drug addicts, all of whom lend the community an aura of rebellion and counter-culture cache, in contrast to the middle-class restraint of Moorabbin. Julian admits that he hangs out in St. Kilda hoping to bump into Martin,

> partly so that I could prove to myself that we were still friends, and partly because I knew I wanted to cross the line, the border between me and the delirious renunciation of that small, constricted self that was always so threatened by Martin's nihilistic presence. (97-98)

Julian perceives Martin's radical lifestyle as a means of escaping his own boring conventionality, which he sees as a product of suburbia.

While drunk and stoned at a party, Julian sees a wanted poster for the West German terrorist Ulrike Meinhof and overhears another student explaining her significance. Julian soon declares he is "in love with the spectre of Ulrike Meinhof ... Grubby, secreted images of war, terror, prison and sex flickered through the darkness" (71). However, despite the seductiveness of the terrorist, Julian begins a relationship with Sally, a fellow student who is middle-class, suburban, responsible, and academically ambitious.[16] After the party, Sally takes Julian back to her parents' house in the upper-middle-class suburb of Malvern. Julian describes the house as understated and tasteful, lacking "the cluttered catastrophe of popular aesthetics ... found in the 'burbs" (72). Sally's family's house is a study in "considered minimalism: polished wood, a dancing Shiva on the mantel, a decorative ceramic dish painted like an arabesque. There was something generous about the place as well: high ceilings, Persian rugs, deep comfortable couches" (72). The positive description of Sally's home is an unusual departure within the novel, since it suggests that not all of suburbia deserves derision, while the cosmopolitan interior decorations and furnishings are reminiscent of both Martin's Elwood house and Kerry and Rachel's Queenslander in *Steam Pigs*.

In the morning, Julian encounters Sally's mother reading Germaine Greer's *The Female Eunuch* and soon learns that she is writing a thesis at Monash University on "Hippies, feminism, [and] the counter-culture" (72). Julian is depressed by the thought of Sally's mother writing a thesis on Greer "and something called 'the counter-culture,'" since Greer "grew up in some bloody awful place on the highway, got out, exported her talent, and never came back" (73). Julian claims that Greer's life "repeated the great tropes of Antipodean longing: education, exodus, envy" and proceeds to disparage her and Clive James, two of Australia's most famous expatriates, observing that James' "unique genius seemed to consist of the fact that he lived in Britain" and quips that the pair were probably "relieved to have escaped to the centre of an empire that had died half a century earlier" (73). Julian's attitude towards Greer is curious, since her escape from suburbia and subsequent success abroad is precisely the trajectory he would like to follow.[17]

When Julian recalls waiting at Malvern station after his first night at Sally's, he indulges in more anti-suburbanism, describing the Sunday timetable as "infrastructure running down in half-hour blocks," which he associates with "deserted stations, sparse, vandalized carriages decked out in olive green and a pale, jaundiced yellow, housing-commission mothers with swollen ankles and varicose veins hobbling about on budgets, lugging their shopping back from obscure outposts of low-grade consumerism" (74). When Julian arrives back in Moorabbin, he describes it as "another post-apocalyptic morning. The shops and houses were still there, but the place made you imagine that a hydrogen bomb had cleared the streets, leaving a remnant race of stunted, industrial types that lived in burrows under the buckling cement pavement" (75). Wetherell argues that this passage stands out from "the novel's universally negative references to the suburb" and "tends to make the reader think that both narrator and writer wish that a hydrogen bomb *would* clear its streets … McCann … is all but calling for drastic action – drop the big one now!" (180, original emphasis). Wetherell notes that the anti-suburban passages in *Subtopia* make him laugh: "not, I suspect, in any way that the author or his narrator might wish to prompt in readers … I can't help thinking that Moorabbin will let this hysterically slung mud slide off its ample back – if it hits the target at all" (179). Wetherell makes two important points here: first, that the anti-suburbanism of the novel is so extreme at times that it is absurd; and second, that most of the residents of Moorabbin will never read the novel or care about the way their suburb is depicted.

Julian's constant conflation of cancer and consumerism pervades his negative depiction of the suburbs. On one occasion, he describes suburbia as

> silent brick-veneer crags multiplying like rogue cells across the southern suburbs, a giant tumour composed of brick and asbestos cement, microscopic fibres … wafting fatally about … in great, invisible clouds, the petrol fumes and exhaust seeping into my liver, the electromagnetic fields of the overhead wires turning the cells of my body into sticky repositories for the countless carcinogens. (75)

Julian imagines that the suburbs are literally killing him. While living in East St. Kilda, a drunk and stoned Julian lies on his bed and sees "images of carcinogens proliferating" as he imagines "dark, shaded groves … being bulldozed, one after the other, to clear space for more sun-drenched brick-veneer and fibro subdivisions" (106). Julian's visions of bulldozers destroying the natural environment recalls Johnston's *My Brother Jack*,

A New Generation Perpetuates the Anti-Suburban Tradition 181

the work of suburban fiction most overtly acknowledged as an influence in *Subtopia*, and other suburban novels that contain images of bulldozers razing the bush to make way for new suburbs, such as White's *Riders in the Chariot*, Winton's *Cloudstreet* and Peter Carey's *The Tax Inspector*.

During his undergraduate years, Julian's frequent companion is Sally's high school classmate Penny Gibson, from whom he borrows the word "corpseworld" (81). Penny is famous for having sex with her literature professor, revels in her reputation as the "departmental vamp," and hails from Brighton, "an affluent but very provincial suburb" (80, 79).[18] Penny's reputation as a radical largely rests upon her sexual escapades, her appearance – "Boots, torn fishnet stockings, moth-eaten jumpers and worn suede" (80) – her obsession with Nick Cave,[19] and her penchant for hanging out in St. Kilda. Julian and Penny spend their weekends "watching junkies and prostitutes drifting along Fitzroy Street as if ... [their] proximity to them could help ... [them] get clear of the burdens of being so terminally middle-class" (81). The two drift apart as Julian becomes more studious and committed to Sally, while Penny becomes a heroin addict and prostitute, eventually dying of an overdose. Thus, it is life in the urban, alternative inner suburb that destroys Penny, rather than middle-class suburbia.

Although Julian is constantly attracted to radical ideas and individuals, and does not embrace suburban ideals, there is little to afford him the status of a radical, apart from "long, untidy hair ... army pants, a tattered shirt" and a Polish solidarity badge (64). The solidarity badge impresses Sally on their first meeting, during which she touches it "as if it were a talisman" (62), and prompts Martin to scoff, "Fuck ... You're a radical" (61). Julian refuses to join Martin in a protest against an American warship simply because he is politically apathetic; he studies diligently at university, completing an honors thesis; he continues to live at home in suburbia with his parents and sister; in short, apart from weekends in St. Kilda dabbling with drugs and alcohol, he lives a comfortable mainstream middle-class suburban life. Meanwhile, Martin stars as an axe-murderer in an amateur pornographic film; plays in a punk band; does not work or study; takes copious quantities of drugs; smokes and drinks to excess; sleeps most of the day; is known around St. Kilda as "The Mongrel"; and lives in a squalid flat with his pierced and dyed German girlfriend, one of his co-stars in the pornographic film.

Julian's most radical action is to attempt to emulate Martin by going on the dole after completing his arts degree, and moving into a shared house in East St. Kilda with an architecture student who insists on being called Satan. Julian describes East St. Kilda as "almost David Meredith-*My Brother Jack* territory" and states that although the house does not have a name like "Avalon," "it looked as if it might as well have" (102). Thus, Julian trades one version of suburbia for another, and one could argue that signing up for the dole after finishing an arts degree is a rite of passage and the expected course of action, rather than resistance to cultural norms, especially in the late 1980s. Moreover, Julian soon finds work in a warehouse, saves a few thousand dollars, and travels to London where he stays in an Earls Court doss house and works as a laborer, following an expatriate path that is so well-worn that it has become a cliché. Even when Julian attempts to break out of his suburban middle class life, he does so in a conventional manner, a fact of which he is well aware:

> The border – we were on one side of it, people like Sally and me, and these people, Penny … Anja … and Martin … were on the other … They were what I had imagined in my vision of exploding bus stops and suburban terror. They were mutants. Free radicals breeding in cells. (101-02)

Moreover, Julian realizes that he will never be able to cross the border and transcend his suburban roots.

After the mandatory stint in London, Julian travels to Berlin to see Martin who has moved there with Anja and is now an unwilling father. In London, Julian heard people rave "about the 'Berlin scene': Bowie and Iggy Pop, Nick Cave … graffiti on the wall, the sniff of world war, Cold

War and genocide" (131). In Berlin, Julian finds Martin living a domestic life filled with dirty nappies and baby-bottles in a tiny flat purchased by Anja's father. In an attempt to resist a bourgeois existence, Martin keeps a mattress in a squat near the Berlin Wall, where he indulges in drugs and escapes his responsibilities. The squat lends Martin some radical credibility, especially as it is located in a neighborhood containing "placards and posters for the PLO, the Autonomen and the Anti-Apartheid movement ... [and] A sparse assortment of punks, lay-about radicals [and] loiterers" (140). Julian is impressed enough to claim that Martin, even as a father, "was still really living on the fringes. Unwashed, a bit pongy, a riot waiting to happen" (145). However, when Julian overstays his welcome and has to spend a night in the squat, he admits that when faced with freezing temperatures and the threat of theft and violence his "utopian fantasies of anarchist squalor [quickly] started to dissipate" (145). Despite the seductiveness of the radical lifestyle, Julian still values middle-class suburban comforts.

While in Berlin, Julian meets Ingrid Gutmann, who quickly becomes his sexual partner and substitute for Ulrike Meinhof. As Sornig puts it, Ingrid is the woman Julian "wishes to be the flesh on the ghost of Ulrike Meinhof" (4). Ingrid establishes her radical credentials by claiming her father was an American soldier who raped her when she visited him in suburban Maryland at the age of fifteen and that she and her former boyfriend were considering joining the Red Army Faction and attended Ulrike Meinhof's funeral. On his first night in Ingrid's bed, Julian fantasizes about "urban guerillas blasting bus stops" (150) and later admits that within less than twenty-four hours he has become intoxicated by the "confluence of sex and politics that [he] projects onto Ingrid" (151).

Believing that Ingrid is a radical involved in clandestine, possibly terrorist activities, Julian fabricates stories to impress her, claiming he torched his uncle's car with kerosene and set off a cigar box full of gunpowder under a police car in rebellion against Australian suburbia, which he tells Ingrid is "'a horrible world,'" a "'facade of sport, leisure and freedom concealing something lurking and ugly'" (157). Julian believes he sees Ingrid pass a package to a woman in an East Berlin bookshop; when he questions her, she claims it is a detonator for a bomb (176, 184). After two claustrophobic months of sex and politics, Julian suspects Ingrid is mentally ill, investigates her past, and calls her sister to stage an intervention. When Ingrid's sister Gabi and her husband Lars arrive, Lars tells Julian that people from the radical group Ingrid is involved with "killed people in Stockholm" (193). However, when Julian visits Ingrid a few years later, she denies involvement in any of the aforementioned activities.

In addition to his relationships, real and imagined, with radicals and terrorists, Julian repeatedly fantasizes about terrorist attacks. Julian's erotic visions of terrorism begin in his youth soon after he questions his father about the Cuban missile crisis. Julian's father, a closet radical, explains "the utopian vision behind the Russian revolution in a way that ... [has Julian] momentarily prepared to call ... [himself] a communist. The hint of resignation in his voice conveyed a melancholic sense of lost opportunity and baffled idealism" (19). Returning home after the party at which he is seduced by the specter of Meinhof, Julian begins

> to fantasize about conflict, crisis and struggle ... a groggy vision of the bus stop outside the station exploding through the funereal calm of the morning. Shattered glass and twisted metal raining down on the pavement. Silence, then sirens, debris strewn across the street, some bleeding bodies bashed about in the wreckage. (76-77)

Julian's fantasy is comprehensive enough to include the aftermath: "line-ups along the streets, boots kicking in doors in the dead of night, guns trained on naked bodies, face down, handcuffed on the floor" (77). Readers will see clear parallels between Julian's imaginings and the erosion of civil liberties in Western societies since 9/11, also reflected in other recent Australian novels, such as Andrew McGahan's *Underground* (2006) and Richard Flanagan's *The Unknown Terrorist* (2006).[20] However, Julian realizes that "the idea that an affluent society could be covertly fascist" is probably "insane," since people are "happy in the suburbs, not oppressed" and thinks of the "backyard barbecue, the Hills hoist and the old shed" as "repositories of shared meaning" (77). This passage is one of the few in the novel that could be interpreted as presenting suburbia in a positive light.

Towards the end of *Subtopia*, when Julian lives with Sally in a suburb of New York City while she writes a doctoral dissertation, he despises the predictability and order of suburbia and yearns for "the filthy squat and the joyous, anarchic squalor of Kreuzberg" (227). Disgusted by the rampant capitalism and excessive consumerism of the United States, Julian fantasizes about a radical strategist, "a Mao or a Lenin," mobilizing the people in mass protests and riots that lead to "the heads of executives paraded on pikes" and angry mobs "charging through the streets" (233). The reality, however, is that Julian spends his days in Queens fighting depression and fears of cancer and trying to write prose in an International House Of Pancakes restaurant. He declares that he is not going to return to Australia, but will become an expatriate, "like Germaine and Clive, doing whatever it is that expats do when they aren't gloating" (214). However, Julian soon hates American life, and later admits he had no idea why he was there, declaring the U.S. is "like a black hole, a centre of cultural and political gravity so intense that it sucks you in and crushes you" (227). When Sally is offered a position as a university lecturer in Melbourne, the couple returns to Australia without hesitation (240-41).

Back in Melbourne, with Penny dead and Martin, Anja and Ingrid in Berlin, Julian finds himself without a radical foil and is unable to successfully reintegrate into Australian society. Julian and Sally rent a house in Carlton, where he is disgusted by "the cretinism of a society obsessed with the wonders of its leisured lifestyle" (244). Julian visits his parents in Moorabbin and describes returning to his home suburb as "like revisiting a hollow in myself, a time that I had repressed or forgotten, or a time that hadn't really happened" (242). Consequently, he returns to Berlin to seek out Ingrid and Martin and make sense of his life. Ingrid has mellowed and put on weight due to prescription medications and Julian accepts the fact that she was never a radical or a terrorist, but suffered from mental illness. More significantly, Julian discovers that Martin has been dead for two years, having developed a brain tumor, undergone surgery, lost many of his mental faculties and motor skills, and committed suicide at the site of a concentration camp. Finally, Julian is forced to confront the fact that his flirtations with radicalism and terrorism are illusory, that he will never achieve transformation, and "Mild discomfort, drowsiness, drunkenness … [and] depression … [are] as close to transformation as … [he is] going to get" (239). After learning of Martin's death, Julian realizes that both he and Martin sought "transformation, metamorphosis, [and] negation"; the difference between them was that Martin was willing "to demolish things if they didn't measure up, and finally he was ready to demolish himself" (10), whereas Julian was unwilling to be an actor rather than an observer.

Despite the fact that Julian's quest for transcendence through radicalism and terrorism ends in failure, and at the conclusion of the novel he settles down to a predictable, comfortable middle-class life with Sally in Carlton, the novel promotes radicalism and rejects mainstream Australian culture. Although McCann does not present radicals and terrorists who succeed in their quest, he depicts the ideals, characteristics and actions of Meinhof, Martin, Penny and Ingrid as more exciting, appealing and worthy of emulation than capitalism, consumerism and suburban life. However, the novel is also simultaneously conservative in its overwhelmingly negative treatment of suburbia, and like Malouf's *Johnno*, Winton's *Cloudstreet* and Lucashenko's *Steam Pigs*, serves to perpetuate the anti-suburban tradition established by Johnston. Although *Steam Pigs* and *Subtopia* are set in different times and places, and the former is a novel with a female Indigenous protagonist written by a female Indigenous author while the later utilizes a white male protagonist and is written by a white male author, the novels are similar in important ways. First, *Steam Pigs* and *Subtopia* are two of the few literary novels published in the past fifteen years that use suburbia as a primary setting; second, both feature young protagonists who reject suburbia; third, both novels present inno-

A New Generation Perpetuates the Anti-Suburban Tradition 187

vative content and provocative ideas within an inherently conservative structure; fourth, they both provide overwhelmingly disparaging depictions of suburbia; and fifth, both novels deliver sharp criticisms of mainstream Australian society. In my next three chapters, I address novels by Gerald Murnane, Peter Carey and Steven Carroll, three Australian writers who have produced innovative novels set in suburbia that reject the anti-suburban tradition and treat suburbia as a site for experimentation and intense engagement with both personal and social issues.

Endnotes

1. Portions of this chapter appeared in different form in two of my previous publications: "Exploring Indigenous Identity in Suburbia: Melissa Lucashenko's *Steam Pigs*" and "McCann Rejects Mainstream Australian Literature."
2. The biographical information in this paragraph is drawn from Austlit's author record for Melissa Lucashenko: http://www.austlit.edu.au/run?ex = ShowAgent&agentId = A(Ub
3. The Brisbane architect James Davidson writes that the Queenslander "is a hybrid dwelling form developed during the height of the British colonial period born out of the syncretism of cultures when the English house met the tropical climes of India and south-east Asia." Davidson notes that "the Queensland house went through a number of local iterations before its final 'settled' architectural form ... where I live, it is common to see a large yard full of Queenslanders lined up next to each other on the backs of semitrailers ready to be purchased and moved to their new site. From an architect's perspective, they are a renovator's dream as their light-weight single-skin timber walls are easily modified."
4. "Murries" is the plural form of the noun "Murri," which refers to the Indigenous peoples of Queensland.
5. Rachel's sentiments about working class vitality echo those expressed by Esson in "Our Institutions." However, unlike Rachel, Esson attacks suburbia and celebrates the working-class slums.
6. For a more detailed analysis of this aspect of the novel, see my article "Exploring Indigenous Identity in Suburbia: Melissa Lucashenko's *Steam Pigs*."
7. In 1966, Vincent Lingiari led a walk-off of the Gurindjii people from the Wave Hill cattle station in the Northern Territory in protest over wages and working and living conditions. The dispute evolved into a national battle for Indigenous land rights. For more information about Vincent Lingiari and the Gurindjii fight for land rights, see http://www.lingiari.org/.
8. Brunswick Street is a major thoroughfare in the inner Brisbane suburbs of New Farm and Fortitude Valley; Yeerongpilly is a southern suburb of Brisbane.
9. As I child, I lived in Rochedale South between 1980 and 1985 and attended primary school in Springwood. Although I had Indigenous

neighbors and classmates, I had little interaction with them and was never made aware that I lived in Yuggera country. I was not even aware of the fact that I lived on stolen land, which I think was pretty typical for a white child living in Australia in the early 1980s.
10. The architecture critic Deyan Sudjic states that the term "subtopia" was used in the 1950s by *The Architectural Review* in what he describes as their "war" on "the suburban dream" (12). Discussing the novel's title, McCann states: "'Subtopia' is a satirical contraction of 'suburbia' and 'utopia.' I wanted to suggest the ways in which urban and suburban environments deliver much less than what they promise us. I also wanted to evoke, ultimately, a politicized consciousness linked to an awareness of that fact. The sense of utopia betrayed is as evident to me in New York City as it is in the outer suburbs of Melbourne or Sydney" (Nicholson 1).
11. Interestingly, the biographical note accompanying one of McCann's recent works of literary criticism, an article in *Overland* entitled "The International of Excreta: World Literature and its Other," describes McCann as "an Australian writer currently teaching in the US and author of *Subtopia*," downplaying his privileged status as an academic at an Ivy league institution, and emphasizing his role as a novelist.
12. Biographical information from Griffin (1) and the AustLit author record for McCann: http://www.austlit.edu.au/run?ex = ShowAgent&agentId = A)M@
13. See http://www.vulgar.com.au/.
14. Andrew McGahan's debut novel *Praise* (1992) is the archetype of Australian "grunge fiction."
15. David Murray-Merry is a fictional Australian celebrity author in *Subtopia* who lives in New York City while writing novels set in Australia, enjoys an international reputation, and frequently returns to Australia for readings and media appearances.
16. During an interview with Michelle Griffin, McCann admits that Sally is the character in the novel most like him: "Anyone who reads the book and knows me will know that's true. I was conscious of those two characters [Julian and Sally] relating aspects of my own experience but there's no question the academically responsible character is the one that more reflects what I have done."
17. However, Greer-bashing is a favorite pastime of the Australian media, and Julian may be reflecting some of the ideas about Greer circulating in the public sphere.
18. McCann grew up in East Brighton.

19. Nick Cave is an Australian musician who has had a major international reputation for almost three decades. He became famous in the early eighties as the leader of The Birthday Party, and since 1984 has fronted Nick Cave and the Bad Seeds. Cave has been based in Melbourne, London, Berlin, Sao Paulo and now Brighton (UK).
20. McCann published an article dealing with both novels: "Professing the Popular: Political Fiction circa 2006." In the essay, McCann argues, "Never before, it seems, has political writing critical of the government, its policies and a prevailing sense of neoconservative status quo appeared to be so attractive" (44).

Chapter 5

Creating Suburban Fantasies

Gerald Murnane's *A Lifetime on Clouds* (1976) and *Landscape with Landscape* (1985)

While the anti-suburban tradition in the Australian novel established by Johnston has been perpetuated by prominent authors such as Winton and Malouf with the help of less prominent writers like Lucashenko and McCann, the experimental writer Gerald Murnane has eschewed mainstream literary traditions, creating unique works of suburban fiction.[1] Murnane's second and fourth books, *A Lifetime on Clouds* (1976) and *Landscape with Landscape* (1985), are predominantly set in Melbourne's suburbs and demonstrate remarkable creative possibilities for suburban fiction that rejects or ignores the anti-suburban tradition. Murnane's biography, critical reputation, influences and aversion to travel all contribute to his unique place within Australian literature and shape his engagement with suburbia. Paul Genoni notes that the biographical details of Murnane's life are often reflected in the lives of his narrators and protagonists (294), while Imre Salusinszky argues that Murnane's fiction remains "securely anchored in the details of his own life, and of suburban Melbourne" (*Gerald Murnane* 2).

Murnane was born in the Melbourne suburb of Coburg in 1939. His family moved to Bendigo in 1944, then to the Western District of Victoria in 1948, returning to the Melbourne suburbs in 1949, where Murnane lived for over sixty years before retiring to a small town in the Western District (Birns, "Reading"). Murnane matriculated from De La Salle College in the Melbourne suburb of Malvern in 1956. Between February and May of 1957, Murnane studied for the priesthood in Sydney; this three-month period was his longest absence from Melbourne's suburbs between 1949 and 2010 (Braun-Bau 44). Murnane lived in the same house in the northeastern suburb of Macleod for over thirty years (Salusinszky, "Gerald Murnane" 234). Although Murnane was raised Catholic and briefly trained for the priesthood, he stopped attending church when he was nineteen, but returned for a few years after his marriage. Murnane has stated that his wife is also an ex-Catholic (Baker 202, 204). Nevertheless, Catholicism plays a crucial role in Murnane's first two novels, *Tamarisk Row* (1974) and *A Lifetime on Clouds* (1976), and also features in *Landscape with Landscape* (1985). In interviews, Murnane rarely mentions training for the priesthood and usually leaves his three-month residency in Sydney out of accounts of his travels.

Unlike his contemporaries Malouf, Carey and Keneally, Murnane has won few awards. He won the FAW Barbara Ramsden Award for the Book of the Year in 1990 for *Velvet Waters* and won the South Australian Festival Award for Innovation in Writing in 2010 for *Barley Patch*. In 1999, Murnane won the Patrick White Award, which is presented to writers whose body of work has not received significant recognition. In 2007, Murnane received a New South Wales Premier's Literary Award (Blackwell 1); in 2008, he received the Australia Council writers' emeritus award, which recognizes the achievements of writers over sixty-five "who have made an outstanding contribution to the field and created an acclaimed body of work" ("Critically" 1). In 2009, Murnane won the Melbourne Prize for Literature. The fact that Murnane has won just two prizes for individual books but four career achievement awards is indicative of his critical reputation, which is now firmly established, but grew slowly. Salusinszky's essay "On Gerald Murnane," the first work of academic criticism on Murnane's writing, did not appear until 1986, twelve years after the publication of Murnane's debut novel.

Murnane established his reputation with his third novel, *The Plains* (1982), which continues to receive more critical attention than his other works.[2] Murnane's work is perceived as difficult and has never sold in large numbers (Genoni 293). When Murnane won the Patrick White Award in 1999, none of his books were in print in Australia ("Gerald Murnane: Adult"). In 1986, Salusinszky declared that Murnane's writing "is difficult, uncompromising, and simultaneously personal and intellectual" ("On Gerald Murnane" 518). In his 1993 monograph, Salusinszky argues that Murnane's "exclusively personal set of meditations and images … will establish his fiction as one of the finest and darkest achievements in the English literature of the last part of the twentieth century" (*Gerald Murnane* 103-04). In 2004, Salusinszky claimed Murnane is "widely regarded as one of the most unusual and original Australian writers of the late twentieth and early twenty-first centuries," declaring that Murnane "has probably aroused as much serious scholarly interest overseas as any living Australian prose writer" ("Gerald Murnane" 232, 237, 239). However, Salusinszky's latter claim is highly exaggerated.[3] Despite the small body of criticism on Murnane's work, he was a contender for the 2006 Nobel Prize for Literature (Hibberd 1). The continued rise of Murnane's critical reputation was evidenced by his appearance in 2008 at the Adelaide Festival's Writers' Week on a program featuring Peter Carey, Ian McEwan and David Malouf ("Gerald Murnane" *Adelaide Festival*). In 2012, Murnane published *A History of Books*, a "fictionalized autobiography" demonstrating his ongoing productivity and experimentation.

Murnane's unusual writing style and subject matter may have developed in part due to his diverse literary influences. Murnane has said that reading Joyce's *Ulysses* "turned him from a would-be poet into a novelist"; he also cites Kerouac,[4] Proust, Emily Bronte, Hardy, Calvino, Borges, Grass, Carver and the philosopher and psychologist Robert Musil as influences.[5] Genoni argues that Murnane has clearly "read very widely" but has "denied knowledge of the theory or practice of postmodernism, which has often been used to frame discussion of his fiction" (293). Murnane's novel *Inland* (1988) reveals that he has read White's *The Solid Mandala*, and thus is familiar with at least one previous work of Australian suburban fiction. In *Inland*, Murnane's narrator mentions a quotation from the French poet Paul Eluard, "*There is another world but it is in this one*," but declares he found the quotation in White's book (100, 101).[6]

Murnane is well-known for spending most of his life in Melbourne's suburbs and rarely traveling. He has "never flown in an airplane" and has not traveled outside of Australia; when asked if he would ever travel overseas, Murnane declares that such travel is "Completely out of the question" since he cannot "relax or feel at home even in a strange suburb of Melbourne" (Salusinszky, "Gerald Murnane" 234; Baker 208). However, Murnane's "legendary" dislike of travel (Salusinszky, "Gerald Murnane" 234) has been distorted and exaggerated. In fact, Murnane has traveled much more than his reputation suggests. A 1987 interview with Murnane revealed that he had been to Sydney twice and once to Adelaide, as well as into New South Wales and South Australia in his youth, in addition to visiting Bendigo every ten years (Baker 193, 208). In a 1992 interview, Murnane reveals that he spent three months of 1957 living in Sydney and that he has "been away from Melbourne a bit more than people know. My wife and I went to Sydney for two days last year ... I've been twice briefly to Adelaide and to Tasmania" (Braun-Bau 44). Murnane spent two weeks in Newcastle in 1990 (Salusinszky, "Newcastle" 25) and returned in 2001. In 2007, he traveled to Sydney to receive an award (Blackwell 1), and he attended the Adelaide Festival in 2008. Thus, in addition to travels within Victoria, Murnane has left the state at least ten times.

Nevertheless, Murnane clearly dislikes travel and was remarkably rooted to his suburb before moving to the country. Murnane declares that when he travels to an unfamiliar location, he is "overcome, or overwhelmed, or even plain confused" (Baker 193). Murnane insists that his aversion to travel and need to stay in familiar locations is "not a pose ... It's my way of thinking about the world. I do a lot of walking around Melbourne. I don't own a car" (Baker 194). Murnane spends much of his time thinking about other places, but travel makes him "numb ... the years are passing, and I still stay in my suburb of Melbourne" (Braun-Bau 44). Murnane's unusual relationship with travel and his fascination with maps and foreign locales are mirrored by the narrators in *Landscape with Landscape*, and, to a lesser extent, *A Lifetime on Clouds*; his intensely personal relationship with Melbourne's suburbs, where he lived for over sixty years, feature prominently in both works.

A Lifetime on Clouds: Suburban Adolescent Fantasies

Murnane's second novel is set in the fictional outer Melbourne suburb Accrington in 1953 and 1954, when the protagonist, Adrian Sherd, is fifteen and sixteen years old.[7] However, Adrian's numerous fantasies take place in the United States, Tasmania, Victoria's Western District, and several real and imagined Melbourne suburbs. In addition to exploring suburban life in the 1950s, *A Lifetime on Clouds* addresses adolescence, masturbation, Catholicism, fantasies and landscapes. Birns notes that ever since its publication, *A Lifetime of Clouds* has been compared to Joyce's *A Portrait of the Artist as a Young Man* ("Do Not" 2) due its confluence of adolescence, Catholicism and sexuality. However, Murnane's novel does not include "the achievement of sexual maturity through sexual experience," which Birns identifies as "a traditional motif of the novel of male adolescence" ("Do Not" 4). In fact, the closest Adrian ever comes to a sexual experience with another person is the moment when Denise McNamara's leg brushes against his during mass.

Salusinszky argues that *A Lifetime on Clouds* is Murnane's funniest and "most accessible" novel, but despite the comedy and satire, it is "an uncompromising and courageous book"; it is not an "attempt to 'come to terms with' or 'salvage some meaning from' a Catholic schooling in the early to mid-1950s: it summons that schooling up from the past in order to spit it out whole" ("That Hilarious" 295). Salusinszky describes the novel as a "documentary account of a lost subculture" and "a marvellous recreation of the atmosphere of Australian Catholicism in the 1950s" ("That Hilarious" 295; *Gerald Murnane* 27, 26). Salusinszky claims that *A Lifetime on Clouds* is Murnane's "most under-rated and least studied book," arguing that it is far more than a story about teenage sexual obsession ("That Hilarious" 294). Murnane's examination of suburbia, sexual fantasies and Catholicism in *A Lifetime on Clouds* illustrates the remarkable creative possibilities for suburban novels that reject the anti-suburban tradition and utilize a suburban setting for fictional experimentation.

A Lifetime on Clouds contains numerous descriptions of Melbourne's suburbs. Almost all of the action of the novel takes place in suburbia, with Adrian only leaving Melbourne's suburbs once, when he travels to his uncle's farm. Genoni argues that Murnane's fiction "is obsessively concerned with 'landscape,' 'place,' 'space,' 'time,' and 'maps'" (294); thus, the novel's suburban setting is entirely consistent with Murnane's other works, even those set on the imaginary plains of "Inner Australia," the United States and Hungary. While the suburbs and the plains are different in many ways, both locations allow Murnane to pursue his obsession with physical surroundings, space and maps, as well as to examine the effects of time on place.

In *The New Diversity*, Gelder and Salzman suggest that Adrian's "Catholic experience of the repressive 1950s is linked to the monotony of an outer eastern suburb from which he escapes in a torrent of daydreaming" (105). However, Adrian's daydreams and nocturnal fantasies are not driven by a desire to escape suburbia; rather, they are driven by sexual desire. Adrian's sexual fantasies are usually set outside suburbia, in the United States, because the objects of his desire are American film stars. Moreover, Adrian does not wish to escape suburbia physically, and the dominant, extended fantasy of the novel centers on his imaginary relationship with Denise McNamara, a Catholic schoolgirl who resides in his suburb and attends his parish church. Salusinszky argues that Murnane's imagination requires "an intensity of the normal, and few things could be more intensely normal, or hold more promise of hidden vistas, than a city whose streets fall into an easy grid" ("On Gerald Murnane" 519-520). Thus, Murnane's grounding in an "intensely normal" Melbourne suburb allows him to construct incredible flights of fancy.

Adrian attends St. Carthage's College in the fictional suburb Swindon, which is located in the inner eastern suburbs. In order to get home from school, Adrian walks half a mile along the tramline from his school to Swindon railway station, then travels five miles by train to Accrington station before walking a mile along the main road to his street (9). Adrian's home suburb, like other new outer suburbs, has few paved roads or footpaths. On Adrian's walk home from the railway station along a dirt path beside the main road, he passes several factories before reaching his street, Riviera Grove, which Murnane's narrator describes as "a chain of waterholes between clumps of manuka and wattle scrub" (9). Builders and deliverymen drive their trucks "over the low scrub, looking for a safe route," but the only residents of the street who can afford a car know better and park on the main road (9). Murnane's description of the partially-developed suburb, based on the suburb where he grew up, contains parallels to the outer suburbs Winton describes in *Cloudstreet* and "Aquifer." Murnane's description of indigenous vegetation and waterholes emphasize the continued presence of the bush and its ongoing destruction.

Adrian's family's house is bordered on one side by a "dense stand of tea-tree scrub thirty feet tall" and on the other by the wooden frame of a partially-constructed house, which stands in front of a "fibro-cement bungalow, twenty feet by ten, where the New Australian Andy Horvath lived with his wife and small son and mother-in-law" (9). Thus, the location of Adrian's outer suburban home literally situates it in the midst of two of the most commonly addressed issues in Australian suburban novels: environmental degradation and immigration. The remnants of the bush are next-door to the Sherds' house, and thus the suburb and the bush are intertwined. The Sherds' house is a "two-year-old double-fronted weatherboard" (9). A lawn bordered by geraniums and pelagoniums occupies the front yard, but the backyard consists almost entirely of "native grass and watsonia lillies" (9).[8] The backyard contains a fowl-run paralleling the back fence, a garden shed, and a weatherboard lavatory (9). Adrian's neat, typical suburban home and front yard contrasts with the thick bush on one side and the partially constructed house of the immigrants on the other, which symbolizes their partial integration into Australian society. The native grass and vegetation in the backyard serve as a reminder of how recently the quarter-acre block was bushland, and how quickly it could revert to that state.

One Sunday afternoon, Adrian's father drags a plank back and forth across the backyard in an attempt to level the soil before sowing it with lawn seed, thus continuing the process of suburbanization and the subjugation of the indigenous vegetation (48). Meanwhile, the Hungarian immigrants next door and their friends engage in "some kind of party in the bungalow behind the Horvath's half-built house" (48). The Hungarians sing "foreign songs" all afternoon and keep returning to one particular song: "The way they sang the chorus made the hair prickle on the back of [Adrian's] ... neck. It was sad and savage and hopeless" (48). Adrian presses his ear against a hole in the fence and hears "the separate voices of each man and woman trying to pick up the song again ... making noises like sobs, as though they couldn't sing for crying" (49). This brief episode powerfully highlights the struggle of immigrants to adapt to a new environment and culture, demonstrates the diversity of suburbia, and reveals Adrian's compassion for the Hungarians and their homesickness.

Adrian occasionally explores the bush near his house, where he observes possums' and bull-ants' nests: "like a scientist ... he kept a diary describing the ants' habits and drew maps to show how far they travelled from their nest" (10-11). One hot afternoon, Adrian sits in the garden shed with the door open, staring "at the listless branches of the wattle scrub over the side fence ... The only sounds around him were the clicking of insects and the crackling of seedpods on the vacant block next door" (79). Murnane presents the sounds of the bush pervading the suburb, again emphasizing the interconnectedness of the bush and outer suburbia: Adrian is simultaneously in suburbia and the bush. If Adrian pushes through the bush to the other side of the lot, he comes up against the Gaffney's side fence. The narrator notes that the Sherds know almost nothing about their neighbors, who are all "what Adrian's parents called young couples, with two or three small children" (11). The fact that the street is full of young parents and small children emphasizes the suburb's youth and the lack of an established community.

The interior of the Sherds' house contains "three bedrooms, a lounge, a kitchen, a bathroom and a laundry ... The lounge-room had an open fireplace, two armchairs and a couch of faded floral-patterned velvet, and a small bookcase" (10). Although Adrian's working-class suburban home is modest, the open fireplace and wooden floors are features contemporary readers may associate with middle-class comfort and affluence. When Adrian returns home from school each day, he is required to take off his school uniform to prevent wear and tear; he changes into his "only other clothes ... the shirt and trousers and jumper that had been his previous school uniform but were now too patched for school" (10). Adrian's lack of clothing signifies his family's thrift, low income and working class status. The presence of factories and the fact that only one family on Adrian's street can afford a car signals the working class character of the suburb. Adrian's family does not own a car and rides the bus to church (22). Adrian's father's occupation is not revealed; however, the narrator states that he was formerly a prison warder (84).

On a typical evening in the Sherds' home, Adrian's father goes to bed early with a book, while Adrian's mother knits by the stove (12). Television has not yet arrived in Australia, so Adrian and his brothers spend their evenings doing homework and playing board games in a house so quiet that the family can hear trains passing a mile away (12). The sound of a car or truck is rarely heard on Riviera Grove (12). Adrian always completes his homework on time and is astonished by his classmates who fail to complete their work and make excuses, claiming they had gone out in the evening, forgotten the time while listening to the radio, been ordered by their parents to talk with visitors, or been sent to bed early because their parents were throwing a party (12). In the Sherds' two years in Accrington, "they had almost never gone out after dark" and Adrian cannot recall any visitors in the evening (12). Adrian's classmates who have activities to pursue other than homework in the evenings reside in suburbs closer to Swindon, suburbs "with made roads and footpaths and front gardens full of shrubs. The suburbs had dignified names ... Adrian imagines the houses in these suburbs full of merry laughter every night of the week" (12-13). Murnane uses both real and imagined names for Melbourne suburbs, which are almost exclusively English and conjure peaceful images.[9]

Birns argues that Adrian is "clearly an authorial surrogate" ("Do Not" 2); his contention is supported by Murnane's admission in an interview that he identifies closely with Adrian, especially his isolation and fantasy life (Baker 200). Murnane states,

> My isolation started in adolescence ... We were completely cut off as teenagers. Outside of school hours there was nothing ... this was the outer suburbs of Melbourne in the 50s, and we lived from books, radio programs and dreams. School work took the place of socializing. (Baker 200)

Adrian's primary activity apart from schoolwork is masturbation. Adrian's fixation on sex pervades his consciousness so thoroughly that when he is not imagining himself having sex, he wonders about the sex lives of others and the possibilities for sex in suburbia. After examining his neighborhood, Adrian decides that

> In all the backyards around Riviera Grove there was no place where a couple could even sunbathe together unobserved ... from what Adrian heard of their conversations in the local bus, it seemed they had no time for fun. The men worked on their houses and gardens ... The women were often sick. (16)

When Adrian contemplates Melbourne's suburbs and the sexual possibilities in suburbia, he divides Melbourne "into three regions – slums, garden suburbs and outer suburbs" (16). On Adrian's mental map, the slums include

> all the inner suburbs where the houses were joined together and had no front gardens. East Melbourne, Richmond, Carlton – Adrian was not at all curious about the people who lived in these slums. They were criminals or dirty or poor, and he couldn't bear to think of their pale, grubby skin naked. (16)

Although Adrian's perception of the inner suburbs reveals misconceptions and prejudices, he does not conform to the view of the slums as being the source of vitality and authenticity, and thus superior to middle-class suburbia, which is traditionally espoused by anti-suburban intellectuals. Adrian's prejudices are not specifically anti-suburban; they are classist and elitist. The garden suburbs, in Adrian's conception, form "a great arc around the east and southeast of Melbourne. Swindon ... was in the heart of them, and most of the boys at his school lived in leafy streets" (16). Adrian envies the residents of the garden suburbs, since he imagines that "the houses and gardens in these suburbs ... [are] ideal for sexual games," although Adrian doubts that they are used for that purpose since the residents of the garden suburbs are "too dignified and serious" (16-17). It is the outer suburbs that Adrian knows best:

> Whenever he tried to imagine the city of Melbourne as a whole, he saw it shaped like a great star with the outer suburbs its distinctive arms. Their miles of pinkish-brown tiled roofs reached far out into the farmlands and market gardens and bush or scrub as a sign that the modern age had come to Australia. (17)

Rather than depicting the outer suburbs as isolated, repetitive and boring, a common trope in suburban novels, Murnane presents the outer suburbs as symbols of modernity and progress.

When the newspapers refer to a typical Melbourne family, Adrian envisions "their white or cream weatherboard house in a treeless yard surrounded by fences of neatly sawn palings" (17). Adrian thinks of the women who reside in the outer suburbs as "not beautiful (although occasionally one was described as attractive or vivacious). They wore dressing gowns all morning, and frilly aprons over their clothes for the rest of the day" (17). Adrian takes a long bike ride through the suburbs in an attempt to abstain from masturbation and finds

> ... temptations even in the bleakest suburbs. Sometimes he saw the backs of a woman's thighs as she bent forward in her garden, or the shapes of her breasts bouncing under her sweater as she pushed a mower. When this happened he slowed down and waited for a glimpse of the woman's face. It was nearly always so plain that he was glad to forget all about her. (22)

The suburban women cannot compete with the American film stars featuring in Adrian's fantasies, demonstrating his distorted ideas of beauty and the power of American cultural influence.

Adrian occasionally encounters non-Catholic teenagers from more affluent suburbs and is intimidated by their confidence and worldliness. On days when Adrian takes the tram from school to Swindon station rather than walking, he finds the tram "crowded with boys from Eastern Hill Grammar School and Canterbury Ladies' College. Adrian knew that these schools were two of the oldest and wealthiest in Melbourne. He felt very ignorant not even knowing where they were among the miles of garden suburbs" (53).[10] In the second half of the novel, once Adrian begins his imaginary relationship with Denise and attempts to live purely, he finds a new group of friends who are "obviously in the state of grace" (90), unlike his former friends, who are self-described "sex addicts" and meet at lunch time to tell dirty jokes, discuss the sex appeal of film stars and report the details of their previous evening's masturbation sessions (5). Adrian's new friends live in garden suburbs and travel home on trams: "They talked a lot about the Junction ... Adrian eventually discovered that this was

Camberwell Junction but he was not much wiser, since he had never been there" (90).[11] The stories Adrian's new friends tell often go over Adrian's head, since "the people or the places in them were known only to the Camberwell boys" (91-92). Thus, Adrian's status as a working class resident of an outer suburb excludes him from the geographical, social and cultural knowledge necessary to enter the world of the garden suburbs.

Adrian's ignorance of the garden suburbs is demonstrated again late in the novel when his class participates in a retreat at a monastery located "in a garden suburb a few miles from Swindon ... he stood at his upstairs window and looked across the huge lawns to the tall front fence and couldn't work out the direction of Swindon or Accrington" (121). Adrian knows the name of the street and the suburb where the monastery is located, but he has never visited the suburb before and "might have walked for miles from the front gate of the monastery before he came to some tramline or railway station that could give him his bearings" (122). Near the novel's conclusion, while riding the tram to Swindon, Adrian gazes "at the enormous houses along the tramline," wondering, "who else beside doctors and dentists and solicitors could be wealthy enough to live in such places. In all his life he had never been inside the front gate of any house like them" (138). Due to Adrian's class, and to a lesser extent, his religion, he is denied knowledge of vast swathes of suburbia.

Although Adrian usually envies the garden suburbs' residents (138), towards the end of the novel he believes Catholic rumors and propaganda about communism and "the end of the world" and "almost" pities them:

> While hundreds of millions of Chinese and Russians were preparing for a Third World War, the people of Melbourne's garden suburbs were going about their business as though there was nothing to worry about. They were thinking of wall-to-wall carpets and radiograms and washing machines. (138)

The suggestion of mindless consumerism in the passage above is about the closest Murnane's novel comes to expressing anti-suburban sentiments.

However, readers are well aware that it is Adrian who is deluded, rather than the garden suburbs' residents. As Adrian's tram climbs a hill, he looks back "at the miles of dark-red roofs and grey-green treetops ... he whispered into the breeze blowing past the tram that they were all doomed. And he saw the end of the world like grey rain bearing down on suburb after suburb" (139). The absurdity of Adrian's apocalyptic vision is emphasized with great humor by Murnane when he writes of Adrian envisioning "the people in their last agony crying out that if only they could have had a Catholic secondary education they might have seen it coming" (139). Murnane conveys much of the novel's humor similarly, through the absurd thoughts of his protagonist.

Adrian's sexual fantasies constitute much of the novel, which begins with Adrian "driving a station wagon towards a lonely beach in Florida" accompanied by three young women, Jayne, Marilyn and Susan (3). Adrian and Jayne swim naked, and soon Adrian finds himself gazing upon the naked bodies of Marilyn and Susan before having sex with Marilyn while the other women watch (4-5). It is not until the third page of the novel that readers learn they have been reading the sexual fantasy of a fifteen-year-old boy, when the narrator states: "Next morning Adrian Sherd was sitting in the Form Four classroom in St Carthage's College in Swindon, a south-eastern suburb of Melbourne" (5). Throughout the novel, Murnane makes many such unmarked shifts between Adrian's present reality and his fantasies, which become more and more elaborate and often contain fantasies within fantasies and fantastical "histories" of masturbation, religion and civilization.

Genoni argues that *A Lifetime on Clouds* develops a recurring theme in Murnane's fiction, "the coupling of the search for the ideal landscape with the search for the ideal woman" (297). During the first half of the novel, Adrian's sexual fantasies feature a series of American film stars in a variety of American landscapes. In the second half of the novel, Adrian engages in an extended fantasy covering a number of years of his imagined marriage to Denise McNamara, in which he places himself and Denise in a variety of Australian landscapes. While Murnane's novel almost exclusively depicts women as sexual objects, readers should remember that Murnane writes from the perspective of a sex-crazed teenage boy. Salusinszky argues that Murnane always "writes from a male position" with "great honesty," which "means that he writes a great deal about the conditioning of males, as children and as adolescents" (*Gerald Murnane* 30; "That Hilarious" 296).

Although Adrian's sexual fantasies are usually set in America, they are launched in his suburban backyard, where Adrian keeps a model railway in the garden shed (10). In the evenings, after finishing his homework, Adrian sets up his model railway track, which overlays a penciled outline of the United States. When the train stops, Adrian makes a mental note of its location, such as Florida, and uses it as the setting for that night's sexual fantasies (13). Even though the map of the United States is "crudely drawn" and the proportions distorted,

> Each few inches of railway track gave access to some picturesque scene from American films or magazines ... Nearly every night Adrian made an American journey ... usually he went in search of American women ... He had seen their pictures in Australian newspapers and magazines. Some of them he had even watched in films. (13)

Adrian uses "the whole of the U.S.A. for his love-life" (8) and associates America with beautiful film stars, liberated women and casual sex, as opposed to the sheltered, predictable reality of his working class Catholic suburban existence.

Birns argues that Murnane presents America "as a fantastic locale of sexual fulfillment and unconstrained imagination, as opposed to the repressive Cold War Catholic milieu shrouding the Australia of its teenage protagonist" (49-50). Birns highlights the anomalous nature of Murnane's text, pointing out that Anglophone writers have rarely "dared to represent America," despite "the bravado of the post-colonial project" ("Indefinite" 50). Anticipating the objections of feminist scholars, Birns notes that "Murnane's seeming idealization of women, his perpetuation of the Petrarchan stereotype of the perfect yet remote beloved, obviously calls his work into question from a feminist perspective" ("Indefinite" 50). Birns argues, however, that Murnane's work "may be compatible with feminism, in both a simple way and on a more sophisticated level," since the author's

> view of women is a stance that deliberately marks out the limits of its applicability. Rather than mounting a pretentious plunge into a Lawrentian *omphalos* of sexual otherness, Murnane retains a certain veil of mystery that is as much an index of cognitive self-discipline as it is of patriarchal mystification. ("Indefinite" 50)

Indeed, Murnane's satire continually highlights the absurdity of Adrian's conception of women and his complete lack of understanding of them; moreover, his idealization of women is linked to his idealization of American spaces.

Murnane emphasizes the dominance of American culture in 1950s Australian suburbia by repeatedly depicting Adrian gathering images for his sexual fantasies from media outlets. After setting the table for dinner, Adrian reads the *Argus* newspaper and searches the front pages

> for the cheesecake picture ... It was usually a photograph of a young woman in bathers leaning far forward and smiling at the camera. If the woman was an American film star he studied her carefully. He was always looking for photogenic starlets to play small roles in his American adventures. If she was only a young Australian woman he read the caption ... and spent a few minutes trying to work out the size and shape of her breasts. Then he folded up the paper and forgot about her. He wanted no Melbourne typists and telephonists on his American joureys. (11)

Adrian's imagined sexual adventures become "a little more outrageous" (15) each night and he eventually concludes that the "kind of sexual activity" he prefers is "not common in real life": "Even after watching an American film, Adrian still thought he might have been a very rare kind of sex maniac" (18). Adrian reads books by authors such as Robert Louis Stevenson, Sir Walter Scott, Alexandre Dumas and Ion L. Idriess, but does not expect to find any proof that men and women behaved "as he and his women friends did in America" (18).[12] However, "an innocent-looking library book eventually proved to Adrian that at least some adults enjoyed the pleasures that he devised on his American journeys" (18). In a book by Idriess, Adrian finds

> a picture of a naked man lolling on the ground against a backdrop of tropical vegetation while his eight wives ... waited to do his bidding. The man was Parajoulta, King of the Blue Mud Bay tribe in the Northern Territory. Although he and his wives were Aborigines, there was a look in his eye that cheered Adrian. (18)

Adrian muses that his fellow suburbanites might consider him crazy if they knew about his dreams of orgies "beside some beach or trout stream in America," but decides that "King Parajoulta would probably have understood" (18).[13]

Later in the novel, while thinking about how masturbation has changed the course of history, Adrian decides that "Not just the things that might have happened, but many important events that actually happened were missing from Australian history books" (58). Although Adrian is specifically thinking about masturbation, the larger point is obvious to Murnane's readers. On the following page, Adrian thinks,

> Of course the Aborigines had been in Australia for centuries before the white men, but no one would ever know their history. They had lived a carefree bestial existence. Some of them, like King Parajoulta of Blue Mud Bay with his eight wives, showed signs of imagination. But without books or films they had no inspiration to do unusual deeds. (59)

Although Murnane uses Adrian's teenage ignorance and narrow 1950s worldview to highlight omissions in Australian history and distorted perceptions of Australia's Indigenous people, he does not directly address issues of Indigenous ownership, land rights or belonging in *A Lifetime on Clouds*.[14]

Adrian's sexual fantasies and his perceptions and experience of suburbia are intertwined with Catholicism. Like Stephen Dedalus in Joyce's *A Portrait of the Artist as a Young Man*, Adrian, a former altar boy, is continually concerned about sin, guilt, salvation and the rules of Catholicism (14, 6). Adrian and his mother and brothers often visit his devout spinster aunt, who prays daily that he will become a priest (39). Since all of Adrian's thoughts and energies are focused on sexual fantasies and he commits only one kind of mortal sin, he has no need to examine his conscience before going to confession: "All he had to do before confession was to work out his total for the month ... Yet he could never bring himself to confess his total" (19). When a priest lectures Adrian's class about the dangers of the secular press, Adrian is certain that the priest is referring to the *Argus*, "which was delivered to the Sherds' house every morning because Mr Sherd said it was the best paper for racing and football" (61). Adrian is terrified that his fellow Catholics will shut down the *Argus* or prevent it from printing suggestive pictures, since he depends on the newspaper "to introduce him to new faces and breasts and legs" (62). After Adrian begins his imaginary relationship with Denise, he becomes extremely devout and imagines himself as a model Catholic husband.

During the retreat at the suburban monastery, Adrian enjoys the isolation and being "hidden for a few days in one of the best suburbs of Melbourne for the purpose of looking into his soul and making sure he was on the right path" (122). Adrian reflects upon his former self and tries to determine "why he had turned ... from a normal Catholic boy in a decent household to a sex-crazed satyr rampaging across America ... he was inclined to blame American films," despite the fact that he has never seen his favorite stars in a film, since he is only allowed to view "five or six films a year," half of which are Disney films, and the remainder selected by his mother because they are "recommended for children" (129). Adrian suspects that the "supposedly harmless films might have started him on his year-long orgy of lust" (129), since they "introduced him to a kind of woman he never came across in Australia – the attractive young woman in her twenties who had no boyfriend but travelled around waiting for the right man to fall in love with her" (132). Here Adrian thinks of his suburban existence as devoid of temptations; the unsavory influences all come from outside suburbia.

When a priest visits St. Carthage's and gives a speech designed to recruit boys into the priesthood, Adrian expresses an interest in talking privately about a vocation (149). He tells himself that he has "just taken the most dramatic step of his life" and is "almost certain" that he possesses "a vocation to the priesthood" (149, 151). Launching into another extended fantasy, Adrian imagines himself serving a parish in the western suburbs of Melbourne, where he delivers fiery sermons (152). In Adrian's priesthood fantasy, he quickly rises through the ranks to become the private chaplain to the Archbishop of Melbourne (154). After the Archbishop is elected to the College of Cardinals and the Pope dies, Adrian accompanies the Archbishop to Rome and advises him on how to cast the deciding vote in the election of the new Pope (154-55). While Adrian's imaginary future self is in Rome, he thinks of Melbourne far away and its "great sprawling suburbs [spreading] from the idly slapping water of Port Philip Bay to the moist leafy hillsides of the Dandenong Ranges. But under the night sky with its fiercely blazing Southern Cross, the city was not at peace" (155), since thousands of young Catholic men masturbate while fantasizing about young Catholic women who "could have inspired the passionate young men to reform their wasted lives if only they had met and understood each other" (155). Adrian's imagined possibility of reform is inspired by the purifying effects he experiences through his imaginary relationship with Denise, which takes up most of the second half of the novel.

During mass one Sunday, a girl's golden stockings brush against Adrian's knee as she approaches the communion rail. The girl wears "the uniform of the Academy of Mount Carmel, in the suburb of Richmond" (72); looking at her, Adrian thinks her face is "angelic" and decides she possesses

> the kind of beauty that could inspire a man to do the impossible. He turned towards the altar and put his head in his hands. Slowly and dramatically he whispered a vow that would change his life, "For her sake I will leave America forever." (72)

While riding his bike home after the encounter, Adrian sings "*Earth Angel*. He sang the words slowly and mournfully like a man pleading with a woman to end his long years of misery" (73). Adrian ceases fantasizing about orgies with American women and makes Denise (whose name he does not yet know) his new obsession. In bed the following night, Adrian thinks of Denise and shelters "in the aura of purity that surrounded her like an enormous halo. In that zone of sanctity no thought of sin would trouble him" (73). He resolves to go to confession the following Sunday "and rid himself for the last time of the sin that had threatened to enslave him," and to spend every afternoon for the rest of the school year catching a different train from Swindon to Accrington in an attempt to "meet up with his Earth Angel on her way home" (73). Adrian thinks that once he knows which train Denise catches, he will be able to catch her train every day (73).

On the last Monday of the school year, Adrian's friend Stan Seskis proposes a competition for the holidays in which all of the boys in the group "would keep a careful count of how many times they did it. They would be on their honour not to cheat, since they all lived in different suburbs and had no way of checking on each other" (73). Adrian refrains from telling his friends he has ceased masturbating, so he agrees to make the scorecards and believes he will be able to keep his blank, since

> The women who had tempted him to sin in the past were only images in photographs. The woman who was going to save him now was a real flesh-and-blood creature. She lived in his own suburb ... For too long he had been led astray by dreams of

America. He was about to begin a new life in the real world of Australia. (74)

Salusinszky argues that "the greatest irony" in the above passage "inheres in the fact that what is presented as a turning away from 'mere images' towards a 'flesh-and-blood creature,' from 'dreams of America' towards a 'real world,' will become the final, decisive retreat into a fantastic dream-world" ("That Hilarious" 296). Thus, rather than rejecting American fantasies and embracing Australian realism, Adrian replaces his American fantasies with an extended Australian suburban fantasy.

During the final weeks of 1953, Adrian catches a different train home each afternoon and searches every carriage "for the girl in the Mount Carmel uniform" but cannot find her (77). Adrian realizes that he has "to endure ... the summer holidays with only the memory of their one meeting ... to sustain him. But he swore to look for her each Sunday at mass and to go on searching the trains in 1954" (77). When Adrian's mother informs him that they will not be taking their annual holiday to her brother-in-law's farm, Adrian takes the news calmly, since "he was secretly pleased to be spending January in the suburb where his Earth Angel lived" (77-78). Adrian spends the holidays looking for Denise at mass and riding his bike around the suburb hoping to find her (78). Adrian decides that the way to keep his nocturnal adventures "pure and sinless" is to "take his Earth Angel with him" and in his fantasy proposes marriage to Denise, who, of course, accepts (80).

Once the 1954 school year begins, Adrian continues searching the trains. He finally finds Denise in "a second-class non-smoking compartment ... his Earth Angel was absorbed in a book. If she loved literature they had something in common already" (81). Attempting to obtain Denise's attention, Adrian stands nearby holding a book entitled *The Poet's Highway*, which contains "the most beautiful poem he had ever read – *La Belle Dame Sans Merci*" (81). As the train rounds a bend, Adrian pretends to lose his balance and leans over so far that "the poem was no more than a foot from his Earth Angel's face. He saw her look up ... He couldn't bring himself to meet her eyes, but he hoped she read the title of the poem" (82). Adrian spends the next few minutes staring at the poem and moving his lips, pretending to memorize it, and "Out of the corner of his eye ... [sees] her watching him with some interest" (82). Adrian puts his anthology in his bag at the last station before Accrington since, "He knew it was unusual for a boy to like poetry and he dreaded her thinking he was queer or unmanly" (82).

Adrian travels in Denise's compartment for the next fortnight, and since she does not change compartments, he convinces himself that she must be interested in him (82). In bed at night, Adrian is reunited with Denise, "not the girl ... but the twenty-year-old woman who was already his fiancé. He spent a long time each night telling her his life story" (84). Denise continues to sit in the same seat on the train throughout February and sometimes glances at Adrian when he enters the carriage (84). On an evening when all the seats in the compartment are occupied, Adrian stands above Denise's seat and takes out an exercise book, which he holds so that the front cover is "almost in front of her eyes" (85). Since Adrian spent half an hour during school going over the letters, the writing on the cover is "large and bold ... It read[s]:

> Adrian Maurice Sherd (Age 16)
>
> Form V
>
> St Carthage's College, Swindon" (85).

Denise looks at the book, and then lowers her eyes, but glances at Adrian's writing twice more during the following minutes. She then takes out her own exercise book and holds it "in front of her with her own name facing him:

> Denise McNamara
>
> Form IV

Academy of Mount Carmel, Richmond" (85).

Apart from brushing legs during mass, the exchange of names is the closest Adrian and Denise ever come to interacting, assuming that Denise actually reads the writing on Adrian's exercise book. Salusinszky argues that Adrian and Denise "come close to exchanging ... a pair of signifiers emptied of content" and describes the signifiers as "emptied twice over" since "they are mere tags, labels, names" and readers "never know for sure whether Denise has any *intention* of revealing her name to Adrian" ("That Hilarious" 299, original emphasis).

However, the information displayed on the covers of the exercise books (name, age, and educational and religious affiliation) is crucial in terms of establishing identity and compatibility, and thus serves an important function, regardless of whether or not Denise reads Adrian's cover or intends to reveal her identifying information. Once Adrian knows Denise's name, he is able to acquire more information. Adrian searches a telephone directory for McNamaras in Accrington and finds two listings: I.A. and K.J. Since Adrian knows "how to tell Catholic names from non-Catholic," he assumes the K.J. stands for Kevin John and decides that K.J., who resides at 24 Cumberland Road, must be Denise's father (86). Adrian looks up Cumberland Road in a street directory and memorizes its location (86).

Each night Adrian walks out of Accrington station "a few paces behind Denise," looks towards Cumberland Road, and finds there is "nothing to see except rows of white or cream weatherboard houses, but just knowing that her own house was somewhere among them made his stomach tighten" (86). Adrian yearns for a glimpse of Denise's home and envies

> the people who could stroll freely past it every day while he had to keep well away. If Denise saw him in her street she would think he was much too forward in his wooing. The only way to see her house was to sneak down Cumberland Road late at night, perhaps in some sort of disguise. (87)

At school, Adrian avoids his former friends and thanks God that they travel home on different trains (89). When Adrian fantasizes about his honeymoon with Denise, he spreads the imagined twelve days of the Tasmanian honeymoon out over several months of nocturnal fantasies (96).

The narrator reveals that Adrian's knowledge of Victoria is limited to the western suburb "where he had grown up and gone to primary school," Accrington, the south-eastern suburbs he passes though on his way to and from school, and "the landscape on either side of the railway line between Melbourne and Colac and a few miles of farmland around his uncle's property at Orford" (105). The only trips Adrian has taken outside Melbourne are the "few brief holidays he had spent on his uncle's farm at Orford, near Colac, in the Western District of Victoria" (58).[15] Adrian decides that none of the places he knows, whether suburbs or rural landscapes, will serve as "a fitting backdrop for the scenes of his married life," and thus draws on places he knows of that are "worthy settings for a great love story," since they are "landscapes so different from the suburbs of his childhood" that against their backdrop "even the trivial events of his married life" will "seem momentous" (105). Adrian fantasizes about being a husband who can "forget all those Sundays when he had come home from mass with nothing to do but climb the solitary wattle tree in the backyard and look across rows of other backyards and wait for the six o'clock *Hit Parade*" (105). The depiction here of suburbia as a boring site devoid of interesting activities is one of the few negative depictions in the novel.

While attempting to find an appropriate location in which to live out his fantasy marriage, Adrian remembers photographs of Victorian landscapes mounted in the compartments of country trains (105-106). In his fantasy marriage, Adrian tells Denise that they will "make their home in a valley beside a waterfall at Lorne or on a hillside overlooking Camperdown ... or best of all, in the trees above a bend in the road near Hepburn Springs" (106). As the September holidays approach, Adrian's mother informs him that she has arranged for him to spend a week on his uncle's farm (112). While Adrian is at Orford, his uncle takes him and his cousins "to visit a place called Mary's Mount ... [in] the steep timbered hills of the Otway Ranges" (113). According to Adrian's uncle, Mary's Mount is a Catholic community comprised of "'modern saints'" who have returned "'to the medieval idea of monasticism ... They bought nearly 600 acres of bush with only two cleared paddocks and they're turning it into a farm to supply them with all their needs ... they share almost everything in common'" (113-114).

Adrian's uncle expresses wonder at the prevalence of "'trashy books and films'" in the city and "'the spread of Communism,'" declaring,

> "The only safe place to bring up a family nowadays is somewhere like Mary's Mount ... If anything can save Australia the move back to the land can do it ... We haven't got much time left. The experts reckon by 1970 at the latest the whole of Asia will have gone Communist. We need a population of at least 30 to 40 million to defend ourselves." (114)

Both Adrian and his uncle fail to realize that the residents of Mary's Mount are essentially communists, adding to the comedy of the episode. Inspired by his visit, Adrian revises the narrative of his fantasy marriage to Denise and has them plan a move from Hepburn Springs to "a Catholic rural co-operative called Our Lady of the Ranges, deep in the Otways" (117).

Eventually Adrian tires of his imaginary marriage, since "the married life of the Sherds was becoming too remote from the daily life of the young Adrian Sherd. Mrs Denise Sherd was a wonderful wife, but perhaps a boy in Form Five needed someone nearer his own age" (140). Adrian begins fantasizing about Denise the schoolgirl, rather than Denise the young woman, and derives "more pleasure from hearing the schoolgirl Denise talk about her likes and dislikes and hobbies than he had once got from imagining her as his wife" (141). After talking to the priest about a vocation, Adrian ends his fantasy relationship. Rather than catching Denise's train, he prays inside the Swindon church until he knows he has missed it (151).

At the novel's conclusion, Adrian decides he has "spent too much time in unreal conjectures ... His dreams had spanned a lifetime. He had spent a lifetime on clouds. Now was the time to think of his real future" (156). Adrian proceeds to imagine himself a "humble parish priest" in a Melbourne suburb (156). Murnane does not depict Adrian's residence in suburbia as the cause of his sexual and religious fantasies. Rather, it is Adrian's Catholicism that prompts his misguided imaginings. Although there are a few passages in *A Lifetime on Clouds* that can be interpreted as negative depictions of suburbia, there are no blatantly, incontrovertibly anti-suburban passages, such as those in Johnston's *My Brother Jack*, Malouf's *Johnno*, Winton's *Cloudstreet*, Lucashenko's *Steam Pigs* and McCann's *Subtopia*. Rather than perpetuate the anti-suburban tradition, *A Lifetime on Clouds* rejects the tradition and demonstrates some of the numerous possibilities for fiction that uses the suburban setting without being constrained by negative preconceptions. Moreover, *A Lifetime on Clouds* is almost certainly the first Australian novel set in suburbia since White's *The Solid Mandala* that is not anti-suburban.

Landscape with Landscape: Imagining, Traversing and Investigating Suburbia

In his fourth book, *Landscape with Landscape*, Murnane continues his explorations of suburbia, rejecting the anti-suburban tradition and once again demonstrating the enormous variety of possibilities for fiction set in suburbia. Salusinszky argues that *Landscape with Landscape* contains "some of Murnane's best writing" and claims that it "is clearly full of bits and pieces of ... [Murnane's] life, as well as ... lives he might have led" ("On Gerald Murnane" 525). Murnane's fictional experiments in *Landscape with Landscape* are even more radical than *A Lifetime on Clouds*; in addition to investigating a range of suburban settings, Murnane experiments with genre, abandoning the traditional form of the novel and utilizing six versions of an unnamed first person narrator to relate six interwoven narratives. Murnane's innovative fictional techniques in *Landscape with Landscape* have inspired debates regarding whether the text is a novel or a collection of stories. The cover of the Penguin edition uses the terms "stories" and "fiction," but does not label the text either a novel or a collection of short stories. The text is comprised of six pieces of fiction, each beginning on a new page with an italicized title. However, the book does not contain a table of contents, and thus the reader is unaware that the first piece, "Landscape with Freckled Woman," is a self-contained narrative until encountering the next narrative.

Niall Lucy argues that the lack of a table of contents is a sign that *Landscape with Landscape* is "not a collection of short stories"; he considers referring to the "stories" as "chapters" but acknowledges that "this is not a very satisfying description of Murnane's text either, since it invokes a set of ... assumptions about novels that the text declines to fulfill" (104). Genoni argues that even though *Landscape with Landscape* is comprised of "separate stories," the text "can be approached as a novel" (298). Likewise, Helen Daniel describes the text as "six stories ... [that] make up a novel" (*Liars* 329). In the last section, "Landscape with Artist," Murnane's narrator directly addresses the issue, stating,

> I had considered again one of the problems that had kept me from showing my manuscripts to a publisher. I tried to decide whether they were a collection of short stories or whether I could combine them and unify them to make them a single novel ... [I] told myself that ... I would ... devise a new form of prose fiction – neither short story nor novel. (218)

Thus, the words of one of the narrators of *Landscape with Landscape* provide the answer to the question of its genre, and henceforth I will refer to the text as a work of prose fiction containing six pieces.

Although the six pieces in *Landscape with Landscape* can be read separately, they are all connected and the narrator of each piece refers to the existence of the next, which he claims to have written. Thus, the narrator of the first narrative, "Landscape with Freckled Woman," states that his "first story, *Sipping the Essence*," will "almost certainly be published" (22); four pages later, readers encounter "Sipping the Essence." The pattern of the narrator of the present piece naming the following piece continues until the sixth narrative in the book, "Landscape with Artist," which refers back to "Landscape with Freckled Woman," which the narrator claims to be carrying in his backpack (267). Lucy suggests that the terms "'First' and 'last' ... need to be placed in inverted commas, because the sequence ... isn't linear but circles back on itself'" (104). Daniel contends that each piece "opens out of its predecessor ... in a strange loop which is never ending" (*Liars* 328). Salusinszky describes the six narratives as fitting "into each other like Chinese boxes" and argues that Murnane's use of an unnamed narrator in all six pieces who is "a young, or youngish, man living in Melbourne and trying (without conspicuous success) to become a published writer, suggests that the book has an allegorical relationship to Murnane's life in the 1960s and early 1970s" (*Gerald Murnane* 58). Indeed, the six narrators are similar to Murnane to such an extent that one is tempted to conclude that they are all simply versions of Murnane.[16]

Daniel argues that the setting for *Landscape with Landscape* is on one level the "real places and suburbs" of Melbourne, such as Fitzroy, Brunswick and Carlton. However, "across the face of Melbourne from the 1950s to the 1980s," Murnane overlays "another city and another level ... a prismatic image of Melbourne ... a private city with suburbs and districts spaced according to his own private coordinates, a Melbourne of his own in the crevices and interstices of the real city" (*Liars* 329). Rather than viewing suburbia as a site unworthy for fiction or a location to disparage, Murnane perceives suburbia as a space in which limitless manifestations of life can be imagined, revised and re-imagined. *Landscape with Landscape* demonstrates that suburbia contains an infinite number of narratives. Because *Landscape with Landscape* contains six narratives, rather than the single narrative traditional novels employ, it is necessary to provide summaries of each narrative in order to demonstrate Murnane's unique explorations of suburbia. Thus, the remainder of this chapter contains both summaries and analysis of the six narratives.

Creating Suburban Fantasies 219

The first narrative, "Landscape with Freckled Woman," takes place in 1975 and focuses on an unnamed narrator who sits in a suburban committee meeting where he is the only male among nine women (1). He has been persuaded to join the committee and serve as treasurer and knows none of the women, although they all live in his suburb (1). The narrator wants each woman to wonder, once she learns he is a writer, whether he has been observing her (1). When the president of the committee introduces the narrator and states that he is available any time because he is a writer who works at home and is "hard at work on a book ... [that] might turn out to be about a suburb very like" their own, he fears he may have been misrepresented. The narrator wonders whether the women on the committee see him as "a man whose eye ... [has] ranged widely over the world but now chose[s] to scrutinise their quiet streets ... or [as] a man who ... [has] failed somewhat in the world at large" and now seeks to "learn from them what they saw beyond their kitchen windows all day or in the greyness of their television tubes late at night" (3). The narrator desires the approval of the suburban women but reveals his sexism by assuming that they stay at home rather than work, watch a lot of television, and view films "every evening" (1).

During the meeting, the narrator finds himself "staring at two freckles low on the neck of one of the committee women" (4), prompting him to recall his history with freckled women. He states that ten years earlier, just before his wedding, he made preparations to burn his collection of pictures of women but "had hesitated" over his favorite pictures, since "the freckled women had always seemed peculiarly ... [his] own" (4). The narrator then indulges in a fantasy in which the freckled woman at the meeting approaches him and asks him what kind of writer he is and where he finds his subjects (6), and he answers by telling a story about his history as a writer, referring to himself as "the young man." The majority of the text of "Landscape with Freckled Woman" is comprised of the fantasy the narrator tells the freckled woman; the physical action of the story consists solely of the narrator sitting in the meeting.

The story the narrator imagines himself telling the freckled woman focuses on a young man who wants to be a writer and believes a writer needs "no more than a landscape of his own" (8). In 1960, the young man rents a room in a south-eastern suburb of Melbourne, later revealed to be Malvern (11), and every Sunday walks to a major intersection where he stands "for five minutes or so beside the traffic-lights, pretending to wait for someone but actually watching for any car that had a young man as driver and a young woman as its only passenger" (8). When the young man sees a car containing a young couple, he imagines their story. In the couple's story, the residents of Melbourne's suburbs are depicted as constantly looking "east or south-east" when they think about "travelling towards the pleasant places that waited all week on the edges of their thoughts" (8). Mount Dandenong serves as "a not-too-distant goal" (8). Closer to the city, there are "gentler folds of hills," of which "the furthest" look "like true countryside from a distance," while the closest are "already marked out with rows of newly built houses" where the young couple dream of living (8-9). In the fantasy within the fantasy, the young couples of Melbourne dream of residing in the newest outposts of suburbia, which spreads towards the horizon.

The young man spends his Sunday afternoons alone in his room, "reading and writing and trying to define his landscape" (9). Eventually, he decides that the southeastern suburbs are "distracting him from his landscape" and resolves "to live in a suburb of Melbourne that offered nothing to the eye: a suburb from which the writer could see only what he himself devised. And he fixed on an inner suburb" (10). In 1960, the young man "had never heard of anyone wanting to settle in an inner suburb," since they were considered slums (10). Young couples "were expected to buy blocks of land in new suburbs," although some newlyweds lived in rented flats "in tree-lined streets" of South Yarra or Hawthorn "while they saved for their newly built houses far away to the east" (10). After searching "the true slums north of the city," the young man chooses "a suburb almost bare of trees, where front doors were an arm's length from the footpath and walls of factories kept whole neighbourhoods in shadow all day" (10).

The young man rents a room in "a single-fronted house in Argyle Street, Fitzroy" (10).

As Murnane once was, the young man in the narrator's imaginary story is a schoolteacher who aspires to be a writer (11). The young man's friend who helps him move asks if he knows what he is doing, prompting the young man to decide that his friend is "only one more of the thousands who knew nothing of true landscapes because they had grown up in the belt of neat suburbs between Port Phillip Bay and Mount Dandenong" (11). Since the young man is "too tired to rebuke" his friend, and "a little alarmed that the man might go back to his bayside suburb thinking the young man's mind had given way," he tells his friend he has moved to Fitzroy in order to "write about reality – about the sort of people in the kitchen downstairs; people who lived lives of elemental passion unhindered by the conventions of the suburbs by the sea" (11). Here Murnane draws on anti-suburban ideas about the slums and the working-class; however, his narrators do not subscribe to notions of working-class vitality and superiority, or promote them. Rather, the ideas are used as an excuse to justify a decision that seems strange to a middle-class suburbanite, who is presented as a member of a class bound by convention.

The young man spends three months living in Fitzroy, and although he continues to teach in a primary school in a south-eastern suburb, he spends most of his free time in his room seeking to "disorder his senses," since he has "read a little about Arthur Rimbaud" (11, 12). After a dispute with "the woman who seemed to be the chief tenant of the house," the young man decides to leave Fitzroy and dreams of moving to a room above a warehouse or shop in "the central business district ... He saw the central city as a blank space from which the true patterns of the suburbs would be visible" (13-14). However, he is unable to find a room in the city and has to "settle for a block of flats about a mile from the city, in St. Kilda Road" (14).

Murnane uses his story within a story to address the issue of the gentrification of the inner suburbs. The young man in the narrator's story notices "people from the outer suburbs finding their way into the inner parts of Melbourne" and speculates that he may have accidentally "been aware years beforehand of the prevailing mood of the late 1960s. Perhaps, blundering into Fitzroy in 1960 ... he had been something of a pioneer" (16). The young man gradually realizes that "what he had thought was the fixed shape of Melbourne was changing" (17). Many of the "shabby houses" in the inner suburbs are now occupied by "teachers and lecturers and ... business and professional couples. On his walks through suburbs where he had once felt safely alone ... he saw the trails and outposts of the people ... who were going to change their surroundings" (17). Thus, Murnane reveals the evolving nature of suburbia.

Around the time that the gentrification of the inner suburbs becomes apparent, the young man marries and has to decide where to buy a house (17). As a married man, he attends social gatherings in renovated terrace houses in the inner suburbs and sees "how the people in them had shaped their surroundings to suit themselves" (17). The young man and his wife live in "a cream-brick block of flats" in the inner suburb of Brunswick (18). During a party in 1970, he comes to realize that "the inner suburbs had become part of a far-reaching landscape such as he had once wanted to write about" (18-19). The young man persuades his wife "to buy a house in the last place left for him, the one place that the dreamers of the new Victoria had disregarded ... the narrow belt of newer suburbs where all the houses were said to look the same" (19). He works on his writing in a brick veneer house in a room with a window that looks upon the window of the neighboring house and thinks of his street as "a narrow valley," assuring himself that "someone looking from the highest point in Carlton across the northern suburbs would see nothing of his insignificant hollow in the land" (19). Murnane's narrator deliberately dwells in the kind of suburb and house that Johnston's narrator vehemently rejects in *My Brother Jack*.

The narrator recalls telling the president of the committee that after writing two novels he has "now turned to the short story" (22). When the president asked if the narrator's work had been published, he told her that his "first story, *Sipping the Essence*, would almost certainly be published" before he finished his committee work (22). The narrator is convinced that "the president's foolish words of introduction would have persuaded" the freckled woman that he is "searching her suburb for characters in some work of fiction" (23). At the conclusion of "Landscape with Freckled Woman," the narrator imagines himself "writing at last about the real world" (24), presenting suburbia as the most authentic setting for fiction.

The second narrative in *Landscape with Landscape*, "Sipping the Essence," begins in Sorrento, at the end of the Mornington Peninsula, where the young narrator and three of his friends rent a holiday flat, planning "to have a wild party on New Year's Eve, the last day of the 1950s" (27). The unnamed narrator believes that he does "not belong in Victoria" and that his "peculiar hopes" can "only be fulfilled … in the far sunlight of Queensland," which he only knows "from pictures in magazines" (29). Of the three other young men, the narrator is closest to Kelvin Durkin, who is the "only person" the narrator knows who reads *Time* and is aware of Nabokov and Kerouac (30). The narrator feels an affinity with Durkin, since they each need "a certain setting" in order to be themselves (33). Each Friday night in 1959, the narrator walked "two miles across the suburbs" to visit Durkin (35). The narrator read to Durkin from Kerouac's *On the Road*, even though Durkin's reading was limited to "the reviews in *Time*" and "short fiction in … *Esquire*" (35). The narrator believes Kerouac's "blend of poetry and craziness would one day take over the world," leading to the recognition of his own talents (35).

On New Year's Eve, two of the narrator's friends attend a dance and return with three girls, two of whom have already paired-off with the narrator's friends, so the remaining girl, Carolyn, spends the night talking with the narrator and Durkin (34). Back in Melbourne's suburbs in early 1960, the narrator yearns to call Carolyn and ask her out; he states that he "wanted urgently to explain" himself "to a young woman" but is afraid to ask one out and perceives the act as "an absurd ritual of the suburbs" (39).

Every day the narrator enters a phone booth intending to call Carolyn, but quickly thinks of reasons to avoid calling, such as his lack of a car (41). Another excuse the narrator devises to avoid calling Carolyn is his idea that "every young woman of the suburbs" hopes to marry her boyfriend, and thus it would be unfair to go out with Carolyn since he plans to quit his job and "hitch-hike up and down the eastern States of Australia" for the remainder of his life (41). Such narrow and sexist views of suburban women are typical of the six male narrators in *Landscape with Landscape*.

When the narrator finally calls Carolyn, she informs him that she has purchased a Morris Minor and can take them anywhere (42). As Carolyn arrives at the narrator's home, he tells himself that he is "a bastard" because he has

> tricked a good-natured girl from a respectable family into spending Saturday night with a man who wanted to tell her that the only good in life was poetic pleasure before he fled to the back roads of Queensland and mocked the conventional domestic life she was dreaming of. (42)

However, within moments of sitting down beside Carolyn in her car, he begins to see "quite a different future" (42, 43). The narrator foresees himself "staying in Melbourne and writing an epic poem set in an imagined Queensland ... going out with Carolyn every night for a year; proposing marriage, becoming engaged, marrying," and establishing a suburban home (44).

However, the narrator's relationship with Carolyn only lasts a few weeks, and she soon becomes Durkin's girlfriend. The narrator resolves that Melbourne's suburbs will become for him what "the entire United States had been for Kerouac ... There seemed space enough in Melbourne for a solitary to travel for years out of sight of those who huddled together" (49). The narrator begins drinking heavily six afternoons per week, having decided that alcohol can show him all he needs to see, and continues to write poetry, which he submits to magazines (59). He remains friends with Durkin, but Carolyn disapproves of his drinking and insists he be kept away from alcohol before her wedding to Durkin; the narrator bitterly dismisses her as

> a timid bitch from the bayside suburbs, terrified of anything unconventional, who had smiled and listened to ... [his] ravings two years before for the same reason that she had spread her legs for Durkin and half a dozen men before him: because she would have tried any means of fulfilling her lifelong ambition to appear as a radiant bride on a sunny Saturday at her local Anglican church. (59)

Here, in the book's most misogynistic passage, the narrator conflates Carolyn's disapproval of his drinking with her suburban upbringing and unfairly characterizes her as solely motivated by the desire to have a public wedding.

A few years later, after the narrator and his girlfriend visit the Durkins at their "contemporary-style timber house in the cheapest subdivision in Mount Eliza," his girlfriend confides that "she considered Carolyn an empty-headed, stuck-up bitch" (61). When the narrator learns that Carolyn does not think his girlfriend is his intellectual equal, he marries her to spite Carolyn (61). Once the narrator is married, he and his wife rarely visit the Durkins, since they live in suburbs on opposite sides of the city (62). Some years later, the narrator and his wife are invited to a farewell party for the Durkins, who are moving to New South Wales (63). In one of the book's numerous echoes of Murnane's own life, the narrator states that he and his wife have "never left Melbourne" and the narrator claims that at "the age of forty" he has "been no further north than Bendigo," where he "had lived for four years as a child" (66). Twenty years after the holiday at Sorrento, the narrator receives a letter from Durkin stating that "Carolyn had left him" (66). When Durkin visits, the narrator informs him that he now writes prose instead of poetry and has "finished a story about the New Australians, the men from Queensland who had set out for Paraguay to found a country of dreams ... *The Battle of Acosta Nu*" (69).

According to Salusinszky, "The Battle of Acosta Nu" is the text's "brilliant centerpiece" ("On Gerald Murnane" 525). The narrator states in the first sentence that he is standing in Melbourne; however, the reader discovers that the narrator is not referring to Melbourne, Australia, but to another Melbourne, located in Paraguay. Murnane prefaces the piece with an excerpt of a letter from one of the settlers who founded the New Australia colony in Paraguay in 1893. Murnane uses the New Australia settlement in Paraguay as the backdrop for his narrator's personal history (Birns, "Gerald Murnane" 79); the narrator believes he is a descendant of the original Australian settlers (Salusinszky, "On Gerald Murnane" 525). Salusinszky argues that the setting "sounds not at all like Paraguay, but very much like the same neck of the woods in which we find all of the adult versions of the narrator in *Landscape with Landscape*" (*Gerald Murnane* 65). The narrator lives in a city of sprawling suburbs that utilizes trams for public transportation, and the Paraguayan landscape is described as if it is Australia, with "bush" containing "listless ironbarks" and "bare flinty soil" (74, 80, 98).

When the narrator stands on a hill "northeast of Melbourne" and looks "across the folds of suburbs towards the Kinglake Ranges," he "almost" believes he is "in Australia after all" (71). The narrator's primary goal is to solidify his Australian identity and imbue Australian identity in his son: "I only wanted to feel in touch with my own past; to be assured that a theme persisted through my confused and fragmented story" (72). As a younger man, the narrator engaged in a quest to find "someone of Australian ancestry among the females of Paraguay," while acknowledging that there is only an "impossibly remote" chance of meeting an Australian woman (72). The narrator's search for identity, longing for a true home, and desire to establish a permanent relationship with a place combine to make "The Battle of Acosta Nu" a synthesis of national and autobiographical themes (Birns, "Gerald Murnane" 79).

As a young man, the narrator lives a life remarkably similar to that of the suburban narrators of the other pieces in *Landscape with Landscape*,

Creating Suburban Fantasies 227

spending Saturday evenings "at the home of a married couple" (73). The narrator has a habit of arriving at the couples' house with a six-pack of beer, sitting down in front of the television, and planning to spend a quiet night with the couple who tolerate him "as some sort of foreigner" (73). However, the husband usually informs the narrator that they have been invited to a party and he must come with them (73). At the parties, "made hopeful by the beer," the narrator rushes "into supposing ... [he] had finally met a female of ... [his] own generation who was at least partly Australian" (73). Having left the party alone, he would be left to wonder "which suburb of ... [their] huge city had swallowed her" (74).

Believing that he needs to keep his true identity secret, the narrator avoids social gatherings, rarely leaves his house, and adopts "the dress and manners of one of the obscure classes of Paraguayans," reading and making notes about Australia in his free time (76). One of the narrator's friends suspects he is mentally ill and persuades him to see a doctor. The narrator informs the doctor that according to Paraguayan science he is mentally ill, but he is in fact "one of a handful of Australians still surviving years after ... [their] grandparents had arrived in Paraguay" (80). The narrator explains to the doctor that "the settlement had failed because ... the Australians had foolishly abandoned the true source of their culture, the land of Australia itself" (80). As the narrator talks to the doctor, he realizes "more clearly than ever before, the peculiar dilemma of the Australian exiles ... [who] yearned for Australia but ... dared not travel towards it for fear of finding it different entirely from ... [their] families' scant traditions and ... [their] own later conjectures" (80-81).

The narrator's son contracts a rare form of blood poisoning and dies in hospital, after which the narrator declares, "I was finished with Paraguay. My only link with that country was broken forever. Already I could see the bare room in an inner suburb of Melbourne where I would spend the rest of my life alone, reading and writing" (120). When the narrator leaves the hospital after his son's death, he walks "beside a busy road that ... [leads] into the centre of Melbourne" and sees ahead of him "the empty spaces of a park" he had "sometimes stared at" from his "son's hospital room," which has "no formal lawns and paths, only a roughly mown paddock with scattered native trees" (120, 121). While walking in the park, the narrator remembers his son's last hours and kneels down to gather a "handful of dust and grass and fallen leaves and scraps of twigs" (121). After standing up and flinging the soil away, the narrator perceives the soil all around him to have changed:

> It was the soil that my son had died on. He had died in that place and he had died fighting. He had fought because he loved his land insanely. And the land he loved was Paraguay. He had died for Paraguay. He was a Paraguayan. (121)

After his epiphany, the narrator decides that if his son is Paraguayan, then he is too:

> And if he and I were Paraguayans, then the people in cars and trams passing a suburban park ... must have been Australians ... They were the exiles and I was the man who had come to his senses after all and stood, sure at last of his whereabouts, in his native land – in Paraguay, the country he had thought for years was only a place he had read about it. (122)

Salusinszky claims "we can be sure" that "The Battle of Acosta Nu" "is physically set in suburban Melbourne" and contends that when the narrator walks from his son's hospital bed to an adjoining park "we know that the hospital is the Royal Children's Hospital, and the park is Royal Park" (*Gerald Murnane* 66; "On Gerald Murnane" 526). However, Salusinszky claims that the narrative has "precious little to do with either of the real places called Australia or Paraguay," arguing that the narrator "has a severe case of solipsism" and that solipsism is "Murnane's great subject ... a force which imposes itself on all his books" (*Gerald Murnane* 66; "On Gerald Murnane" 526).

Murnane's fantastic explorations of suburbia continue in "A Quieter Place than Clun." The piece begins with the narrator describing what was for "twenty-three years ... the most important event" of his life, which occurred "on a basketball court behind a Catholic church in an outer southeastern suburb of Melbourne" (123). In his youth, the narrator joined a basketball team in a Catholic young men's league believing it would allow him to meet Catholic girls. He endured "long trips by train to distant suburbs" where he sat on the bench anticipating the end-of-season social gathering (124). However, when arrangements are made for the bus trip to Mount Donna Buang, where a picnic will be held with the girls, the narrator watches his team-mates order pairs of tickets and realizes he has wasted his time, since the young men and women are already paired-off (123, 124).

However, the narrator's realization that the desirable young women are already taken is not the most important event of his life. Rather, the crucial event is his utterance on the basketball court of the phrase "literary landscape," which he says as though he is "naming" his "lost homeland" and announcing his destination:

> I decided that ... I would devote my life to poetic emotion rather than philosophy or theology. From that moment I was much less anxious about my Catholic soul and much less interested in golden pagan skin. I felt myself filling up with all the branching greenness of the English literature I was going to read. (133, 135)

For the narrator, the study of literature is not just a transformative path to a more fulfilling life, but a process through which literature colonizes the body. In the narrator's case, his Australian body is colonized by English literature in a highly allegorical manner.

On Saturday mornings, the narrator travels from the suburbs into the city to visit bookshops. One day an attractive young woman brushes past him and takes "a small book from a shelf in Standard Authors" (130). The narrator believes the young woman took "one of Thomas Hardy's novels, almost certainly *The Woodlanders*," so he buys a copy (130). The book has a "soothing dark-green" cover, and when the narrator returns home, instead of reading the novel he stares at the cover imagining "the woman somewhere in Melbourne reading at that very moment the words behind the dark-green" (130). The narrator develops a habit of spending hours in the bookstore every Saturday but never sees the young woman again; however, each week he purchases another of the green-covered editions of Hardy, eventually acquiring the entire set (130). While searching "for books that would extend the zone of green between ... [himself] and ... [his] surroundings," the narrator discovers A.E. Housman's *A Shropshire Lad* and describes the morning when he purchases it as "almost as decisive ... as the evening on the basketball court" (136). The narrator's discovery of English literature causes him to be "reconciled" to his life "at last" (137). The weather is no longer able to change his mood since "greenness" has "filled up all the spaces inside" him and he has found a way to "live continually in a landscape of literature" (137).[17]

As a young man living in "the third bedroom of a suburban house twelve miles south-east of the city of Melbourne," the narrator resolves "to live as Housman had lived" (138, 141). He reads poetry on the train and recites it as he walks to work from the station (141). The narrator overhears his colleague Warwick Whitbread describing his weekend, which consists of working in the garden and taking his family to the Mornington Peninsula or the Dandenongs (146). The narrator declares that he "felt a keen pity for Whitbread and his kind" as he perceives their struggle "to grow lawns and shrubs" and habit of visiting "scenic spots beyond Melbourne" as proof that "even they felt an obscure yearning for landscapes" (146). While the narrator may be misguided to interpret suburban gardening as evidence of a yearning for landscapes, the visits to scenic locales outside the city can be plausibly interpreted as evidence of a yearning to engage with nature.

The narrator indulges in suburban rituals of his own, taking regular Sunday walks. The route of the narrator's walk takes him past the house of a police officer, whom he sees every Sunday "in overalls and a frayed police shirt, pushing a rusty hand-mower over his swampy lawn or pulling weeds from flower-beds" (147). The narrator always walks slowly past the policeman's house, hoping to see the wife "push open the front door with the torn fly-wire and show herself," since he is "affected" by her face and thinks of her "as a type of all the attractive young matrons of Melbourne who looked out on straggling gardens late on Sunday afternoons" (147). The narrator spends his evenings and weekends "reading, writing drafts of poems, and studying maps and photographs of landscapes, mostly English" (151). The narrator's fascination with English landscapes is the product of his immersion in English literature and serves as a reminder of the pervasive influence of English culture on Australia.

When the narrator is twenty-one, he enrolls in a course that will qualify him to work as a primary school teacher. He declares that teaching does not interest him and states that his motivation for becoming a teacher is to "get away from Melbourne and into a new landscape" (151). While undertaking the course, the narrator studies "lists of remote schools and large-scale maps of Victoria," trying to decide where he will teach (151). The narrator envisions himself spending forty years drinking "every afternoon between four and six o-clock with stolid working-men in a small town whose tree-lined main street trailed away into gently undulating grasslands" (151). He envisions daily drinking sessions followed by a solitary meal in a café, after which he will walk to his "self-contained bungalow behind the house of a silent elderly couple," where he will sip beer and write, pursuing his "lifelong task of writing poetry" (151). After studying maps of Victoria, the narrator decides that Casterton, in the state's far west, is the location where he can turn his fantasy into reality (152).

However, when the narrator completes his course and appointments are announced, he learns that he will not be leaving Melbourne, but will be teaching in Frankston, "the last of the suburbs that followed the southeastern curve of Port Phillip Bay" (152).[18] However, the narrator adapts his Casterton fantasy to Frankston and carries out his "plans for living as an unknown poet" (152). He rents a sleepout in a suburban backyard, drinks every afternoon at a hotel with three other teachers, and becomes an alcoholic (152, 153). The narrator retains his habit of visiting bookstores on Saturday mornings and buys Jung's *Memories, Dreams, Reflections* (156). Although Jung does not make much sense to the narrator, he is "taken by the coloured mandalas in the illustrations" and resolves to write and live "by the light of ... [his] mandala. In its glow, any detail of the world might seem significant" (156, 158). Murnane's reference to Jung and the narrator's fascination with mandalas clearly allude to White's *The Solid Mandala*, which Murnane refers to directly in *Inland*, and is the Australian suburban novel with which Murnane's work shares most in common.[19]

The narrator's encounter with Jung and discovery of his mandala leads him to resolve to "write only prose in future," since "a poem seemed a stunted, greenish thing compared with a huge, tangled, many-coloured novel" (157). While living in Frankston, the narrator reads a review of Gunter Grass' *The Tin Drum* and decides that the novel is "a message" to his "nervous system from the teeming, glowing world outside" (157-58). He keeps the review but does not actually read the novel, declaring,

> It was enough for me to know that a German with a resonant, evocative name had written a book to prove that everything in the world was worth looking at and touching. In any case, I had to begin my notes for a novel that would do for Melbourne what Grass had done for Danzig. (158)

As part of his project to write a Melbourne novel similar to *The Tin Drum*, the narrator applies for positions in inner-suburban schools, and by 1963 is living in Carlton (158). The narrator rents his Carlton room from a man he calls "the Danziger," whom he met during the summer holidays while

> walking from one hotel to another around the edge of the city, buying a pot of beer in each and looking around for a circle of drinkers who seemed like characters from *The Tin Drum*, whose clothes and gestures and words derived from elaborate mandalas. (158)

After drinking together from midday until early evening, the Danziger takes the narrator home and makes him repeat to his wife his plans for his Melbourne novel, explaining that "the characters would squeeze boils, and vomit, and smash windows with their voices. The Danziger told his wife to tidy their spare room, and ... [the narrator] moved in with [his] clothes and books next day" (158-59).

After moving in to the Danziger's house, the narrator buys *The Tin Drum* and reads it aloud to the Danziger and his wife (159). After the three finish the novel, "the Danziger, who considered himself a philosopher and an atheist," reads Bertrand Russell's *History of Western Philosophy* to his wife and the narrator (159). In an echo of "The Battle of Acosta Nu," on Saturday nights the Danziger and his wife attend parties in the suburbs, urging the narrator to accompany them and "bring back a woman"; however, the narrator always returns home "in a taxi with just the Danziger and his wife" (159). Eventually, the narrator befriends the art teacher at his school and asks her to accompany him to the horse races (161). After a successful afternoon, the art teacher invites the narrator to her flat, where they talk and drink until after midnight (161). However, a lasting relationship fails to develop.

In the final years of his twenties, the narrator becomes a statewide relieving teacher, "at the disposal of the Education Department," and spends "months at a time" teaching in country schools (163). He finds himself living a version of his Casterton fantasy "in country hotels with only a suitcase of clothes and a pad of blank pages as ... possessions" (163). The narrator is occasionally assigned to a school in a provincial city or a Melbourne suburb, where the male teachers "would defer a little" to him during their weekly drinking sessions, because he "was a man who had not been trapped by marriage (as they affected to think they had been) and was not burdened with mortgage payments and lawn-mowing and home handyman jobs" (165). Although Murnane presents suburban life as restrictive here, his use of an unreliable narrator makes it difficult to determine whether the men actually feel constrained by suburban life, or if that is simply the narrator's misguided interpretation.

When the narrator is thirty-four, a magazine publishes his story entitled *Charlie Alcock's Cock* (which, of course, is the next piece in *Landscape with Landscape*); he describes the narrative as having "begun as a section in the huge novel I had not even half-finished. It was a mostly imaginary story about a man I might have been if things had gone differently " (166).[20] The narrator's description of his story also serves as an apt description of all six pieces in *Landscape with Landscape*, which can be read as six versions of Murnane's life. Now that he is a published author, the narrator applies for jobs where he might encounter "literary people" and receives an appointment as "an assistant publications officer with the Department of Main Roads" (166). He works in a city office and lives in a South Yarra flat, "in the cheaper quarter south of the Toorak Road post office" (167). The narrator is successful in finding "literary people," as a senior colleague who has published poetry invites him to a gathering at his house, located "in one of the better parts of South Yarra" (167).

The narrator tells the colleague and his guests that he has moved to South Yarra because he believes he belongs "on the margins of things" and wants to "live as a tenant in a suburb of mostly transient people" (167). He declares that the "sound of the Dandenong trains at night" brings his childhood as close as he wants it and the "wind from the sea" is sometimes enough to warn him "away from the bayside suburbs, where ... [he] had once spent two miserable years" (167). The narrator concludes that his place is "Melbourne and its hinterland to the north and west," stating, "I had never been anywhere else; my hair was turning grey and I had never crossed the borders of the State of Victoria" (169). Murnane's repeated use of narrators who have never left Melbourne or Victoria has surely contributed to the exaggerated accounts of his aversion to travel.

The fifth piece, "Charlie Alcock's Cock," is the only one in which Murnane devotes a considerable portion of the narrative to the narrator's childhood; the other five narratives focus on their narrator's lives as adults.

Creating Suburban Fantasies 235

The narrator spends his first ten years "in a suburb of Melbourne so quiet" that he believes people could not survive "on the far side of their trimmed privet hedges unless their wardrobes were stuffed" with secret, mysterious items, "a world that poked up into Melbourne in the dark corners of bedrooms and the shadowy spaces under fruit-trees and behind fowl sheds in backyards wholly hidden from the street" (172). The narrator is convinced that suburbia hides a secret world that he can access if he can discover how. On Sunday afternoons during the late 1940s, the narrator's mother takes him on tram trips to visit aunts and great-aunts (172, 174). The aunt that the narrator and his mother visit most often lives in Hawthorn, and every month the narrator and his mother get off the tram at "the corner of Riversdale and Glenferrie Roads" and walk down narrow side-streets to the aunt's house (173).

During visits to his aunt's house, the narrator sometimes takes his young male cousin for a walk (174). The narrator pauses "at points among the half-dozen streets in the north-eastern right angle between the Glenferrie Road and Riversdale Road tramlines" and waits for his cousin to tell him "something that would cure" his "strange unhappiness as the afternoon turned to evening and the houses and yards still gave nothing away" (174). While walking the quiet suburban streets, the narrator yearns "to hear what a woman or a girl might cry out in a backyard … when she forgot for the moment that her side fence adjoined the street with the strange name and the dark hedge" (174). On a quiet street, the narrator and his cousin kneel "in the very middle of the deserted roadway" and place their "heads against an iron grating to hear the trickling and gurgling of unseen sluggish water on some unthinkable route" (174). All around him, the narrator perceives spaces and knowledge which he cannot access.

Trams and tramlines fascinate the narrator, since they promise access to unknown suburbs. The northern suburb where the narrator lives as a child developed around a tram terminus (174). All the trams the narrator saw in his suburb were "either arriving from the city or setting out for the city along the same straight route. But Hawthorn, east of Melbourne, was crossed by more than one tramline" (174). The narrator thinks of Hawthorn as superior to his own suburb because the presence of numerous tramlines signals the possibility of access to more destinations and their secrets. He derives pleasure from reading the destination signs on the trams: "ST KILDA BEACH, KEW COTHAM ROAD, BURWOOD, WATTLE PARK ELGAR ROAD" (175). Although the narrator has not been to any of the places named on the signs, he associates the names with "open spaces and trees" and thinks of the trams "as bound for some quarter of an immense, park-like landscape" (175).

When the narrator's family has to sell their house, the narrator and his mother move in with his aunt and cousins in Hawthorn while the narrator's father looks for a new home (175). The narrator finds Hawthorn remarkably quiet at night, since cars rarely pass the house, but the trams run regularly: "I could hear the pairs and pairs of steel wheels bumping over the right-angled crossing at Glenferrie and Riversdale Roads. When a tram gathered speed I tried to decide which route it was following" (176). Lying in bed listening to the trams, the narrator thinks about his favorite street, the Boulevard, which is the only street he knows of in Hawthorn that curves and does "not fit neatly in the commonplace grid surrounding it" (176). The narrator prefers the Boulevard to straight streets and "sometimes feared that the streets wherever" he goes will be "too simply arranged to lead to the mystery that hung over certain afternoons" (176). He imagines "streets riddled with strange by-ways and short cuts needing years to explore" and hopes to hear in his "sleep the sounds of trams multiplied, the patterns of their routes made more complex, and all their destinations called into question" (176). For the narrator, suburbia's infrastructure signifies endless possibilities for exploration and the discovery of secret knowledge; this notion contrasts markedly with anti-suburban depictions of suburbia as conformist, repetitive and shallow.

The narrator's older female cousins occasionally invite him on walks and show him their favorite sites, including a cage of canaries, "a greenhouse full of orchids" and a "house they called the Hollywood mansion" (177). The narrator's female cousins call the sights they show him "treats," but he believes he is being deceived, that his cousins want him to believe they have shown him "everything worth seeing in their suburb" (177). The narrator suspects his cousins want him "to see no more than a child should see" and suppose that he knows "nothing about the insides of wardrobes or the dark spaces undermining their house and their suburb" (177-78). The narrator yearns to know what his female cousins talk about when they stand on the street corner in the mornings "waiting for the tram to take them far to the east along Riversdale Road to one of those suburbs where the dark-green of hedges seemed to meet in the middle of the roadway" (178). Envisioning himself the keeper of secret knowledge, the narrator imagines walking with his female cousins "in the Boulevard, following its gradual curve" and stopping them before they could see what lay beyond the curve, "describing all they should expect ahead of them" (178-79).

As part of his quest to discover and share secret knowledge, the narrator takes his male cousin beneath the lemon tree in the backyard, tells him they are "being shut out of the best places around" them, exposes his penis, then encourages his cousin to do the same, wanting them to sit there until he "began to share the urge ... to explore some part of the elaborate network of the places just out of ... reach" (180). However, the boy grabs the narrator's penis and asks him what he calls it; the narrator tells his cousin that it is called a "cock" and the boy begins repeating the word, then chanting and shouting it (180-81). The narrator's aunt hears her son, resulting in the narrator being the recipient of both his mother and aunt's wrath (182). After the embarassing episode, the narrator's family leaves Hawthorn and moves into a house "in an outer suburb among sandy paddocks and factories built of galvanized-iron and cement-sheet," located "a mile from the railway station and ten miles by train from Hawthorn," making Sunday visits to Hawthorn "rare events" (182).

After the narrator finishes school and begins working in a government department, he learns that his male cousin plans to become a priest (188).

A few years later, the cousin enters the seminary and the narrator leaves home to live in rented rooms near Hawthorn (189, 192). The narrator meets his first girlfriend at work when he is "only a few years short of thirty" (194) and begins taking her to visit his cousin (195). After the cousin is ordained and presides over his first mass, his family holds a party at the Hawthorn house, which has been renovated and contains new rooms "where the back lawn had been," although the lemon tree still stands (199-200). The narrator thinks of himself and his cousin as having taken divergent paths, the cousin making "his way towards an idea of God" while the narrator searched "for a certain suburb in a Melbourne of dreams" (201). The narrator admits that from his

> earliest years ... [he] had hoped to find an actual place where the mystery would reveal itself: a suburb at the end of an unmapped tramline, a street bordered with hedges and curving in on itself like a pathway in a maze, even a corner of a backyard or a cupboard in a room made somber by the sunlight of late afternoon. (197-98)

All his life, the narrator has sought to discover the secrets of suburbia.[21]

Once the narrator and his girlfriend marry, the cousin visits "once a month from his parish in the western suburbs" (203). The narrator believes that as a married man he sees "clearly at last" and that he once searched for "Shadowy landscapes interwoven among actual streets and suburbs" solely because he "was baffled by the strangeness of females, having no sister and not even a girl-cousin" of his "own age who might have sat under her lemon tree" with him (203). During the late 1960s, the narrator and his wife purchase their own house "in an outer suburb" and within five years have a son and a daughter (204, 208). The narrator's cousin, who has developed "a considerable reputation as a marriage counselor," holds a position in a diocesan office arranging "conferences for married couples" (207-08). The narrator no longer considers himself happily married, but "could not have explained why" (209).

When the narrator considers leaving his family, he does not think of other women; rather, he has begun to envy the life of his priest-cousin (209). The narrator is uninterested in his cousin's religion, but would like to live like his cousin "in a building ... clearly different from the suburban houses around it" (209). The narrator studies Melbourne's presbyteries and inspects five or six each weekend (209). Although the narrator has "come to despise the Catholic religion," he admires "the sites and structures and surroundings of the homes of Catholic priests" and declares, "I could have wished for a presbytery in every street of every suburb: a place to vary the repetitive pattern of houses of married couples, to hint at other patterns" (210). Eventually the narrator informs his wife that he is leaving in order to "live as a single man in a building that would seem not a part of the suburb around it," where he will work on his writing, which has "developed" to the point where he is on his "way to finishing what later ... [becomes his] first published piece of fiction: *Landscape With Artist*, a story about a man who had travelled backwards and forwards over his territory" (214).

Salusinszky describes "Landscape with Artist," the final piece in *Landscape with Landscape*, as "a hilarious satire on the bohemians who gathered in the semirural Melbourne suburb of Eltham in the 1960s and 1970s" ("Gerald Murnane" 236). The narrator begins his story in 1970 by stating that he is "in the backyard of ... [his] three-bedroom house in the City of Heidelberg, on a gentle slope that ... [he] insist[s] is the first of the foothills of the Kinglake Ranges" (217).[22] The narrator chose his house, where he intends to live for two decades, because it is almost "half-way between the centre of Melbourne and the district of Harp Gully" (217). Whenever he is "half-drunk," the narrator tells his wife and friends that he belongs at Harp Gully, unfolds his favorite map, and points to the line he has "plotted from the inner northern suburb where ... [he] was born to the outer north-eastern suburb where ... [he] now live[s]" (217). He explains that the line represents his lifelong movement in a "north-east direction at an average velocity of 0.75 kilometres per year" and moves his finger across the map to show where he should be by the age of fifty (217).

The narrator states that he is currently stationary in his suburban house because his wife wants their children to have "a good education," but he intends to "catch up again with the projection of the graph" of his life by 1990 and "settle at Harp Gully, on a dry and stony hillside in the rain-shadow of the Kinglake Ranges" (217). The action of "Landscape with Artist" shifts between events that take place in 1960, 1970 and 1980, with the narrator making several trips between Melbourne's suburbs and Harp Gully. In 1960, the narrator sits "on the back veranda of a weatherboard cottage on a hilltop in the district of Harp Gully," where, from the rooftop, he would be able to see in the south-west, "on the hills around Heidelberg, the outer edge of ... the suburban sprawl" (219). The narrator has read *On the Road* twice and constantly carries it with him (220). He drinks wine instead of beer as part of his "program for imitating Jack Kerouac" and believes "that of all young men in Australia," he is "the closest in spirit to Kerouac" (220).[23]

The narrator describes two main groups he is involved with, the scrags and the artists. The scrags are bearded young men who "are the nearest Australian equivalent to the Beats of the USA. The best of them are dedicated to feeling the qualities of particular places and moments" (220). The narrator tries to think of the scrags as distinct from the artists, whom he thinks of as "nothing but pretenders," but admits that he is probably the only person who cares about the distinction, since the "two groups mix freely" and many young men with "wild hair and paint-spattered trousers would regard ... [themselves] as both artist and scrag" (220, 221). The narrator considers himself a scrag, but envies the "self-styled artists," amongst whom he is "never comfortable," since he thinks of himself as a writer (221).

Despite perceiving himself as a writer, the narrator feels that nothing he sees around him belongs in his writing (221). He describes his writing as "landscapes of the mind," which are "a sort of prose-poem made by arranging words from a private collection" (221). When the narrator reads Dylan Thomas' poetry for the first time, he believes that he "devised quite independently, at the age of twenty-one, a way of writing at least comparable to his" (222). Despite his literary ambitions, the narrator does not know any writers, his closest contact with writers being the photographs he sees "each week in the book review pages of *Time*" (223). The narrator plans to quit his "school-teaching job and move to Harp Gully" once his "writing is being published regularly" (227). He lives in the inner suburb of Fitzroy, writing "until long after midnight" on weeknights (236).

During a visit to Harp Gully in 1960, the narrator's friend, the Existentialist, encourages him to bring one of the young female teachers from his school for the weekend (227). However, even when he is drunk, the narrator "cannot imagine" himself "approaching a young woman from the suburbs" and does not think that he "could persuade such a woman to give up her hopes of marriage and a house and garden just to consort with a man of the road, even if he was a published writer" (227). Like the narrators of "Landscape with Freckled Woman" and "Sipping the Essence," the narrator of "Landscape with Artist" mistakenly believes that all suburban women desire marriage and a house above all else.

During the same year, the narrator finds himself drinking "in a hotel lounge in a northern suburb of Melbourne" with colleagues (235). It is the first time the narrator drinks with the other teachers, since he usually travels into the city to drink with scrags (235). In an allusion to "Landscape with Freckled Woman," he finds himself seated next to a young woman with "freckles low on her throat" and finds the suburban hotel lounge a "warm and pleasant place," and when "the sun outside shines between the spring showers" he sees "a rich yellow glow all around" him and decides that the bar "represents the comfortable refuge" he "might have found in the suburbs if ... [he] had not been called to a life on the road" (235-36). The narrator reveals his misogynistic and narrow views of suburban life again when he thinks of the freckled young woman as representative of "all those small-minded but not ungenerous females who might have been content to do the dishes at night and sit in front of the television set and keep ... [him] supplied with cold bottles" of beer while he writes in his room (236). On the train home from Harp Gully a few days later, the narrator writes "a draft of a letter" to the freckled young woman, claiming he is writing "beneath a tree somewhere between Harp Gully and Melbourne" and that he wants to spend his "time in future sipping quiet beers with a sane young woman like herself" (266).

In 1980, the narrator, who has recently left his family, takes his twelve-year-old son on a weekend expedition to Harp Gully, where they stay with an artist; it is his "first night away from Melbourne" since moving out of his family home (228). The narrator, who now describes himself as "an alcoholic failed writer," meets a woman at the artist's home and obtains her address, telling her that he wants to "send her a copy of the best thing" he has "written in twenty years as an unpublished writer of fiction" and that the main character in it "is only an imagined version" of himself (264). "Landscape with Artist" concludes with the narrator traveling home to the suburbs. During the journey, he states, "I ask myself what lies behind me. If I mean to answer my question literally, I might mention a photocopied typescript of a piece of fiction called *Landscape With Freckled Woman*. (It lies in the pack on my shoulders)" (267).

The narrator imagines the artist painting a landscape that includes the narrator walking away; in the painting the figure walking away is "planning to write a piece of fiction" which describes the view of him in more detail. However, the narrator declares he has

> read enough to know that such fiction would seem nowadays merely modish, that my self-conscious narrator would seem only a figure of artifice and not a means of telling the truth. And so I decide never to write such a story. And I keep to my decision. (267)

Murnane's narrator's discussion of fictional techniques is an excellent example of why critics refer to him as a postmodernist and demonstrates a strong understanding of contemporary fiction and criticism, despite Murnane's claims that he lacks knowledge of postmodernism.

Critics of Murnane's work pay significant attention to his narrative technique and praise him highly for his experimentation. Paolo Bartoloni suggests that Murnane's "refusal to conform to conventional narratives by ... stripping his fiction of names, dialogues and clear plots" testifies "to an uncompromised search for a medium through which metaphysical and philosophical preoccupations can be firmly engaged" (115). Likewise, Lucy emphasizes Murnane's unique style and technique, deeming *Landscape with Landscape* "one of Australian fiction's most beautiful lies" and arguing that it "retains its innocence" and is "untainted by trans-Atlantic irony" (105). While acknowledging the importance of Murnane's style and technique, Genoni posits that the critical emphasis on Murnane's style "risks submerging consideration of his place within the broader sweep of Australian literature," arguing that analysis of Murnane's work often overlooks "the extent to which he embeds his quest for self-discovery in images that convey a rich range of meaning associated with being 'Australian'" (302). Indeed, Murnane's descriptions of suburbia include numerous details that emphasize the Australianness of his work. Genoni argues that while Murnane "may not consciously write as part of a national literature, his intensely personal fictions paradoxically mobilize issues of nationhood as effectively as those of his contemporaries who have self-consciously mined the seams of the postcolonial state" (302).

Although *A Lifetime on Clouds* deals with religion intensively and briefly engages with immigration and environmental degradation, Murnane's engagements with suburbia are intensely personal. He does not address in detail many of the common topics in the Australian suburban novel, such as immigration, environmental degradation, Indigenous ownership, non-Indigenous belonging, domestic violence, drug and alcohol abuse, or expatriation. In fact, the only common topics in suburban fiction that Murnane engages with closely are religion and the role of the artist in society, both of which were first addressed in the suburban context by White. Nevertheless, Murnane's repeated use of suburbia as the setting and subject of his unique fictional experiments demonstrate the remarkable possibilities open to writers who reject the anti-suburban tradition. Murnane is certainly not the only Australian writer to reject the anti-suburban tradition, although he is the most unique. My study now moves from a relatively obscure writer's engagement with suburbia to that of Peter Carey, arguably Australia's most prominent contemporary writer.

ENDNOTES

1. Critics widely consider Murnane to be a postmodern writer. See Birns ("Indefinite" 48), Bartoloni (122), Anderson (83), Braun-Bau (48) and Genoni (293). However, Murnane dislikes the label, and in a conversation with Salusinszky declared, "I swear I don't even know the meaning of that fucking expression *post-modern*!" ("Newcastle" 39, original emphasis).
2. Bibliographic information in this and the preceding paragraph is from the AustLit database: search conducted July 13, 2012. *The Plains* has been the subject of more than thirty works of criticism and has been published twice in the United States, by George Braziller in 1985 and New Issues in 2003; reissued in Australia by Penguin in 1984, McPhee Gribble in 1990, and Text in 2000 and 2012; and translated into Swedish in 2005.
3. The MLA database lists just thirty-three works about Murnane, whereas there are 228 works of scholarship listed concerning Malouf and 208 works about Carey. Search conducted July 16, 2012.
4. Kerouac features prominently in *Landscape with Landscape*, and although Kerouac and Murnane are markedly different writers with radically different life experiences, Murnane claims a deep connection to Kerouac: "when I was twenty-one, and working as a primary school teacher ... at the weekends I would try to live what I thought was the way Jack Kerouac would have lived ... Kerouac has had a strange and deep influence on me. Even to this day if I see a new book on him I have to buy it and read it. I think of Jack at least once every day of my life ... Because I think in a silly way that he is my missing part" (Baker 215). When Baker asks if Murnane means "the expansive, travelling part," he replies in the affirmative (215).
5. See Salusinszky (*Gerald Murnane* 1); Baker (216); Braun-Bau (43, 48); Genoni (293) and Salusinszky ("Newcastle" 30). Critics cite Murnane's literary precursors and influences as Borges, Calvino, Beckett, Camus, Kafka, Sartre, Emily Bronte, Samuel Butler, Hardy, Dostoevsky, and Nabokov (Salusinszky, *Gerald Murnane* 2, 27; Anderson 85; Genoni 293; Zawacki 2-4).
6. I am indebted to page 112 of Paolo Bartoloni's article on Calvino and Murnane for this point.

7. Accrington is located five miles east of the real suburb of Caulfield (27), which makes it a substitute for Mount Waverley, Waverley or Glen Waverley.
8. Watsonia is the name of a suburb adjacent to Macleod, Murnane's home suburb for more than thirty years.
9. Examining the names of Melbourne's suburbs reveals that the majority of the inner and middle-belt suburbs have English names, such as Kew, Kensington, Richmond, Collingwood and Camberwell, while few suburbs have Indigenous names. Newer, outer suburbs are much more likely to have Indigenous names, such as Dandenong, Warrandyte and Kurunjang, reflecting White Australia's changing relationship with Indigenous cultures. For more on the use of Indigenous place names, see: Furphy, Sam. "Aboriginal House Names and Settler Australian Identity."
10. Eastern Hill Grammar School and Canterbury Ladies' College are both fictional schools; however, they are thinly-veiled references to Melbourne Grammar School and Presbyterian Ladies' College.
11. Camberwell is an expensive eastern suburb of Melbourne usually associated with the upper-middle class and tree-lined streets. Camberwell Junction is the intersection of Camberwell, Burke and Riversdale roads and the commercial and social locus of the suburb.
12. Ion L. Idriess (1889-1979) was a best-selling Australian author who wrote adventures and historical novels such as *The Red Chief: As Told by the Last of His Tribe* (1953), *Madman's Island* (1927), *Headhunters of the Coral Sea* (1940), and *Nemarluk, King of the Wilds* (1951).
13. Parajoulta seems to be a fictional character; however, Blue Mud Bay is located in the Northern Territory, on the Gulf of Carpentaria, and was the subject of a Native Title ruling in 2005 in which the Federal government's National Native Title Tribunal recognized the Yolngu people's native title rights to the area ("Traditional Rights").
14. However, Murnane addresses Indigenous issues in a remarkable fashion in his short story "Land Deal," which presents the arrival of European settlers in the area now known as Melbourne from the point of view of the Indigenous inhabitants.
15. Orford is indeed a town in the Western District of Victoria, but it is nowhere near Colac; in fact, it is 160 kilometers west of Colac.
16. The narrator of "Landscape with Freckled Woman" imagines himself telling a story about a young man "trying to finish his first novel before he reached the age of thirty. It was the novel of his childhood. He had been born in a northern suburb of Melbourne. His parents had taken him inland

to Bendigo at the age of five and moved back to Melbourne four years later. He had lived in Melbourne ever since" (17). This passage corresponds almost exactly to the facts of Murnane's life.

17. In an article published in March 2008, Murnane writes that when he was in his twenties he "committed to memory all the poems of A.E. Housman in order to save ... [himself] from having what was called in those days a nervous breakdown" and read Thomas Hardy's novels "in order to keep ... [himself] from falling back into the religious beliefs of ... [his] childhood" ("Save Us" 15).
18. Frankston is no longer the last of the suburbs stretching southeast along the Port Philip Bay shore of the Mornington Peninsula. The suburbs now stretch for fifty kilometers from Frankston to Sorrento, which was once an isolated holiday town at the tip of the peninsula.
19. *Landscape with Landscape* and *The Solid Mandala* both examine the role of the artist in society, feature aspiring artists living isolated lives in suburbia, and engage with spirituality.
20. According to Murnane, his third novel, *The Plains*, begun as "part of a chapter in a much larger book which was never published and almost certainly never will be, a novel called *The Only Adam*" (Baker 195).
21. Readers familiar with Borges' work will see many similarities between his concerns and Murnane's, especially the fascination with labyrinths, gardens, books and secrets.
22. The City of Heidelberg was a local government area that was abolished in 1994 and contained the suburbs of Macleod (where Murnane lived for three decades) and Heidelberg, Heidelberg Heights, Heidelberg West, Ivanhoe, Ivanhoe East, Rosanna, Viewbank and Yallambie. Heidelberg is well-known as the location of the Heidelberg School, which consisted of a group of painters, including Frederick McCubbin, Tom Roberts and Arthur Streeton, who painted in Heidelberg during the 1880s and 1890s and remain among Australia's most revered artists. In "Landscape with Artist," Murnane clearly alludes to the painters of the Heidelberg School, who are famous for their landscapes.
23. See note 5 above.

Chapter 6

Taking Suburbia Seriously

Peter Carey's *Bliss* (1981) and *The Tax Inspector* (1991)

While Malouf and Winton have written anti-suburban novels and perpetuated the anti-suburban tradition, Carey is the first prominent living Australian author to reject the anti-suburban tradition and write novels addressing the complexity of suburban life. Malouf and Winton are the only contemporary Australian novelists with national and international reputations comparable to Carey's. Although Malouf and Winton have won numerous national and international awards and have been shortlisted for the Booker Prize, neither of them have won it, unlike Carey, who is one of only two authors who have won the Booker Prize twice, the other being J.M. Coetzee. Carey has been described as "Australia's greatest living writer" (Verghis 15), and, as Bliss notes, "is generally acknowledged" as one of "the Anglophone world's most accomplished and important writers" ("Peter Carey" 283).

Carey was born in Bacchus Marsh, Victoria, in 1943. He was educated at Geelong Grammar School before attending Monash University, dropping out after a year of studying chemistry, and began working in advertising. Carey was exposed to literature by colleagues in a Melbourne advertising agency and began writing fiction in the early 1960s. Carey established his reputation in the 1970s with two collections of short fiction, *The Fat Man in History* (1974) and *War Crimes* (1979). Carey's highly experimental short stories are unlike any previous Australian fiction (Hassall, "Peter Carey" 54). Craig Munro, the former University of Queensland Press editor, describes Carey as "the most spectacular talent to emerge in the 1970s" (Qtd. in Gelder and Salzman, *Diversity* 15). *Bliss*, Carey's first published novel, won two major awards in Australia, the Miles Franklin and the New South Wales Premier's Literary Award, and was runner-up for the National Book Council Award. Hassall notes that *Bliss* "consolidated Carey's growing Australian and international reputation as one of the most exciting and imaginative of contemporary writers" (*Dancing* 64). Carey's second published novel, *Illywhacker* (1985), was short-listed for the Booker Prize and won five major Australian awards, establishing Carey "as a novelist of international stature"; his "spectacular rise to fame reached its apogee in 1988" when his third published novel, *Oscar and Lucinda*, won the Booker Prize (Hassall, *Dancing* 3).

In 1993, *Oscar and Lucinda* was "judged the second best, after Salman Rushdie's *Midnight's Children*, of the then 25 Booker Prize winners" (Hassall, *Dancing* xix). In the same year, Turner described Carey's "level of visibility" as "exceptional" and argues that he was "a national figure" by the end of the 1980s ("Nationalising" 132). Carey has published nine novels and three other books since *Oscar and Lucinda* and won numerous awards; as a result, his reputation has grown to the point that he is among the most renowned living Anglophone writers, part of an elite group including Salman Rushdie, J.M. Coetzee and Ian McEwan. Australian novelist and critic Nicholas Jose argues that Carey represents Australia "on the literary map, as Margaret Atwood represents Canada and Salman Rushdie India," declares that he has watched Carey's "brilliant career with appreciation and pride," and characterizes Carey as "a daredevil, a dealer, an investigator, a spin-doctor, a phantom, an opportunist – a literary Houdini" (140, 141, 137).

Carey moved to New York in 1989, where he continues to live while writing almost exclusively about Australia. Carey hates the term "expatriate" and prefers to be referred to as "a writer living overseas" (Verghis 16). Carey's literary influences include Borges, Barthelme, Vonnegut, Marquez, Faulkner, Kerouac, Joyce and Nabokov (Daniel, *Liars* 152). Given Carey's international reputation and influential stature, his engagements with suburbia carry more weight than those of any other contemporary Australian novelist and have the potential to shape both reader's attitudes and other writers' engagements with suburbia. While Murnane uses suburbia as a setting for highly personal fictional experiments, Carey utilizes suburbia to directly engage important issues in contemporary Australian society, including the effects of capitalism, consumerism and American imperialism; incest, child sexual abuse and domestic violence; sexuality and family relationships; immigration; environmental degradation; and both organized and petty crime.

Bliss: Life and Death in Mt. Pleasant[1]

Between 1977 and 1981, Carey lived in a commune near Yandina in southern Queensland. While living in the commune, Carey wrote fiction and continued to work in advertising, spending one week per month in Sydney. *Bliss* was written in the commune, which, along with the advertising industry, plays a major role in the novel (Daniel, *Liars* 151; Hassall, "Peter Carey" 54, *Dancing* xvi). Describing the publication of *Bliss* in 1981, Jose declares, "It was addressed to the world we lived in and was an immediate hit: bright, zesty and atmospheric; a classic piece of contemporary fiction ... people argued about it around dinner tables" (143). Despite the awards and positive popular and critical reception, some reviewers of the novel "were disconcerted by the change of genre," since they had pigeonholed Carey as a short fiction writer, were not aware that he had written five unpublished novels, and did not know that "his ambition had always been to succeed as a novelist" (Hassall, "Peter Carey" 55).[2]

The settings Carey utilizes in *Bliss* play crucial roles in the construction of meaning and the development of themes; however, critics have paid little attention to the specific settings of the novel, especially the suburban setting, other than the pastoral setting of the commune in the final thirty-page section, which comprises just ten percent of the text. Carey does not specifically name the nation, states, or city in which the action of *Bliss* take place; moreover, the only specifically named locations in which the novel's action occurs are the commune at Bog Onion Road and Harry Joy's suburban home at 25 Palm Avenue, Mt. Pleasant (60).[3] Nevertheless, critics agree that *Bliss* is set in Australia.[4] Hassall argues that *Bliss* is "recognisably Australian," and while the setting is "resolutely non-specific," he sees it as "a deliberate conflation of Sydney, Brisbane, Townsville and Cairns" (*Dancing* 72). Jose declares that *Bliss* is "Set in a magical zone on the north coast of New South Wales" and that the characters are "late-twentieth-century Australians" (145, 144). Theodore Sheckels notes that *Bliss* is "set in Australia in the 1960s or 1970s" and claims that it is difficult to precisely locate both the time and place of the novel, since "there are only a few clues that point to the Australian setting" (89).

However, the novel actually contains numerous clues to its Australian setting, including place names, the names of vegetation, descriptions of architecture, and references to colonialism, England and America.[5] For example, the novel contains many references to vegetation found in the Australian sub-tropics, including flame trees, jacarandas, mangoes, bananas, bougainvillea, poinciana, pawpaws, mangroves, lantana bushes, avocados and papaya.[6] On several occasions, references to the weather, seasons and specific dates definitively place the setting of the novel in a subtropical latitude in the Southern Hemisphere, where winters are like European summers, there are wet and dry seasons, rather than four distinct seasons, and September marks the end of winter (30, 59, 225, 255, 267). The Australian setting of the novel is abundantly clear in the novel's final section, which refers to rainforests, cyclones, yellow box and eucalypt trees, and repeatedly mentions "the bush" (277, 295, 296).[7]

Sheckels notes that if the primary setting of the novel is located in New South Wales, "then the ecotopia [Bog Onion Road] must be somewhere up in Queensland" (89). Sheckels' contention is supported by the text, especially the scene in which Harry pursues Honey Barbara after she runs away from Palm Avenue. Harry finds Honey "one hundred miles up Highway One" and drives her the further 400 miles north to Bog Onion Road (248). Highway One is the coastal highway that circumnavigates Australia and serves as the most direct route between Sydney and Brisbane. On their way to Bog Onion Road, Harry and Honey drive "through Sunday traffic past giant fiberglass pineapples and bananas" (249). Here, Carey clearly alludes to two well-known tourist attractions, the Big Pineapple near Nambour in Queensland and the Big Banana at Coffs Harbour in New South Wales. The Big Pineapple is less than ten miles from Yandina, where Carey lived from 1977 to 1981, while the Big Banana is just over three hundred miles south of Yandina. Thus, if Bog Onion Road is based on Yandina, then Harry's fictional hometown would lie somewhere between Port Macquarie and Coffs Harbour.

Although the critics who have paid attention to the novel's setting have largely focused on the bush setting of the final section, the vast majority of the novel's action takes place in an unnamed coastal city and one of its suburbs, Mt. Pleasant, where the protagonist Harry Joy lives with his wife Bettina and children Lucy and David. The unnamed urban area is referred to as both a town and a city, and neither its population nor its geographical size is specified. However, many clues suggest that the city is quite large, such as the presence of a freeway (236), ships moored in the river (47), numerous suburbs (102), "factory-lined streets" (188), traffic reports on the radio (261), crowded city streets (249), a Hilton hotel, and neon signs atop "glossy, black-windowed" buildings in the city center (79). When Honey Barbara angrily gets out of Harry and Bettina's Jaguar at a busy intersection in the city (186), she walks streets lined with used-car yards and warehouses and through department stores and a fish market (204). She climbs "above the coastal plain" to the top of Mount Sugar Loaf and walks "the unnamed streets ... where the unemployed, hippies, junkies, and even the respectable poor lived amongst the smell of unsewered drains, half-buried shit, uncollected garbage, jasmine, honeysuckle and frangipani" (204). In the city square, Honey finds a phone box and telephone directory and locates Harry's house in Palm Avenue; she finds a street directory in the square and discovers that she is three miles from Harry's suburban home (205).

The novel opens with Harry dying of a heart attack on his suburban front lawn and having an out-of-body experience, rising high above his suburb. From his vantage point, Harry sees a

> blue jeweled bay eating into what had once been a coastal swamp ... [a] long meandering brown river ... quiet streets and long boulevards planted with mangoes, palms, flame trees, jacarandas, and bordered by antiquated villas in their own grounds, nobly proportioned mansions erected by ship-owners, sea captains and vice-governors. (11-12)

This description of the city indicates that the setting is sub-tropical and contains evidence of colonialism, capitalism, urban development, and alteration of the natural environment. The city is described as being "on the outposts of the American Empire," and Harry conducts

> his business more or less in the American style, although with not quite the degree of seriousness the Americans liked. Telexes which began their journeys in Chicago, Detroit or New York found their way to him up river, where he interpreted these requests in a manner which ... suited local conditions. (13)

The depiction of the city as an outpost of "the American Empire" alludes to the late-twentieth-century American dominance of Australian culture and commerce, and the description of messages from the centre of the empire reaching Harry "up river" on the margins, where he acts according to "local conditions," echoes the situation and behavior of Kurtz in Conrad's *Heart of Darkness*.

Harry's wife Bettina hates her hometown and dreams of moving to New York. She hates her city's

> wide colonial verandahs, its slow muddy river, its sleepy streets, its small-town pretentions. She loathed the perpetual Sunday afternoons, the ugly people, the inelegant bars and frumpy little frocks. Here, marooned on the edge of the Empire, she had spent ten years waiting for Harry's promise that they would go to New York. (24)

After his heart attack, Harry convalesces in the local hospital awaiting surgery. The hospital is located beside the river in an "old building" with verandahs that are "smothered in bougainvillea and surrounded by big old flame trees, frangipanis and mangoes" and banana trees (23, 25). However, Bettina sees "no charm" in a building and grounds that many would describe as peaceful and beautiful (23). Harry does not share his wife's hatred of the city and its residents, and frequents a restaurant called Milano's, which he considers his "favourite place in the world" (65). After Harry's heart bypass surgery, his "second death," he wakes up believing he has gone to Hell, and comes to think of Milano's as "a sanctuary ... where one could momentarily forget the tribulations and terrors of the unknown continent" (65, 68), making a blatant allusion to the early European settlers' fears of Australia.

Although more that half of the action of *Bliss* takes place in the fictional suburb of Mt. Pleasant, the vast majority of the scholarship on the novel ignores Carey's engagement with suburbia. Unlike Johnston, Malouf, Winton, Lucashenko, McCann and others, Carey does not depict suburbia in an overwhelmingly negative manner. In fact, *Bliss* does not contain any explicitly anti-suburban passages, although on a few occasions Bettina briefly expresses disgust with suburbia and its residents. While visiting Harry in hospital, she fantasizes about picking up the nurses "by their necks" and shaking them "for their dreary ambitions and their dreary lives ... They went back to the suburbs and had families" (26). On another occasion, while arguing with her daughter, Bettina declares, "'You are going to be a social worker and you'll just get your degree and end up with a line of children and a house in the suburbs'" (102). However, most of Bettina's hatred is directed at other people generally, rather than suburbia or suburbanites specifically. Moreover, since Bettina is a suburban wife and mother with thwarted ambitions, her hatred of other suburbanites may well be a manifestation of self-loathing.

Bliss contains many negative depictions of the society in which it is set, but the negativity is aimed either at the city or at capitalism, rather than suburbia. Obviously, suburbia is part of the capitalist system and an extension of the city, but Carey does not single out suburbia for direct criticism. In fact, the word "suburbia" does not even appear in the novel. The fact that Carey does not follow the anti-suburban tradition and attack suburbia, even though his suburban characters engage in negative behaviors, including infidelity and incest, suggests that he takes suburbia seriously as the site in which most Australian lives are lived, and the scene in which a great variety of human activities take place. Of all the criticism on *Bliss*, only one article addresses suburbia in any detail. Interestingly, the article in question, "Utopia in Peter Carey's *Bliss*," by Don Fletcher, is by a political scientist, not a literary critic. However, Fletcher's analysis is quite superficial and does not acknowledge the complexities of suburbia or Carey's ambivalent representation of it. Fletcher reads suburbia as a "site of consumption," labels Harry a "happy consumer," and focuses on Harry's fondness for silk shirts and fine wine, which tempt him on his return to suburbia after his family commit him to a mental institution (41).

On the first page of the novel, Harry Joy dies of a heart attack "in the middle of ... [his] green suburban lawn" (11). Harry's "first death" lasts for nine minutes before his heart is restarted by electric shock (12). Carey presents Harry looking down on his body from "a certain height above the lawn," noticing that the lawn is "very, very green, [and] composed of broad-leaved tropical grasses, each blade thrillingly clear" and wonders "why everyone else had forsaken it for the verandah" (11). Harry and his family live in a middle-class "straight-laced suburb where people brought home alcohol in special little cases ... The children, what few there were, all had clean nails and in many houses they still said grace" (34, 193-94). Hassall argues that Harry's first death "is presented as a fall from a primal, albeit suburban, innocence" (*Dancing* 72). Before his heart attack, Harry lives a happy, naïve life in suburbia: "he thought himself happy, and why shouldn't he? He had a wife who loved him, children who gave no trouble, an advertising agency which provided a good enough living for a man with an almost aristocratic disdain for mercantile success" (13). Bruce Woodcock argues that Harry's existence before his "first death" was "structured around his own self-satisfaction and complacency" (44). It is not until after Harry's surgery that he understands that his family is dysfunctional and he has a distorted view of his life.

However, Harry begins questioning the value of his life before undergoing surgery, when he writes a farewell note to his family and prints the address as "Bettina and Lucy and David Joy, 25 Palm Avenue, Mt Pleasant" (49). He thinks of "His whole world" as being

> contained in those ten words ... It seemed nothing, a life so pitiful and thin that it was an insult to whoever made him. It was not so much that he had achieved nothing, but that he had seen nothing, remembered nothing. A series of politenesses, lunches, hangovers, dirty plates and glasses, food trodden into carpets, spilt wines. (49-50)

Harry reaches "the sour realization that he had made a fool of himself and done things he hadn't meant to" (50). However, Harry's loss of innocence, new awareness of his family's problems, and realization of his past errors are not specific criticisms of suburban life; rather, they are more broadly applicable to the life of any person in any time or place who has failed to pay attention to his or her daily existence.

After his successful heart surgery, Harry becomes convinced that he has died and is in "Hell" (52). During his convalescence in Palm Avenue, Harry conducts "tests" and writes observations in spiral-bound notebooks, which he keeps locked in ammunition boxes in the garage: "Harry Joy is running checks. He is comparing his life (termed 'life' in the books) with his other life, that is the days and years before he entered the operating room" (55). Having become disgusted with his family's behavior, Harry leaves his family and retreats "to a suite on the twenty-first floor of the Hilton" (115). At the hotel, Harry lives lavishly and spends a small fortune on food, alcohol and the prostitute Honey Barbara, who lives for the majority of each year in a commune at Bog Onion Road, where she was born and raised. Harry's family and his American business partner Joel, who is having an affair with Bettina, contrive to have Harry committed to a mental institution. After Harry is released, he and Honey both take up residence at Palm Avenue, as do Bettina's lover Joel and Lucy's boyfriend Ken. The narrator reveals that the neighbors are aware that "something decadent" is going on, but the "only firm sign" they have is Ken's "great derelict Cadillac parked in the middle of the once neat lawn. Around this Cadillac they had watched Lucy and her new boyfriend dance with wrenches and electric drills, but they did not see that as the problem, more as a symbol" (193). Here Carey alludes to the surveillance activities of the neighbors and the ways in which the Joy family and their lovers deviate from suburban norms.

While living with his family and their companions in Palm Avenue, Harry marvels "at the richness and variety of life in Hell" (197). In *Bliss*, Carey never presents suburbia as boring or repressive. Despite her hatred of capitalism and consumerism and her belief in the superiority of rural life, Honey Barbara develops "a taste for expensive wine" and gets "sucked into the madness which took place around the dining table at Palm Avenue" (225). Much to the alarm of her "silent Victorian heart," Honey starts to enjoy life in suburbia, complains "triumphantly about her hangovers" and even enjoys the "shouting and arguing which would have been considered boorish at home" (226). Interestingly, life in the commune is more polite and reserved than life in middle-class suburbia, and on several occasions, Honey is described as having "Victorian" morals (213, 226), despite her drug use and annual season of prostitution. Honey thinks of the residents of Palm Avenue as more alive than her companions in the commune, who spend much of their time "sitting back zonked out on dope" (226).

Although Carey names Harry's suburb and indicates that it is middle class, he does not describe Mt. Pleasant in any detail. However, Harry's house is described extensively. The Joy home is

> an old planter's house, designed to cool off quickly in the evening ... built on high stilts so that air circulated beneath the floor and the walls were only clad on one side, the inside, so that the uprights and cross-bracings became a decorative element to the exterior walls. (223)

The house has "high-ceilinged rooms," wide verandahs in the front and back, and is described as "charming" and "expensive but not of the first rank" (58, 59, 92, 103, 257). Although the term does not appear in the text, the house is a Queenslander, similar to that owned by Kerry and Rachel in Lucashenko's *Steam Pigs*. The garden is also described in detail; it contains flowerbeds, "honeysuckle and frangipani," a "hammock stretched from the red flaming poinciana to the side fence" and "pawpaws on the tree outside the kitchen window" (58, 59, 92). The narrator describes the air in Harry's backyard as "so fragrant that ... one could have imagined that the grass was perfumed" (59). The backyard is "thick and glossy with the luxurious semi-tropical vegetation people fly half-way round the world for" (59). Harry's suburban garden is depicted as a sub-tropical paradise in stark contrast to the unappealing suburban gardens in the novels by Johnston, Lucashenko and McCann.

The interior of the Joys' house signals the family's affluence and middle-class taste. The dining table, which serves as the focal point for much of the action of the suburban sections of the novel, is "Georgian, made from English Ash and imported by a sea captain from a certain Percy Lewis Esq." (102). Not only does the antique dining table represent affluence and solidity, it also functions as a reminder of English colonialism. The narrator reveals that before Harry's heart attack and surgery,

Bettina was "fastidious about the house," since she possessed a "strong streak of very-small-town politeness and a serious concern for what the neighbours thought, although she would have violently denied it" (62). During Harry's convalescence, Bettina leaves "pictures to hang crooked" and "floors unswept" (62). Harry had always preferred that the house and garden be kept neat; he liked "the grass trim, the floors polished, the magazines in their rack" (191). However, after returning from the mental institution, he is pleased to see the house "in disarray ... At least there was some external sign of change ... There were empty tins everywhere and, on the front lawn, an ancient Cadillac with a crumpled tail fin ... The back garden was high with weeds" (191).

When Harry is released from the mental institution after Bettina makes a deal with him and pays off the management, he decides that he can no longer live in suburbia (207). However, he quickly changes his mind, realizing that his suburban home provides security and sanctuary (207). When Honey arrives at Palm Avenue, she declares that she will stay for three months and do all the cooking (209). She discards the food in the Joys' kitchen, intending to replace it with healthier alternatives (211). Honey takes food extremely seriously and divides "the world into people who ... [eat] shit and people who ... [eat] good food" (214). Not only does Honey change the Joys' eating habits, she physically alters their house and garden. In order to plant a vegetable garden, she takes to "the back lawn with a spade," transforming "it into something useful" (255). She starts a compost heap, mulches with hay, and purchases "seedlings from Garry at the Zen Inn" (225). Inside the house, Honey changes the bedroom she shares with Harry by painting "the frames of the three windows three different colours" and beginning a mural above the bed depicting a scene from the commune at Bog Onion Road (229). In an attempt to "make the bedroom a peaceful place" she furnishes it with cushions and candles, burns incense, and installs wind chimes (230).

A number of critics, including Jose and Daniel, view Harry Joy as an everyman representative of the average Australian. Jose describes Harry as "one of us, a local Hamlet, crawling between heaven and earth, a middling man in the middle of his existence" (146). Daniel argues that Harry is "a Good Bloke, a conventional family man, living in a conventional house and style, in a conventional job. He is blind to the faults in others and to the injustices of the world which is surely conventional too" (*Liars* 159). Following Jose and Daniel's line of reasoning, one may conclude that Carey uses suburbia as the primary setting because it is the location where the average Australian life is lived. Despite his representativeness, Harry, according to Hassall, is a "complex and compelling" character "who is both a loser and a winner" (*Dancing* 63). Early in the novel, before Harry's enlightenment and transformation, the narrator describes him as a thirty-nine-year-old who believes what he reads in the newspapers, "someone of note but not of importance, occupying a social position below the Managing Director of the town's largest store and even the General Manager of the canning factory" (13). Harry's "great talent in life" is to be "a Good Bloke" (13). He can enter a room and everybody is "happy to have him, even if all he ever" does is smile, since he projects the aura of being "intelligent enough to be critical," yet never criticizes (13).

Harry enjoys a reputation as "something of a story-teller," is popular with women, lets "himself be seduced" by them, and accepts "their praises without embarrassment" (13, 14). The narrator declares that Harry is "not particularly intelligent, not particularly successful, not particularly handsome and not particularly rich. Yet there was about him this feeling that he belonged to an elite" (14). Harry does not read books, but acquires his skill as a storyteller from his father Vance, who was "born in New York State and had traveled the world" (38, 19). Despite running a fairly successful advertising agency, Harry is not ambitious. The narrator describes Harry's business as a "slightly decrepit ... old boat drifting with the current down a slow muddy river" (24). Harry gets out of the boat "every now and then" and pushes "it away from the bank" but has no desire to compete at a high level (24). In an interview with Philip Nielsen, Carey states that "Harry is a fool" who

> basically reacts to things that happen. It becomes more and more apparent that he is an extraordinarily passive character in many respects and it is the women that have the drive and the ideas. I like Bettina, she is a much more interesting character than Harry is and she has got more passion, more drive. (69)

Harry's wife Bettina is in many ways his opposite. While he is easygoing, humorous, passive and popular, she is ambitious, serious, active and abrasive. The women whom Harry has affairs with "could never understand how he had married Bettina, who always seemed to speak badly of everyone and everything" (14). Bettina is also unfaithful, although she does so "less cleanly ... less gracefully" than Harry (14). Bettina is loud and coarse "and her aggressions, normally so well hidden beneath a pancake make-up of niceness, cracked and broke on the third martini" (14). Bettina is well aware of her own nature, and states: "'I was never a sweet little wifey. I was a hard ambitious bitch'" (184).

Since her adolescence, Bettina has dreamed of moving to New York and becoming a "hot-shot" in the advertising industry:

> And while she waited she became more American than the Americans. She supported their wars, saw their movies, bought their products, despised their enemies ... She believed in the benevolence of their companies, the triumph of their astronauts, the law of the market-place and the twin threats of Communism and the second-rate. (100)

As part of her New York dream, Bettina cultivates Americans, reads their magazines, and saves money "in a special account" (25). Although Harry has vaguely promised to sell the business sometime in the future, Bettina fantasizes about Harry quietly dying in his sleep so that she will be free to move to New York (25). Bettina's daughter Lucy, a communist for most of the novel, is irritated by her mother's "elitist attitudes" and asks her, "'What's the matter with being ordinary? ... Why do you want to be special?'" (102). Bettina replies, "'I couldn't bear to be second rate'" (102).

Harry meets Honey Barbara while residing in the Hilton suite; when he calls an escort agency for a prostitute, she is sent to his room. Honey is "tall and straight ... [and] from instant to instant, severely plain then astonishingly beautiful, and her most beautiful and obvious feature was her very large, almost impossibly large, brown eyes" (126). Honey tells Harry that she is a "'gifted amateur,'" which is not strictly true, since prostitution is

> her one commercial talent and once a year, for two months, she came down to the city and signed up with the Executive Escort Agency. She felt as ambivalent about it as she felt about the city itself, sometimes looking back on it with nostalgia and forgetting that daily life was normally spent in fear and homesickness. (129)

Honey earns three hundred dollars per "trick," which goes a long way in the commune at Bog Onion Road, where it is "enough to live on for six weeks ... a roof. A water tank. A stove ... thirty avocado trees. Half a horse" (129). Harry becomes Honey's regular client, and she visits his suite each morning (133).

Honey has come down to the city with Damian, a fellow resident of the commune, who is responsible for selling the annual marijuana crop. Honey worries about Damian, who is "immersing himself in a whole lot of city shit ... eating Kentucky Frieds and Big Macs ... soon he would be covered with poisonous fat from cancered chickens and Big Macs" (133). Although Honey views the city as the source of innumerable poisons, "each year when the wet ended she found herself looking forward to it again," having forgotten the "dreadful fear she felt in the city. She remembered the bars and restaurants and movies and even the junk food seemed tasty in her memory" (135). While living in the commune, Honey forgets "how damn miserable" the city-dwellers "looked and how dirty the air was and most of all ... the anger. They seemed knotted in anger, and the whole of the city seemed like it was about to uncoil itself in a paroxysm of fury" (135). Honey thinks of the city as "a force, half machine, half human, exuding poisons" (135). The negative descriptions of the city conveyed through Honey and other characters are not accompanied by negative depictions of the suburbs. If one reads *Bliss* as an attack on the built environment, it is the city, rather than the suburbs, which bears the brunt of the criticism.

Like White and Murnane, Carey uses suburbia as a setting in which to examine issues concerning religion and spirituality. Daniels notes that at the beginning of the novel, "Carey sets up the double notions that are our landmarks ... Life and death, pleasure and pain, Heaven and Hell, bliss and punishment" (*Liars* 159). Daniel goes on to argue that *Bliss* "explores the existential horror lying just below the surface of the ordinary life of a Good Bloke" and describes *Bliss* as "a post-Christian fable" that "opens with a gathering of myths ... of innocence and purity ... that no longer hold" (*Liars* 161, 160). Likewise, Hassall describes *Bliss* as "a religious allegory," albeit one that is situated "in a late-twentieth-century, post-Christian outpost of the 'American Empire'" (*Dancing* 72). Ryan-Fazilleau also notes the frequent use of binaries that Daniel identifies, arguing that Carey "plays on the binary opposition between heaven and hell that is part of" the Western tradition "and also an element of the Australian heritage" in that Australia, "since the beginning of white settlement ... has regularly been described as either a hell on earth (for convicts) or a heaven on earth (... 'working man's paradise,' 'lucky country')" (78). According to Ryan-Fazilleau, before Harry's heart attack and operation, he "lived in an illusory Garden of Eden surrounded by his loving family" (79). John Eustace argues that Harry's "desire to understand the world in terms of a binary between good and evil ... arises from a desire to absolve himself of responsibility for an oblivious, immoral life and for the vice of his family" (111).

As Harry lies in hospital after his heart attack awaiting surgery, he contemplates death, but is less concerned about dying than about where he will go after he dies (23). While in hospital, Harry asks Bettina if she believes in God; she does not answer his question, but the narrator provides her thoughts: "If she had been religious she would have believed in Satan and would have found him, in her terms, 'generally less boring.' But religion represented all the goody-goody two-shoes and she found it embarrassing even to talk about" (28). Harry reveals to Bettina that he had an out-of-body experience during the heart attack and declares that it is "'a warning ... I saw Heaven and Hell. There is a Heaven. There is a Hell'" (28-29). However, once Harry is out of hospital, he decides that the Hell he finds himself in "is not the childish Hell of the Christian Bible with its flames. Here ... they planned more subtle things" (56). Harry does not return to the Christian church in which he was raised and does not adopt any religion during the remainder of his lifetime. However, he determines to be "Good" and attempts to live a moral life. Ryan-Fazilleau argues that even though Harry's ordeals in the hospital and mental institution have taught him to recognize "the difference between Good and Evil, he still cannot muster the necessary force of character to give up his decadent world and face the rigours of the lifestyle in Honey Barbara's hippie community at Bog Onion Road" (80), where he has promised to go with her.

One of the central themes of Carey's investigation of suburbia, both in *Bliss* and *The Tax Inspector*, is that of dysfunctional families. Before Harry's heart attack and surgery, he "was never heard to criticize anyone ... He exhibited a blindness towards the faults of people and the injustices of the world" (14). Harry's blindness prevents him from seeing the dysfunctional relationships and behaviors within his family. Harry's seventeen-year-old son David is a drug dealer and his fifteen-year-old daughter Lucy engages in an incestuous relationship with her brother, exchanging oral sex for marijuana (36). After a scene in which Lucy performs fellatio on David, the narrator states that Harry has "never seen his family as you, dear reader, have now been privileged to" (37). Harry's marriage is also dysfunctional; not only do Harry and Bettina both have affairs, but his refusal to allow her to join his advertising agency is the source of great contention. Early in the novel, Harry is "not sorry" that he had not allowed Bettina to join the business, since he "had offered her enough money to start a little boutique instead" (48). Harry tells Bettina that he did not let her into the business because she did not have the necessary experience, "But the truth was ... [that] he did not want his wife around the office undermining his dignity" (49). The narrator reveals that Harry and Bettina have been arguing about whether or not she could join the business for five years before his heart attack, that "Bettina had been deeply offended by his refusal," and that "It was a rejection more painful than any she had ever experienced and she could not forgive him" (100).

After Harry returns home from the hospital believing he is in hell, he observes his family as if for the first time and begins to perceive and understand the magnitude of their problems. Harry detaches himself from his family and withholds "his vast, blind, uncritical love" (57). Finding their love unreciprocated for the first time, Harry's family punish him

> with a fury that puzzled them and left them guilty and shaken, offering apologies that could not be accepted, the rejection of which, in turn, produced greater hurts, ripped scar tissue before it was healed, and ended in scenes of such emotion and frenzy that the neighbours turned off their lights and came out into their gardens. (57)

Eventually, Harry's family decide to ignore him and he finds himself isolated and alone, prowling the lawn, haunting the garage, and staring at the television (61).

As part of his observations and "tests," Harry pretends to board a flight for a business trip and then leaves the plane at the last moment, returning home to climb a tree beside his house and conduct a "Final Test" (107).[8] While in the tree, Harry sees his wife having an affair with his business partner and his daughter performing oral sex on his son (110). After his "Final Test," Harry curses his family and checks in to the Hilton (112, 115). Huggan notes that Harry "sees his whole world fall apart; his illusions of 'success' and 'goodness' are completely, devastatingly, shattered. No indignity is spared him" (*Peter Carey* 6). Likewise, Hassall argues that Harry's "fall into the nightmare world of Experience involves a major deconstruction of the stories he has been telling himself about his business and his family" (*Dancing* 73). While at the Hilton, Harry learns that the products of one of his clients, Krappe Chemicals, cause cancer, and decides, as part of his new commitment to being good, to drop their business, worth two million dollars per year (123). Harry's unilateral decision to fire his agency's biggest client, combined with his excessive spending, lead his family to have him committed to a mental institution. Commenting on Harry's family's decision to institutionalize him, Hassall argues that while "they could live with Harry as a Good Bloke, they cannot tolerate his newfound knowledge of their true natures, and his enthusiasm for Goodness, which is not at all the same as being a good bloke" (*Dancing* 73).

Before Harry is committed, Honey says that she should take him to Bog Onion Road with her, but declares: "'you wouldn't like it: mud and leeches ... no electricity, no silk shirts'" (143). However, Harry promises Honey that he will go with her (181). Harry's plans change, however, when Bettina secures his release from the institution as part of a deal that allows her to pursue her ambition to create advertisements (182). While in the institution, Harry ceases to care about advertising and finds it "astonishing that he had once thought ... [advertisements] were important" (183). He is now preoccupied by thoughts of "Bog Onion Road, Honey Barbara, wholemeal bread. He wanted to be safe. He did not care about his house, his business, his car" (183). However, Bettina imposes a further condition on Harry; he has to sell the advertisements for her (183). When Honey learns the details and conditions of Harry's deal with Bettina during the drive from the mental institution to Palm Avenue, she jumps out of the car and runs away. After examining Bettina's advertisements and realizing they are brilliant, Harry sees them as a ticket to financial security and safety (192-93). Despite her anger at Harry's decision to return to Palm Avenue and advertising, Honey joins Harry in Mt. Pleasant, where she witnesses his family's dysfunction.

Honey is shocked by the way Harry is treated by his family, even though she does not realize how badly he is being treated:

> She did not know that Harry had been, all his life, a protected species ... Yet this was the way it was going to be at Palm Avenue for as long as they all lived there ... arguing, shouting, laughing, vomiting, attacking, counter-attacking, all too loud, too late, too abrasively. (220)

Honey believes Harry's return to advertising is having a negative affect on his behavior, declaring, "'You're getting poisoned with this shit you're doing Harry. You can't fuck around with it. You're catching it. You're becoming one of them'" (231). By the time Honey has lived in Palm Avenue for three months, Harry spends more and more time away from home due to the remarkable success of his work with Bettina, which has led Harry and Bettina to become "involved in the social life of the town" and Harry to be "elected as a trustee" of the State Gallery; "In less than six months they had moved up that impossible last rung of the ladder and entered the very inner circle of society" (233). Harry is seduced by luxuries such as leather seats, silk shirts and fine wines, and does not want the life at Bog Onion Road, which includes "blistering heat, mud, leeches and hard work" (236-37).

Honey's nadir at Palm Avenue occurs when she allows herself to be seduced by David:

> She had come to this, this seedy betrayal, and she knew it was time to leave these people who had such trunk-loads of dreams, ideas and ambitions but never anything in the present, only what would happen one day, and it was time to get away from it and face whatever might be waiting for her at home and hope that it might be as it had been. (242)

The authors of *The Oxford Companion to Australian Literature* claim that Honey's energy is sapped by "the unhealthy aspects of modern city life," the dysfunctional Joy family, "and Harry's rapid moral deterioration," all of which combine to spur her to return to the commune (Wilde et al. 94). Although Harry catches up with Honey and drives her home, he returns to Palm Avenue.

While Carey does not explicitly critique suburbia in *Bliss*, he repeatedly attacks capitalism and consumerism, especially through descriptions of the role of advertisers and multinational corporations in knowingly selling products that cause cancer. Huggan posits that advertising "plays a central role in Carey's moral allegory of consumer culture" (*Peter Carey* 26). Likewise, Woodcock argues that the advertising industry functions in the novel as "the embodiment of the imperialist forces of Western capital" (45). Sheckels suggest that Carey's decision to make the Australian setting of the novel implicit rather than explicit "is deliberate, for what the novel depicts is a business world that has become amoral if not immoral. Carey wishes to suggest that this lack of morality is not exclusively Australian; rather, it is characteristic of the industrialized world" (89). Huggan argues that Carey uses cancer to illustrate "the grotesque disjunction between capitalism's utopian rhetoric and the disease it helps to spread within the collective social body. Cancer is the monstrous by-product of corporate ambition" (*Peter Carey* 70). Likewise, Woodcock claims that the theme of cancer is the aspect of the novel "which reveals the nature of capitalist delusions most explosively ... The linkage between capitalism and cancer is part of the satirically apocalyptic side to the novel" (45). Carey depicts the link between capitalism and cancer unequivocally; the only character who questions the link develops terminal cancer.

Harry first learns about the prevalence of cancer during the period between his operation and his retreat to the Hilton. Aldo, the waiter at Milano's, tells Harry that he is dying of cancer, names a number of other people he knows who are also afflicted, and declares,

> "there is a great deal of it around and it makes me wonder ... My theory is that it is being sent to punish us for how we live, all this shit we breathe, all this rubbish we eat. My theory, if you are inter-

ested, is that cancer is going to save us from ourselves. It is going to stop us eating and breathing shit." (67)

Later that evening, as Harry rides home in a taxi and crosses a bridge, "the river below appeared as black as the Styx. Barges carried their carcinogens up river and neon lights advertised their final formulations against a blackening sky" (79). From the moment of its first mention in the novel, cancer is repeatedly linked with capitalism, consumption and environmental degradation. When Harry first learns from his employee Alex Duval that their client Krappe Chemicals produces carcinogenic products, he ignores Alex, but as he spends more time in "Hell," he comes to accept the truth about the link between his client and the increasing incidence of cancer in his community, and becomes more aware of the pollution caused by capitalism (91).

Eventually, Harry takes action and summons Adrian Clunes, the Marketing Director of Krappe Chemicals (120). Harry tells Adrian he is firing Krappe Chemicals because he has evidence that their products cause cancer (123). Adrian does not deny it; rather, he openly admits the products are carcinogenic and declares,

> "The whole of the Western world is built on things that cause cancer. They can't afford to stop making them ... Mobil have benzine in petrol which is carcinogenic ... And every time an announcement is made that something causes cancer, it makes people *less* worried because they can't believe that half the things they breathe and eat are carcinogenic." (124, original emphasis)

In order to prove his point, Adrian produces a cancer map that "'shows the incidence of cancers according to place of residence and place of work. There is a damn cancer epidemic going on ... They will not even sell these maps any more'" (125). Horrified, Harry is unable to "disbelieve the map" and does not take the time "to study the relative proportions of tumours or understand all the accompanying statistics," since he is focused on the fact that he and Adrian are currently located "in the epicenter of Hell" (125). Adrian informs Harry that his own wife has cancer and angrily declares:

"'This,' he tapped the paper, 'is what we get for how we live. And believe me, it is just hotting up'" (125).

Bettina, who grew up above her father's petrol station, accepts pollution as normal and does not believe "'all this rubbish about cancer,'" since she is "convinced that the whole cancer theory ... [is] a Communist conspiracy" (217, 226, 227). However, she privately admits to being terrified of developing cancer and undergoes annual tests (226). When Bettina visits her doctor to obtain the results of her annual check-up, he informs her that she has developed a kind of cancer caused by the benzine in petrol and might have a year to live (251, 252). Bettina is enraged and decides that her "whole life" has "been built on bullshit" (252). Rather than accept her fate, Bettina pursues revenge. She takes "three large bottles of petrol" into a meeting with the board of Mobil, who are her clients, and blows them up, killing the board members and herself (253). Hassall describes the murder-suicide as "semiotically brilliant" and argues that Bettina's development of cancer "just at the moment when her career is about to take off" is "both appropriate, and cruelly ironic" (*Dancing* 77). Ryan-Fazilleau considers Bettina's revenge "spectacular" and claims that she is a victim of "capitalism's conspiracy of silence despite her loyal service" (81, 80).

In the aftermath of Bettina's murder-suicide, the members of the household at 25 Palm Avenue are investigated by the police, who believe Bettina did not act alone and declare that the household "has been harbouring two terrorists, possible more" (260). Convinced he is going to be charged as an accomplice, Joel commits suicide (259). After Bettina's death, Harry continually repeats the phrase, "'She had cancer'" (261) and becomes convinced of cancer's all-pervasiveness:

> Harry could feel the cancer in the air. It had been here all the time. It was impregnated in the walls, like spores, like a mould, invisible but always there in what they breathed, what they ate. He could feel

the cells in his own body rising, multiplying, marshalling against him, to make him beg for mercy, for death, for release. (261)

Harry's newfound obsession with cancer is echoed in McCann's *Subtopia*, in which the protagonist, Julian, also develops an obsession with cancer, although, like Harry, he does not become a victim.

During what the narrator describes as "possibly the lowest, most shameful period" of Harry's life, he fights David for a fifty percent share of David's savings, steals Ken's Cadillac, and flees to Bog Onion Road, abandoning his children, home and business (262, 263). David also flees, using a ticket to New York stolen from Joel, and is later executed in Columbia for gun smuggling (261, 264, 248). On one of the last pages of the novel, the house at Palm Avenue is described as "deserted," but Ken and Lucy's fate is not revealed (292). The narrator provides a glimpse into an apocalyptic future, claiming that Harry's behavior is "much milder" than the panic that ten years later sweeps through "the Western world (and parts of the industrialized East) ... when the cancer epidemic" arrives during "a time of deep recession, material shortages, unemployment and threatening nuclear war" and proves to be "the last straw for the West" when "the angry cancer victims" cannot be controlled and take to the streets (262). Ryan-Fazilleau argues that Harry's flight to Bog Onion Road is driven by fears of imprisonment and cancer, rather than an ideological rejection of capitalism (81). Likewise, Eustace suggests that Harry sees "going bush" as "the only way of preserving himself" (112). Harry's escape to Bog Onion Road is not a rejection of suburbia, which is the site where Harry felt most secure and comfortable. Rather, it is a simple act of self-preservation.

The sixth and final section of *Bliss*, "Blue Bread and Sapphires," is set entirely in the commune at Bog Onion Road and spans a period of thirty-five years in just thirty pages, in contrast to the first five sections of the novel, which cover less than a year. The Bog Onion Road section of *Bliss* is the aspect of the novel most frequently discussed by critics, with many reading the final section as the key to the novel's meaning.

Indeed, in an interview in which Carey discusses critical responses to the novel's conclusion, noting that some critics have argued that because the conclusion is "lyrical and pastoral, it ... [is] in some way not intellectually rigorous," Carey declares that "the whole book stands or falls" on the final section (Nielsen 70). Rather than being an idyllic, peaceful pastoral retreat, Bog Onion Road is a hybrid community, part-retreat, part-fortress, part-communist and part-capitalist. Although Bog Onion Road is physically beautiful, located in secluded rural bushland and containing rainforest, the community is guarded with a "barred gate and, sometimes, a lookout" (270), and the oft-paranoid residents are fearful of strangers and the police.

Harry's introduction to Bog Onion Road is anything but peaceful. On the morning after his flight from the city, he is found by Daze, one of the commune's residents, who has to carry Harry down a hill to the nearest dwelling, since he is physically incapacitated by heat stroke and exhaustion. The second person Harry meets at Bog Onion Road, Clive, declares that if Harry is a spy he will hang him from a beam and disembowel him (272). Clive brags that he has a machine-gun that he will not hesitate to use on intruders (273). Honey Barbara's father, Paul Bees, defends Harry and offers to take responsibility for his welfare (277). Harry stays with Paul in his hut in the rainforest, which is considered a safe place to hide a "hunted terrorist," since it is "guarded on its edges by lantana ... and even from the air, it was thought, the dark roof of the hut would be invisible. The visitor was forbidden to leave the rain forest" (276, 277).

Since Harry seeks security, he is content to stay in the rainforest and eventually has to be ordered to leave it in order to work in other areas of the commune (277). The residents of Bog Onion Road are engaged in a project of planting trees on the old forest roads in order to restrict access to their community and thwart aerial surveillance; Harry is given a job as a tree-planter (279). As Harry becomes a member of the community, he plans and builds a hut, and through the process of design and construction comes to "know his neighbours and make new friendships" (282). Although Harry finds "a new happiness" in the commune, he is burdened by his past:

> he had done bad things in Hell. The guilt he felt about his past was the worst of the pains he now carried, but not the only one, for he had, if not daily, at least weekly, the reminder of Honey Barbara's hostility towards him. (285)

Harry feels "some guilt, some remorse, about almost everybody he had known in Palm Avenue," but through his work with the trees and gradual integration into the community he discovers love and tries to make amends (285). Not only does Harry make new friends, he becomes a necessary member of the community, both through the knowledge of trees he acquires and his skill as a storyteller (290).

Harry constructs new stories "grown on their soil" (291). In addition to his role as storyteller, Harry comes to know "as much about trees as anyone in Bog Onion" (292). Harry's transformation from middle-class suburban businessman to forest worker is so complete that the narrator declares, "He was a bushman" (291). After a number of years, Harry and Honey are reconciled and have children together. He lives through "thirty more wet seasons, seven droughts and two cyclones" (295). After thirty-five years at Bog Onion Road, Harry dies his third and final death at the age of seventy-five, when a limb of a yellow box tree "known to forest workers as widow-makers ... because of their habit, on quiet, windless days ... of dropping heavy limbs," performs "the treacherous act of falling on to the man who planted it" (295). When he dies, Harry rises "higher and higher" through the trees (296). As he ascends, the leaves stroke him "like feathers" and he has no desire "to return to his body" (296). Rather, he spreads himself "thinner, and thinner, and thin as a gas" until the trees breath in and take him into them "through their leaves ... so that, in time," he becomes "part of their tough old heart wood" (296). Thus, in death, Harry becomes part of the bush.

Eustace argues that Harry "quite literally goes bush through his death, attaching himself to the land in a profoundly spiritual way" (108). Recognizing that the pastoral ending is "the most critically controversial aspect of the novel," Eustace suggests that "Carey invites readers to recognize the territorial implications of going bush" (108-09). Eustace argues that when Carey declares, "the whole book stands or falls" on the pastoral ending, he is "calling attention to the way his deployment of the pastoral is crucial to the novel's aesthetic and thematic resolution" (109). Eustace reads Harry's "journey toward pastoral bliss" at Bog Onion Road "as an elaborate cultural performance" and "a ritual of cultural legitimacy and territorial consolidation" through which Harry becomes indigenous (110). Thus, Eustace posits that Harry is engaged in (and representative of) the ongoing European Australian project of establishing indigeneity, which I discussed in my analysis of Winton's *Cloudstreet*. Gelder and Salzman argue that *Bliss* "turns away from history in its attempt to offer a kind of ecological vision of fictional production: Harry Joy goes into the forests to turn stories into myth, to plant his stories and make them grow" (*Diversity*, 124). However, Eustace convincingly demonstrates that Carey's engagement with indigeneity, belonging, legitimacy and consolidation in *Bliss* has everything to do with history.

Eustace argues that when the narrator describes Harry as "a bushman, his transformation and idealization seem complete" (113). The fact that there are no Indigenous Australians at Bog Onion Road, or anywhere else in the novel, conveniently positions the bush as *terra nullius*, "empty" land ready to be occupied and claimed. In the final line of *Bliss*, the reader learns that the novel has actually been narrated by "the children of Honey Barbara and Harry Joy" (296), rather than a third-person omniscient narrator. Eustace presciently asserts that Harry's children are "narrators with a vested interest in recuperating him as an ethical subject and legitimizing his position as the patriarch of the meaningful, indigenizing rituals at Bog Onion Road" (112). Thus, the children of Harry and Honey perform a storytelling role similar to the historians and novelists who have constructed Australia's national narratives, adding, omitting and shaping incidents as necessary in order to construct a narrative that establishes a legitimate relationship with, and ownership of, the land. In a similarly allegorical vein, Hecq reads *Bliss* "as a medium through which those Australian values, traditions and rituals which were expunged by American imperialism, can be recovered" (102), while Turner argues that Harry's function within the commune "can be regarded as a kind of model for the writer within the Australian culture, providing fictions, Australian dreams" ("American" 441).

Although critics agree that the novel's conclusion is both pastoral and allegorical, there is disagreement over whether Carey's use of the pastoral is effective and whether the commune provides a viable model or alternative to urban life and capitalism. Eustace argues that the novel is structured around "the central binary ... [of] the city and the bush" (111), and thus sees Bog Onion Road in opposition to the city. However, the commune, like the city and the suburbs, contains a mixture of positive and negative elements; none of the three sites is ideal, let alone superior, and the commune is dependent on the city, rather than separate from it. Ryan-Fazilleau argues that Bog Onion Road "is not a Garden of Eden ... and nature is neither innocent nor accommodating there" (81-82). Huggan points out that Bog Onion Road "is a disputed territory, a locus of competing cults" and argues that by "escaping there, Harry Joy has only exchanged one form of captivity for another; in 'opting' out of city life, he is merely contending with other warring alternatives" (*Peter Carey* 42-3). Moreover, the community is surrounded by a variety of threats, from the police to neighboring communities and cults; as Carey himself states, "there are evil fuckers around the place. There're guns and there is witchcraft going on" (Nielsen 70). Carey has indicated that his preferred title for the novel was *Waiting for the Barbarians* and argues that it "would have placed the ending in the right context," presumably by indicating that the peace and security of the community was threatened, and further claims that the ending of *Bliss* may not have "been misinterpreted" if he had been able to use his preferred title (Nielsen 70).

Woodcock argues that Bog Onion Road "is hardly ... a plausible alternative to the corruptions of the business world" (49) and notes that the commune is "dependent on the capitalist world it rejected" (39). Although the commune claims to have rejected capitalism and the city, it depends on the city for income from the marijuana crop and Honey Barbara's prostitution. Huggan argues that the commune "is deluded in seeing itself as an anti-material enclave" and claims that *Bliss* reveals "a paucity of alternatives" to capitalism, illustrating "the paradoxical uniformity of western consumer society, a society in which commodities dominate all aspects of social life" (*Peter Carey* 6, 27). Hassall claims that Harry does not undergo "a conversion from the values of late capitalism to pastoral communalism, but simply wants to survive at any cost" (*Dancing* 80). Likewise, Huggan suggests that "Carey's redemptive allegory is too coy ... to be taken unduly seriously" (*Peter Carey* 6). Huggan reads Carey's work as "both a critique and an ironic celebration of consumer frenzy" and argues that *Bliss* "is his most explicit satire on contemporary consumer society, and on Australia's location on the outskirts of a global commodity culture" (*Peter Carey* 25). Thus, *Bliss* addresses the negative impact of capitalism and consumerism, rather than suburbia.

Carey neither rejects nor celebrates suburbia in *Bliss*; rather, through his examination of capitalism, consumerism, morality, family relationships, alternative lifestyles and the pastoral, he demonstrates the centrality of suburban life to Australian culture. Moreover, through his use of the suburban setting, Carey not only reveals some of the numerous themes available to writers willing to reject the anti-suburban tradition, but memorably demonstrates that authors can engage with serious social issues while employing satire and experimenting with narrative technique and the form of the novel. *Bliss* is irrefutable proof that the suburban novel is anything but boring, conventional and predictable.

The Tax Inspector: Exposing Suburban Secrets

Between the publication of *Bliss* (1981) and his fourth published novel, *The Tax Inspector* (1991), Carey published two novels, *Illywhacker* (1985) and *Oscar and Lucinda* (1988), which catapulted him to global prominence and established him as a celebrity author within Australia. Carey's rapid rise to fame and his first Booker Prize win, combined with his move to New York in 1989, undoubtedly fostered the conditions that caused *The Tax Inspector* to receive a controversial reception in Australia. Upon the publication of *The Tax Inspector*, Carey became the first internationally acclaimed Australian author since White to set the majority of a novel in an outer suburb of an Australian city, and the first prominent author to write about a suburb and its inhabitants without ridicule or judgment, thus rejecting the anti-suburban tradition. Not only was Carey's decision to set the novel in the fictional outer Sydney suburb of Franklin a risky departure from the mainstream of Australian literature and his own previous work, his choice of a single, heavily-pregnant Greek-immigrant tax inspector as his heroine, and his engagement with incestuous child sexual abuse and political corruption signaled a willingness to challenge his audience and take risks. Moreover, the contemporary setting and the short time-frame of *The Tax Inspector*, the action of which covers just four days, marked a radical departure from the epic neo-Victorian historical novel that preceded it.

Hassall argues that Carey "does not repeat himself" and declares, "no one would have expected the sequel to *Oscar and Lucinda* to be a violent and confronting pyschothriller" ("Peter Carey" 58). Likewise, Woodcock claims that "reviewers seemed to want ... another prize-winning great Australian novel set safely in the past with humour and distance, rather than the savage piece Carey had written" (169). Turner posits that since "the marriage between national author/celebrity and national audience" had been "celebrated through the widespread acknowledgement of *Oscar and Lucinda*'s success, the publication of *The Tax Inspector* must have seemed like an act of betrayal," especially as it coincided with Carey's move to New York ("Nationalising" 135). Turner notes that it "has become conventional wisdom ... that the novel received bad reviews in Australia," but argues that the reviews "were not so much bad as bewildered. For some reviewers ... what mattered was that Carey seemed no longer to be 'writing in the national interest'" ("Nationalising" 135).

Hassall notes that the reception of *The Tax Inspector*, which is the only one of Carey's twelve published novels that has not won major prizes or been shortlisted for them,[9] led to "something of a downturn" of Carey's reputation, since it "was greeted in Australia with little enthusiasm and indeed some dismay, one reviewer describing it as 'brutish and nasty'" (*Dancing* 4). Hassall argues that the "favorable response by English and American reviewers left the local response open to the charge of lopping a tall poppy, though it was clear that some Australian reviewers were puzzled and disappointed rather than hostile" (*Dancing* 4). Woodcock argues that it "has become almost a commonplace to assume that the reviews ... were favourable in America and the UK, but were damning or bad in Australia" and notes that there were "some complimentary Australian reviews ... but many were highly critical" (167). However, the foreign reviews were certainly not all favorable: writing for *Newsweek*, M. Jones, Jr. describes reading the novel as "like ogling an epic wreck," dismissing it as "a shambles of a book" (60), while Bill Marx declares that the novel "rattles along ... like an apocalypse on cruise control" (347).

Although the tremendous success of *Oscar and Lucinda*, Carey's Booker win, and his expatriation to New York all played a role in the negative reception of *The Tax Inspector*, the novel's subject matter is the primary reason for the poor reader response. When Larsson describes the novel as "relentlessly brutal" and Woodcock declares that it is "Carey's most savage novel to date," they are not exaggerating ("'Years Later'" 178; 89). As Hassall notes, the novel "sets a grimly detailed account of three generations of incest in the Catchprice family against a broader account of public venality and corruption in Sydney" ("Peter Carey" 58). While child sexual abuse perpetrated by parents is no longer a taboo subject and has received increased media attention in recent decades, the topic remains sensitive, and, as Hassall notes, "part of the negative reaction to the book in Australia resulted from the public's dislike of the deliberate breaking into this particular silence, and of the suggestion that this private indecency was symptomatic of a wider social decay" (Hassall, "Peter Carey" 58). Turner argues that the novel placed new emphasis on "aspects of Carey's view of the world which had troubled reviewers of the short stories and *Bliss*," namely, "the incipiently gothic mixture of absurdity and romanticism, and the complicated attitude to Australian contemporary culture which seems to both celebrate and fear the rich details of suburban life" ("Nationalising" 135).

Hassall argues that some readers struggled "with the portrayal of violence and sexual deviance" due to the narrative's lack of framing and distancing devices, such as those used by Conrad in *Heart of Darkness* ("Peter Carey" 58). Moreover, Turner claims that "Australians are always going to read Carey's work in an especially direct relation to the specific social context in which it was written" ("Nationalising" 135). Thus, Australian readers are confronted directly with a shocking portrayal of child sexual abuse and corruption that they may interpret as an attack on their society, and, by extension, themselves. Indeed, Australian readers are not alone in interpreting the novel as social criticism; Woodcock, a British academic, interprets the novel as an "investigation of the state of the Australian nation at the beginning of the 1990s" (90), and Andreas Gaile, a German critic, argues that *The Tax Inspector* comes across as "intensely critical" of Australia ("Introduction" xxii).

Carey himself is well aware of the novel's negative reception and has discussed it in a number of interviews. Carey told Gaile that he has "never forgotten" the reader response ("The 'Contrarian Streak'" 9) and in an interview with Radhika Jones acknowledges that Australian readers and critics "got upset about *The Tax Inspector*": "They thought I didn't like my country, because I said some things about Sydney being continually corrupt from its beginnings. It's an edgy, unsettling sort of book" (143). Likewise, in an interview with Ray Willbanks, Carey declares, "I absolutely don't hate Australia" and states,

"They think I've said I hate this city; therefore, they're upset. They take it personally. It's not surprising the novel gets read this way; in the end it won't be read this way at all. I think finally this book will survive quite well in Australian society and have a useful place in Australian culture." ("Peter Carey" 14)

The Tax Inspector remains Carey's most disturbing, honest and intense examination of late-twentieth-century Australian society and perhaps will, in time, be acknowledged and respected as such.

Despite the many negative reactions to the novel, a number of critics have acknowledged Carey's achievement. Citing Veronica Brady, who reviewed *The Tax Inspector*, Turner agrees with her contention that the novel is "adventurous" and declares that it is "a bold rejection of the linear development widely constructed for ... [Carey's] work since the short stories" ("Nationalising" 135). Woodcock contends that *The Tax Inspector* contains "an urgent narrative ... which, along with the urgency of the social issues, marks a dramatic and adventurous shift of direction" and goes so far as to claim the novel "is perhaps the most adventurous of Carey's career so far, and an indication that the acclaim for his work has in no way compromised the risks he takes" (89, 107). Larsson argues that the novel is "extremely rich and adds new dimensions to the themes that recur throughout Carey's literary production" ("Cross References" 65), while Michael Heyward regards the novel as "a quantum leap in the development of Carey's art" (Qtd. in Woodcock 92).

The Tax Inspector focuses on the Catchprice family, owners of Catchprice Motors, a heavily indebted car dealership in Franklin (modeled on the outer southwestern Sydney suburb of Campbelltown), which was once a country town surrounded by farmland and bush, but has been swallowed by the suburban expansion of Sydney and transformed into a working-class suburb. The matriarch of the family, Frieda (Gran) Catchprice, has called the Tax Office to report possible irregularities in the family business' accounting practices in an attempt to avert her daughter Cathy's attempts to have her committed to a nursing home. Maria Takis is sent to audit Catchprice Motors, and over a bizarre four days is embroiled in a series of disturbing and violent events involving the severely dysfunctional Catchprice family. The outer suburban setting of the novel allows Carey to engage with a number of the common issues in the Australian suburban novel, including the development of suburbia, environmental degradation, immigration, class, sexuality, family relationships, violence and crime.

However, despite Carey's focus on some of the most negative aspects of suburban life, such as child sexual abuse, violent crime and environmental degradation, he does not depict suburbia in an overtly negative manner and his narrator does not deliver the kind of diatribes against suburbia that are prevalent in anti-suburban novels such as Johnston's *My Brother Jack*. Rather, Carey treats the residents of suburbia seriously and sympathetically, even those characters that could easily be demonized and disparaged. Carey departs from the mainstream of Australian literature by using the fictional suburb of Franklin as the primary setting, recognizing that for the majority of Australians, the suburban experience is the Australian experience. By deeming an outer suburb of a large city a viable setting for a work of fiction, Carey highlights the importance, influence, and prominence of suburbia in the lives of ordinary Australians and thus breaks with the anti-suburban tradition by treating the suburb as one of the most important sites within Australia.

It is important to note that the western suburbs of Sydney are stigmatized in Australian culture. In *Out West: Perceptions of Sydney's Western Suburbs*, Diane Powell examines media representations of the western suburbs, as well as the development of the suburbs' negative reputation and the physical development and social history of the suburbs. Powell argues that Sydney's western suburbs are "seen as the repository of all those social groups and cultures which are outside the prevailing cultural ideal: the poor, the working class, juvenile delinquents, single mothers, welfare recipients, public housing tenants, Aborigines, [and] immigrants" (xviii). Not only are the western suburbs stigmatized, they are also the site of rapid development and population growth, which has serious social consequences regarding immigration and environmental degradation, both of which Carey addresses. Writing about Sydney's western suburbs in 1997, Deborah Chambers states that they comprise "the fastest growing region in the country with 45 per cent of Sydney's total population now living there. It is estimated that over 90 per cent of Sydney's development will take place in western Sydney over the next twenty years" (86).

Powell demonstrates that during the 1990s articles regularly appeared in the print media concerning "the problems of urban sprawl to the west and south-west of Sydney. The large population, housing estates and industry have apparently created a severe strain on the city, polluting rivers and air, and destroying the natural environment" (33). Noting that the western suburbs bear the brunt of the blame for environmental degradation in the greater Sydney area, Powell argues that authors of articles

> about the problem of urban sprawl never describe the typical housing and lifestyles of people living in wealthier Sydney suburbs which have sprawled (or climbed) to the outer north and south of the city. It seems it is not the quarter-acre personal rainforest complete with double garage, in-ground pool and tennis court that is the problem. (34)

In *The Tax Inspector*, Carey explores both the destruction of the natural environment by suburban development and the conflicting emotions residents of suburbia experience as they witness the simultaneous development and destruction. The Catchprices have lived in Franklin since it had "a population of 3,000 people and limited commercial potential" (6) and witness its transformation from a country town "twenty miles from Sydney and in the bush" to a suburb "twenty miles from Sydney and almost in the city" (6). The westward expansion of the city consumes the rural and natural environments; moreover, the suburbanization of Franklin causes the demolition of old buildings to make way for the new (a process also described in Malouf's *Johnno* and Winton's *Cloudstreet*), and the paving-over of farms and bulldozing of bushland to create housing estates. Hassall links Carey's Franklin to White's Sarsaparilla due to both locations being defined by "near-city farmland overrun ... by suburban sprawl" (*Dancing* 147).

Although the development of Franklin results in a massive influx of population (including immigrants from Europe and Asia) and the construction of new freeways, office buildings, and retail outlets, other parts of Franklin are decaying, causing social and economic problems. Catchprice Motors is "stranded out on the north end of Loftus Street opposite the abandoned boot-maker's and bakers" while the "commercial centre had shifted to a mall half a mile to the south" (7); this commercial shift contributes significantly to Catchprice Motors' demise from a relatively successful business to one seriously indebted. Additionally, the displacement of the once well-known local business creates a situation in which newcomers to Franklin have never heard of Catchprice Motors, leaving the family both literally and figuratively disconnected from their community. The construction of freeways, commercial buildings and housing estates contributes to the destruction of Franklin's natural environment, disconnecting the Catchprices from their rural past and eradicating their connection with nature.

The effect of suburbanization on the natural environment is best illustrated by the transformation of the once-pristine swimming hole known as the Wool Wash. As a child, Benny Catchprice walked along a path across "little hills which had once been known as 'Thistle Paddocks'" on his way "to the clear waters of the Wool Wash pool" (115). However, the paddocks have been paved-over and replaced with a housing estate named Franklin Heights, cutting off the walking path from Catchprice Motors to Benny's sanctuary. The collision of the suburbs and the bush leaves the Wool Wash surrounded by "bullet-scarred, yellow garbage bins" and "POLLUTED WATER signs"; its banks are littered with "beer cans and condoms and paper cups" (116). What was once a peaceful recreational site has become an abused gathering place for suburban youth who abandon stolen cars, lose their virginity, and buy and sell illegal drugs (116). The narrator declares that the Wool Wash is "the sort of place [where] you might find someone with their face shot away and bits of brain hanging on the bushes" (116). Not only can Benny no longer walk to the Wool Wash, he can no longer swim there either. Suburbanization has transformed a beautiful, clean and treasured environment into a site of pollution, crime and danger, eradicating one of the only positives in Benny's tragic life.

In addition to the destruction of the bush, suburban development severs the physical and emotional connection between characters and the natural environment. The Wool Wash served as a sanctuary for Benny as a child, allowing him to escape from the emotional and sexual abuse he suffered inside his home at the hands of his father and symbolically purify himself by swimming in the Wool Wash. While walking at night with the Armenian immigrant Sarkis Alaverdian, Gran Catchprice hails a taxi and asks to be taken to the Wool Wash, which she declares is "'the most lovely part of Franklin'" (97). However, neither the driver nor Sarkis have heard of the Wool Wash, causing Gran Catchprice to be "stricken with that horrible feeling that sometimes came to her on her night-time walks. It was as if all her past had been paved over and she could not reach it" (97). As a young woman, Gran Catchprice dreamed of owning a flower farm; however, the land she purchased was used as a poultry farm instead for twenty years before being partially used to build Catchprice Motors and the rest subdivided to create an estate named Catchprice Heights (86-89). Gran Catchprice tells her grandson Vish (named Johnny before he became a Hare Krishna) that she never wanted the car dealership: "'I wanted little babies, and a farm. I wanted to grow things ... It was your grandfather who wanted the business'" (163). Gran tells Vish that concrete was poured "'over perfectly good soil'" in order to construct the car yard, "'and that's what upsets me. It's like a smothered baby'" (164). In Carey's Franklin, the interaction between the natural and suburban environments causes both locales to suffer, rather than one triumphing over the other.

In her study of the western suburbs, Powell briefly discusses *The Tax Inspector* and erroneously claims that "Carey's view of the west relies on the stigmatized image; a concrete wasteland, polluted and brutal, where there is no sense of community, nothing attractive about life at all, and nobody who cares about the place" (131). However, Cathy and Howie are the only characters who express any desire to leave Franklin, and their reason for wanting to leave is to pursue success on the road with their band, Big Mack, rather than dissatisfaction with their home suburb. Sarkis and his mother have recently moved to Franklin voluntarily, and Benny has no intention of leaving. Although his short tragic life has provided him with a plethora of reasons for wanting to escape suburbia, Benny dreams of being successful on home ground. Benny tells Vish that he is "'going to buy a double block at Franklin Heights. There's some great places up there now. They got tennis courts and everything. Vish, we could do so fucking *well*'" (102, original emphasis). Hassall argues that Benny's desire to take over the family business and make it a success indicates his acceptance of "the crude ideology of capitalism" and notes that Benny has no desire "to leave for the eastern suburbs or the northern beaches. He wants to stay in the west, to live in a house at Franklin Heights, and make two hundred thousand dollars a year selling cars" (*Dancing* 153). Benny envisions himself rescuing Catchprice Motors "and carry[ing] it into the twenty-first century. He was the one who was going to find the cash to pay for their old people's home ... He would care for them the way they never cared for him" (6).

Like other suburban novels that preceded it, such as White's *Riders in the Chariot* and *The Solid Mandala* and Murnane's *A Lifetime on Clouds*, *The Tax Inspector* examines immigration. In fact, a realistic novel set in Sydney's western suburbs would be remiss if it did not address immigration. In 1986, Campbelltown, the model for Franklin, had a population of 121,297, with 26,132 of those residents (21.5%) being foreign-born (Powell 141). A study conducted in 2003 by the Centre for Population and Urban Research found that "Sydney's ethnic minorities are being locked into 'concentrations of the suburban poor' that are becoming even more concentrated as English-speaking migrants drift towards an 'Anglo heartland' on the city fringes" (Millett 1). The study contends that Sydney "is battling to cope with the pressures of a national migration intake of more than 100,000 a year" and reports that immigrants "with poor work and language skills are being 'trapped' in the sprawling western and south-western suburbs" while Australian-born residents and English-speaking immigrants are moving out of these suburbs (Millett 1). Woodcock notes that *The Tax Inspector* "gives a significant presence to the non-Anglo/Celtic Australia of the various immigrant communities such as those represented by Sarkis and his mother, or Maria and her father" (97). The novel contains a number of immigrant characters: Maria Takis and her family; Maria's parents' Greek immigrant friends; Sarkis Alaverdian and his mother; Pavlovic, the Yugoslavian taxi driver; Gino Massaro, the Italian grocer who almost buys a car from Benny; and Tahleen and Raffi, an Armenian couple who own a corner store in Franklin.

Maria Takis is the most prominent and developed of the immigrant characters. Carey depicts the Greek immigrants as hard-working and part of a close-knit community, yet homesick and unconvinced that life in Australia is an improvement. Maria immigrated to Australia as a young girl with her parents and sister. She has "a very dark olive-skinned face" which her mother describes derogatively as "Turkish," prompting Maria to develop a style of dress that incorporates "gold rings and embroidered blouses," thus accentuating the "look that her mother was so upset by" and instigating her mother to declare, "'You look like a gypsy'" (24). When Maria is twenty, she runs away from "her marriage and her mother" and returns to Greece for six weeks, staying on her home island of Letkos with her mother's uncle (32). While in Greece, Maria tells her relatives stories of walking the streets of Newtown, a working-class inner-suburb of Sydney, looking for work with her mother in a heat "like hell ... so hot and poisonous you could not breathe," but her relatives will not listen because it is "not their way of thinking about Australia" and they believe all Australians are rich (32).

Maria grew up "mourning" for the "beautiful little house" on Letkos, which is "the place her mother meant when she said, 'Let's go home,' whispering to her husband in bed in a shared house in Sydney" (33). Maria's mother often says "Let's go home" to her husband, but there is no chance that the family will ever return, since "fifteen men from the village had come to Australia and they were all working on the production line at the British Motor Corporation in Zetland. They were like men in a team" (33). Maria's mother likes to declare, "Your father is crazy," especially while she trudges the streets with her daughters looking for work "in the merciless heat … She had no English and Maria would walk with her to interpret" (33). According to Maria's mother, life was better in Greece, where the family owned a house and there was "'better oil, better fruit'" (34). Maria's father and his Greek immigrant friends often spend the evening talking in the kitchen: "They were all from Agios Constantinos. They said, remember the year this happened. Remember the time that happened. They never talked about Australia" (34).

The Greek women from Letkos cannot read English, and thus cannot read the employment columns in the newspapers, so they walk the streets of Enmore, Alexandria and Surry Hills "going from factory to factory, following up the rumours … It was all piecework, and her mother hated piecework. Childhood friends competed against each other to see who would get the bonus, who would get fired" (35). Maria's mother loses 85% "of her hearing in one ear in a Surry Hills sweat-shop … She would say, this machine is deafening me. The owner was Greek, from Salonika. He would say, if you don't like it, leave" (36). While her mother is in hospital dying from cancer, Maria visits her daily and brings her "flowers and Greek magazines and gossip that would cheer her up" (36). She believes her relationship with her mother is improving and her mother is softening, so she reveals "what she had previously thought she could never reveal – her pregnancy" (36). Maria had imagined that her mother "had moved, at last, to a place which was beyond the customs and morality of Agios Constantinos"; however, when Maria reveals that she is pregnant, her mother stares at her with "steely grey" eyes like "a village woman, standing in a dusty street" and declares "'We'll kill you'" (36-37). Hassall argues that Maria's family narrative is one that "offers no forgiveness, no escape, no movement to a kinder country, no softening of a brutal village morality. Like Benny, Maria is a victim" (*Dancing* 157).

Sarkis Alaverdian, an Armenian, is the other fully-developed immigrant character. Sarkis moves to Franklin with his mother from the northern suburb of Chatswood six months before the action of the novel begins because his mother wants to get away from the Armenian community (82). When Sarkis meets Gran Catchprice, whom he finds standing at the foot of his backyard one evening, he is "depressed and unemployed" (82). However, Sarkis is "normally optimistic" and possesses the ability to "lose three jobs and not be beaten ... he always had a way forward. He was a member of a race which could not be destroyed. He had energy, intelligence, resilience, enthusiasm" (85-86). Sarkis is twenty years old and has been forced to wait on the back steps of the house he shares with his mother because she is having sex with a Yugoslavian taxi driver named Pavlovic (82). When Sarkis was employed as a hairdresser, he had been in Pavlovic's taxi, and he knows that Pavlovic comes to Franklin looking for women who are "abandoned and lonely and often just getting used to the idea that they ... [will] now be poor for ever" (82-83).

The narrator states that Sarkis' mother, who is only thirty-six, is "celebrating her independence from the Armenian community" by "wearing short skirts and smoking in the street" (85, 84). She is also unemployed, having lost her job when "Ready-snap Peas" closed down (84). Sarkis' mother moved to Franklin because she believed there were no Armenians living in the suburb, but the first people she met were an Armenian couple, Tahleen and Raffi, who run a corner store (84). Sarkis believes that his mother's hatred for the Armenian community, the reasons for which are never specified, clouds her judgment and cannot change the fact that she is one of them, no matter how hard she tries to assimilate and reinvent herself as an Australian (84). Sarkis' mother is optimistic and cheerful, and "Even in the worst of the time when his father disappeared, she never cried or despaired. When she lost her job she did not cry ... She triumphed in the face of difficulties" (218). Carey's portrayal of Sarkis' mother is consistent with his portrayal of Greek and Italian immigrants who continue to work hard and hope for a better future, despite setbacks, discrimination and difficult living conditions.

After Sarkis meets Gran Catchprice and walks her home, she offers him a job as a salesman and he reports for work at Catchprice Motors the following day. Sarkis and Benny work together attempting to sell a car to Gina Massaro, an Italian immigrant, but when Benny attempts to squeeze several thousand dollars profit out of Gino through a deceptive financing arrangement, Sarkis uses body language to warn Gino, who pulls out of the deal (175). Furious, Benny lures Sarkis into his cellar where he straps him to a fiberglass contraption he has constructed in imitation of a picture in a pornographic magazine, and tortures Sarkis for eight hours (207). Before Benny tortures Sarkis, he states, "'I am in control of you,'" to which Sarkis responds, "'Hey, come on – what sort of talk is that?'" only to receive the reply "'English'" (175). Woodcock links Benny's treatment of Sarkis to "the colonial origins of the continuing exploitation of immigrant communities in Australia" (97). Benny's treatment of Sarkis can certainly be read as symbolic of the treatment of both convicts and immigrants by the English and their descendants, and the torture scene is also reminiscent of the mock-crucifixion of Himmelfarb in White's *Riders in the Chariot*. Woodcock describes Benny as "the victim of a victim who has become a victimizer" and notes that after the torture Sarkis "feels a 'prisoner' of the Catchprice estate, trapped in the grid of history embodied in streets named after members of the Catchprice family" (97).

The most controversial aspect of *The Tax Inspector* and the primary reason for the poor reception of the novel is Carey's engagement with child sexual abuse. As Karen Lamb notes, most Australian reviewers of the novel focused heavily on the child abuse (50), leading to unfavorable reviews. Apparently, many Australian critics did not approve of Australia's dirty suburban laundry being aired on the international stage by one of its most famous authors; perhaps such critics would prefer Australian authors to write fiction that does not reflect the serious social problems in Australian suburbia. When Benny is three years old, his mother, Sophie, catches his father, Mort, sucking Benny's penis (105). Sophie responds by picking up a rifle and demanding that Mort hand Benny to her. When Mort refuses, Sophie attempts to shoot Mort, but misses and shoots Benny in the shoulder (105-06). Sophie's response is to try to kill herself by putting the rifle barrel in her mouth and pulling the trigger, but the bullet passes through the back of her neck, missing her spine, and she runs away (107). Benny and his brother grow up without a mother and are both sexually abused by Mort.

During the four days spanned by the action of the novel, Benny tries to seduce Mort as part of a deluded attempt to take control of his life. Mort knows that his actions are wrong, but points out Benny's complicity and the complex identity of a child molester:

> I am the one trying to stop this stuff and he is crawling into bed and rubbing my dick and he will have a kid and do it to his kid, and he will be the monster and they'll want to kill him. Today he is the victim, tomorrow the monster. They do not let you be the two at once. (158)

Throughout the course of the novel, it is revealed that Mort and his sister Cathy were both sexually abused by their father, Cacka, and that their mother, Frieda, "let Cacka poison her children while she pretended it was not happening" (167).

Although Carey's decision to address the sexual abuse of children stirred controversy and contributed greatly to the novel's poor reception, a number of critics have recognized the complexity of Carey's presentation of the issue and praised him for it. In his discussion of domestic violence, incest and sexual perversion in suburbia, Hartley argues that *The Tax Inspector* is "one of the most sustained and telling analyses of this aspect of suburban life" (212-213). Likewise, Hassall argues that Carey "portrays the incestuous Catchprices with a degree of insight, compassion and imaginative sympathy that complicates but does not forestall moral judgement" (*Dancing* 144). Woodcock argues that Carey presents child sexual abuse in a complex manner that "belies the response of reviewers and critics who, like Peter Pierce, thought this treatment 'reductive,' or who, like Robert Dixon, challenged the representation of sexual abuse" (95). Commenting on the novel's reception, Hassall claims that "the public conscience seems more tolerant of systemic corruption than it is of the private abuse of children" and argues that Carey complicates "social judgement by insistently humanising his family of child molesters" and declares that the only devils in *The Tax Inspector* are "the guests at the Rose Bay dinner party" (*Dancing* 150).

In a number of interviews, Carey addresses his portrayal of child sexual abuse. Carey describes *The Tax Inspector* as being "about a hellish family situation" and declares that writing about incest was "horrible" (Meyer 87). Carey reveals that during the composition of the novel he "spent a lot of time depressed" about what he was doing, wondered whether it was worth it, and "lived with a lot of doubt" (Meyer 87). He admits that he was upset by the negative response to the novel in Australia, but, with the benefit of hindsight, believes that writing *The Tax Inspector* "was really worth doing" and he is "very proud of it" (Meyer 87). When Carey was asked in a separate interview if he felt a "moral imperative" when addressing violence and incest in *The Tax Inspector*, Carey replied:

> "Well, yes. There had been a sadistic rape and murder in Sydney – really, really horrible. At the same time, my first son was born. I had the idea of putting these two things in magical opposition ... I wanted in my simplistic, sentimental heart for birth to triumph." (Jones 144)

Carey reveals that he began with the idea that Benny's psychological problems were due to him being abused as a child, but was not aware of the "morass" he was creating:

"If he had been abused, how had he been abused? Do you really want to think about that? Do you really want to see the mother finding the father sucking the little boy's penis? Oh no. I really didn't want to think about that, and it took me forever to write it. It was the most difficult thing I've written." (Jones 144)

In her article on child sexual abuse in *The Tax Inspector*, Barbara Bode argues that Carey utilizes incestuous sexual abuse "as a key element to show the ultimate corruption and downfall of an Australian family" (107). Bode points out that at the apocalyptic conclusion of the novel, when Gran Catchprice, aided by Vish, uses gelignite to blow-up the dealership, Cathy, Mort, Vish, and Frieda are all "huddled together like a heap of ill fortune that does not leave room for any other person, not even Cathy's husband Howie" (108). Cathy and Mort's brother Jack, who was not molested by Cacka, is the only family member other than Benny who is absent, symbolizing his distance from the corruption at the heart of the family. Benny is not huddled together with the other family members who are victims, perpetrators and enablers of child sexual abuse, since he is busy terrorizing Maria in his cellar (behavior which is surely a result of the abuse he suffered). Hassall argues that Benny's cellar "is an appallingly vivid image of the abuse he has suffered and of his junk status in the family" (*Dancing* 150). Bode points out that Jack has become "so far removed from his family" that he is able to use the abuse of his brother and sister by his father as a topic for dinner conversation with Maria (108). Bode reads the sexual abuse in the novel as "a metaphor for the corruption ... in the Catchprice family, who with their deviousness along with their great helplessness, represent Western society" (109-110). Bode is correct to assert that the sexual abuse represents the moral corruption within the family; however, she is incorrect to claim that the Catchprices represent Western society. There is no evidence in the novel to support such a claim, and it would be difficult to prove that the Catchprices represent Franklin or Sydney, let alone Western society as a whole.

Although Dixon praised Carey's engagement with the issue of child sexual abuse in his review of *The Tax Inspector*, describing it as "one of the great achievements of the novel" (Qtd. In Woodcock 95), he criticizes Carey's portrayal of child sexual abuse in his article, "Closing the Can of Worms: Enactments of Justice in *Bleak House, The Mystery of a Hansom Cab* and *The Tax Inspector*." Dixon argues that *The Tax Inspector* "creates the impression that sexual violence can be taken as a symbol – the symbol – of corruption in Sydney," claims that Carey has a "fascination with incest in the western suburbs," and declares that despite

> all its social compassion, *The Tax Inspector* demonstrates once again that narratives of sexual transgression are seriously flawed as vehicles for analysing the complex problems of social decline. Inevitably, they offer individual acts of sexual violence as metaphors for problems that are really of a different order. ("Closing" 43, 44, 45)

Dixon notes that *The Tax Inspector* reveals the connections between Sydney's wealthy "and the 'sewers' that lie beneath their lives. The extent of institutional corruption is suggested by numerous characters and events, but Carey does not develop these leads" ("Closing" 41). Moreover, Dixon argues that the novel "is driven" by the incest in the Catchprice family and that the "revelation of this secret displaces the blame that properly belongs to the wealthy and powerful on to the low-life characters of the western suburbs" ("Closing" 41). However, both Woodcock and Greg Ratcliffe correctly point out that Dixon mistakenly conflates child sexual abuse with political corruption (96; 191). Woodcock argues that the Catchprices, especially Benny, are not depicted by Carey as "the cause of corruption, but rather as its perpetrators and victims" (96). Moreover, Woodcock argues, the various types and levels of corruption depicted in the novel "are related, interlinked, [and] juxtaposed, but are not necessarily equated with each other" (96). *The Tax Inspector* "does not offer the simple paradigm that because Mort is a child abuser he will necessarily be involved in corrupt business" (Woodcock 96). Likewise, Ratcliffe claims that Dixon incorrectly argues that Carey's use of incest "displaces the blame for political corruption that properly belongs to the upper classes onto the low-other" (Dixon, "Closing" 41), contending that the novel actually "demonstrates the pervasiveness of corruption which cannot be attributed to any one group" (Ratcliffe 191).

Carey portrays political corruption, tax evasion and connections between the wealthy, politicians and organized criminals as quite removed from the Catchprice family as a whole. Jack Catchprice, the property developer and only member of the family to escape the dealership, is involved in corrupt and possibly criminal business dealings and is so well-connected that he can make contact with Wally Fischer, the organized crime boss, with just a few phone calls, and stops the audit of Catchprice Motors in the same manner. However, Jack operates in very different circles than the rest of his family, who are corrupt only in the moral sense. Moreover, the child sexual abuse that has been repeated for generations in the Catchprice family is not presented as representative of Franklin or of suburbia in general. While child sexual abuse certainly occurs in suburbia, it is also perpetrated in the city and the bush, and Carey does not present it as a specifically suburban perversion. In fact, since the abuse has been perpetuated by at least four generations of Catchprice males, and the Catchprices were originally a rural family, if the novel places child sexual abuse as originating in any geographic location, it is the bush, not suburbia.

In addition to child sexual abuse and institutionalized corruption, Carey addresses the prevalence of crime and violence within suburbia. Huggan notes that sites such as the Wool Wash are associated with violence (*Peter Carey* 43). However, suburbanization has not only turned the Wool Wash into a dangerous place; the entire suburb of Franklin has become a location for violence and crime. For example, Sarkis is fully aware that he resides in a dangerous community, even though he has only lived in Franklin for six months. Sarkis is described as "young and strong," yet he refuses to walk alone at night in Franklin and is scared of "homeless kids wandering around with beer cans full of petrol" (87). When Sarkis goes for a night-time walk with Gran Catchprice, he takes a spanner with him for protection and thinks her family should be ashamed to let her wander the streets alone at night (87). While walking the streets of Franklin, Sarkis and Gran encounter a group of "twelve-year-olds ... ripping the insignia off a Saab Turbo" (93). Sarkis thinks of the twelve-year-olds as

> like dogs in a pack ... They were feral animals. He was scared of them, even now, twenty metres past the Saab. There was a dull thudding noise. They were running over the roof of the Saab and jumping on its hood and if the owners were smart they would stay in their house and wait for the cops to come. (93)

When Sarkis and Gran take a shortcut across a "burnt-out Kmart lot," he hopes she will keep her voice down because the "piss-smelling [concrete] pipes might hide Nasties, people without a human heart. They might beat you because they thought you had money, or a job, or a handsome face you did not deserve" (94).

The narrator reveals that Benny shares a penchant for petty crime with other suburban youth and has been in trouble for "lying, cheating, truancy, shop-lifting, selling bottled petrol for inhalation, [and] trying to buy Camira parts from the little crooks who hung about in Franklin Mall" (66). Hassall argues that the "gangs of doped-up twelve-year-olds who strip cars in their owners' driveways are too close to the daily police record to dismiss as exaggerated fantasy" (*Dancing* 145). However, Powell contends that the behavior and welfare of suburban youth is "Central to the image of western Sydney and to the stigma surrounding the working class" (87). Since Carey has not lived in the western suburbs of Sydney, his depiction of criminal youth may draw on exaggerated media reports and the distorted reputation of the western suburbs that circulates in popular discourse. The presence of crime in the suburbs demonstrates that it is not confined to the city or the bush, but the reception of Carey's novel suggests many Australians are uncomfortable with such associations. In her essay "The Suburban Problem of Evil," Jennifer Maiden also links the suburbs with violence, discussing her experience with murder and gang violence in Sydney's western suburbs in relation to her novel *Play with Knives* (1991), which is "about a suburban girl who has killed her younger siblings at the age of eleven ... [and] her relationship with her male probation officer" (116). Maiden notes that it took eight years to find a publisher for her novel, one "rejecting it on the grounds that the Mt. Druitt setting was 'too parochial' for an intelligent reader to accept" (116). Significantly, the publisher did not reject the novel because it contained violence, but because it was set in the suburbs. The anti-suburban tradition is clearly present amongst publishers, in addition to writers and critics.

The final violent, criminal act of the novel is Benny's kidnapping of Maria, whom he holds hostage in his cellar at gunpoint and plans to rape. However, once Benny has Maria imprisoned in his cellar, he no longer wants to rape her, and when the stress of the ordeal triggers early labor, he assists with the birth and lavishes the baby with affection. Hassall argues that Benny's kidnapping of Maria is the "end result of the family's refusal to confront the reality of its child abuse" (*Dancing* 158). Furthermore, Hassall compares the climactic cellar scene to the mock-crucifixion of Himmelfarb in White's *Riders in the Chariot* and argues that "the battle between Maria and Benny in the cloacal atmosphere of the cellar is a tour de force in its audacity as well as in its horror" (*Dancing* 160).

A final example of Carey's serious and detailed engagement with suburbia is his decision to show middle class characters who reside in affluent inner suburbs disparaging the working class outer suburbs. Not only is such condescension a tradition within Australian literature, it is also reflected in the common usage in Australian society of derogatory terms such as "westies" and "bogans" to refer to residents of outer suburbs. When Maria tells her colleague and friend Gia over cocktails that she has been assigned to investigate the Catchprice dealership in Franklin, she exclaims:

"They sent me to Franklin. Can you believe that?"

> "Franklin. My God. Who's in Franklin?"
>
> "No one's in Franklin. It was some shitty little G. M. dealer."
>
> ... "They looked like they were Social Welfare clients, not ours." (77)

Not only does the mere mention of Franklin elicit disgust from the middle-class Gia, Maria perceives the residents of Franklin to be worthless people who could pass more easily for "Social Welfare clients" than tax evaders. Powell notes that "in Australian culture, to live in some suburbs is to suffer an equivalent stigma to that borne by people living in the ghettos of Europe and North America" and explains that the negative image "is generated through publicity given to real events but these events are represented through the discourse, experience and knowledge of the dominant culture, interpreted by people outside the ghettos" (xiv). Thus, the residents of the western suburbs rarely have the opportunity to speak for suburbia in the public sphere; Powell and Maiden are rare exceptions.

The middle-class perception of the residents of the outer suburbs is readily apparent to Cathy Catchprice, who tells Maria, "'You come to Franklin and you've decided, before you even get off the F4, that we are all retards and losers - unemployed, unemployable'" (139). Cathy seeks to convince Maria that the residents of Franklin are valuable individuals with significant lives and dreams, rather than "retards and losers" to be dismissed and ignored. Hassall argues that Cathy's defense of Franklin "is at least as persuasive as Maria's defence of the Tax Office" (*Dancing* 150). While defending and explaining her role as a tax inspector to Jack Catchprice, Maria states,

> "I hate all this criminal wealth. The state is full of it. It makes me sick. I see all these skunks with their car phones and champagne and I see all this homelessness and poverty. Do you know that one child in three in Australia grows up under the poverty line?" (216)

Maria declares that she did not become a tax inspector in order to "piddle around rotten inefficient businesses like ... [Catchprice Motors]. I never did anything so insignificant in my life. I won't do that sort of work. It fixes nothing'" (216). Hassall claims that Maria's "heartfelt apologia" presents her as both an idealist and a snob, arguing that "her contempt for the pettiness of auditing Catchprice Motors sounds uncomfortably like contempt for the Catchprices, Franklin, Western Sydney, and the very people that a fair tax system is supposed to champion" (*Dancing* 155).

Despite Carey's bleak depiction of Franklin and its residents, his decision to write without judgment about the kind of place where many Australians live and the social and personal problems they face deserves respect. Australian writers have ignored or disparaged suburbia for far too long. In contrast to his peers Winton and Malouf, predecessors such as Johnston, and younger writers like Lucashenko and McCann, Carey rejects the anti-suburban tradition and treats the outer suburbs as one of the most important places in Australia. Because the vast majority of Australians "make sense of their lives" within suburbia, as Fiske, Hodge, and Turner argue (52), Australian writers who seek to write realistic fiction about their nation severely limit their choice of subject matter if they choose to disparage the suburbs and their inhabitants, or ignore them altogether. Since the publication of *The Tax Inspector*, short fiction writers such as Liam Davison, Jonathan Bennett and Neil Boyack have followed Carey's example of rejecting the anti-suburban tradition, setting their fiction in suburbia and realistically dealing with issues such as unemployment, factory work, family relationships, drug use, and the Australian dream of owning a new home. The recent engagement with suburbia by short fiction writers has been paralleled by a handful of novelists who have followed the lead of Carey and Murnane and abandoned the anti-suburban tradition, producing works that realistically depict the suburban lives of Australians. The new suburban novelists are Elliot Perlman (*Three Dollars*), Damian McDonald (*Luck in the Greater West*), Christos Tsiolkas, whose 2008 novel *The Slap* won several major prizes and was short-listed for the Booker prize, and Steven Carroll, who published a trilogy of suburban novels during the first decade of the twenty-first century: *The Art of the Engine Driver* (2001), *The Gift of Speed* (2004) and *The Time We Have Taken* (2007). Carroll's "Glenroy trilogy" represents a new approach to suburbia and is the focus of my next chapter.

Endnotes

1. Antonella Riem Natale notes that the title of Carey's novel connects it with Katherine Mansfield's short story "Bliss" (341); similarly, Teresa Dovey claims, "the title of the novel ... is surely taken from Katherine Mansfield's story of the same name" (201). However, Carey has stated that his preferred title for the novel was *Waiting for the Barbarians* (Nielsen 70); J.M. Coetzee's novel *Waiting for the Barbarians* was published the year before *Bliss*, and thus Carey was unable to use his preferred title.
2. In a 2006 interview with Radhika Jones, Carey reveals that he had not intended to write a novel at the time, but did so due to market forces: "... my agent told me that it would be easier to sell the stories if I said I was writing a novel. So I said, Sure. But of course I just wanted to sell the stories. I had no intention of writing a novel ... Then I started to worry about it, and I thought about this failed short story about this complacent bourgeois who thinks he's died and gone to hell and hasn't" (127).
3. The "Pleasant" in Mt. Pleasant serves to convey Harry's conception of life in suburbia before his heart attack. There is a Mt. Pleasant in Wollongong and a Mt. Pleasant in Ballarat. Carey may have borrowed the name from one of these real suburbs.
4. See Sheckels (89), Hassall ("Peter Carey" 55; *Dancing* 72), Jose (145), Gelder and Salzman (*Diversity* 124), Ryan-Fazilleau (78), and Turner ("American" 436).
5. Sue Ryan-Fazilleau argues that *Bliss* includes "numerous linguistic, onomastic and environmental details [that] suggest, to the Australian reader at least, that ... [the novel] is set in Australia" (78).
6. See pages 12, 23, 25, 59, 92, 102, 172 and 225.
7. Although the phase "the bush" is also used in Africa and Canada, there are numerous details in *Bliss* that indicate definitively that the novel is not set in Africa or Canada.
8. The scene is possibly inspired by Murray Bail's 1975 short story "Life of the Party," in which the unnamed narrator invites a group of friends to his house for a barbecue and watches from a treehouse as his guests arrive and proceed to have a party in his back yard, thinking he is absent.
9. Here I am excluding Carey's latest novel, *The Chemistry of Tears* (2012), which was published too recently to have won any awards.

Chapter 7

Celebrating Suburbia

Steven Carroll's *The Art of the Engine Driver* (2001), *The Gift of Speed* (2004) and *The Time We Have Taken* (2007)

Steven Carroll was born in Melbourne in 1949 and grew up in the suburb of Glenroy. He attended La Trobe University and has worked as a high school English teacher, professional musician, playwright, university lecturer and theatre critic. *The Art of the Engine Driver* (2001), the first of the novels in the Glenroy trilogy, is Carroll's fourth novel, and the first for which he was shortlisted for a major award, the Miles Franklin. Carroll's critical reputation grew throughout the first decade of the twenty-first century, as *The Gift of Speed* (2004) was also shortlisted for the Miles Franklin and *The Time We Have Taken* (2007) won the award in 2008. Carroll followed his Glenroy trilogy with *The Lost Life* (2009), a novel set in England, which was shortlisted for both the Australian Literature Society Gold Medal and the Barbara Jefferis Award, and *Spirit of Progress* (2011), a prequel to the Glenroy trilogy, which was longlisted for the Miles Franklin. Carroll's Miles Franklin shortlistings and win, combined with shortlistings for the Prix Femina, The Age Book of the Year Award, the Victorian Premier's Literary Awards and the

Australian Literary Society Gold Medal, along with his 2008 Commonwealth Writers Prize win, established him as one of Australia's leading novelists. However, despite numerous accolades and positive reviews in prominent newspapers, magazines and journals, to date not a single work of academic criticism focuses in detail on Carroll's fiction.[1] However, Carroll's extensive explorations of suburbia in his Glenroy trilogy demonstrate that not only has he rejected the anti-suburban tradition, but that Carroll has established suburbia as a rich setting for fiction that contains limitless possibilities. Despite the fact that the Glenroy of Carroll's novels is a small suburb and he uses a limited cast of characters, he devotes over one thousand pages to exploring the lives of ordinary Australians in a suburb similar to those millions of Australians call home. For Carroll, suburban life is significant, complicated, beautiful and worthy of both examination and celebration.

Like much suburban fiction, the Glenroy novels are semi-autobiographical, set in Carroll's childhood suburb during the years of his own childhood and adolescence. The impetus for writing the novels was a vivid dream Carroll experienced; in the dream, "he was a child in the late 1950s, walking along his boyhood suburban street with his parents, on their way to a neighbourhood party" ("Inspiration" 8). Carroll became fascinated with "the suburban frontier" and began investigating the possibility of writing a novel "about the sensations of growing up ... in the new Australian suburbs in the Menzies era" ("Inspiration" 8). Carroll's dream provided the basic plot for *The Art of the Engine Driver*, and he soon discovered that not only was it possible to write a novel set in suburbia in the 1950s, but that he had enough material for three novels. Carroll has stated that he loved writing about suburbia and its residents (Sorensen). Clearly, Carroll's inspiration for writing his suburban trilogy does not have its roots in the anti-suburban tradition, and, unlike writers such as Johnston, Malouf, Winton, Lucashenko and McCann, he does not disparage suburbia or suburbanites. Jason Steger argues that Carroll is "a rare beast" since "he writes with great affection and understanding about life in the suburbs" ("The Critical Eye" 12).

Helen Elliott contends that the "specifically Australian world" of a "post-war suburb full of refugees" that Carroll focuses on in his trilogy had not been explored seriously by other Australian writers "because of its perceived ordinariness." While Elliott overlooks Murnane's suburban fiction, she correctly notes the powerful and widespread influence of the anti-suburban tradition and recognizes Carroll's rare achievement. Although Carroll is not the first Australian novelist to seriously explore suburban life, he is the first to write three consecutive novels with a suburban setting and thus has engaged with suburbia more thoroughly than any other Australian novelist. Moreover, Carroll's exploration of suburbia is ongoing. *Spirit of Progress*, Carroll's most recent novel, is a prequel to the Glenroy trilogy, using many of the same characters and settings, but the sections of the novel focusing on Glenroy take place before the suburb develops, and thus the novel focuses more on Melbourne's inner suburbs than the outer suburb of the trilogy. Furthermore, Carroll has stated in interviews that he is writing a fifth Glenroy novel. While Carroll eschews the anti-suburban tradition, his work contains much in common with all of the suburban novels discussed in this book. Many of the common themes of the Australian suburban novel are present in Carroll's trilogy, including immigration, environmental degradation, the effects of colonialism, non-Indigenous belonging, Indigenous displacement, family relationships and class. Carroll's novels also explore the importance of sport in Australian culture, an aspect of suburban life largely absent from previous suburban novels.

The Art of the Engine Driver

The action of the first novel in Carroll's trilogy takes place over a single weekend in 1957. The novel begins with the central characters Rita, Vic and their son Michael walking along their suburban street en route to an engagement party at the home of their neighbor George Bedser, an English immigrant. At the time the novel is set, Vic is forty, Rita is thirty-three, and Michael is twelve (4). Vic is an engine driver for the railways, Rita demonstrates washing machines for a department store (6), and

Michael is obsessed with cricket. Michael practices his bowling relentlessly and imagines bowling the perfect ball, which "will become known" throughout the suburb "as the ball that Michael bowled" (36). Michael dreams that his speed bowling "will one day carry him along his street, out of the suburb" (35).

The Art of the Engine Driver contains numerous descriptions of the physical environment of the suburb in which it is set. Although Carroll has made it clear in interviews that the novels are set in Glenroy and the novels are marketed as "the Glenroy Trilogy," the suburb is never named in the novels. Carroll repeatedly emphasizes the evolving nature of the suburb, which is in a transitional state somewhere between a farming community and a fully-established suburb. The suburb has its roots in a farming community established around 1870 just nine miles north of Melbourne's CBD (7). The main street of the town is an old wheat road leading to the flour mills, which are connected by rail to Melbourne (7). The main street "contains two imposing, double-storey shops," which are the sole remnants "of the 1880s land boom" (7). Until about 1950, the community changed little, then after the Second World War a factory was constructed "near the railway station and the owner [Webster] built himself a large house on expansive grounds not far away" (7). The construction of the factory brings workers to the community, which in turn leads to the construction of new houses and shops, and then more factories, causing the process to repeat itself (8). By the time the action of the novel begins in 1957, the suburb is rapidly developing: "All around, a suburb is being born ... Like all booms it will soon turn into a rush, a land grab, and, within a few years, cheap workers' homes will be thrown up" (8).

Remnants of the farming community share the suburban space with new streets and houses. Old bluestone farmhouses occupy "the few vantage points of the low, broad valley on which the community sits" (7). However, the spatial arrangement of the community is being transformed by the ongoing development:

> ... the new lines of the suburb are taking shape. Streets and salubriously named dirt avenues have been carved out of the paddocks and houses have begun to appear; red roofs, white weatherboards and instant gardens, sprouting like fold-out models. Cattle refuse to accept the newly drawn suburban boundaries and graze where they always have, even if it is now somebody's front yard. (7)

Vic, Rita and Michael live on a street exemplifying the transitional state of the suburb; it contains both newly constructed homes and open paddocks, and is close to a golf course, flour mills and a railway line (3, 4). Carroll depicts the evolving suburban environment positively, beginning the novel by describing the family "walking under a cloudless peach sky, ripe and glowing. The sun is low and their shadows almost stretch back to the family house at the golf course end of the street" (3). The narrator informs the reader that "Years later, Michael will dream of ... [the] evening. It will be vivid. He will go back to the suburb in dreams" (10). The image of the family walking along their suburban street at sunset is repeated in *The Time We Have Taken*, the concluding novel of the trilogy.

The characters in *The Art of the Engine Driver* are often conscious of their suburb's evolution. Rita contemplates the state of her environment prior to suburban development and thinks of the open paddocks near her home as "part of wide, open country, as they were before the suburb arrived" (43). A few pages later, Vic thinks about the close proximity of open, undeveloped space, "beyond the mills, beyond the houses. Out where there's nothing but paddocks of Scotch thistle" (44). Vic thinks of the only paved road in the suburb, the main road that divides the suburb in half, as forming a connection between the open spaces just two miles away and the developing community comprised mostly of young working class families (44-45).

Like other suburban novels set in the 1950s, *The Art of the Engine Driver* contains a number of immigrant characters. Moreover, the majority of the residents of Vic and Rita's street are immigrants. George Bedser, the host of the party that forms the novel's narrative core, is an English immigrant who lives in a house situated "in a small hollow at the end of the street. It is made from plain weatherboard, painted white, and has a small rose garden" (169). A native of Liverpool and a welder by trade, Bedser immigrated in 1950 with his daughter Patsy after his wife suddenly left him (170). At the age of twenty-one, Patsy is getting engaged and Bedser has decided to invite his neighbors to the party since all his relatives still live in Liverpool (170). Bedser has lived in the street for five years and feels that "If he has a sense of family ... of community, it is the community of the street he has come to live in" (171). Carroll emphasizes the sense of community developing in the street, depicting the families leaving their houses to make their way to Bedser's party: "... one after the other, the front doors and front gates of the street are opening out onto their lawns, footpaths and nature strips, as all the families ... step onto the dusty dirt road and form a modest procession" (5). The families have all moved to the suburb from other places, whether older suburbs of Melbourne or European nations, and by accepting the invitation to Bedser's party participate in the process of forming a new community through a shared celebration.

Another immigrant, the Dutchman Peter van Rijn, plays an even larger role than Bedser in forming a community in the new suburb. Van Rijn is an electrical engineer with a shop in the commercial heart of the suburb, where he repairs radios and sells televisions. It is Van Rijn who brings television to the suburb, and it is television that makes his business successful (134-135). Van Rijn sets up a television in his shop window and families who have not yet purchased a television gather outside and watch as if they were at the cinema (135). However, van Rijn's success is not appreciated by all members of the community; on the night of the party his shop is vandalized, the front window smashed by a brick, and the word "commie" written in large red print on the floor (136). Although van Rijn is disheartened by the attack, especially because he had "left Holland after the war with the precise intention of leaving ... hatred behind," he resolves to attend the party anyway, despite the fact that his wife, also a Dutch immigrant, proclaims loudly "as if to the whole street, that no, she will not go to the party. She will not mix with people who could do this" (136, 138). The motive for the attack on van Rijn's shop is never explained, and the identity of the perpetrator is not revealed until the third novel in the trilogy. However, the episode is an acknowledgment of the tensions regarding immigration that existed in Australia during the 1950s and of the occasionally violent expressions of xenophobia. Although the attack on van Rijn's shop is much less violent, it recalls the mock crucifixion of Himmelfarb in White's *Riders in the Chariot*. In addition to Bedser and van Rijn, there are a number of other immigrants living on the street, including a Ukrainian family whose children are Michael's friends (157); Mary Younger, a twenty-seven-year-old Irish immigrant with five children (66); and Mr. Malek, a Polish immigrant who speaks little English, gets drunk on home-made liquor and keeps to himself (148, 149).

Although the prevailing tone of the novels in the trilogy is nostalgic and celebratory, Carroll certainly does not depict suburbia as a flawless environment or a space that is loved by all its inhabitants. Of the central characters, Rita has the most contentious relationship with the suburb. She is repeatedly depicted as wearing dresses that are "too good" for the suburb (4) and as not sharing the tastes and attitudes of her neighbours. Rita grew up in an inner suburb of Melbourne south of the Yarra River and has not yet learnt to consider her new suburb home. Rita's relationship with the environment of her childhood and adolescence is contrasted with her attitudes towards her new suburban environment in a passage written from her point of view:

> My sisters all stayed south of the river, the river that slips away from me every night when my train leaves the platform and we curve across the city to Spencer Street, North Melbourne, Newmarket and on. When, at the end of the suburban line, I see the flour mills in front of me towering over the flat paddocks and square houses, I should feel like I'm coming home but I don't. And when I step off the train and see the wide, open paddocks and the

> timber houses, looking like they could all be swept away by a good storm, I still wonder what I'm doing here. (98)

Rita has lived all her life in suburbia, and thus her dissatisfaction is not with suburbia per se, but with the new, outer suburb in which she now lives. Compared to her former inner, established suburb, the new suburb feels temporary and flimsy, largely because she has not yet established a strong sense of belonging.

Rita is aware that she lacks a strong sense of belonging to her community, both the physical environment and the people who live in it, and wonders if she will ever be able to make the new suburb her emotional home:

> Rita looks at the Millers on the other side of the street. They should feel like neighbours but they don't. The street should feel like home, but it doesn't ... she wonders if the street will ever feel like home. (98)

From Michael's perspective, his mother's lack of a strong sense of belonging is at least partially due to her own behaviour and personality, rather than a product of the suburb. According to Michael, Rita "is not very good at making friends" and can create the impression that "she prefers to keep to herself" (164). However, Rita has managed to make at least one friend on the street, a young woman named Evie Doyle. Evie and her husband Dennis are newcomers to the street, having lived for just six months in a house named "Eden" (163).[2] When Rita and Evie's husbands work the night shift, the women are in the habit of sitting together on the front porch talking. During their conversations, Evie often talks about "going somewhere," but when pressed for specifics is unable to provide an answer (165-166). Evie also claims that "she keeps on forgetting she's alive" and together with Rita talks "a lot about going places. Together and alone. But they never say exactly what it is they are so intent on leaving" (165-166). The desire for escape and dissatisfaction with life expressed by Evie and Rita can certainly be interpreted as the consequence of a deficiency in suburbia; however, there are other plausible explanations for their malaise, such as marital problems, ennui and unrealistic expectations.

Later in the novel, Rita decides that once Michael has grown up and left home she will separate from Vic and explore the world beyond her suburb:

> ... she will go to it, that great, wondrous world that lies beyond the suburb, and the poky houses and the prying eyes. And all those small minds that look you up and down if you try to look a little smart, that take it personally like an insult and brand you a snob if you look a bit stylish. (190)

Rita's desire to see the world beyond the suburb is intertwined with her perception that her suburb is in some way repressive. Since the reader is not privy to the thoughts of the majority of the residents of Rita's street, let alone the suburb, it is not clear whether Rita's belief in the small-mindedness of her neighbours is justified. It is entirely possible that Rita mistakenly believes that her neighbours are judging her appearance. Rita is also dissatisfied with some of the physical characteristics of the suburb. She yearns for some trees to populate "the low grassy paddocks" that "go on forever" so that there is some visual variety, "Something to break the flat lines of the paddocks, the dirt streets and the square houses that sit on them" (198). In a direct reference to the environmental degradation caused by suburban development, the narrator states, "The trees have all been swept away to make room for the square houses" (198). The destruction of the natural environment due to suburban development is not an issue Carroll foregrounds in his trilogy; nevertheless, it is mentioned on several occasions and always depicted negatively.

Rita is not the only character to express negative feelings about the suburb. Michael often overhears the Barlows next door yelling at each other, and Mrs. Barlow always loudly delivers the same list of complaints: "The house is wrong. The suburb is wrong. The street is ghastly. The suburb is stuck out on the edge of the world. She is ashamed of the address" (34). During a drive into the countryside north of the suburb, Patsy Bedser notes that the street along which she drives is treeless, "like most of the streets in the suburb, for they were cleared away to make room for the houses" (71). As Patsy watches "the street recede in the rear-vision mirror," she realizes that she hates it and is happy to leave it behind, since she considers the houses to be "plain and ugly," the gardens "pathetic," "the dirt road like a cattle track. She wished they'd never come. She was a city girl, from Liverpool ... And this was a frontier settlement" (72). The complaints of both Mrs. Barlow and Patsy focus on the peripheral location of the suburb, the unfinished infrastructure, the modest houses and the lack of established trees and gardens; over time, all of these characteristics of the suburb change. Thus, the aspects of the suburb that some of the characters perceive as negative transform as time passes and the criticisms cease to be valid. In *The Time We Have Taken*, Carroll reveals how the attitudes of the characters towards the suburb change markedly as time passes and the suburb changes to such an extent that the inhabitants grow to love their suburb and feel a deep sense of belonging.

Marriage and family are major themes in *The Art of the Engine Driver*. Vic and Rita have a poor relationship and both frequently contemplate separating once Michael has left home. Vic comes to perceive marriage and parenthood as a burdensome trap and an economic drain. After coming home drunk, a frequent occurrence, Vic advises Michael to never marry, declaring: "'This is what happens when you get a house and a family. You wind up with ten lousy shillings. Never get a house and a family. Stay free'" (118). On another occasion, Rita plans to go out for the evening and waits at home for Vic, already "dressed to go out," but Vic comes home late "too drunk to go anywhere" (131). Vic falls over onto the floor of the lounge room and remains there while Rita yells and insults him: "He knew it was coming and he didn't care ... Eventually, having exhausted her anger ... [Rita] had given up. It was pointless and she had left him there to sleep on the floor" (131). Despite witnessing such scenes, Michael has a relatively happy childhood and gets along well with his parents. Carroll depicts a family who are neither happy nor miserable; he presents neither a rosy picture nor an extremely negative one. Rather, he realistically depicts a family that experiences both ups and downs. Carroll's depiction of suburban family life is actually positive in comparison to Johnston's *My Brother Jack*, Lucashenko's *Steam Pigs* and Carey's *The Tax Inspector*.

In their analysis of *The Art of the Engine Driver*, Gelder and Salzman argue that the party at the heart of the novel "should be the moment during which settlement establishes itself and a sense of community prevails"; however, in their view, "community is both offered ... and taken away" (*Celebration*, 46). Gelder and Salzman contend that the families on the street are estranged from each other and that the neighborhood is haunted by "a yearning to be elsewhere ... It is as if the novel is heading in quite the opposite direction to the kind of fully embodied occupation of a house we find in *Cloudstreet*" (*Celebration*, 46). However, Gelder and Salzman fail to recognize that the community is in the early stages of an ongoing process of establishing community and belonging, one that is developed by Carroll over the course of three novels, and thus it is misguided to expect to find an established, fully-embodied community at the end of the first novel in the trilogy.

The Gift of Speed

The second novel in Carroll's trilogy is set four years after *The Art of the Engine Driver*. *The Gift of Speed* begins in October 1960 and concludes in February 1961. The novel is set against the backdrop of the West Indies cricket team's tour of Australia, beginning with Michael watching the team arrive in Perth on television, and concluding with the team's farewell parade in Melbourne. Michael is now sixteen years old and still obsessed with cricket and bowling the perfect ball, one that "will become known all across the suburb as the ball that Michael bowled" (7). *The Gift of Speed* focuses much more on Michael and his cricket obsession than the other novels in the trilogy, while also serving as a transitionary narrative exploring the ongoing development of the suburb and the establishment of community. Speaking in an interview about the composition of the novel,

Carroll states that "Speed operates in lots of different ways in the book but one is actually the suburb itself, and it's a phase of history [when] the country seemed to go into fast-forward from about 1946 onwards, and these suburbs just bloomed and sprung up" ("The Inspiration" 10).

Due to the ongoing development of the suburb, the old wheat road has become the Old Wheat Road, simultaneously a landmark, a major thoroughfare and a reminder of the suburb's origins. Vic rides his bike to the Old Wheat Road to go shopping, traversing a route that has become "a familiar path, past the school, its red-brick classrooms quiet under the peppercorns, past the tennis courts, freshly raked and sprinkled, and up into the Old Wheat Road. It's an easy and pleasant ride" (150). Over just four years, the suburb evolves from a frontier community with only one paved road to an established community replete with well-maintained tennis courts. The Old Wheat Road is no longer "like the main street of a wild west town, all weeds and dirt and long swaying grass"; it has become "just like anywhere else" (151). Vic and Rita now live in a world "of neat new lawns and glistening weatherboard houses" and the young families on the street look "like they've arrived at their stop and their journey is over" (151). Not only has the suburb become established, it is now a final destination and the space in which young families chose to spend the rest of their lives.

In *The Gift of Speed* Carroll depicts a suburban community in which children, adolescents and adults live pleasant, comfortable lives. Midway through the novel, Michael contemplates the community on his street:

> All around him the houses, the street, the suburb itself, are quiet. The children who play their games in the street are sleeping. The girls who gather outside Younger's house to talk in whispers about boys have gone to their beds. So too have the boys who stand near listening to their talk. (204)

Here, the suburb is a self-contained world filled with pleasure, innocence, friendship and budding romance. Carroll also depicts the adults in the suburb as members of a community united by common experiences and daily routines. Late at night, the last train of the day "clatters over the track that leads down into the city. It is a distant sound" that "draws them all together" (225). The train is heard by Webster, Michael, Vic's mother, Kathleen and Rita (225-226). Vic's mother thinks of the train as "a welcome sound, a familiar comfort" (226). While in Nat's barber shop, Michael listens to the cricket on the radio with Nat and the bicycle repair shop owner and looks "out across the street to where the butcher, the chemist and the newsagent are gathered around the butcher's radio, and he imagines that all along the street, and all across the suburb, everybody is doing exactly the same thing" (235). When the match ends in a dramatic draw, "the barber shop, the butcher shop, and all the shops and houses across the suburb, burst into life and the tension that has been curled up inside everyone is suddenly released in a carnival of sound" (236). In this instance, the community is united by a historic sporting event that they are all able to experience together. Throughout *The Gift of Speed*, Carroll repeatedly emphasizes the increasing development of community in the suburb. By the end of the novel, Vic acknowledges that although he is not friends with his neighbors they are "good people" who help each other in times of need (335).

In addition to the ongoing development of a sense of community, Carroll depicts characters establishing long-lasting connections to the suburb and a sense of permanent settlement. The "settling in" is partially achieved through the establishment of gardens, such as Vic and Rita's backyard, which now contains mature plum, apricot and lemon trees (8), but also through modifications to houses. Rita decides to add French windows to the house, even though Vic does not approve (11). Vic knows that the neighbors "will talk about the changes to the house and he will be called upon to explain" (12). Rita is well aware of what the neighbors will think, but does not care, since she thinks of the street as "damned, bloody stupid" and she "barely talks to anybody" (15). Rita acknowledges that the trees are growing, the streets have been paved, and concrete footpaths installed, which has all "made a difference," yet she believes that the suburb "will always remain a backwater" (15-16). However, just a page later the reader learns that Rita thinks "The street might not be the end of the world as it once was" and takes comfort in the planned renovations to the house: "The new windows, the brass fittings, the painted patio, will all be waiting for her, sparkling in the night so that anybody passing in the street will pause to look" (16). Again, Rita is concerned about how the neighbors will perceive the house, but in this case considers that the improvements will inspire envy.

The Gift of Speed contains numerous reminders of the former state of the land now occupied by the suburb. A creek that runs through the golf course near Vic and Rita's house "once ran through the whole suburb," and children on their way to school used to jump the creek, but now the creek is mostly covered over and "runs unseen and unheard beneath the footpaths and the roads of the suburb" (22). Michael attends a picnic with his love-interest Kathleen at a farm north of the suburb. The farm has not yet been reached by the suburban sprawl,

> but it has the look of a place that is about to disappear and pass into local history ... the frontier of the suburbs is ever moving and moving closer with every day ... Like an arrow that has already been fired, the city is heading towards them, and it is not difficult for Michael to imagine streets and salubriously named avenues being carved out of the open field upon which they are now standing. (95-96)

Although the ongoing suburbanization that constantly alters the landscape could be read as negative, Carroll depicts the process ambivalently, simultaneously acknowledging the loss and recognizing the positive aspects of suburbanization.

Carroll devotes a considerable portion of *The Gift of Speed* to developing the character of Webster, the factory owner who has played a significant role in the establishment of the suburb. Webster built the suburb's first factory, which takes up a whole block "at the intersection of the two main streets of the suburb," and is one of the largest employers (27, 73).

Although Webster is wealthy enough to live anywhere he chooses, he decided to live in the suburb

> ... because he liked the look of the land. And there was no shortage of wide rambling mansions left over from the previous century when the suburb was a farming community. Here he could have the mansion and the sprawling grounds that he'd always sought. (73)

Webster's mansion and the surrounding grazing land formerly "belonged to the descendents of an old pioneering family, a family that had once possessed wealth and power" (74). The mansion on Webster's estate is transformed from a symbol of colonialism, settlement and the pastoral elite in to a symbol of post-war industrial capitalism. Webster's estate is surrounded by a "high sandstone wall" that "runs almost the full length of the block" and contains indigenous trees that reached maturity long before the suburb existed (265).

Not only is Webster's estate a secluded sanctuary in the heart of suburbia, it is a physical remnant and reminder of the physical environment as it existed before suburbanization. When Michael visits Webster's estate while knocking on doors to raise money for his cricket team, he experiences an "immediate feeling of being in another country. The grounds are vast. He can see no end to them. Lawns, paths, gardens, wooded sections like small forests, go on and on as far as he can see" (266). On Webster's estate, Michael feels "out of his territory" and the "endless lawns ... small forests ... [and] winding paths" all seem to "belong to someone's private country" (266). Webster's estate is not the only physical location in the suburb that existed before suburban development. Michael's love-interest, Kathleen Marsden, is an orphan who lives in a Catholic Girls' Home. Like Webster's mansion, the Girls' Home is a colonial era building "set back from the street in a world of its own," including "cast-iron balconies, tall, closed doors and wide grounds" (40). The fenced grounds and the front gate shut "the rest of the neighbourhood out"; from Michael's perspective, the Girls' Home "is a distant building, the most distant in the suburb" (40). Not only is the Girls' Home distant, it is a reminder of another time, a time when the suburb did not exist: "there is no suburb here, only what might have been twenty, thirty, forty or fifty years before the suburb ever came" (184). The presence of Webster's estate and the Girls' Home in the suburb demonstrate that suburbia is not a homogenous environment comprised solely of weatherboard single family houses on quarter-acre blocks. Rather, the physical environment and infrastructure of suburbia is diverse and varied, just like the residents who make up the community.[3]

Webster owns an expensive and powerful sports car that he is in the habit of driving around the suburb late at night and at high speeds along a mile-long straight stretch of road. The sound of the sports car's powerful engine accelerating through the darkness and quiet of the night is familiar to many of the suburb's residents. After Webster crashes his car and dies, the local newspaper describes him as a "giant" of the community and the residents agree (301-302). When Vic hears about Webster's death, he is deeply affected, not because he knew Webster or worked for him, but because he interprets the death as a sign that the suburb is changing

> ... and can no longer absorb the things it could when it was on the frontier. A suburb is tamed by time, subdued by its own speed. In the flicker of a bored eye, a paddock becomes a suburb, the frontier shifts, and all the types that the place was once wild enough to take in, must either adapt or go. (301)

Vic comes to see the suburb as an environment that no longer suits him, since he is not willing to settle down permanently and plans to retire alone to a small fishing community in northern New South Wales after Michael leaves home.

Since Michael plays a much larger role in *The Gift of Speed* than in *The Art of the Engine Driver*, the second novel contains a number of passages that reveal Michael's feelings about his suburb, which range from alienation to appreciation. Each time Michael leaves cricket training and returns to "the everyday life of the suburb," he feels like he is "stepping back into some foreign world" that is not "meant for him and which has merely claimed him again for the time being" (47). For Michael, cricket is the source of beauty and represents the hope of a more exciting future, so leaving the cricket field and returning to normal daily life feels like a transition from the sublime to the mundane. Nevertheless, the suburb is Michael's home and intimately familiar territory. Like Johnston's *My Brother Jack* and McCann's *Subtopia*, Carroll's trilogy contains scenes depicting characters traversing suburbia on commuter trains and musing about their environment. While the train journey scenes in Johnston and McCann's novels allow the characters to express their hatred for suburbia, Carroll's train passages are ambivalent. While Michael rides the train home from the city,

> He watches the sun melting onto the rooftops of Kensington and Newmarket – old suburbs, old houses, squashed together in rows. He knows the stops by heart after years of taking the dusty red train to and from the city. Then he watches the same sun yet again settle onto the rooftops of Essendon and all the suburbs that follow, and soon he sees the flour mills of his suburb glowing in the distance like the medieval towers of a medieval town, and all the houses become flat and square and dull and he knows he is nearing home. (57)

Michael's intimate knowledge of his suburb is often expressed in territorial terms. For example, Michael thinks of his suburb as really being two suburbs: "his side of the railway line and the other side, east and west. And whenever he crosses the railway line he feels, for that time, out of his territory" (26).

The passages of the novel narrated from Michael's point of view contain expressions of the beauty that he experiences in his suburb, such as "the sweet smell of watered lawns" (99). While gardening is depicted in Johnston's *My Brother Jack* as an activity representative of conformity, narrow-mindedness and an excessive concern with keeping up appearances, Carroll focuses on the role gardening plays in enhancing the natural environment and cultivating the beauty within suburbia:

> In those few hours ... [Michael] was away ... they were out – all of them. The gardeners of the suburb. They were out watering their lawns and gardens and filling the air with the scent of cut grass, damp concrete, flowers, gravel and wet bitumen, which is the rich, dense scent of a suburb and a suburb alone. (100)

The concluding paragraph of the novel is a Wintonesque description of the suburb at twilight that suggests the importance of community, the ability to perceive the familiar from a new perspective and to reassess what one had previously understood as ordinary:

> And the light, slanting across the shopfronts and rooftops, piercing the venetian blinds of all the lounge rooms beyond the street, is a different light. It is part of something that is still there and which won't go away. For Michael, standing at the top of the Old Wheat Road, with the flour mill and the railway station just behind him, there will always be a trace of this summer left behind ... this vague, nagging feeling that we all might just be a bit better than we thought we were. (348)

The Time We Have Taken

The final installment of Carroll's trilogy won the 2008 Miles Franklin award, garnered much critical praise, and established Carroll as the leading novelist of Australian suburbia. Gillian Dooley describes Carroll's prose as possessing "a remarkable, hypnotic stillness" and argues that his style "is quite extraordinary in its subtlety and poise" (1, 3). Debra Adelaide compares Carroll to Murnane, notes the presence of many "small and beautiful epiphanies" in the novel, and argues that it is Carroll's "creation of a larger concept of suburban life in all its astonishing transcendent possibilities that makes ... [the] novel so special. Carroll's revelations of these beautiful insights into our utterly ordinary world make him a writer worth cherishing." Similarly, Lyndall Nairn notes Carroll's innovative, revelatory and celebratory engagement with suburbia, arguing that "Those who consider the suburbs to be boring have not read ... *The Time We Have Taken*" (95, 94).

The novel is set in 1970. Michael has left home and almost completed university, Vic has retired to northern New South Wales, and Rita remains alone in the family home. The novel begins with Peter van Rijn having a remarkable idea while driving to work, "an idea of such significance to the suburb that it will become the reference point for all official events in the coming year. And the unofficial" (6). While thinking about the time that has passed since he settled in the suburb, the establishment and development of his business, and the changes that have taken place in the suburb, Van Rijn recalls "A photograph in the local newspaper of a road junction, a few farm houses on a wide landscape, and ... the first wooden store to come to the community. And beneath that the date: 1870" (7-8). Van Rijn decides that the construction of the first shop in the community in 1870 marks the beginning of the suburb:

> A shop marks the arrival of Progress. A shop brings with it all the latest wonders the production process has to offer. A shop is, in short, the flag of settlement. It was – this single, wooden general store (and his conviction is absolute) – the point at which the suburb could look back and say that is where we began. And, in a flash ... he knows that this is the year to pronounce the suburb one hundred years old. (8)

Van Rijn immediately shares his idea with the suburb's mayor, Harold Ford, and together they decide to form a committee of local dignitaries to plan celebrations and commemorations. Although the Mayor does not like Van Rijn, he is enamored with the idea and seduced by fantasies of "fat government cheques and a whole suburb transformed into the very emblem of Progress" (82). In the Mayor's fantasy, he sees "his suburb, his people, all brought together in mutual celebration, under the beaming gaze of the mayor whose vision had made it happen" (82). Mayor Ford realizes that the celebration of the suburb's centenary is "his doorway into local history" where he will take "a shining place at the very centre of the suburb's story" (82). Although Ford and Van Rijn do not question the veracity of the claim that the suburb is one hundred years old, Carroll makes it clear that the notion is a construction, a fictional narrative that the people of the suburb tell themselves because it confirms and enhances their self-perception. Most of the characters, however, take it for granted that the suburb's history "is a grand and dignified matter" (83). However, when Mrs. Webster, the widow of Webster the factory owner, is invited to serve on the committee planning the centenary events, she immediately questions the idea: "Is the suburb really a hundred years old? The age of the suburb is not something she has ever pondered. And how can anybody know such a thing anyway? Where do you start?" (52).

When the centenary committee meets, their discussion focuses on the development of the suburb and its transformation from a farming community into an established residential community. The committee concludes that the suburb is "the very picture of Progress," noting that just twenty years earlier the suburb was "a frontier community of stick houses and dirt tracks," but has become "a wide, solid community of lawns and gardens and tree-lined streets ... What was once a frontier outpost is now, indeed, the Toorak of the North that the estate agents of a hundred years ago had promised all their grandparents" (83). Enamoured with the idea of their suburb being a hundred years old, the committee exaggerates both the status of the suburb and their personal connections to it. Comparing Glenroy to Toorak, arguably Melbourne's most expensive and prestigious suburb, is absurd, and since almost all of the committee members are relative newcomers to the area (and one of them an immigrant), it is quite a stretch to claim that any of their grandparents were potential buyers of land in the area in 1870. Moreover, while claiming that the suburb is a hundred years old, the committee members also acknowledge that the community did not exist in its present form twenty years earlier. Thus, while it might be plausible to claim that the community is one hundred years old, it is simply not true that the suburb is one hundred years old.

Celebrating Suburbia

In addition to deciding to celebrate the centenary of the suburb, the committee, adopting a suggestion by Van Rijn, also decides to label the suburb "Centenary Suburb" (85). Van Rijn argues that the title "tells everybody what they need to know" and conveys both "a sense of history" and "a sense of debt," in addition to celebration (85). After making the resolution, the committee begins to think of their suburb as Centenary Suburb, and as they leave the meeting

> ... it is as though those two words have already transformed the suburb. The mayor is struck by a sense of its solidity and history that he has never appreciated before, and the two priests are discussing the farms that once existed where the houses and shops and garages of the suburb now stand, and Peter van Rijn is contemplating the frail wooden structure that first brought commerce to the community and thereby heralded the beginning of settlement. (86)

The simple act of naming the suburb Centenary Suburb causes the committee to see it anew and appreciate its beauty: "all across the suburb, rich and profuse gardens of bright red, pink and yellow roses ... the rattle of trains comes and goes; shop doors open and close ... this suburb of theirs, now transformed into a grand achievement" (87-88). After the renaming, the suburb becomes a "perfectly functioning organism" and "a grand tale, calling ... for recognition" (88).

In the third novel of his trilogy, Carroll addresses one of the most significant issues in contemporary Australian society, the treatment of the Indigenous peoples and the theft of their land by European settlers. Carroll first raises the issue by revealing that Van Rijn subscribes to the concept of terra nullius and does not even think about the former Indigenous inhabitants. For Van Rijn, the shop constructed in 1870 is the starting point for the settlement because it is "the focal point of a group of people who have decided to settle in one place and call that place home" (86). Van Rijn

> ... gives no thought to the fact that others were there before them all and too called this place home; that earlier inhabitants, for millennia, walked the very ground that they have, just now, collec-

> tively decided to call Centenary Suburb. He simply does not think of it. When he thinks of the suburb before they all came to it he thinks only of open country and vacant land. As open and vacant as the blank page upon which their history will be written, for History begins with a blank page. As well as open country and vacant land. (86)

Here Carroll clearly introduces the concepts of Indigenous ownership and belonging, displacement, terra nullius, settler denial and forgetting, without naming any of the issues explicitly. The subtle manner in which Carroll deals with such contentious issues is consistent with the understated, meditative tone of the trilogy. The novels are not overtly political or controversial, yet Carroll openly acknowledges the role the suburbs have played in displacing Indigenous peoples and occupying Indigenous land. Carroll engages with the Indigenous issue again at the conclusion of *The Time We Have Taken*, discussed later in this chapter.

As part of their celebrations and commemorations, the Centenary Suburb Committee commissions a mural depicting the suburb's history "from its sheep-farming origins" to the present "as if the suburb has spoken *through* them" (114-116, original emphasis). The mural is referred to as "the grand narrative of the suburb" (221). Michael, who is asked to join the Centenary Suburb Committee because he is young and grew up in the suburb, suggests that his housemate Mulligan, an artist, receive the commission (103). While Mulligan is working on the mural, a process that takes many months, other events and celebrations occur, more

> ... than anybody could remember, for, once the idea had taken off, everybody wanted to be part of it. Small groups and societies that nobody even knew existed were writing to the committee applying to be part of the celebrations ... Tiny religious organisations that seemed to have mushroomed overnight, sporting groups, amateur science foundations, reading groups – it was a revelation to the committee just what was going on in the suburb ... the whole place was humming. (281)

The number and variety of events, celebrations and organizations reveals the diversity and complexity of the suburban community, as well as the pride that the residents take in their suburb and their desire to participate in the celebrations. The above passage clearly reveals the absurdity of the notion that suburbia is boring and devoid of culture. One of the events held to celebrate the centenary is an exhibition of the history of Webster's factory, held in Webster's mansion and curated by Rita. The exhibition is successful "Beyond anyone's imaginings" (282). The narrator reveals that the success of the exhibition is due to the fact that it

> ... had touched a spot in the suburb that the suburb didn't even know was there, because it's easy to overlook the ordinary, familiar things that are around you every day of the year ... Until someone or something alerts everybody to the possibility that they just might not be so ordinary after all. (282)

The newfound ability of the residents of the suburb to see the sublime in the ordinary and to appreciate the beauty of everyday life can be read as a meta-commentary on Carroll's trilogy in that one of the major elements of the novels is Carroll's exploration of the "ordinary" world of suburbia and repeated revelation of suburbia's beauty and complexity.

During the first two novels of the trilogy, Michael often thinks about leaving the suburb after finishing high school and of an escape enabled by his cricket skills, "the gift of speed." However, it turns out that it is not speed that takes Michael "out of his street and his suburb," but the pursuit of a university degree (111). While living in an inner suburb in accommodation shared with other students, Michael travels by taxi to a party with his girlfriend Madeleine. The party is in a suburb unfamiliar to Michael, and being out of his territory causes him to miss his home suburb: "... he is filled with a fierce, illogical longing for his old street and the children's voices that he and his friends once had when they were young and the street was a world unto itself" (39). Being away from his home suburb allows Michael to appreciate the environment he once considered ordinary, and as the novel progresses he becomes increasingly nostalgic for his suburban childhood and adolescence. Michael becomes an English teacher at his old high school and spends an increasing amount of time in the suburb (75). As a member of the Centenary Suburb Committee, he is the representative of the generation that grew up in the outer suburbs, advocates change, and represents progressive political action, such as protesting against the Vietnam War and voting for Gough Whitlam.

Michael brings Madeleine home to his suburb to show her where he grew up, "the world that he comes from and which he will take with him wherever he goes" (147). The visit takes place on a glorious day as "a ripe morning sun … pours its warmth onto the gardens, lawns and hedges of the suburb" (137). Michael is drawn back into the world of the suburb by visiting his old street, seeing himself as "ten, twelve and sixteen all over again" (138). He notices how much the suburb has developed, changed and become established, realizing that it "is no longer at the edge of the known world," that the "frontier bleakness is gone … The gardens have grown, the streets are paved, and the houses themselves have achieved a solidity that they never had when they were" being constructed "when, all around them, a suburb was being born" (139). While visiting his childhood home, Michael hears the voice of the neighbor Mrs. Barlow, whose complaints about her house, street and suburb have remained "consistent down through the decades"(145). The narrator reveals that Mrs. Barlow has now lived in the suburb for "so long she can now no longer leave"; however, she can never admit this fact to herself, since an admission "would be to concede that she is, in fact, home" (145). As the decades have passed, Mrs. Barlow and the suburb "have meshed, grown into each other, to such an extent that she would now be lost without it. Sometime, during all the years she fought so hard against the place, it became her centre" (145). Carroll's depiction of Mrs. Barlow's gradual development of a deep sense of belonging echoes Winton's depiction of the Lambs and Pickles' evolving relationship with their house in *Cloudstreet*, a novel which appears to have strongly influenced Carroll's trilogy.

Carroll's suburban novels are also influenced by Johnston's *My Brother Jack*, although Carroll's work is clearly not anti-suburban, unlike Johnston and Winton's. In *The Time We Have Taken*, Carroll makes a number of direct references to Johnston and his novel. One of Michael's colleagues gives him a copy of *My Brother Jack* after repeatedly observing Michael reading English novels. Soon after beginning to read Johnston's novel, Michael realizes that

> ... he is doing more than reading just another book. There is something about the reading of this book that feels like what he can only call an event ... For when he reads this book, he sees, for the first time in his reading life, the world from which he comes. His world – his past and present (and quite probably his future) – has been made different by a book. (230-231)

For the first time, Michael has read a novel set in Melbourne's suburbs, and although Johnston's work is set several decades before Michael's adolescence and outside his suburb, the novel describes the suburbia that he comes from and knows intimately. Michael begins to understand that his suburban world can also be the setting for serious, life-changing literature. While reading *My Brother Jack* in his shared student house in an inner suburb of Melbourne, Michael is transported to "somewhere else, both home and not home" and comes to the realization that whether he wants to or not,

> ... he will carry home wherever he goes, will be forever going back to it, or being dragged back to it, while forever just wanting to be rid of the whole damn place. And it is, he knows, the same for the character in this book, and its author, this Johnston. (232)

Here Carroll focuses on the deeply ambivalent relationship that Michael has with his suburb, a relationship Michael believes he shares with David Meredith and George Johnston. By the end of the novel, Michael thinks of *My Brother Jack* as "the book that will give him a place to go when a place to go is needed in the hollow years afterwards" (344). Part of the message of Carroll's trilogy is that people are created and shaped by their environments and that as much as one might try, one can never sever the relationship with one's formative place. Carroll seems to suggest that one can only find contentment after coming to terms with the place from which one comes.

Throughout *The Time We Have Taken*, Rita lives by herself in the family home in the suburb, despite the fact that during the first two novels she was eager to leave. In addition to living alone, the other major change in Rita's life is that she no longer works in the city, but is now the housekeeper at the Webster mansion (16-17). Like Mrs. Barlow and so many other residents of the suburb, Rita has established a deep connection to the suburb over time and feels that she now belongs. During a scene in which Rita strolls along her street, which "has mellowed into a pleasant walk" (16), she contemplates the fact that it has "been hers for just over fifteen years" and thinks about the changes that have taken place both in her life and to the physical infrastructure of the suburb:

> She came here as a young wife with a young husband and a young child in those distant days when the suburb marked the frontier of civilized life, a place so primitive she could never conceive of it as ever feeling like home. Now she is alone. Vic has gone north as he always said he would, Michael left the suburb as soon as he was old enough, and the house that was theirs became hers. And the street and the suburb that has always been beyond the pale, slowly, unobtrusively, became home. (14)

Rita has developed such a strong sense of belonging that she even worries about what will happen to the house after she dies and who will take care of it (15).

Michael constantly asks Rita why she stays, but she is unable to tell him, not because she does not know the answer, but because she feels unable to reveal the depths of her emotional connection to the house, that she believes leaving the house "would be a betrayal ... To live in another, almost an infidelity" (15). Rita now possesses the "house she has always wanted (as a child, as a young wife) ... The finest house in the street. The house of her dreams" (15). She is finally able to admit that her dream life is a suburban life. In a scene near the end of the novel, Rita stands in her front yard and thinks "My world ... My world. From the golf course to the station, from the Webster estate back to the Old Wheat Road. A rectangle no more than a mile long and a half mile wide" (333). However, a short time afterwards Rita sells the house without explanation and moves back to where she grew up, an inner suburb south of the Yarra (365). One might be tempted to read Rita's return to an inner suburb as a rejection of outer suburbia; however, her motives are not explained and it is not possible to determine the exact reason for her decision.

However, Rita's sale of the house might be explained by the fact that Mrs. Webster had sold her late husband's factory not long before, and thus an era is ending and major changes are occurring in the suburb. The site of Webster's factory will be cleared and "the factory levelled as though it had never existed" in order to make way for a new department store (363). After the store is constructed, "the drapers by the post office, the clothing store by the station and the small shoe shop ... will disappear from the landscape one by one" (363). The suburb has matured and is undergoing a surge of redevelopment, a process which might serve to weaken the connection older residents have to the suburb. Nevertheless, much like *The Gift of Speed*, *The Time We Have Taken* concludes with a nostalgic paragraph that emphasizes the physical characteristics of the suburb, a strong sense of belonging, and the community that has been established:

> The house, the yard on summer nights, the passionfruit vine where the spider indifferently spun its web, the street that started bare and filled overnight with weatherboard box houses and gardens that bloomed while you watched, the open farm land that hovered for a few years between town and country, the dances, the songs, the tennis, the cricket, the coming and going back from the station, work, school and home, throughout the years that saw a suburb born – that, that exotic tribe, was us. And the time we have taken, our moment. (376)

The conclusion emphasizes the fact that a strong community existed in the suburb, regardless of whether or not the community continues to exist in the same form. Carroll repeatedly emphasizes both the idea of the suburb as an evolving organism and the constancy of change.

In Adelaide's review of *The Time We Have Taken*, she argues that Carroll quietly signals the "inevitability of change," a process that speeds up towards the end of the novel "when in a masterstroke" he introduces Gough Whitlam, "the mighty symbol, focus" and agent of change. As part of the centenary suburb celebrations, Whitlam, who will in just a few short years become Australia's most progressive prime minister, agrees to visit the suburb to open a new sports ground (283). "The mountain of Whitlam" flies to Melbourne's new Tullamarine airport, from where he is driven to Centenary Suburb (312). Although Whitlam has more important tasks to perform than opening a new sports ground, he makes the journey because he knows that the "fringe suburbs are his territory. It is suburbs such as these that house or once housed Michael and his kind, and it is Michael and his kind who will one day soon push the mass of Whitlam to power" (313). Thus, the new outer suburbs are where the progressive new generation was raised and often continues to reside, making them the base of support for politicians who wish to overthrow the old order. Rather than being peripheral, both literally and figuratively, the outer suburbs become the heartland of support for the political changes that begin to occur at the time the novel is set.

The political differences between the generations, as well as radically different understandings of settlement and history, are clearly revealed when Mulligan's mural is unveiled. The foyer of the town hall, where the mural has been painted, is packed with citizens of the suburb for the unveiling ceremony, including Mayor Ford, the member of parliament, the council, Mrs. Webster, local business owners, religious leaders, bankers, local sports heroes, "and the everyday faces of the suburb itself " (352). The suburb's citizens have come to the unveiling because the mural tells "their story" (352). Before the unveiling, the mayor gives a speech celebrating the suburb and questioning those who would criticize it:

> And for those people ... who might be tempted to smile at the very idea, to those young people not here today ... let us pose them the question – was it so bad, this world we gave you? This world of trimmed lawns and modest gardens, of brick and timber block houses that have stood the test of time better than anybody thought, of paved streets and footpaths upon which you can stroll and survey this society that we – the Age – gave you. Was it so bad, after all? (354)

Once the curtains are opened and the mural revealed, the crowd begins to read the visual narrative displayed before them, progressing chronologically along the wall from left to right. The mural tells the "grand tale" of the suburb from its "very beginnings," depicting "open land, open country, just the way the leaders of the suburb imagine it all" (356). However, the citizens soon notice that the narrative contains elements they had not expected to see:

> For there are, in fact, figures on this landscape that Mulligan has created. And these figures, these earlier inhabitants, are hunting, fishing, painting, or simply standing still and looking over the valley out there in the old thistle country. People. Whole families. Just living. Just doing the ordinary and extraordinary things that everybody does. And the mayor is staring intently at the wall because this is not part of his grand story at all. (356)

Mulligan's depiction of the Indigenous inhabitants as an established community that is settled on the land and clearly belong to it is a radical act for the time in which the novel is set. The majority of the citizens present at the unveiling are stunned, since their conception of Australian history, especially local history, does not include any acknowledgment that the land was already inhabited by Indigenous peoples when the first European settlers arrived. As Carroll's narrator notes,

> This is not History as most of those gathered in the foyer of the town hall understand it. No, History begins with an open field. Nobody in it. An open field, thinks Peter van Rijn, waiting to receive the footprints of settlers. Settlers who will carve something out of this open field, create a farm, then a community, and finally a shop. This is how History works. It begins with an untamed open country. Then people arrive. Not before. (356)

The citizens' shock is partly allayed as they continue reading the mural and see that the Indigenous inhabitants "are no sooner in the picture than they are out of it" (357). They have been "Written out of the picture" by the arrival of European settlers; "Fences have gone up, farm houses where there was an open field. Then more fences, more settlers and houses. A community forms" (357). Streets, houses, more shops, the flour mill and the railway all soon follow and the suburb assumes a form recognizable to everyone present at the unveiling (357). However, while viewers focusing on the parts of the mural depicting recent decades may be able to temporarily forget the presence of the Indigenous people, they cannot ignore the fact that they were the first inhabitants.

The final scene of the mural depicts a group of local leaders and dignitaries: "the mayor, Webster ... councillors, the sitting member and shop and factory owners" (359). However, in another unforeseen twist in the narrative, the figures are all staring backwards, instead of forwards, "not in the direction of the unwritten, out there off the wall, where Progress lies waiting to take whatever form it will" (359). Thus, Mulligan, and by extension Carroll, depicts the leaders of the community as backward-looking, fixated on the past and unable to foresee the future. Understandably, the residents of the suburb are divided with regard to their reaction to the mural and the story it tells about them and their community. Some residents "dare to admire" the mural while others "can't bear to look upon it"; some are quietly amazed "that a thing such as this has entered their world," while others want the mural erased (360). Nevertheless, the mural survives and over time becomes known around the suburb as "Mulligan's

Wall," and even those who were opposed to the mural learn to accept it (360).

The gradual acceptance of the mural by the entire community echoes one of the major messages of the trilogy; namely, acceptance of one's community, regardless of its negative qualities. Carroll suggests that Australians need to celebrate and embrace their community, but not in a manner that is blind to the atrocities of the past or pretends that they did not occur. Rather, Carroll's trilogy argues that Australians should accept their community and learn to belong, while recognizing and acknowledging the unpleasant realities of their community and its history. Through his Glenroy trilogy, Carroll provides the most extensive engagement with suburbia in Australian literature. Carroll eschews the anti-suburban tradition established by Johnston and follows Murnane and Carey's lead by engaging seriously with suburbia. Carroll's trilogy provides abundant proof that suburbia is the site in which many of Australia's important and difficult social issues are confronted, and that it is a setting that provides almost infinite possibilities for writers interested in exploring life in Australian society.

Endnotes

1. Gelder and Salzman's *After the Celebration: Australian Fiction 1889-2007* contains a roughly two-page analysis of Carroll's fiction.
2. The ironic name for the house is similar to Johnston's depiction of house-naming in *My Brother Jack*, a novel mentioned on several occasions in Carroll's *The Time We Have Taken*.
3. Both Webster's estate and the Girls' Home are reminiscent of Xanadu, Miss Hare's estate in White's *Riders in the Chariot*, and Bangalore, the Turley's mansion in Johnston's *My Brother Jack*.

Conclusion

The preceding analysis of fourteen novels by nine authors demonstrates the importance, diversity and complexity of representations of suburbia in the contemporary Australian novel, and of suburbia itself. The fourteen novels examined provide ample evidence of the wealth of material available to writers due to Australia's status as the world's most suburban society. *Exploring Suburbia* proves that although Australian narratives are rarely suburban, a number of Australia's most canonical and popular novels, such as *My Brother Jack*, *Johnno* and *Cloudstreet*, are suburban narratives that occupy a central position in Australian culture. While I have shown that literary novels set in suburbia comprise a small portion of Australian literature, and that Australia's novelists and literary critics have often ignored suburbia due to the dominance of the anti-suburban tradition, I have also demonstrated that suburbia contains a vast array of subjects for future novels and that suburbia is a subject addressed in many Australian novels that has been under-analyzed by literary critics. Since the topic of suburbia is clearly important globally, within literary studies and other academic fields, it is time for new investigations of suburbia in Australian literature, not just within novels, but also within poetry, short fiction, drama, creative non-fiction and autobiography. I have demonstrated that the anti-suburban intellectual tradition has influenced Australian culture as a whole and heavily influenced both the literature dealing with suburbia and the criticism of that literature. The anti-suburban tradition continues to pervade and influence Australian literature and be perpetuated by it. The most singular effect of the anti-suburban tradition is that it has caused Australian writers to set the vast majority of their works *outside* suburbia.

Despite the decision by the majority of Australian novelists to ignore suburbia and the tendency of writers such as Johnston, Malouf, Winton, Lucashenko and McCann to disparage it, Murnane, Carey and Carroll have taken suburbia seriously and engaged with it in a detailed and nuanced manner. Utilizing a combination of canonical and little-known works written by both internationally-recognized and emerging authors, I have revealed a progression within the suburban novel over five decades from *Riders in the Chariot* (1961) to *The Time We Have Taken* (2007), demonstrated that Johnston established the anti-suburban tradition with *My Brother Jack*, and shown how the anti-suburban tradition has been perpetuated by Malouf, Winton, Lucashenko and McCann. *Exploring Suburbia* began with an analysis of two novels by Patrick White, since he was the first prominent Australian novelist to use a suburban setting and has often been labeled anti-suburban. By examining two of White's novels, I demonstrated that White is not anti-suburban, that he did not establish the anti-suburban tradition in the Australian novel, and that suburbia was a central concern for White. By providing a new interpretation of *Riders in the Chariot*, *The Solid Mandala* and White's attitudes towards suburbia, which I demonstrate are much more ambivalent and nuanced than critics have acknowledged, I hope to initiate a new understanding of White's work.

Exploring Suburbia has examined novels set in suburbs around Australia, namely in the suburbs of Perth, Brisbane, Sydney and Melbourne, which include representations of a variety of types of suburbs, including inner, outer, working-class, middle-class, established and newly-developed. I have shown that the suburban novel encompasses a variety of styles, from White's high Modernism to Johnston's journalistic realism to Murnane's experimental post-modernism. Moreover, I demonstrated that the suburban setting allows Australian novelists to address important social issues, such as environmental degradation, immigration, Indigenous land rights, non-Indigenous belonging, capitalism and consumerism, religion and spirituality, domestic violence, class, and sexuality. *Exploring Suburbia* has addressed a long-neglected and under-examined area within Australian literature and analyzed some of the most important Australian novels from a new perspective. I provided new insights and interpretations of fourteen novels, several of which are canonical works that other critics have analyzed extensively.

The scope of this project has not permitted an analysis of every Australian suburban novel, and there are novels that other scholars may choose to examine or re-examine after reading this book, such as Christos Tsiolkas' *The Slap*. I did not plan to write primarily about male authors; the novels I focused on were chosen for many reasons, including subject matter, date of publication, critical reception and place within the body of suburban novels. The gender of the author was not a consideration when selecting the novels. However, once it became apparent that I had selected only one novel by a female author, I decided against adding others novels by female authors simply in order to create a gender balance. However, Australia's female authors have not failed to write novels set in suburbia. Novels by female authors that are set wholly or partially in suburbia include Amanda Lohrey's *Camille's Bread* (1995); Lillian Ng's *Swallowing Clouds* (1997); Elizabeth Jolley's *The Newspaper of Claremont Street* (1981); Judy Pascoe's *Our Father Who Art in a Tree* (2002); Sonya Hartnett's *Of a Boy* (2002); Barbara Hanrahan's *The Scent of Eucalyptus* (1973), *Sea-Green* (1974) and *Kewpie Doll* (1989); Jessica Anderson's *Tirra Lirra by the River* (1978); Helen Garner's *Monkey Grip* (1977); and Joanna Murray-Smith's *Sunnyside* (2005). I did not address these novels because they often focus on domestic issues rather than social issues such as immigration, environmental degradation, Indigenous rights and religion, all issues I wished to explore. I certainly do not wish to suggest that domestic issues and feminism are not vitally important; rather, I want to stress that I focused primarily on novels by male authors because those novels focused on issues I wanted to address, not because I sought to exclude female authors, which was certainly not the case. The novels by

Anderson, Lohrey, Ng, Jolley, Pascoe, Hanrahan, Garner, Murray-Smith and Hartnett contain ample material for a fascinating study of domestic relationships and spaces in the Australian novel, a project that I hope another scholar will pursue.

Indeed, work on suburban novels by female authors has already begun. In 2011, Belinda Burns published "Untold Tales of the Intra-Suburban Female," an article in which she notes the influence of the anti-suburban tradition and identifies the common representation of suburbia as a feminized domain as a consequence of the influence of the anti-suburban tradition. Burns identifies three narrative categories in suburban fiction focusing on female protagonists, namely "linear flight from suburbia, non-linear flight from suburbia, or non-flight whereby the protagonist remains inside suburbia." Of course, the idea that suburbia is a space that one must escape is central to the anti-suburban tradition. However, Burns argues that the body of work produced by contemporary Australian female authors "may signal a re-examination of the suburban female within, not outside, her suburban setting" and "may also reveal a weakening of … anti-suburban critiques."

Hopefully, *Exploring Suburbia* will lead to a reassessment of the novels and authors addressed and inspire further research into suburbia in Australian literature. I hope to reinvigorate the debate regarding suburbia in Australian literature and move it beyond Gerster, Kinnane and Wetherell's calls for Australian authors to engage more closely with suburbia. I have shown that the authors who have explored suburbia since 1961, even those who wrote anti-suburban novels, have moved the Australian novel in a new direction, away from the traditional focus on the bush and the city, demonstrating that the space between the city and the bush contains some of the most interesting and important subjects within Australia. The novels I have addressed and my analysis of them clearly demonstrate that suburbia is not homogenous, repetitive, shallow and boring; rather, suburbia contains a wealth of fascinating, diverse and constantly evolving lives, including much worth celebrating.

BIBLIOGRAPHY

Primary Sources

Carey, Peter. *Bliss*. 1981. New York: Vintage International, 1996. Print.

---. *The Tax Inspector*. 1991. New York: Vintage International, 1993. Print.

Carroll, Steven. *The Art of the Engine Driver*. Sydney: HarperCollins, 2001. Print.

---. *The Gift of Speed*. 2004. Sydney: Harper Perennial, 2006. Print.

---. *The Time We Have Taken*. 2007. Sydney: Harper Perennial, 2008. Print.

Esson, Louis. "Our Institutions." *The Time is Not Yet Ripe*. 1912. Ed. Philip Parsons. Sydney: Currency Press, 1973. Print.

Johnston, George. *My Brother Jack*. 1964. Sydney: Angus and Robertson, 1993. Print.

Lucashenko, Melissa. "A Whiter Shade of Pale – Being Aboriginal in 2002." *Queensland Performing Arts Centre*. 20 Feb. 2008. n. pag. Web.

---. "Black on Black." *Meanjin* 59.3 (2000): 112-118. Print.

---. "Gender, Genre and Geography." *Southerly* 58.4 (Summer 1998): 50. Print.

---. "Many Prisons." *Hecate* 28.1 (May 2002):139-144. Print.

---. "Not Quite White in the Head." *Where the Rivers Meet: New Writings from Australia*. Ed. Larissa Behrendt, Barry Lopez and Mark Tredinnick. Special Issue of *Manoa* 18.2 (2006): 23-31. Print.

---. *Steam Pigs*. St. Lucia, Queensland: University of Queensland Press, 1997. Print.

Malouf, David. *Johnno*. 1975. New York: George Braziller, 1998. Print.

---. "Preface." *Johnno*. New York: George Braziller, 1998. vii-xiii. Print.

---. *12 Edmondstone Street*. London: Chatto & Windus, 1985. Print.

---. "A Writing Life: The 2000 Neustadt Lecture." *World Literature Today* 74.4 (Autumn 2000): 701-705. Print.

McCann, A.L. *Subtopia*. North Carlton, Victoria: The Vulgar Press, 2005. Print.

Murnane, Gerald. *A History of Books*. Artarmon, New South Wales: Giramondo, 2012. Print.

---. *A Lifetime on Clouds.* 1976. Ringwood, Victoria: Penguin, 1986. Print.

---. *Inland*. Richmond, Victoria: Heinemann, 1988. Print.

---. "Land Deal." *Velvet Waters*. Ringwood, Victoria: McPhee Gribble, 1990. Print.

---. *Landscape with Landscape.* 1985. Ringwood, Victoria: Penguin, 1987. Print.

---. *The Plains*. 1982. Kalamazoo, MI: New Issues, 2003. Print.

---. "Save Us from Text Maniacs." *The Australian Literary Review* 3.2 (March 2008): 14-16. Print.

White, Patrick. *Flaws in the Glass: A Self-Portrait*. 1981. London: Penguin, 1988. Print.

---. "The Prodigal Son." *Australian Letters* 1.3 (Apr. 1958): 37-40. Print.

---. *Riders in the Chariot.* 1961. New York: New York Review Books, 2002. Print.

---. *The Solid Mandala.* 1966. New York: Avon, 1975. Print.

Winton, Tim. *Cloudstreet.* 1991. Camberwell, Victoria: Penguin, 1998. Print.

---. *The Turning: New Stories.* 2004. New York: Scribner, 2005. Print.

Secondary Sources

"ABR Favourite Australian Novels." *Australian Book Review* 318 (Feb. 2010): 25. Print.

Bibliography

Ackland, Michael. "Patrick White." *Dictionary of Literary Biography 260. Australian Writers, 1915-1950*. Ed. Selina Samuels. Detroit: Thomson Gale, 400-415. Print.

Adelaide, Debra. Rev. of *The Time We Have Taken*, by Steven Carroll. *The Australian* 17 Feb. 2007. n. pag. Web.

Anderson, Don. "Wrestling with an Angel: Gerald Murnane's Fictions." *Real Opinions: Polemical and Popular Writings*. Ringwood, Victoria: McPhee Gribble, 1992. 83-92. Print.

Andersson, Lars. "Burglary in Shady Hill and Sarsaparilla: The Politics of Conformity in White and Cheever." *Australian Literary Studies* 22.4 (Oct. 2006): 432-442. Print.

Anthony, Marilyn. Rev. of *Cloudstreet*, by Tim Winton. *Westerly* 2 (Winter 1992): 92-93. Print.

Antor, Heinz. "David Malouf's *Johnno* (1975): A Study of Post-Colonial Self-Constitution in Modern Australia." *Intercultural Encounters: Studies in English Literatures*. Ed. Heinz Antor and Kevin L. Cope. Heidelberg: Carl Winter Universitatsverlag , 1999. 509-531. Print.

Archer, John. "Colonial Suburbs in South Asia, 1700-1850, and the Spaces of Modernity." *Visions of Suburbia*. Ed. Roger Silverstone. London: Routledge, 1997. 26-54. Print.

Arens, Werner. "Destruction and Regeneration as Blakean Contraries in Patrick White's *Riders in the Chariot*." *Anglistentag 1988*. Tubingen: Niemeyer, 1989. 126-145. Print.

Ashbolt, Allan. "Godzone 3: Myth and Reality." *Meanjin* 4 (Dec. 1966): 373-388. Print.

Ashcroft, Bill. "The Horizonal Sublime." *The Sacred in Australian Literature*. Ed. Bill Ashcroft, Frances Devlin-Glass and Lyn McCredden. Special Issue of *Antipodes* 19.2 (Dec. 2005): 141-151. Print.

Badcock, Blair. "Home Ownership and the Illusion of Egalitarianism." *A History of European Housing in Australia*. Ed. Patrick Troy. Cambridge: Cambridge University Press, 2000. 254-268. Print.

Bail, Murray. *Contemporary Portraits and Other Stories*. St. Lucia, Queensland: University of Queensland Press, 1975. Print.

Baker, Ali Gumillya and Gus Worby. "Aboriginality since Mabo: Writing, Politics and Art." *A Companion to Australian Literature Since 1900*. Ed. Nicholas Birns and Rebecca McNeer. Rochester, NY: Camden House, 2007. 17-40. Print.

Baker, Candida. "Gerald Murnane." *Yacker 2: Australian Writers Talk About Their Work.* Ed. Candida Baker. Woollahra, New South Wales: Pan, 1987. 188-217. Print.

Banerjee, Jacqueline. "A Reassessment of Patrick White's *Riders in the Chariot.*" *The Literary Half-Yearly* 20.2 (1979): 91-113. Print.

Bartoloni, Paolo. "Interstitial Narratives: Italo Calvino and Gerald Murnane." *Westerly* 45 (2000): 111-124. Print.

Bennett, Bruce. *Australian Short Fiction: A History*. St. Lucia, Queensland: University of Queensland Press, 2002. Print.

Ben-Messahel, Salhia. *Mind the Country: Tim Winton's Fiction*. Crawley, WA: University of Western Australia Press, 2006. Print.

Bentley, Nick, ed. *British Fiction of the 1990s*. London: Routledge, 2005. Print.

Beston, John. "Unattractive Saints and a Poor Devil: Ambivalence in Patrick White's *The Solid Mandala.*" *The Literary Half-Yearly* 14.1 (1973): 106-114. Print.

Bird, Delys. "New Narrations: Contemporary Fiction." *The Cambridge Companion to Australian Literature*. Ed. Elizabeth Webby. Cambridge: Cambridge University Press, 2000. 183-208. Print.

Birns, Nicholas. "Do Not Ask For Names: Gerald Murnane and Noncommodified Fiction." (Translated into Swedish by Lars Ahlstrom as "Fraga Inte Efter Namn"). *ARTES (Journal of Swedish Academy, Stockholm)* 28. 4 (2002): 9pp. Print.

---. "Indefinite Desires: Love and the Search for Truth in the Fiction of Gerald Murnane." *Southerly* 55.3 (Spring 1995): 48-62. Print.

---. "Gerald Murnane and the Power of Landscape." *New Literatures Review* 18 (1989): 73-82. Print.

--. "Reading Gerald Murnane." *Context* 23 (2011): n. pag. Web.

---. "*The Solid Mandala* and Patrick White's Late Modernity." *Transnational Literature* 4.1 (Nov. 2011): n. pag. Web.

Birns, Nicholas and Rebecca McNeer, eds. *A Companion to Australian Literature Since 1900*. Rochester, NY: Camden House, 2007. Print.

---. "Introduction." *A Companion to Australian Literature Since 1900*. Ed. Nicholas Birns and Rebecca McNeer. Rochester, NY: Camden House, 2007. 1-13. Print.

Blackwell, Eoin. "Winning Works Feature Tales of Displacement." *Festival News: Newsletter of the Sydney Writers' Festival*. 17 Mar. 2008. n. pag. Web.

Bliss, Carolyn. *Patrick White's Fiction: The Paradox of Fortunate Failure*. New York: St. Martin's, 1986. Print.

---. "Peter Carey." *A Companion to Australian Literature Since 1900*. Ed. Nicholas Birns and Rebecca McNeer. Rochester, NY: Camden House, 2007. 281-292. Print.

Bode, Barbara. "Angels and Devils - Child Sexual Abuse in Peter Carey's *The Tax Inspector*." *Antipodes* 9.2 (Dec. 1995): 107-110. Print.

Boyd, Robin. *The Australian Ugliness*. Revised Edition. Ringwood, Victoria: Penguin, 1963. Print.

Brady, Veronica. "God, History, and Patrick White." *The Sacred in Australian Literature*. Ed. Bill Ashcroft, Frances Devlin-Glass and Lyn McCredden. Special Issue of *Antipodes* 19.2 (Dec. 2005): 172-176. Print.

---. Rev. of *The Tax Inspector*, by Peter Carey. *Overland* 125 (1991): 80-83. Print.

Braun-Bau, Susanne. "A Conversation with Gerald Murnane." *Antipodes* 10.1 (1996): 43-48. Print.

Brennan, Bernadette. "*Riders in the Chariot*: A Tale for Our Times." *JASAL* 7 (2007): 32-45. Web.

Brook, Susan. "Hedgemony? Suburban Space in *The Buddha of Suburbia*." *British Fiction of the 1990s*. Ed. Nick Bentley. London: Routledge, 2005. 209-225. Print.

Brotherson, Lee. "Three-dimensionality and *My Brother Jack.*" *Australian Literary Studies* 18.1 (May 1997): 84-89 (6pp). *InfoTrac OneFile.* Thomson Gale. Western Michigan University Libraries. 4 Jan. 2008. Web.

Burns, Belinda. "Untold Tales of the Intra-Suburban Female." *Suburbia.* Ed. Angela Lin Huang, Emma Felton and Christy Collis. Special issue of *M/C Journal: A Journal of Media and Culture* 14.4 (Aug. 2011): n. pag. Web.

Carroll, Steven. *Spirit of Progress.* Pymble, New South Wales: HarperCollins, 2011.

Carter, Paul. *The Road to Botany Bay: An Exploration of Landscape and History.* New York: Knopf, 1988. Print.

Chambers, Deborah. "A Stake in the Country: Women's Experiences of Suburban Development." *Visions of Suburbia.* Ed. Roger Silverstone. London: Routledge, 1997. 86-107. Print.

Chapman, Edgar L. "The Mandala Design of Patrick White's *Riders in the Chariot.*" *Texas Studies in Language and Literature* 21.2 (Summer 1979): 186-202. Print.

Chellappan, K. "Self, Space and Art in a Few Novels of Patrick White." *The Literary Endeavour* 7.1-4 (1985): 48-58. Print.

Coad, David. "Intertextuality in Patrick White's *The Solid Mandala.*" *Commonwealth* 17.2 (1995): 111-116. Print.

Coleridge, Samuel Taylor. "Khubla Khan." *The Norton Anthology of Poetry.* Third edition. Ed. Alexander W. Allison, Herbert Barrows, Caesar R. Blake, Arthur J. Carr, Arthur M. Eastman and Hubert M. English, Jr. New York, Norton, 1983. 564-565. Print.

Collins, Jock. "Migrant Hands in a Distant Land." *Images of Australia: An Introductory Reader in Australian Studies.* Ed. Gillian Whitlock and David Carter. St. Lucia, Queensland: University of Queensland Press, 1992. 103-128. Print.

Conrad, Joseph. 1902. *Heart of Darkness.* New York: Penguin, 1987. Print.

Craven, Peter. "Critically Acclaimed Writers Honoured with Top Literary Prize." *Australia Council for the Arts*. 11 Feb. 2008. 8 Mar. 2008. n. pag. Web.

Crouch, David. "National Hauntings: The Architecture of Australian Ghost Stories." *Spectres, Screens, Shadows, Mirrors*. Ed. Tanya Dalziell and Paul Genoni. Special Issue of *JASAL* (2007): 94-105. Web.

---. "Writing of Australian Dwelling: Animate Houses and Anxious Ground." *Journal of Australian Studies* 80 (2004): 43-52. Print.

Dalziell, Tanya. "Australian Women's Writing from 1970 to 2005." *A Companion to Australian Literature Since 1900*. Ed. Nicholas Birns and Rebecca McNeer. Rochester, NY: Camden House, 2007. 139-153. Print.

Daniel, Helen. *Liars: Australian New Novelists*. Ringwood, Victoria: Penguin, 1988. Print.

---. "Narrator and Outsider in *Trap* and *Johnno*." *Southerly* 37.2 (June 1977): 184-195. Print.

Davidson, James. "The Queenslander House." Message to the author. 6 May 2008. E-mail.

Davison, Graeme. "Australia: The First Suburban Nation?" *Journal of Urban History* 22.1 (1995): 40-75 (21pp). *Academic Search Elite*. EBSCOhost. Kellogg Community College Library. 27 Nov. 2002. Web.

---. "Colonial Origins of the Australian Home." *A History of European Housing in Australia*. Ed. Patrick Troy. Cambridge: Cambridge University Press, 2000. 6-25. Print.

Davison, Graeme and Tony Dingle. "Introduction: The View From The Ming Wing." *The Cream Brick Frontier: Histories of Australian Suburbia*. Ed. Graeme Davison, Tony Dingle and Seamus O'Hanlon. Clayton, Victoria: Monash Publications in History, 1995. 2-17. Print.

Davison, Graeme, Tony Dingle and Seamus O'Hanlon, eds. *The Cream Brick Frontier: Histories of Australian Suburbia*. Clayton, Victoria: Monash Publications in History, 1995. Print.

Dever, Maryanne. "Artist and Nationality in G. Johnston's Trilogy." *Commonwealth* 7.2 (Spring 1985): 19-30. Print.

Dewey, Joseph. "Patrick White (1912-1990)." *World Writers in English, Volume II: R. K. Narayan to Patrick White*. Ed. Jay Parini. New York: Scribner's, 2004. 747-65. Print.

Dixon, Robert. "Closing the Can of Worms: Enactments of Justice in *Bleak House*, *The Mystery of a Hansom Cab* and *The Tax Inspector*." *Westerly* 37.4 (Summer 1992): 37-45. Print.

---. "James McAuley's New Guinea: Colonialism, Modernity, Suburbia." *Writing the Everyday: Australian Literature and the Limits of Suburbia*. Ed. Andrew McCann. Special Issue of *Australian Literary Studies* 18.4 (1998): 20-40. Print.

---. "The Logic of the Excluded Middle." *LiNQ: Literature in North Queensland* 18.2 (1991): 133-41. Print.

---. "Tim Winton, *Cloudstreet* and the Field of Australian Literature." *Westerly* 50 (Nov. 2005): 240-260. Print.

Dooley, Gillian. Rev. of *The Time We Have Taken*, by Steven Carroll. *Transnational Literature* 1.1 (Nov. 2008): 1-3. Web.

Dovey, Teresa. "An Infinite Onion: Narrative Structure in Peter Carey's Fiction." *Australian Literary Studies* 11.2 (Oct. 1983): 195-204. Print.

During, Simon. *Patrick White*. Melbourne: Oxford University Press, 1996. Print.

Eagle, Chester Arthur. "Myth, Mockery and Expatriation - Love/Hate of Australia in George Johnston's *My Brother Jack*." *Commonwealth* 6.2 (1984): 35-41. Print.

Edgecombe, Rodney Stenning. "No Gift for Words: The Role of Miss Hare in Patrick White's *Riders in the Chariot*." *World Literature Written in English* 25.1 (1985): 52-66. Print.

---. *Vision and Style in Patrick White: A Study of Five Novels*. Tuscaloosa, AL: University of Alabama Press, 1989. Print.

---. "The Weeds and Gardens in *Riders in the Chariot*." *Patrick White: The International Legacy*. Ed. Carolyn Bliss. Special Issue of *Antipodes* 6.1 (1992): 25-31. Print.

Eliot, T.S. *Selected Poems*. 1954. London: Faber and Faber, 1975. Print.

Elliott, Helen. "Poet in Suburbia." *The Australian* 10 Feb. 2007. n. pag. Web.

Ellmann, Richard. *James Joyce*. Revised edition. New York: Oxford University Press, 1983. Print.

Eustace, John. "Going Bush: Performing the Pastoral in Peter Carey's *Bliss*." *Antipodes* 20.2 (Dec. 2006): 108-116. Print.

Felski, Rita. "Nothing to Declare: Identity, Shame and the Lower Middle Class." *PMLA* 115 (Jan. 2000): 33-45. Print.

Ferber, Sarah, Chris Healy and Chris McAuliffe, eds. *Beasts of Suburbia: Reinterpreting Cultures in Australian Suburbs*. Carlton, Victoria: Melbourne University Press, 1994. Print.

Field, Michelle. "Tim Winton: 'I Got a Jump on My Generation.'" *Publishers Weekly* May 29, 1995. 62-63. Print.

Fishman, Robert. *Bourgeois Utopias: The Rise and Fall of Suburbia*. New York: Basic, 1987. Print.

Fiske, John, Bob Hodge and Graeme Turner. *Myths of Oz: Reading Australian Popular Culture*. Boston: Allen & Unwin, 1987. Print.

Fitzgerald, Michael. "Fate and the Little Guy." *Time* 18 Oct. 2004. n. pag. Web.

Flanagan, Martin. "The Writer in the Landscape." *Tim Winton: A Celebration*. Ed. Hilary McPhee. Canberra: National Library of Australia, 1999. 11-16. Print.

Fletcher, Don. "Utopia in Peter Carey's *Bliss*." *Social Alternatives* 26.1 (2007): 39-42. Print.

Fogelson, Robert M. *Bourgeois Nightmares: Suburbia, 1870-1930*. New Haven, CT: Yale University Press, 2005. Print.

Francois, Pierre. "Psycho-ontological Evil in Patrick White's *The Solid Mandala*." *Commonwealth* 18.2 (1996): 104-17. Print.

Fry, Robert. Rev. of *Voss*, by Patrick White. *Australian Letters* 1.3 (Apr. 1958): 40. Print.

Furphy, Sam. "Aboriginal House Names and Settler Australian Identity." *Journal of Australian Studies* 72 (2002): 59-68, 267-68. Print.

Gaile, Andreas. "Introduction." *Fabulating Beauty: Perspectives on the Fiction of Peter Carey*. Ed. Andreas Gaile. Amsterdam and New York: Rodopi, 2005. xix–xxxv. Print.

---. "The 'Contrarian Streak': An Interview with Peter Carey." *Fabulating Beauty: Perspectives on the Fiction of Peter Carey*. Ed. Andreas Gaile. Amsterdam and New York: Rodopi, 2005. 3-16. Print.

Genoni, Paul. "Gerald Murnane." *A Companion to Australian Literature Since 1900*. Ed. Nicholas Birns and Rebecca McNeer. Rochester, NY: Camden House, 2007. 293-304. Print.

Gelder, Ken and Paul Salzman. *The New Diversity: Australian Fiction 1970-88*. Melbourne: McPhee Gribble, 1989. Print.

---. *After the Celebration: Australian Fiction 1989-2007*. Carlton, Victoria: Melbourne University Publishing, 2009. Print.

"Gerald Murnane." *Adelaide Festival* 17 Mar. 2008. n. pag. Web.

"Gerald Murnane: Adult Fiction Author." *Golvan Arts: Literary and Artists Agency*. 17 Mar. 2008. n. pag. Web.

Gerster, Robin. "Gerrymander: The Place of Suburbia in Australian Fiction." *Meanjin* 49.3 (1990): 565-575. Print.

Gilbert, Alan. "The Roots of Anti-Suburbanism in Australia." *Australian Cultural History*. Eds. S.L. Goldberg and F.B. Smith. Melbourne: Cambridge University Press, 1989. 33-49. Print.

Goldsworthy, Kerryn. "Fiction from 1900 to 1970." *The Cambridge Companion to Australian Literature*. Ed. Elizabeth Webby. Cambridge: Cambridge University Press, 2000. 105-133. Print.

Griffin, Michelle. "Behind the Scene." *The Age* 24 Sep. 2005. n. pag. Web.

Guy, Elizabeth. "A Conversation with Tim Winton." *Southerly* 56.4 (1997): 127-133. Print.

Gzell, Sylvia. "Themes and Imagery in *Voss* and *Riders in the Chariot*." *Australian Literary Studies* 1.1 (1964): 180-195. Print.

Hartley, John. "The Sexualization of Suburbia: The Diffusion of Knowledge in the Postmodern Public Sphere." *Visions of Suburbia*. Ed. Roger Silverstone. London: Routledge, 1997. 180-216. Print.

Hassall, Anthony J. *Dancing on Hot Macadam: Peter Carey's Fiction*. Third edition. St. Lucia, Queensland: University of Queensland Press, 1998. Print.

---. "Peter Carey." *Dictionary of Literary Biography 289. Australian Writers, 1950-1975*. Ed. Selina Samuels. Detroit: Thomson Gale, 2004. 53-62. Print.

Hayward, David. "The Reluctant Landlords? A History of Public Housing in Australia." *Infoxchange.net.au* 24 July, 2007. n. pag. Web.

Head, Dominic. *The Cambridge Introduction to Modern British Fiction, 1950-2000*. Cambridge: Cambridge University Press, 2002. Print.

Healy, Chris. "Introduction." *Beasts of Suburbia: Reinterpreting Cultures in Australian Suburbs*. Ed. Sarah Ferber, Chris Healy and Chris McAuliffe. Carlton, Victoria: Melbourne University Press, 1994. xiii-xvii. Print.

Hecq, Dominique. "Myth-Taken Paths and Exits in Peter Carey's *Bliss*." *Commonwealth* 18.2 (Spring 1996): 99-103. Print.

Henderson, Margaret. "Subdivisions of Suburbia: The Politics of Place in Melissa Lucashenko's *Steam Pigs* and Amanda Lohrey's *Camille's Bread*." *Writing the Everyday: Australian Literature and the Limits of Suburbia*. Ed. Andrew McCann. Special Issue of *Australian Literary Studies* 18.4 (1998): 72-86. Print.

Herring, Thelma. "Self and Shadow: The Quest for Totality in *The Solid Mandala*." *Southerly* 26.3 (1966): 18-89. Print.

Hibberd, Georgina. "Australian Literature on the Nose?" *ON LINE Opinion: Australia's E-Journal of Social and Political Debate* 9 Oct. 2006. 3 Apr. 2008. n. pag. Web.

Horne, Donald. *The Lucky Country: Australia in the Sixties*. Revised Edition. Ringwood, Victoria: Penguin, 1966. Print.

Hoskins, Ian. "Constructing Time and Space in the Garden Suburb." *Beasts of Suburbia: Reinterpreting Cultures in Australian Suburbs*.

Ed. Sarah Ferber, Chris Healy and Chris McAuliffe. Carlton, Victoria: Melbourne University Press, 1994. 1-17. Print.

Huggan, Graham. *Australian Literature: Postcolonialism, Racism, Transnationalism*. New York, Oxford University Press, 2007. Print.

---. *Peter Carey*. Melbourne: Oxford University Press, 1996. Print.

Hu, Wenzhong. "The Myth and the Facts: A Reconsideration of Australia's Critical Reception of Patrick White." *Australian Literary Studies* 16.3 (May 1994): 333-341. Print.

Indyk, Ivor. *David Malouf*. South Melbourne, Victoria: Oxford University Press, 1993. Print.

Jacobs, Lyn. "Tim Winton and West Australian Writing." *A Companion to Australian Literature Since 1900*. Ed. Nicholas Birns and Rebecca McNeer. Rochester, NY: Camden House, 2007. 307-319. Print.

Johnston, Anna and Alan Lawson. "Settler Colonies." *A Companion to Postcolonial Studies*. Ed. Henry Schwarz and Sangeeta Ray. Oxford: Blackwell, 2000. 360-376. Print.

Jones, Dorothy. "Canon to the Right of Us, Canon to the Left of Us." *New Literatures Review* 17 (Summer 1989): 69-79. Print.

Jones, Jr., M. "The Down-Under Car Dealers from Hell." *Newsweek* 27 Jan. 1992: 60. Print.

Jones, Radhika. "Peter Carey: The Art of Fiction No. 188." *The Paris Review* 177 (Summer 2006): 119-147. Print.

Jose, Nicholas. "*Bliss* and Damnation." *Fabulating Beauty: Perspectives on the Fiction of Peter Carey*. Ed. Andreas Gaile. Amsterdam and New York: Rodopi, 2005. 137-147. Print.

Joyce, James. *A Portrait of the Artist as a Young Man*. 1916. London: Minerva, 1992. Print.

---. *Ulysses*. 1922. New York: Vintage International, 1990. Print.

Jurca, Catherine. *White Diaspora: The Suburb and the Twentieth-Century American Novel*. Princeton: Princeton University Press, 2001. Print.

Kane, Paul. "Postcolonial/Postmodern: Australian Literature and Peter Carey." *World Literature Today* 67.3 (Summer 1993): 519-522. Print.

Kapferer, Judith. *Being All Equal: Identity, Difference and Australian Cultural Practice*. Oxford: Berg, 1996. Print.

Keats, John. "Sleep and Poetry." *The Works of John Keats*. Ware, Hertfordshire: The Wordsworth Poetry Library, 1994. 43-53. Print.

King, Anthony D. "Excavating the Multicultural Suburb: Hidden Histories of the Bungalow." *Visions of Suburbia*. Ed. Roger Silverstone. London: Routledge, 1997. 55-85. Print.

Kinnane, Garry. "The Reconstruction of Self: Background and Design in George Johnston's Meredith Trilogy." *Australian Literary Studies* 11.4 (Oct. 1984): 435-446. Print.

---. "Shopping at Last! History, Fiction and the Anti-Suburban Tradition." *Writing the Everyday: Australian Literature and the Limits of Suburbia*. Ed. Andrew McCann. Special Issue of *Australian Literary Studies* 18.4 (Oct. 1998): 41-55. Print.

Kinnane, Josephine Jill. "George Johnston." *Dictionary of Literary Biography 260. Australian Writers, 1915-1950*. Ed. Selina Samuels. Detroit: Thomson Gale, 169-178. Print.

Kirby, Stephen. "Homosocial Desire and Homosexual Panic in the Fiction of David Malouf and Frank Moorhouse." *Meanjin* 46.3 (Spring 1987): 385-393. Print.

Kuchta, Todd. "Semi-Detached Empire: Suburbia and Imperial Discourse in Victorian and Edwardian Britain." *Nineteenth-Century Prose* 32.2 (Fall 2005): 173-208. Print.

Lamb, Karen. *Peter Carey: The Genesis of Fame*. Pymble, New South Wales: Angus & Robertson, 1992. Print.

Larsson, Christer. "Cross References: Allusions to Christian Tradition in Peter Carey's Fiction." *Fabulating Beauty: Perspectives on the Fiction of Peter Carey*. Ed. Andreas Gaile. Amsterdam and New York: Rodopi, 2005. 53-70. Print.

---. "'Years Later:' Temporality and Closure in Peter Carey's Novels." *Australian Literary Studies* 19.2 (Oct. 1999): 176-185. Print.

Lawson, Alan. "Meaning and Experience: A Review-Essay on Some Recurrent Problems in Patrick White Criticism." *Texas Studies in Literature and Language* 21.2 (Summer 1979): 280-295. Print.

---. "Unmerciful Dingoes? The Critical Reception of Patrick White." *Meanjin* 32 (1973): 379-392. Print.

Leer, Martin. "At the Edge: Geography and the Imagination in the Work of David Malouf." *Australian Literary Studies* 12.1 (May 1985): 3-21. Print.

Ley, James. "A Job Lot." *Australian Book Review* 265 (Oct. 2004): n. pag. Web.

Lock, Charles. "Patrick White: Writing Towards Silence." *The Kenyon Review* 23.2 (Spring 2001): 72-84. Print.

"Lucashenko, Melissa." *AustLit: The Australian Literature Resource*. 12 Jan. 2006. 14 Sep. 2010. n. pag. Web.

Lucy, Niall. Rev. of *Landscape with Landscape*, by Gerald Murnane. *Westerly* 2 (June 1987): 103-05. Print.

Maiden, Jennifer. "The Suburban Problem of Evil." *Writing the Everyday: Australian Literature and the Limits of Suburbia.* Ed. Andrew McCann. Special Issue of *Australian Literary Studies* 18.4 (1998): 115-125. Print.

Malouf, David. "Castle Hill Lear: Patrick White Reappraised." *The Times Literary Supplement* 3 Jan. 2007. 14 Jan. 2007. n. pag. Web.

---. "Introduction." *Riders in the Chariot.* Patrick White. 1961. New York: New York Review Books, 2002. v-x. Print.

"Mandala." *The Oxford English Dictionary*. 3rd ed. 2000. n. pag. Web.

Marr, David. *Patrick White: A Life*. New York: Knopf, 1992. Print.

Marx, Bill. "Dystopia Down Under." *Nation* 16 Mar. 1992: 346-348. Print.

Matthews, Brian. "Introduction." *My Brother Jack*. George Johnston. 1964. Sydney: Angus and Robertson, 1993. Print.

"McCann, A.L." *AustLit: The Australian Literature Resource*. 7 July. 2008. 16 July. 2012. n. pag. Web.

Bibliography

McCann, Andrew. "Decomposing Suburbia: Patrick White's Perversity." *Writing the Everyday: Australian Literature and the Limits of Suburbia.* Ed. Andrew McCann. Special Issue of *Australian Literary Studies* 18.4 (1998): 56-71. Print.

---. "The Ethics of Abjection: Patrick White's *Riders in the Chariot.*" *Australian Literary Studies* 18.2 (Oct. 1997): 145-155. Print.

---. "How to Fuck a Tuscan Garden: A Note on Literary Pessimism." *Overland* 177 (Summer 2004): 22-24. Print.

---. "The International of Excreta: World Literature and its Other." *Overland* 186 (Autumn 2007): 20-24. Print.

---. "Introduction: Subtopia, or the Problem of Suburbia." *Writing the Everyday: Australian Literature and the Limits of Suburbia.* Ed. Andrew McCann. Special Issue of *Australian Literary Studies* 18.4 (Oct. 1998): vii-x. Print.

---. "Professing the Popular: Political Fiction circa 2006." *New Reckonings: Australian Literature Past, Present, Future. Essays in Honour of Elizabeth Webby.* Ed. Leigh Dale and Brigid Rooney. Special Issue of *Australian Literary Studies* 23.2 (Oct. 2007): 43-57. Print.

McDonald, Damian. 2007. *Luck in the Greater West.* London, Quercus, 2008. Print.

McGahan, Andrew. *Praise.* 1992. New York: Carroll and Graf, 1993. Print.

Meyer, Lisa. "An Interview with Peter Carey." *Chicago Review* 43 (Spring 1997): 76-89. Print.

Millett, Michael. "Migration Fuels Sydney Divide." *Sydney Morning Herald* 5 July 2003. n. pag. Web.

Molitorisz, Sacha. Rev. of *Subtopia*, by A.L. McCann. *Sydney Morning Herald* 5 Nov. 2005. 18 Apr. 2006. n. pag. Web.

"Murnane, Gerald." *AustLit: The Australian Literature Resource.* 12 Nov. 2009. 13 July. 2012. n. pag. Web.

Murray, Stuart. "Tim Winton's 'New Tribalism': *Cloudstreet* and Community." *Kunapipi* 25.1 (2003): 83-91. Print.

Murray-Smith, Joanna. *Sunnyside*. Camberwell, Victoria: Viking, 2005. Print.

Nairn, Lyndall. "Finding Meaning in the Mundane." Rev. of *The Time We Have Taken*, by Steven Carroll. *Fear in Australian Literature and Film*. Ed. Nathanael O'Reilly and Jean-Francois Vernay. Special Issue of *Antipodes* 23.1 (June 2009): 94-95. Print.

Natale, Antonella Riem. "Harry Joy's Children: The Art of Story Telling in Peter Carey's *Bliss*." *Australian Literary Studies* 16.3 (May 1994): 341-347. Print.

Nicholson, Kara. "Subtopia: Interview with Andrew McCann." *Wordpower.co.uk* 13 Apr. 2006. n. pag. Web.

Nielsen, Philip. "Waiting for the Barbarians: An Interview with Peter Carey." *LiNQ: Literature in North Queensland* 15.3 (1987): 66-73. Print.

O'Reilly, Nathanael. "Environmental Degradation, Indigenous Displacement, and Non-Indigenous Belonging: Suburbia in Tim Winton's 'Aquifer' and Liam Davison's 'Neary's Horse.'" *Commonwealth Essays and Studies* 32.2 (Spring 2010): 47-60. Print.

---. "Rejecting and Perpetuating the Anti-Suburban Tradition: Representations of the Suburbs in *The Tax Inspector*, *Johnno* and *Cloudstreet*." *Antipodes* 20.1 (June 2006): 20-25. Print.

---. "McCann Rejects Mainstream Australian Literature." Rev. of *Subtopia*, by A.L. McCann. *Antipodes* 20.2 (Dec. 2006): 199-200. Print.

---. "Exploring Indigenous Identity in Suburbia: Melissa Lucashenko's *Steam Pigs*." *JASAL* 10 (2010): n. pag. Web.

Palmer, Vance. *The Legend of the Nineties*. 1954. Melbourne: Melbourne University Press, 1966. Print.

Perlman, Eliot. *Three Dollars*. 1998. New York: Riverhead, 2007. Print.

Phillips, A.A. "*The Solid Mandala*: Patrick White's New Novel." *Meanjin* 25 (March 1966): 31-33. Print.

Pierce, Peter. "Australian Literature Since Patrick White." *World Literature Today* 67.3 (Summer 1993): 514+ (5 pp). *EBSCOhost*. Western Michigan University Libraries. Kalamazoo, MI. 21 Sep. 2002. Web.

---. "David Malouf's Fiction." *Meanjin* 41.4 (Summer 1982): 526-534. Print.

---. Rev. of *Subtopia*, by A.L. McCann. *The Bulletin*. 7 July 2005. 18 Apr. 2006. n. pag. Web.

Powell, Diane. *Out West: Perceptions of Sydney's Western Suburbs*. St. Leonards, New South Wales: Allen & Unwin, 1993. Print.

Ralph, Iris. "A Green Flaw in the Crystal Glass: Patrick White's *Riders in the Chariot*." *Colloquy: Text Theory Critique* 12 (Nov. 2006): 28-42. Print.

Randall, Don. *David Malouf*. Manchester: Manchester University Press, 2007. Print.

Ratcliffe, Greg. "Urban Cannibals: Peter Carey's *The Tax Inspector*." *Journal of Australian Studies* 57 (1998): 184-193. Print.

Read, Peter. *Belonging: Australians, Place and Aboriginal Ownership*. New York: Cambridge University Press, 2000. Print.

Rome, Adam. *The Bulldozer in the Countryside: Suburban Sprawl and the Rise of American Environmentalism*. New York: Cambridge University Press, 2001. Print.

Rooney, Brigid. "David Malouf." *Dictionary of Literary Biography 289. Australian Writers, 1950-1975*. Ed. Selina Samuels. Detroit: Thomson Gale, 2004. 214-222. Print.

Rossiter, Richard and Lyn Jacobs, eds. *Reading Tim Winton*. Sydney: Angus and Robertson, 1993. Print.

Rossiter, Richard. "In His Own Words: The Life and Times of Tim Winton." *Reading Tim Winton*. Ed. Richard Rossiter and Lyn Jacobs. Sydney: Angus and Robertson, 1993. 1-14. Print.

---. "The Writer and the Community: An Interview with Tim Winton." *Westerly* 49 (Nov. 2004): 29-38. Print.

Rowse, Tim. "Heaven and a Hill's Hoist: Australian Critics on Suburbia." *Meanjin* 37.1 (Autumn 1978): 3-13. Print.

Rutherford, Jennifer. "Being for the Nation: Masculine Sacrifice in *My Brother Jack*." *Meridian* 17.1 (May 1998): 109-127. Print.

Ryan-Fazilleau, Sue. "The Adman Who Wanted to Compile a Cultural Heritage: Peter Carey's *Bliss*." *Commonwealth* 27.1 (Autumn 2004): 77-88. Print.

Said, Edward. *Culture and Imperialism*. New York: Vintage, 2003. Print.

Salter, Elizabeth. "The Australianism of Patrick White." *The Commonwealth Writer Overseas: Themes of Exile and Repatriation*. Brussels: M. Didier, 1976. 231-241. Print.

Salusinszky, Imre. *Gerald Murnane*. Melbourne: Oxford University Press, 1993. Print.

---. "Gerald Murnane." *Dictionary of Literary Biography 289. Australian Writers, 1950-1975*. Ed. Selina Samuels. Detroit: Thomson Gale, 2004. 232-239. Print.

---. "That Hilarious Supplement: Gerald Murnane's *A Lifetime on Clouds*." *Australian Literary Studies* 15.4 (Oct. 1992): 294-303. Print.

---. "On Gerald Murnane." *Meanjin* 45.4 (Summer 1986): 518-529. Print.

---. "The Newcastle Freeway Tapes." *Southerly* 55.3 (1995): 25-42. Print.

Scheckter, John. "'Before it is Too Late': George Johnston and the Doppler Effect." *Australian and New Zealand Studies in Canada* 5 (Spring 1991): 115-130. Print.

Schneiders, Ben. "A Generation's Home Dream Vanishes." *The Age* 13 Nov. 2007. n. pag. Web.

Schultz, Julianne. "Colliding Worlds of People Unlike Us." *Griffith Review 8: People Like Us* (Winter 2005): 6-10. Print.

Sheckels, Theodore F. "The Difficulties of Translating Peter Carey's Postmodern Fiction into Popular Film." *Fabulating Beauty: Perspectives on the Fiction of Peter Carey*. Ed. Andreas Gaile. Amsterdam and New York: Rodopi, 2005. 83-100. Print.

Shore, Teri. "An Aussie on Easy Street." *San Francisco Review of Books* 17.2 (1992): 43-44. Print.

Simons, Margaret. "Ties That Bind." *Griffith Review 8: People Like Us* (Winter 2005): 13-36. Print.

Silverstone, Roger. "Introduction." *Visions of Suburbia.* Ed. Roger Silverstone. London: Routledge, 1997. 1-25. Print.

---. "Preface and Acknowledgements." *Visions of Suburbia.* Ed. Roger Silverstone. London: Routledge, 1997. ix-x. Print.

Sorensen, Rosemary. "Steven Carroll Wins Miles Franklin Literary Award for The Time We Have Taken." *The Age* 19 June 2008. n. pag. Web.

Sornig, David. "Specters of Berlin in A.L. McCann's *Subtopia* and Christos Tsiolkas's *Dead Europe.*" *Antipodes* 21.1 (June 2007): 67-71. Print.

Spigel, Lynn. "From Theatre to Space Ship: Metaphors of Suburban Domesticity in Postwar America." *Visions of Suburbia.* Ed. Roger Silverstone. London: Routledge, 1997. 217-239. Print.

Strickler, Breyan. "'Burbs in the Bush': Environmental Rhetoric in Contemporary American and Australian Fiction." Diss. Pennsylvania State University, 2004. Print.

Stretton, Hugh. *Ideas for Australian Cities*. Melbourne: Georgian House, 1975. Print.

"Suburb." *The Oxford English Dictionary*. 2nd ed. 1989. n. pag. Web.

"Suburban." *The Oxford English Dictionary*. 2nd ed. 1989. n. pag. Web.

"Suburbia." *The Oxford English Dictionary*. 2nd ed. 1989. n. pag. Web.

Sudjic, Deyan. *The 100 Mile City*. San Diego: Harcourt Brace, 1992. Print.

Tacey, David. "Patrick White: The Great Mother and Her Son [*The Solid Mandala*]." *Critical Essays on Patrick White*. Ed. Peter Wolfe. Boston: G.K. Hall, 1990. 122-141. Print.

Tan, Shaun. *Tales from Outer Suburbia*. New York: Arthur A. Levine Books, 2009. Print.

Taylor, Andrew. "An Interview with Tim Winton." *Australian Literary Studies* 17.4 (Oct. 1996): 373-377. Print.

---. "The Bread of Time to Come: Body and Landscape in David Malouf's Fiction." *World Literature Today* 74.4 (Autumn 2000): 715-723. Print.

"The Critical Eye." *The Gift of Speed*, by Steven Carroll. 2004. Sydney: Harper Perennial, 2006. P.S.: 12-13. Print.

"The Inspiration." *The Gift of Speed*, by Steven Carroll. 2004. Sydney: Harper Perennial, 2006. P.S.: 8-10. Print.

Thurley, Geoffrey. "*My Brother Jack*: An Australian Masterpiece?" *Ariel* 5.4 (1974): 61-80. Print.

Thompson, Jay. Rev. of *Subtopia*, by A.L. McCann. *Colloquy: Text Theory Critique* 11 (May 2006): 278-280. Print.

"Top Forty Australian Books." *Bookworm.com.au*. 25 July 2007. n. pag. Web.

"Traditional Rights Recognised for the Land and Sea in Arnhem Land." *National Native Title Tribunal* 11 Oct. 2005. 20 Mar. 2008. n. pag. Web.

Tredinnick, David. "David Malouf: A Confession." *Meanjin* 61.1 (2002): 165-174. Print.

Troy, Patrick, ed. *A History of European Housing in Australia*. Cambridge: Cambridge University Press, 2000. Print.

Tsiolkas, Christos. *The Slap*. Crows Nest, New South Wales: Allen & Unwin, 2008. Print.

Turner, Graeme. "American Dreaming: The Fictions of Peter Carey." *Australian Literary Studies* 12.4 (Oct. 1986): 431-441. Print.

---. *National Fictions: Literature, Film and the Construction of Australian Narrative*. Second edition. St. Leonards, New South Wales: Allen & Unwin, 1993. Print.

---. "Nationalising the Author: The Celebrity of Peter Carey." *Australian Literary Studies* 16.2 (Oct. 1993): 131-139. Print.

Vanden Driesen, Cynthia. *Writing the Nation: Patrick White and the Indigene*. Amsterdam: Rodopi, 2009. Print.

Van Toorn, Penny. "Indigenous Texts and Narratives." *The Cambridge Companion to Australian Literature*. Ed. Elizabeth Webby. Cambridge: Cambridge University Press, 2000. 19-49. Print.

Verghis, Sharon. "The Many Lives of Peter Carey." *Good Weekend* 19 Jan. 2008: 13-18. Print.

Wallace-Crabbe, Chris. "Melbourne." *Current Affairs Bulletin* 32.11 (October 1963): 168. Print.

Ward, Russel. *The Australian Legend*. 1958. Melbourne: Oxford University Press, 1981. Print.

Watson, Betty L. "Patrick White, Some Lines of Development: *The Living and the Dead* to *The Solid Mandala*." *Australian Literary Studies* 5 (1971): 158-167. Print.

Watt, George. "Shadows Without Light: Zen and Blackfellas in *Cloudstreet*." *NUCB Journal of Language, Culture and Communication* 6.1 (2004): 59-69. Print.

Webby, Elizabeth. "Introduction." *The Cambridge Companion to Australian Literature*. Ed. Elizabeth Webby. Cambridge: Cambridge University Press, 2000. 1-18. Print.

---. "Our Invisible Collosus." *The Australian* 2 May 2007. 20 May 2007. n. pag. Web.

Wetherell, Rodney. "Subtopia or Sunnyside?" *Meanjin* 65.2 (2006): 174-180. Print.

White, Richard. "Inventing Australia." *Images of Australia: An Introductory Reader in Australian Studies*. Ed. Gillian Whitlock and David Carter. St. Lucia, Queensland: University of Queensland Press, 1992. 23-53. Print.

Whitlock, Gillian and David Carter, eds. *Images of Australia: An Introductory Reader in Australian Studies*. St. Lucia, Queensland: University of Queensland Press, 1992. Print.

Whitman, Walt. *Leaves of Grass: The First (1855) Edition*. Ed. Malcolm Cowley. New York: Penguin, 1986. Print.

Wilde, William H., Joy Hooton and Barry Andrews. *The Oxford Companion to Australian Literature*. Melbourne: Oxford University Press, 1991. Print.

Willbanks, Ray. *Australian Voices: Writers and Their Work.* Austin: University of Texas Press, 1991. Print.

---. "Peter Carey on *The Tax Inspector* and *The Unusual Life of Tristan Smith*." *Antipodes* 11.1 (June 1997): 11-16. Print.

Wimsatt, W.K. and Monroe C. Beardsley. "The Intentional Fallacy." *Critical Theory Since Plato*. Revised edition. Ed. Hazard Adams. Fort Worth: Harcourt Brace Jovanovich, 1992. 945-951. Print.

Winter, Garry. "Queensland Literature: Is It Different?" *LiNQ: Literature in North Queensland* 15.3 (1987): 45-51. Print.

Woodcock, Bruce. *Peter Carey.* Second edition. Manchester: Manchester University Press, 2003. Print.

Zawacki, Andrew. "Foreword." *The Plains*. Gerald Murnane. 1982. Kalamazoo, MI: New Issues, 2003. 1-6. Print.

INDEX

abortion, 138, 142
adolescence, 205, 314
advertising, 51, 267
alcohol abuse, 139
A Lifetime on Clouds, xxxviii, 191–192, 195–196, 204, 208, 216, 243, 286
ambivalent, 52, 124
America, United States of, xii, xvi, xxiii, 4, 36, 177, 205, 207–208, 210–211, 252, 279, 298
Americans, xv–xvi, 112, 254, 262
American culture, xv, 206
American literature, xii, xvi–xvii
anti-suburban criticism, xv
anti-suburban tradition, xii, xviii, xxv–xxvii, xxix–xxxiii, xxxv, xxxvii–xxxviii, 16, 39, 80, 83, 85, 103, 108, 113, 116–118, 125, 131, 133, 137, 139, 152, 165–166, 173, 186–187, 191, 196, 216, 244, 249, 256, 277–278, 282, 297, 299, 304–305, 333, 335–336, 338
architecture, xiii, xv, 6, 12, 99, 147, 182, 252
artists, xiii, xxvi, xxxviii, 7, 10, 29–32, 39, 56–59, 66, 91–92, 107, 113, 173, 233, 281, 300, 303–307, 312–313, 318, 337
Australian culture, xv, xxv–xxvi, xxviii, xxxi–xxxiii, xxxviii–xxxix, 7, 28, 70, 109, 174, 186, 254, 276–277, 281–282, 298, 305, 335

Australian dream, xxiii, 163, 299
Australian literature, xii–xiv, xvii, xxxiii, xxxvii–xxxix, 1, 3, 5, 10, 36, 114, 118, 120, 124, 165–167, 191, 243, 268, 278, 282, 297, 303, 333, 335, 337–338
Australian novelists, xii, xxxiv–xxxv, xxxix, 85, 249, 336
Australian society, xi–xii, xiv, xviii–xix, xxiv, xxx, xxxix, 3, 6–8, 10–12, 28–29, 33, 36, 39–40, 51, 56, 76, 85, 118, 128, 133, 161, 164–166, 170, 185, 187, 198, 251, 281, 297, 323, 333
autobiography, 85, 90, 107, 110, 137–138, 161, 226, 304

belonging, xvii–xviii, 13, 53, 74, 116–117, 119–120, 122–123, 127–133, 137–138, 159, 163–166, 208, 243, 275, 305, 310, 312–313, 324, 326, 328–329, 337
Bildungsroman, 85, 110, 137
Bliss, xxxvi, xxxviii, 22, 36, 38, 41, 46, 61, 66, 68, 126, 249–252, 255–256, 258, 264–265, 269, 272, 275–277, 280
bohemian, 92, 239
boredom, xxxii, 37, 54, 106, 111, 114, 139, 141, 167, 172, 178, 201, 214, 258, 265, 277, 318, 321, 325, 338

Brisbane, xxii, xxv, 36, 108–114, 116, 124, 131, 137–140, 152–153, 159–160, 164–165, 174, 252–253, 336
British literature, xiv, 167
bulldozers, 37, 104, 124, 126, 180–181
bush, 124, 198, 273, 284

cancer, 176, 180, 185, 267, 269–272, 288
capitalism, 73, 176, 185–186, 251, 254, 256, 258, 269–272, 276–277, 286, 317, 337
Carey, Peter, xxxv–xxxvi, xxxviii, 108, 168, 181, 187, 193, 244, 249–251, 256, 266, 269, 276–281, 295
Carroll, Steven, xxxv–xxxvi, xxxviii, 187, 299, 303
cartography, 195–196, 198, 231, 270
Catholicism, 25, 27, 192, 195–196, 202–205, 208–209, 213, 215, 229, 239, 317
celebrates, 16, 41, 118–120, 122–123, 130, 132–133, 164, 173, 277, 289, 303–304, 308, 313, 321, 323, 331, 338
child abuse, 139, 162, 290, 297
childhood, xxix, 21, 26–27, 37, 69, 71–72, 78, 90, 124, 126, 141–144, 159, 199, 205, 208, 228, 240, 250, 253, 256–257, 272, 274–275, 291–292, 309, 314, 316, 325
Christianity, 15–16, 21, 25, 31, 51, 67, 71, 264–265
city, xv, xviii–xxii, xxiv–xxv, xxix–xxx, xxxiii, 110, 113, 124, 163, 168

class, xiii, xv, xviii, xx–xxi, xxiv–xxv, xxx, xxxiv, xxxviii–xxxix, 5, 9–10, 12, 17–18, 24, 27, 38, 45, 47, 49, 53–55, 59–60, 63, 75, 84, 86, 92, 94, 96, 98, 100–101, 103, 111–112, 118–119, 126, 138–143, 146–147, 149–151, 154–156, 160, 164, 166–167, 171, 177–178, 181–183, 186, 199, 201, 203, 205, 208, 211, 221, 256, 258–259, 274, 281–282, 287, 296–298, 305, 307, 336–337
Cloudstreet, xxxiv, xxxvi, xxxviii, 83, 102, 112, 117–124, 128, 130–133, 137, 166, 170, 181, 186, 197, 216, 275, 284, 313, 326, 335
Coetzee, J. M., 117, 249–250
colonial, xix–xxiii, xxvii, 12, 78, 88, 100, 123, 128, 165–166, 205, 255, 290, 317
colonialism, 12, 122, 157, 159
communism, 215
community, xxiv, xxix–xxx, xxxii, 8, 25, 36, 41, 54, 60–61, 64, 71–72, 77, 119, 123, 128, 132, 139, 141, 143, 148, 162, 164, 178, 199, 215, 265, 270, 273–274, 276, 284, 286–287, 289, 295, 306–308, 310, 313–315, 317–318, 320–323, 325, 329–333
conformity, xvii, xxviii, xxxi, xxxiv, 26, 38, 45, 53, 69, 92, 95, 102, 105, 127, 319
consumerism, xxvi–xxvii, 1, 18, 27, 39, 152
corruption, 278–280, 292–295

cosmopolitan, xxvii, xxix, xxxiv, 92, 125, 153, 173–174, 179
country, xi, xvii, xix, xxii, xxvii, xxix, xxxii, 5, 8, 10, 19, 28, 50, 69, 71, 104, 110, 114, 122–123, 125, 128–129, 140, 157, 163–165, 194, 214, 225, 227–228, 233, 264, 280–281, 283, 289, 307, 314, 317, 324, 329, 331–332
crime, 201, 295
critical reception, 3, 5, 38, 191–193, 279, 303
criticism, xiii–xv, xxvi, xxxii–xxxvii, 3, 11, 13, 16–17, 27, 40–41, 73, 79, 85, 99, 173, 193, 242, 256, 264, 280, 304, 335
cultural cringe, xxvii, 109

detached house, xxii, xxiv, 318
development, xviii–xxi, 7, 12, 37–38, 49–50, 77, 86, 104, 121, 126, 131, 162, 170, 252, 282–283, 285, 306–307, 311, 317
discrimination, 13, 290
diversity, xiv, xxx, xxxiv, 33, 46, 114, 116, 153, 196, 198, 250, 275, 325, 335
domestic space, 144, 146, 338
domesticity, xxvi, xxxi, xxxiii, 15, 55
domestic violence, xxxix, 22, 48, 89–90, 138–139, 143–145, 152, 157, 162, 165, 243, 251, 291, 337
drugs, 141, 143, 151, 178, 181–183, 285
drug abuse, 139

education, 5, 31, 48, 147, 166, 249
elitism, 55, 57, 76, 78
employment, xv, xvii, xxi, xxviii–xxix, xxxiii, xxxvi, xxxviii–xxxix, 1–3, 5–6, 10–11, 16, 20, 28, 31–32, 34, 48, 53, 57–58, 60–61, 68, 73, 79–80, 84–85, 90–91, 96–97, 106, 108–109, 115, 117–119, 126, 129, 140, 145, 150–152, 154, 159, 164, 181–182, 192–194, 199–200, 203, 206, 208, 217, 219, 222–223, 230–232, 238–239, 243, 251, 268, 270, 273–274, 277–278, 280–282, 287–288, 290, 299, 304–305, 310, 321, 327, 329, 336, 338
English literature, 193, 229–231
enlightenment, 148, 165
environmental degradation, xxxix, 112, 116, 162, 197, 243, 251, 270, 282–283, 305, 311, 336–337
escape, xvi, xxxiii, 27–28, 70–71, 86, 97, 115, 124, 141, 147–148, 154, 162, 165, 169, 171, 173–175, 179, 196, 272, 285–286, 289, 295, 310, 325, 338
Esson, Louis, xxvi
expatriation, 95, 115, 179, 182, 185, 251
experimentation, xiv, 8, 187, 193, 196, 243

family, xiv, xxii–xxiv, 10, 12, 15–16, 23–26, 45, 50, 53–56, 61, 63, 65, 68, 70–76, 84, 86–88, 90, 93–94, 97–98, 111–112, 119–120, 127, 130, 138, 140–142, 146, 151, 157–158, 164, 168, 173, 179, 192, 197, 199, 202, 215, 224, 230, 236–239, 242, 251, 256–259, 261, 264–268, 277, 279, 281–282, 284, 286–290, 292–297, 299, 305, 307–309, 312–313, 317–318, 321, 328
family relationships, 10, 45, 53, 251, 277, 282, 299, 305
fantasies, 132, 169, 173, 175, 184, 196, 200, 204, 209, 211, 214–215, 219–220, 231, 233, 296, 321
feminism, 147, 153, 155, 158, 165, 205–206

gardens, 52, 103, 230, 319–320
genocide, 48, 52, 183
gender, xviii, 138, 147–149, 155, 163, 165, 337
gender roles, 147–148
genre, 163, 216–217, 251

hedonism, 119

home, xvi, xx, xxii–xxvi, xxix–xxx, 7–9, 14–15, 19, 25–28, 30, 34–37, 50–54, 56, 59, 61, 69–72, 74–75, 78, 86–88, 93–94, 97–101, 111, 115–116, 120, 126, 128, 130, 139–140, 151, 153, 159, 164–165, 170–171, 174–175, 179, 181, 184–185, 194, 197–199, 202, 210–211, 213–214, 219, 224, 226–227, 229, 233, 236, 238, 242, 252, 254, 256, 258–260, 266, 268–270, 272, 282, 285–288, 290, 299, 304–305, 307, 309–312, 317–319, 321, 323, 325–329
home ownership, xx, xxiii–xxiv
homogenous, xxx, 114
homophobia, 148
homosexual, 29
housing, xxii–xxiii, xxv, 9, 30, 142, 179, 282–284

Indigenous, 10–12, 17, 28, 33, 117–123, 128–133, 142, 149, 152–166, 207, 275, 282, 323, 332
Indigenous belonging, 128–129, 159, 163, 165, 208, 243, 324
Indigenous culture, 128, 149, 162
Indigenous displacement, 305
Indigenous history, 156, 159, 163
Indigenous identity, 28, 129, 155–156, 158, 275
Indigenous knowledge, 163
Indigenous land, 13, 120, 128, 130, 132–133, 158, 163–165, 208, 337
infrastructure, 77–78, 176, 179, 236, 312, 318, 328

imagination, xiii, xvi, 32, 117, 196, 205, 207
imperialism, 109, 251, 276
immigration, xvi, xx, xxxix, 10, 22, 25, 45, 53, 69, 107, 116, 197, 243, 251, 282–283, 286, 305, 309, 336–337
immigrants, 19, 287
incest, 251, 256, 279, 291–292, 294
income, 73–74, 96–97, 99, 115, 120, 127, 138, 140, 150–152, 262, 266, 296, 317
influences, 191, 193, 251
innovation, 192
inspiration, 7, 10, 60, 207, 304, 314
intellectuals, xxxvii, 7, 56

Jews, 10–11, 23–28, 46, 57, 72, 75, 107
Johnno, xxxiv, xxxvi, xxxviii, 83, 102, 108–111, 113–119, 125, 131, 137, 153, 169–170, 174, 186, 216, 284, 335
Johnston, George, xxvii, xxxvi–xxxviii, 83–84, 327
Joyce, James, 113, 193, 195, 208, 251

Kerouac, Jack, 240
Kureishi, Hanif, xiv

land rights, 13, 120, 122, 128–133, 158–159, 163–165, 208, 275, 317, 323–324, 331, 337
landscape, 118, 195, 204–205, 214, 221, 230–231, 238, 240
Landscape with Landscape, xxxviii, 191–192, 195, 216–218, 223–224, 226, 234, 239, 243
leisure, 174, 183
lesbian, 148, 153

literary critics, xii, 335
literary criticism, xxxiii
literary influences, 193, 251
literary studies, xiii, xxxvii, 3, 5, 335
London, xx–xxii, 6, 84, 106, 109–110, 113, 125, 182
lower middle class, xv, xxv, 54–55, 59–60
Lucashenko, Melissa, xxxvi, xxxviii, 133, 137

Mabo, 164
Malouf, David, xxxvi, xxxviii, 83, 108, 168, 193
marginalized, 33, 116–117
marriage, 86, 105–107, 192, 204, 211, 214–215, 224, 233, 238, 241, 265, 278, 287, 312
masculinity, 55, 92, 155
materialism, xxvii, xxxi, xxxiii, xxxix, 10, 15, 25, 45, 107, 152, 167, 174, 176, 180, 185–186, 203, 251, 258, 269, 277, 337
McCann, A.L., xiii, xxvi, xxxiii–xxxviii, 2, 12, 27, 36, 39, 86, 102, 108, 131, 133, 137, 166–173, 176–177, 180, 184, 186, 191, 216, 255, 259, 272, 299, 304, 319, 336
Melbourne, xviii–xxii, xxv, xxxii, 15, 36, 84, 86, 91–92, 96, 99, 106, 110, 166–170, 172, 174–176, 178, 185, 191–192, 194–197, 200–204, 206, 208–209, 214, 216, 218, 220, 222–235, 238–242, 249, 303, 305–306, 308–309, 313, 322, 327, 330, 336

middle class, xiii, xv, xxxviii, 54–55, 59–60, 146–147, 150, 171, 182, 259, 297
misogyny, xxxi, 148, 225, 241
mobility, 139
Modernism, xxvii, 2, 8, 38
money, xxiv–xxv, 151, 199, 277
mothers, 15
multicultural, 10, 36, 107, 116
Murnane, Gerald, xxxv–xxxvi, xxxviii, 187, 191–194, 196–197, 205, 216, 218, 226, 228, 239
My Brother Jack, xxxiv, xxxvi, xxxviii, 83–85, 89–90, 100–101, 107–108, 110, 112–113, 116, 118–119, 127, 133, 137, 169–170, 173–175, 180, 182, 216, 222, 282, 313, 319, 327, 335–336

naming, 86, 218, 229, 323–324
narrative technique, 16, 41, 46, 79, 243, 277
nationalism, 55, 69, 168, 226
national narratives, xi, 275
Native Title, 13, 120, 122, 128–133, 158–159, 163–165, 208, 275, 317, 323–324, 331, 337
natural environment, xxxi, 10, 12–17, 21, 107, 124, 132, 169, 205, 222, 230, 262, 269, 276, 284, 306, 308
New South Wales, xxii–xxiii, 137, 160, 192, 194, 225, 250, 252–253, 318, 321
New York, 169, 176, 185, 251, 254–255, 261–262, 272, 278–279
non-Indigenous, 117, 120, 123, 129–130, 133, 149, 161, 166

non-Indigenous belonging, 117, 120, 243, 305, 337

outback, xi, xxxiii, 29
outer suburbs, xviii, xxv, xxxii, xxxviii, 7, 54, 59, 77, 102, 111–112, 116, 119, 124, 138–141, 143, 165, 174, 195–197, 199, 201, 203, 222, 229, 237–239, 278, 281–282, 297, 299, 305, 310, 326, 329–330, 336

pastoral, 252, 273, 275–277, 317
Perth, xxv, 118–120, 124–127, 131, 313, 336
place, xi, xiii, xxiv, xxvii, xxxi–xxxii, xxxiv, xxxviii, 2–3, 7, 9, 17, 24, 35, 51–52, 60, 73, 85–87, 104–105, 109–110, 113–115, 117, 119, 122–123, 125, 127–131, 133, 146, 148, 150, 153–154, 160, 162, 165, 169–170, 173–174, 179–180, 191, 195–196, 200, 215, 219, 222, 226, 228, 234–235, 238–241, 243, 252–253, 255–258, 260, 270, 273, 276, 281, 283, 285–286, 288, 295, 299, 305, 316, 318, 321, 323–324, 326–328, 337
poetry, 58, 61, 66–67, 92–93, 111, 211–212, 224, 231–232
postcolonial, xxiii, 165, 205, 305, 317
postmodern, 194, 242
poverty, 11, 19, 64, 110, 126, 141–142, 154, 157, 160–161, 201, 254, 279, 282, 286–287, 289–291, 312
pregnancy, 52, 141, 288

Index

property, xviii, xx, xxiv–xxv, 13, 130, 214, 295
public housing, xxii–xxiii, 282

quarter-acre block, xxii, 8, 163–164, 198
Queensland, 108, 143, 159–160, 165–166, 223–225, 250–251, 253
Queenslander, 146–147, 174, 179, 259

radicalism, 169, 176, 178, 182–184, 186
race, xiii, 140, 143, 147, 155, 180, 289
racism, xxxii, 19, 21, 29, 36, 162
rape, 292, 297
rationalism, 77
real estate, 96, 152, 170
realism, xxxviii, 8, 211, 336
refugees, 19, 107, 123, 305
religion, xiii, xxxix, 10, 15–16, 22, 25–28, 45, 51, 53, 63, 67, 69, 71, 75, 107, 116, 119, 203–204, 239, 243, 264–265, 337
Riders in the Chariot, xxxvi, xxxviii, 1–2, 10–12, 14, 22, 32, 38–41, 45, 47, 49, 51, 53, 55, 63, 66, 80, 83, 85, 105, 116, 170, 181, 286, 290, 297, 309, 336
rural, xi, xv, 6, 8, 23, 77, 106, 119–120, 123, 125, 175, 214–215, 258, 273, 283–284, 295

security, xxvi, 34, 127, 155, 177, 267
self-loathing, xxvii, 78, 107, 256

settlement, xix, xxi, 37, 77, 87, 119–120, 131–132, 226–227, 264, 312–313, 315, 317, 321, 323, 330
settlers, 121–123, 128, 226, 255, 323, 331–332
sexism, 224
sexuality, xxxi, 21, 29, 59, 92, 95, 97, 148, 155, 178, 181, 183–184, 195, 200, 202, 204–205, 207–208, 210, 265–266, 289
sexual abuse, 139, 170, 251, 278–280, 282, 285, 290–295
short fiction, xii, 7, 217, 250, 280–281
single-family home, xxii
skin color, 160
social issues, xxxviii, 45, 47, 80, 107, 116, 138, 187, 277, 281, 333, 336–337
space, xiii–xiv, xxix, xxxix, 12, 27–28, 91, 121–122, 131–132, 147–148, 161, 165, 173, 180, 196, 218, 221, 224, 306–307, 309, 314, 338
spirituality, xxxix, 10, 14–16, 63, 67, 264, 337
sport, 178, 306, 313, 315, 317–319, 325, 329
status, xxviii, xxxi, 1, 3, 5, 27–28, 47, 54, 59, 64, 75, 84–86, 108, 112, 132, 147, 177, 181, 199, 203, 293, 322, 335
Steam Pigs, xxxiv, xxxvi, xxxviii, 133, 137–139, 144, 147, 150, 152, 155, 160, 162, 164–166, 169–170, 174, 179, 186, 216, 259, 313
stolen generation, 132, 156

suburbanism, xi, xxvi–xxx, xxxiii, 1, 7, 16, 38, 117, 166, 170, 179–180
suburbanization, xv–xvii, xix, xxiv–xxv, 104, 198, 283–285, 295, 316–317
suburban development, xix–xxi, 12, 37–38, 77, 121, 126, 131, 162, 283, 285, 307, 311, 317
suburban environment, xxxvii, 123, 125, 307, 309
suburban fiction, xxxiii, xxxviii, 1, 22, 89, 107, 120, 124, 166, 181, 191, 194, 243, 304–305, 338
suburban life, xii, xiv–xv, xxix–xxxii, xxxvii, 2, 7–8, 45, 47, 69, 77, 89, 104, 106, 116, 123, 125–127, 154, 171–172, 181, 186, 195, 233–234, 241, 249, 257, 277, 280, 282, 291, 304–305, 320, 329
suburban novel, xi–xii, xvi–xvii, xx, xxiv, xxx, xxxvi–xxxviii, 1–2, 5, 7, 17, 37–39, 45, 80, 83, 102, 107–109, 113, 116, 118–119, 133, 162, 169, 181, 186–187, 196–197, 201, 249, 259, 282, 286, 300, 304–305, 307, 309, 327, 335–338
suburban setting, xxxvi–xxxvii, xxxix, 1, 10, 45, 53, 80, 86, 97, 119, 138, 147, 157, 168, 196, 216, 252, 277, 282, 305, 336, 338
suburban values, 12–13, 15, 17, 27, 55, 95, 105, 107
Subtopia, xxxiv, xxxvi–xxxviii, 102, 133, 137, 166–170, 172, 174–176, 180–181, 185–186, 216, 272, 319

suffering, xxxiii, 10, 17, 21, 30, 32, 35, 67–68, 89, 113, 119
suicide, 28, 121, 186, 271
surveillance, 258, 273
Sydney, xviii–xxi, xxiii, xxv, 1, 5, 8–9, 21–23, 30, 32, 55, 58–59, 61, 77–78, 84, 108, 110, 125, 192, 194, 251–253, 278–283, 286–288, 292–294, 296–297, 299, 336

Tasmania, xi, 194–195
television, xiii, 48, 52–53, 76, 84, 139–141, 156, 158, 199, 219, 227, 241, 266, 308, 313
terrorism, 176, 184, 186, 271
The Tax Inspector, xxxvi, xxxviii, 126, 181, 249, 265, 277–281, 283, 286–287, 290–294, 299, 313
The Art of the Engine Driver, xxxviii, 300, 303–307, 312–313, 318
The Gift of Speed, xxxviii, 300, 303, 313–316, 318, 325, 329
The Solid Mandala, xxxvi, xxxviii, 1–2, 41, 45–47, 49, 51, 53, 62, 65, 73–75, 79–80, 83, 93, 116, 125, 194, 216, 232, 286, 336
The Time We Have Taken, xxxviii, 300, 303, 307, 312, 320–321, 324, 327–330, 336
travel, 29, 32, 72, 78, 91, 140, 191, 194–195, 202, 214, 224, 227, 234

unemployment, xxv, 96, 141, 151, 253, 289, 298

university, 23, 53, 108, 114, 138, 147, 149–150, 156, 158, 161, 166–167, 174–175, 178–179, 181, 185, 249–250, 303, 321, 325
upper class, xx, xxxviii, 140
urban, xi, xiii, xv, xxii–xxiii, xxv, xxxiv, xxxvi, 6, 25, 33, 91–92, 94, 109, 112, 116, 121, 125, 131–132, 152–153, 165, 168, 181, 183, 253–254, 276, 283, 286

Victoria, 84, 160, 192, 194–195, 214, 222–223, 231, 234, 249
violence, xxxix, 19, 22, 36, 47–49, 52, 89–90, 92, 119, 138–139, 141, 143–145, 149, 152, 157, 162, 165, 177, 183, 243, 251, 280, 282, 291–292, 294–297, 337

vitality, xxix, 6, 38, 47, 60, 77, 87, 91, 103, 154, 171, 201, 221

White, Patrick, xxvii, xxxv, xxxvii–xxxviii, 1–3, 5, 9–11, 22, 33, 36, 38, 41, 45–47, 61, 66, 68, 83, 116, 192–193, 336
Winton, Tim, xxxv–xxxvi, xxxviii, 83, 117–119, 132
work, 30, 73, 75, 96, 150–151, 288
working class, xxxviii, 47, 54, 118–119, 138, 140–141, 146–147, 149–151, 154, 164, 199, 203, 205, 282, 296–297, 307

www.ingramcontent.com/pod-product-compliance
Lightning Source LLC
Chambersburg PA
CBHW060549230426
43670CB00011B/1753